GEORGE W.
HAMILTON, USMC

George W. Hamilton, USMC

America's Greatest World War I Hero

Mark Mortensen

McFarland & Company, Inc., Publishers
Jefferson, North Carolina, and London

LIBRARY OF CONGRESS CATALOGUING-IN-PUBLICATION DATA

Mortensen, Mark.
　　George W. Hamilton, USMC : America's greatest World War I hero / Mark Mortensen.
　　　　p.　　cm.
　　Includes bibliographical references and index.

　　ISBN 978-0-7864-6321-3
　　softcover : 50# alkaline paper ∞

　　1. Hamilton, George W. (George Wallis), 1892–1922.
2. United States. Marine Corps. Regiment, 5th. Company, 49th — Biography.　3. United States. Marine Corps — Officers — Biography.　4. World War, 1914–1918 — Campaigns — France.
5. World War, 1914–1918 — Campaigns — France — Belleau, Bois de.　6. World War, 1914–1918 — Regimental histories — United States.　I. Title.
D570.3485th.M67　　2011
359.9'6092 — dc23　　　　　　　　　　　　　　　　2011020761

BRITISH LIBRARY CATALOGUING DATA ARE AVAILABLE

© 2011 Mark Mortensen. All rights reserved

No part of this book may be reproduced or transmitted in any form or by any means, electronic or mechanical, including photocopying or recording, or by any information storage and retrieval system, without permission in writing from the publisher.

Front cover: United States Marine Corp insignia; U.S. Employment Service/American Red Cross World War I poster, Dan Smith artist (Library of Congress)

Manufactured in the United States of America

McFarland & Company, Inc., Publishers
　Box 611, Jefferson, North Carolina 28640
　　www.mcfarlandpub.com

To my source of inspiration, my family:
Laura, Wait and Adam
May they never forget true heroes

Table of Contents

Acknowledgements ix
Preface 1

1. Early Years 9
2. Central High 19
3. Off to College 23
4. Becoming a Marine 27
5. A Soldier of the Sea 37
6. America Enters the Great War 45
7. To France and a Time on Land 52
8. Belleau Wood: Château-Thierry Sector June 6–26 —
   Paris Is Saved 74
9. Soissons: July 18–22 — The Long March 92
10. Saint-Mihiel: September 1918 — The World's Most
    Awesome Bombardment 107
11. Blanc Mont: Champagne Sector October 1918 —
    The Acts of a Former United States President 120
12. The Meuse River and Armistice: Heroes to the End 149
13. Assessment of the AEF 170
14. The March to Germany: Belgium, Luxembourg and
    Christmas Letters 174
15. Germany and Court Trials: Through Spring 1919 184
16. His "Boys" Come Home: 1919 Summer and Beyond 195
17. Days of Discontent: 1920 215
18. Time to Fly: 1921 224
19. Wings and Prayers: 1922 231

| 20. Funeral | 239 |
| 21. Life Goes On | 243 |

Epilogue	253
Appendix A	259
Appendix B	262
Notes	269
Bibliography	285
Index	291

Acknowledgments

I am not the first author to admit that writing a book is much more than putting words on paper and binding them together. The process involved much more, including newfound special friendships, which are the essence of life. I have not had the occasion to meet most of these folks face to face, but that has not diminished my appreciation for their time, efforts and consideration assisting me with this venture. Receiving personal letters rather than bills in the mail is as exciting as ever. I am most thankful for their friendship.

Before reaching a final decision to write a book about George W. Hamilton, I asked my wife what she thought of the idea. She is the true writer in the family with a degree from the University of North Carolina at Chapel Hill, School of Journalism. Her approval and confidence in my ability nudged me to give the project my full commitment.

I cannot thank Roger C. Barnard Jr. enough for all of his assistance. When I first approached him with the thought of writing a biography of his uncle, he was naturally a bit surprised. Before long I had gained his trust and friendship, which means so much to me. Through free flowing correspondence, he shed some light on the extended Hamilton family, including the initial connection to the Wrights. There were also some letters that his mother had saved that were both personal and historical, which he willingly shared. His assistance was also exceptionally valuable in obtaining his uncle's military personnel records.

I would like to thank historian and author George B. Clark, who offered so much support and encouragement along the way.

My honorable congressman, Howard Coble, loves heroes. Through guidance, his local staff members, Lindsay Morris and Kathy McClellan, helped me to obtain valuable records from the National Archives. I am very grateful for their professional service and communication, as trying to obtain records from the era before social security numbers were issued can be a daunting task.

Robert V. Aquilina, who serves as the head of the Reference Branch of the Marine Corps History Division, Quantico, Virginia, was very willing to assist me from day one. He provided me with reference material on hand and allowed me to communicate freely with his professional staff, including his assistant Annette D. Amerman.

One very fine woman within the History Division, whom I just cannot thank enough, is Beth L. Crumley, a knowledgeable source on World War I Marine Corps history. She was able to locate specific information very quickly. It was a sheer pleasure corresponding with her, as she is exceptionally enthusiastic and truly enjoys her profession. I hope she writes her own World War I book in the future.

Another friendship started several years ago when I made contact with Lt. Commander Robert Wallace Blake, USNR (Ret). The 1941 MIT graduate proudly served his country in World War II and made valuable contributions to aviation. He has many of the fine personal qualities of his father, Robert Blake, who as a lieutenant in the 17th Company of the First Battalion, Fifth Regiment (1/5), was commended for his fine service at Belleau Wood and later as a captain commanded the 66th Company of 1/5 during the final Meuse-Argonne push breaking the Hindenburg Line and crossing the Meuse River.

A few library research departments were instrumental with assisting my efforts, searching and compiling information of days past. The first two are where I spent much time.

1. The University of North Carolina at Greensboro, Walter Clinton Jackson Library. Mark Schumacher, "Mr. Stanford," and his fine associates were always very gracious and willing to assist with my needs.
2. Wake Forest University, Z. Smith Reynolds Library. The energetic student staff eagerly assisted me and answered all my questions. Go Deacons!
3. Winchester, Massachusetts, town library. Unfortunately I do not recall the name of the woman who provided me with Ove Mortensen's war letter back in the 1980s. Recently, Janet Nelson assisted me with a piece of needed information.

Robert Lowell Goller, the town and village historian for Aurora, New York, was as professional as anyone that I dealt with. Mr. Goller provided me with an abundance of material pertaining to Charles A. Hamilton, including his close bond with Grover Cleveland.

Michael J. Crawford with the Department of the Navy, Naval History and Heritage Command, promptly answered my questions.

Marie G. Kutch, the administrator for the Theodore Roosevelt Association, provided me with hard copy information that I was looking for. The Roosevelt family was certainly one to emulate.

Joseph Keating, of Winchester, Massachusetts, has kept me informed about local issues, Marine books and updates with the new Winchester Veterans Memorial. He lived down the street from the Mortensens during World War II and fondly sent a photo of himself lying on their family dog, appropriately named "Major." He is another new friend.

The *New York Times* and the *Washington Post* archives not only provided me with an enormous wealth of knowledge and facts, but also a true feeling of the World War I era.

Anyone who has written a book that is supported by photographs has a true appreciation for the folks who assist with obtaining photos. Vast quantities of old photos remain in storage yet to be sorted and categorized. Some photos tell a story of their own. I am thankful for those folks who devoted their time.

Lena Kaljot, historian, Marine Corps History Division, Quantico, Virginia, provided me with a large photo selection.

John Thorpe Richards Jr. is very proud of his grandparents. He shared with me a special photograph of their formal wedding party in which Hamilton served as an usher.

Marcene Molinaro, the curator of collections of the Marshall Museum in Lexington, Virginia, went out of her way to assist me with a copy of a special drawing by John W. Thomason Jr.

I have made every attempt to avoid errors; however, if a mistake is present, it is unintentional and my fault alone. If I have omitted a person of notable interest within the AEF or the Marine Corps, it was only because I did not see the person as having a close association to George W. Hamilton. There were many other U.S. Army personnel and "Devil Dogs" in all ranks that deserve proper credit.

The United States Marines
(Dedicated to Maj. George W. Hamilton, Fifth Marines)

They damned their food, and they damned the war.
And they damned the cursed Hun.
By whom they were known as the "Devil Dogs";
And they feared not Fiends, and they feared not gods.
Nor the fires of hell undone.
And little they cared, as they recklessly dared.
And they always damned the damn;
But oft their swear was more a prayer,
These marines of Uncle Sam.

They came from the East and from the West,
And they came from the South and the North,
They sprang to the colors on every hand.
They offered their service throughout the land;
But only the best went forth,
For only the best could have stood the test,
In that baptismal hell.
At Belleau Wood, where they made the good.
When they sounded the Hun's death knell.

The brave, brave French had striven hard,
They had fought, but could fight no more.
The war had been fierce and the struggle long;
Their legions were crushed, and their hope was gone;
For them the strife was o'er.
Through the valley poured that German horde,
Bringing wrack and revolting scenes.
When into the fray there rushed that day The United States marines.

They came as conquering armies come;
Undaunted and unafraid,
With full free swing in their courage great.
For the time was short and the hour late.
And naught their steps delayed.
As they marched along to the lilting song,
"Send the word, send the word, to beware!"
With keen, cold, steel, they made them feel
The weight of our force "over there."

Pompus, and blatant and arrogant,
Bedecked in their new array;
So sure were the Huns in their thick-skulled pride
That nothing on earth could stem the tide,
Or block them on their way.
Eight thousand men were pitted then
'Ganst the Prussian Guard of fiends.
In the power of might for the cause of right
Went the Fifth and Sixth marines.

Awful and fierce the combat raged,
As the Huns came, wave on wave,
Against our men, and steel to steel,
'Mid shot and shell, they'd break and reel,
And at last before us gave.
Our loss was great, but it sealed the fate
Of the Huns — and the world esteems.
Like Spartans of old this tale will be told
Of Uncle Sam's marines

by Isabel Likens Gates,
from the *Washington Post*, 12 August 1919

Preface

Centennial events surrounding World War I will give Americans a unique opportunity to reflect once again upon a war we have learned to forget. In its time the first global war was known as the Great War, the war to end all wars. A war today, overshadowed not only by the preceding Civil War, but by World War II and other wars to follow.

America was in the midst of becoming the great shining nation when President Woodrow Wilson declared war, and America's greatest sons, full of patriotism, were soon off to fight. Athletes and intellectuals from the nation's top colleges and universities along with working men abandoned their education, jobs and careers to join the cause. Heroes were on the horizon. When the war was over Americans quickly tried to put the Great War behind them and move on to a bright future, and they successfully accomplished both.

A man can be labeled a hero for a single act. One notable example was U.S. Army Corporal Alvin C. York, who fully deserved the Medal of Honor he received.[1] However, a person who displays continuous acts of heroism throughout the entire war is nothing short of a role model for all. In the aftermath of the Great War, there were many rousing speeches noting that such brave men would forever be remembered; however, in the forgotten war, sadly the names of many true heroes are also forgotten.

If you were able to travel back in time and view the war through the eyes of just one American, who would that person be? To start, there were about 4,800,000 men from the U.S. Army, U.S. National Guard, U.S. Navy and U.S. Marines who served in the Great War. For the sake of this question let's eliminate past relatives as a personal choice. Before you offer an answer let me detail my choice by reasons of deduction, as you most likely do not know this man.

First, my choice would be an American who lived through the war, as I would want to experience the entire adventure. Those who witnessed the natural beauty of France as well as the mud, the gas, the cold steel, and the death and destruction of war would continue to call the event an adventure like no other.

Second, I would pick a man who fought on land, as the main battles were fought on land rather than at sea or in the air. This was, however, the first war in which airplanes were used by the military. Some of Yale University's best men, along with many others, were instrumental in this venture. The naval battles of World War I were fought predominately prior to the United States entering the war. German U-boats were a constant irritation, but overall the seas were not where the action took place. World War I was a war to be decided on the ground.

Third, I would choose a member of the American Expeditionary Forces (AEF) fighting on the Western Front in France. This was a world war and, although Americans served their country in several locations, the battlefields of France were obviously where all the central action occurred. About 2,086,000 military personnel were sent to France.[2]

Fourth, my chosen man would be a U.S. Marine. The Marine Corps was established on November 10, 1775; however, it was during World War I that the Marines solidified the reputation that continues with them today. Starting with their initial major assault, they proudly earned their reputation the hard way.

Finally, I would pick a high-ranking officer who not only made decisions, but was also in the thick of the major battles at all times. The man would be a commanding officer of a company or a battalion commander. Any higher ranking officer would not be in a position to put his life in jeopardy near the front lines, and a lower ranking officer would not have had nearly as much responsibility.

During World War I many Marine officers achieved great recognition. Some are known as legends of the "Old Corps" and some are household names throughout America today. So which individual would fill my requirements and be my overwhelming choice? That man is George Wallis Hamilton.

From my initial investigation I knew George W. Hamilton was the undeniable role model of the Great War, and I did not need additional validation. However, when I was well past the midway point in my research I came across a very special letter dated 25 years after America's initial major battle of World War I. In 1943 several of Hamilton's personal items were donated to the U.S. Marine Corps Museum by one of his sisters. The letter of acceptance, written by Colonel Clyde H. Metcalf, USMC, who four years prior, in 1939, authored *A History of the United States Marine Corps*, stated: "The above listed objects are received for the purpose of displaying them in the Marine Corps Museum and preserving them as mementos of the late George W. Hamilton, USMC, who, in the opinion of the undersigned, was the most outstanding Marine Corps hero in World War I."[3]

Of the six U.S. Marine battalions to serve actively in France, Hamilton's battalion was the first to set foot on French soil, and the timing of this landing coincided with the arrival of the first U.S. Army troops. On June 6, 1918, when Belleau Wood, the biggest Marine battle and first major American assault, began, Captain Hamilton was one of just two company commanders to shove off in the first wave at 0350. The other company commander died within hours. Hamilton carried a personal rifle with him at all times, and he used it often. On October 4 Major Hamilton, commander of the First Battalion, Fifth Regiment, survived "The Box," during one of the bloodiest days in Marine Corps history. On the evening before the Armistice, he led two battalions of men across the Meuse River under extremely heavy fire, and when word of the Armistice came he was most assuredly the final ranking officer in the entire American Expeditionary Forces to receive official notice that the Great War was over. The Western Front was then silent. From the very start to the final finish, he was in the thick of it all as a fighting commander and highly respected authoritative officer. He was a leader and warrior like no other.

Hamilton was twice recommended to receive the Medal of Honor by two great Marine Corps legends. On the first occasion, the official paperwork was processed by the future 14th commandant of the Marine Corps. The second request was officially filed by the presiding 13th commandant, along with support paperwork from the future 14th commandant. For reasons that will be explained, no U.S. Marine Corps commissioned officer serving with the ground troops would receive the Medal of Honor.

Like James Dean and Norma Jeane Mortenson (aka Marilyn Monroe), George W. Hamilton also died young when immense future success and recognition were all but certain. They achieved fame and were from Hollywood, but Hamilton was an American hero who just so happened to be a Marine. One prominent historian said of Hamilton, "He was highly respected by everyone, officers and men alike, handsome (often referred to by his command as 'our Hollywood actor') and the bravest of the brave."[4]

He lived through the war, receiving numerous awards along with individual citations, and died before the general public got to know him. In that respect he was never truly thanked for his generous service to our country. He served the Corps in all capacities, as "The Marine's Hymn" states, "In the air, on land, and sea."[5] Not many Marines, or for that matter any member of the military service, past or present, can say that. If you are not familiar with the man, you are missing the story of one great American, not just of World War I, but of all time.

As we look into the life of George W. Hamilton, an undeniable pattern emerges that gives true insight into his character. If there was one word to describe Hamilton it would be "competitive." Competition was a part of the

DNA from which he lived and breathed. "Dash" was a very popular word in his time, and, as you will see, he had plenty of it to go along with his display of courage.

I was personally intrigued by Hamilton because little is truly known about him. One Arlington National Cemetery website stated a couple of simple facts followed by a statement declaring they were actively seeking further information. What little information the public was previously given concerning Hamilton's past was often sketchy and to some extent contained unintended errors. With this book I intend to clarify that information. I do, however, applaud those who have not forgotten Hamilton and have continued to praise him.

This is the complete story of George Wallis Hamilton, which encompasses his life before joining the Corps, his acts of bravery and military service representing our country during the war, as well as his final days.

By design, I have avoided the day-by-day events that would distract the reader from the focus of the book. The book follows Hamilton's path and therefore is not meant to be a comprehensive account of the entire Marine Corps in World War I. There are numerous excellent books in publication that cover parts of the war and a few that have tackled the entire Marine involvement.

I treat three main events of World War I with the same emphasis. These are the battles of Belleau Wood in the Château-Thierry sector, Blanc Mont along with St. Etienne in the Champagne region, and the crossing of the Meuse River. In my estimation you can't single out one of the three events with regard to initial sheer courage prior to jumping off at H-hour or when the final objective was complete look back and say this was the toughest assignment. Hamilton served above and beyond the call of duty in each of the three battles, and, in fact, he had the qualifications to receive the Medal of Honor in each.

Much has been written about the battle of Belleau Wood. During that first battle several bold quotes from notable characters have lasted through the decades as a part of Marine Corps lore. Hidden in the depths of the past is another quote, which came from Captain Hamilton himself during the initial hours in the heat of that battle: "Who said I was dead. Send me the mortars and a thousand hand grenades."[6]

But beyond Belleau Wood, there were events just as exciting that were never fully recorded, during a period when Captain Hamilton became Major Hamilton and was given command of one and later more than two battalions of men. It's fascinating history that every American should be proud of.

Lately there has been a small core group of Marines who consider George W. Hamilton one of the toughest warriors in Marines Corps history, as noted in the *Leatherneck* magazine article "TOP-10" BADASS* MARINES." The noted top ten were intentionally not ranked in order, but most certainly some individuals might rank Hamilton as number one. The praise for George W. Hamilton read: "Rated no less a Marine than John A. Lejeune as the Marine Brigade's best combat officer in France as a company and battalion commander. Hamilton led from the front. Never asked anyone to do anything he wasn't prepared to do himself ... and do better. Personally wiped out a German machine-gun crew with a rifle and bayonet at Belleau Wood. Navy Cross. His Marines loved him and trusted him without reservation."[7]

These folks have done their homework, but Hamilton did much more during World War I, and those who consider him to be one of the toughest Marines will be the first to admit they know very little of his personal life or background outside the Marine Corps. There was a sincere gentlemanly side to him. It's possible for one to possess both the traits of a gentleman and a top warrior, as noted by a few of our great presidents.

Hamilton did not leave a personal diary. In searching his past I followed the trail wherever it led me. His father rose to become known as the dean of the Congressional press corps. Hamilton's extended family members were also achievers. One first cousin became a vice admiral in the U.S. Navy; another first cousin also became a vice admiral in the U.S. Navy; and still another first cousin had a stellar journalistic career that came close to the success of Charles A. Hamilton.

Walk into any new or used bookstore and look for the World War I section. There is plenty of space for the American Revolution and in a narrow space between the large selection of Civil War and World War II books is the Great War. Generally it's about enough space to accommodate a thinly sliced loaf of bread.

It is not so much that there is a lack of interest in World War I history as it is that many stories, close to 100 years later, have yet to be told. The media were different from today. In-depth interviews were exceptionally rare, and most volunteers and noncommissioned officers did not talk of the war after it was over. As in so many wars, history is often recorded through the eyes, minds and voices of top generals, who are often far removed from the front lines and therefore miss so much of the true adventure.

This biography is intentionally melded into an overall American tale of the times. In order to fully drift back in time and delve into Hamilton's past, it is important to listen to and absorb the words of the men who surrounded him. Life in the United States, just 100 years ago, was much different from that of today in many respects. To gain insight into Hamilton's personality, drive and ambition, it is also important to understand and view the broad scope of other national events that were taking place across America, as much of this filtered down and factored into his life through his prominent father.

It is very possible that the 20th century will go down in history as the golden years of American society. If so, it is imperative that Americans understand what events caused the United States to be recognized as the pinnacle nation of the world. A country that has lost its rudder, forgotten its roots, its compass and overall path to success, is destined for a decline of unprecedented proportion. It all ties together with the First World War, so it is therefore necessary that all American citizens retrace their steps to understand the early part of the century when so many sacrifices were made for future generations.

The years leading up to the global war were an amazing time to be alive, especially if you were an American.[8] It appeared as if something magical was in the air around 1900, transitioning from the 19th century and springboarding to the 20th century. With little or no government assistance, hard working immigrants were arriving at Ellis Island and other locations to live in the land of opportunity and freedom, calling America home. They readily accepted and adopted American family values, traditions and democratic way of life. The "melting pot" society was excited about the future of the nation. Money from tariffs, not income taxes, was the number one source of revenue for the nation. The United States was a breeding ground for creative thinking and many thoughts and dreams became a reality, which, along with the American work ethic, led to American industrial development setting an example for the rest of the world.

When the Great War started in Europe in 1914, the United States was on its way to becoming the leading nation of the world. This war would be unlike any previous war, as for the first time ever, countries throughout the world would be involved on a grand scale using new technology and weapons development. However, as in ages past, much of the war would be decided by the will of the individual warrior.

Great nations rise, experience golden years, and then fall. Famous empires usually do not fall by military force, but rather their fall is often due to cultural changes prompting a decline in culture, a lack of great leadership, vision, role models, work ethic, motivation, along with increased political corruption and a weakened tax base, resulting in basic self-destruction from within. History, as we well know, often repeats itself.

In the book *The Lessons of History* it was mentioned that over the past 3,421 years of recorded history there have been wars in every year except for 268. As the book was published in 1968, most folks are familiar with current world conflicts.[9] Prolonged peace, as wonderful as it would be, unfortunately seems to be universally unsustainable. Future British prime minister Winston Churchill, who would later deal with the Second World War, reflected upon society and war by saying: "But the world is like a tired old horse plodding down a long road. Every time it strays off and tries to graze peacefully in some nice green pasture, along comes a new master to flog it a bit further along."[10] And a historian and top American staff member in the First World War pointed out: "When you are ill you turn to the doctor. When you are at war you turn to the trained soldier. It is as easy to forget the one when you are well as to forget the other in times of peace."[11]

All civilizations too often find easy means to start wars, but it is generally the rising nations that start wars. My reason for writing this book is not to delve into why wars are fought. Disputes, disagreements and varying opinions abound prior to the start of a war and last long after the recorded history of the war. It is, however, very important for one to understand that wars unfortunately are inevitable, and therefore a strong military force is required to protect society. Where there are wars there will be heroes.

The same countries that start wars have much more difficulty ending them. World War I is a classic case in point. For opposing nations to agree that the First World War would end on a specific day and time was, for lack of words, unusual. Throwing all sorts of ammunition at an enemy up until a set hour will probably never happen again.

Throughout the war, Private Elton E. Mackin was always assisting Hamilton as a message runner. When the war was over he wrote a book that is a masterpiece, *Suddenly We Didn't Want to Die*, which I feel portrays the realistic adventure as well as the horror of war even better than the classic *All Quiet on the Western Front*, by the German author Erich Maria Remarque. Mackin's book is also a favorite of Hamilton's only nephew, Roger C. Barnard Jr. This easy to read book should be included in school reading lists.

1. Early Years

George W. Hamilton's paternal grandparents came from England to America through Canada around 1866 or 1867. Sometime after this venture, his grandfather remarried and it is unclear as to when or why. Possibly his first wife died, but the issue is not a concern for this story. Before long his grandfather settled in the Buffalo, New York, area of Erie County. With American citizenship and a proficient use of language, his grandfather was appointed to a position within the U.S. Internal Revenue office.

The elder Hamiltons had several children, one of whom was a son, Charles Alexander Hamilton, born May 13, 1856, in Islington, England. As a youth, Charles remained in England to continue his education at the Mercers' (Guild) School in London, while his parents established residence in America.[1] Charles soon found out that his lot in life was not going to be dependent upon others, and he matured quickly.

First it is important to understand portions of the life and background of Charles Hamilton. George Hamilton's father, Charles, was a very accomplished individual in his own right, and he was a unique influence throughout George's entire life. One can not ignore this relationship. Through knowing the father you can identify where a few of his son's character traits came from.

In 1869 at the age of thirteen, Charles stepped on board the North German sailing ship *Fortune* destined for America. The ship was also Dutch in part, being registered at The Hague. The small brig departed on May 26 from Liverpool carrying a hundred barrels of ginger and 365 hogsheads of sugar, as well as some other commodities. Charles soon realized that as the only passenger on board he was to participate with the crew of 11 hardened sailors by sharing in the duties during the roughly month-and-a-half-long voyage. Young Charles did not mind this too much as it helped pass the day, and basically he walked about saying, "Aye, aye, sir."

One of his duties was tending to the signal flags. Charles studied the manual "Code of Signals for Mercantile Marine of All Nations" by Capt. Marryat. The top flag on the mast always read "2938," which was code for "What is your longitude?" Ship captains would then test their chronometers for accuracy. At times a second flag displayed "2643," which translated to

"Have you seen icebergs?" Along the voyage Charles did see several icebergs, atop which sat seals and walruses, and passengers on a passing ship had even spotted a polar bear.

While off the banks of Newfoundland on July 1, Charles noticed some large debris floating in the water. The Dutch captain maneuvered over and realized they had come across parts of a ship's cabin. Charles noticed a box containing a complete set of signal flags and brought them on board.

By this point in the voyage, Charles was getting rather bored, and he decided to have some fun playing amateur pirate by putting the newly found flags to use. He scoured the signal book for the proper code words and corresponding numbers until he found what he was searching for. While the watchman was at the ship's wheel Charles pulled down the current flags, and in their place he ran up "2574" and "7083." Before long another ship noticed the flags and questioned the *Fortune*'s Dutch captain as to what was going on because the numbers translated to "Heave to, or I will send a shot across your bows!"[2] Needless to say Charles' Dutch captain was not very pleased with the young English fellow.

After 43 days the ship landed at the Pierrepont Docks in Brooklyn, New York, on July 9, 1869. Charles paid his passenger fare of $77.00 and made his way to Buffalo to reconnect with his parents.

Charles enrolled at the county academy at East Aurora and quickly found a job as a newspaper boy selling papers in the local Buffalo area. One of his many customers was the law office of thirty-two-year-old Grover Cleveland. Mr. Cleveland noted Charles' keen qualities and instantly gave him additional responsibilities of running personal errands.[3] Continuing with the paper route, Charles decided to further his education by taking courses in the medical department at the University of Buffalo. The newspaper business was in Charles' blood, however, and before long his medical studies went by the wayside.

In 1880, at the age of 24, Charles moved within Erie County to East Aurora, New York, and purchased the *East Aurora Times* newspaper. The young man was not only enjoying the business side of newspapers but also the journalistic side. Sometime during his days in East Aurora he met his future wife, Ida Margaret Persons. Ida, four years younger than Charles, was born in East Aurora in January 1860.

The quaint village with only about 1,100 residents had some history of its own with yet another local lawyer. Around 1820, Milliard Fillmore, who had recently married Abigail, built a home in town and began his law practice. He served as the 13th President of the United States from 1850 to 1853.

The newspaper flourished with good journalism and a growing community. One headline event was the July 2, 1881, shooting of President James A.

Garfield, who died a few months later. His assassin, Charles J. Guiteau, was convicted and hanged on June 30, 1882, in Washington, D.C.

Creative thinking was abundant and as folks put their ideas to practice, technological inventions followed. Many of these achievements became the predominant headline news. Thomas Edison was working with direct current electricity, and in the fall of 1882, a new coal commercial power station in lower Manhattan supplied electricity, mainly for nighttime lighting, to 59 residents and businesses within a mile radius.

A lot was happening in the nation's capital, and with the telegraph as a proven means of communication, a great journalist wanted to be where the action was. The *Buffalo Commercial Advertiser* wished to send Charles to Washington, D.C., as their correspondent. He accepted the position and sold the *Aurora Times*.

On January 16, 1883, Charles was given his card as a prestigious member of the Congressional Press Gallery by Maine Senator William Frye, the chairman of the Senate Rules Committee. He cherished the card, keeping it in his back pocket at all times. The card stated:

> 47th Congress, 2nd Session
> Reporters' Gallery,
> This Entitles
> Mr. Charles A. Hamilton,
> Correspondent for the
> Buffalo Commercial Advertiser,
> Admittance to the Gallery until
> Otherwise ordered by the Com-
> mittee on Rules
> (No person interested in leg-
> islation is eligible to be a seat)
> (signed) WM. P. FRYE
> Chairman,
> Washington, D.C., Jan. 16, 1883[4]

Charles went right to work on the 16th, by sitting in a three-hour-long Cabinet meeting, and on the same day, President Chester A. Arthur signed the Civil Service Act. Of all the Presidents that Charles would meet throughout his life, President Arthur, he said, was the best dressed. One statement attributed to President Arthur was "If it were not for the reporters, I would tell you the truth."[5]

Comfortably settled into Washington, Charles looked to enhance his life. On May 9, 1883, Charles and Ida were married back in East Aurora, New York, at the home of Margaret Wallis, a family relative. Ida's mother, whose maiden name was Wallis, passed away when Ida was just two years old.

Ida and Charles would have five children, all of which were born in

Washington, D.C. Their first, a daughter, Mary Elizabeth, was born in May 1884. Ida managed the home, while Charles remained very active with his correspondence.

Grover Cleveland, who had taken a liking to Charles, was continuing his political career and, in the fall of the year, was elected President of the United States. When President Cleveland was sworn into office on March 4, 1885, the journalistic career of Charles A. Hamilton was on a roll and the doors to the White House were wide open to him.

In March of 1886, Ida gave birth to a son named Edwin Persons. Unfortunately, the infant died several months later in September.

At 49 years old, Grover Cleveland was getting married for the first time, and many residents in Washington's upper social circles were wondering who he had been courting. On June 2, 1886, the president got married in the Blue Room of the White House. This was the first wedding in the mansion. His bride, Frances Folsom, who was about to turn 22, was the young daughter of a former law partner in Buffalo.[6] The guest list was strictly limited to only about 40 people, including family, friends, selected dignitaries and Cabinet members. One invited guest was another old law partner from Buffalo, W. S. Bissell. Charles was certainly familiar with both the new bride and Mr. Bissell from his days in Buffalo. The Marine Corps Band, known as "The President's Own," wore their familiar ornate red jackets and blue trousers and performed under the direction of 32-year-old John Philip Sousa.

In 1888, after years of construction, the Washington Monument was officially opened. It weighed over 81,000 tons, and at 555 feet it was the tallest free standing masonry structure in the world. It was quite the talk of the city.

The following year, in February, another son, Charles Burwell, was born into the Hamilton family. To avoid any confusion between the two fellows named "Charles" in the family, the newborn son would often be called "Burley."

To escape from the city, Charles and Ida soon purchased a summer cottage in Cape May, New Jersey. They relished the retreat away from the fast-paced lifestyle as a location for which they could be alone as a family.

On February 24, 1891, 11 men, including Charles A. Hamilton, officially filed proper paperwork with the recorder of deeds for a certificate to incorporate the National Capital Press Club. At the end of the year, Charles was elected as one of three governors of the club for a three-year term.

With two children Charles and Ida wished to expand the family. At 36 years old, Charles, a man full of life and ambition, was to have a son with similar drive and perseverance, yet this son would choose his own very different path in life. On July 5, 1892, George Wallis Hamilton, the subject of this book, was born in the Le Droit Park section of the Capital City. Some publications list his middle name as Wallace or Washington, but his middle name was definitely Wallis, the family name from the lineage on his mother's side of the family. The old adage that true leaders are born cannot be fully explained, but George was in fact a "born leader," and over the course of his lifetime, he would apply this special gift.

As pioneer residents in the Le Droit Park area, Charles and Ida were now firmly settled into the community. In the fall of the year, following one of the less-heated political campaigns, Grover Cleveland defeated incumbent Republican President Benjamin Harrison and was sent back to the White House to serve a second term.

Journalism was expanding and the local *Washington Post* relocated to a brand new building. The proprietor of the building had a vacancy, and Charles, who also represented the *Sioux City Journal*, became the second occupant of the building. Once he had moved in, the building was dedicated on November 23, 1893, with a luncheon and half hour concert by the Marine Corps Band.

A few years later, on November 16, 1895, the Hamiltons' last child, Margaret Dorothy, was born. The family, with four living children — Mary, Burley, George and Margaret — was now complete.

Innovation was now taking place with two types of electricity: direct current, which could only travel a couple of miles, and alternating current that theoretically could travel much further. General Electric was a new company favoring Edison's idea of DC, and they competed against the newly formed Westinghouse Company, which promoted Nikola Tesla's vision of AC. America's biggest new venture was a project to take power from Niagara Falls and transmit it 22 miles away to the city of Buffalo. On November 15, 1896, the power grid was complete, and the city celebrated its recognition as the recipient of the first successful long distance transmission of commercial electricity. With electricity, Buffalo could now attract many new industries and see prosperous growth.

In 1898, when Hamilton was six, Colonel Theodore Roosevelt fought with his First United States Volunteer Cavalry, commonly known as the regiment of Rough Riders, in the Spanish-American War on the island of Cuba. Roosevelt's book *The Rough Riders*, published the following year, was similar to a modern day adventure novel. Most young boys gravitated towards this best selling book rather than some of the classics of the time. The historical book detailed the recruitment of the all-volunteer regiment:

> All — Easterners and Westerners, Northerners and Southerners, officers and men, cowboys and college graduates, wherever they came from, and whatever their social position — possessed in common the traits of hardihood and thirst for adventure. They were to a man born adventurers, in the old sense of the word.[7]

When the Spanish-American War ended, the signed treaty gave the southern shore of Cuba, called Guantanamo, where the Marines camped, to the United States. Americans did not know what the future held, but the war would serve as the nation's last major conflict before entering the World War.

In 1899 the Hamilton family was together for Christmas at their home at 1205 Kenyon Street in the District of Columbia. Little Margaret was 4 years old, George was 7, and Burley 10. Mary, who was 15 and attending the Moravian Seminary in Bethlehem, Pennsylvania, was coming home with a friend from school. The end of this year was also the end of the 19th century and the start of the 20th. It was to be a memorable New Year's Eve across the entire world. Hamilton's local newspaper, the *Washington Post*, described the local atmosphere:

> With a faint and feeble sputter, the candles of 1899 were snuffed as the clocks struck the hour of 12 last night, and the faded glories of the dying year gave place to the bright promise and glowing prospects of the new year. The blowing of steamboat whistles on the river, the clanging of bells upon street cars, the blasts of tin trumpets in the hands of enthusiastic youths, the songs of joy and gladness in many churches, and the happy greetings in millions of homes heralded the dawn of the year of our Lord 1900, which marked the beginning of the end of a century filled with remarkable history.[8]

Most churches held "watchnight" services, which started around 10 P.M. and lasted until midnight. It was noted that in eleven days Russia would finally celebrate the New Year. The Hebrews and the Chinese, who did not acknowledge the Roman calendar, would celebrate the New Year and new century much later in 1900.

One other front page story, "Price for Danish Islands," was noteworthy as it gave an indication of the current economic conditions of America. Danish Captain Christmas, as a formal representative of Denmark's King Christian IX, was offering to sell the Danish West Indies to America for a firm price of $4,000,000. America declined the offer and chose to wait 17 years to purchase Saint Croix, Saint Thomas and Saint John as a national strategic defensive measure during World War I, paying the increased price of $25,000,000.

News of gasoline engine technology was spreading, and all of society would be changed forever. Automobile companies were being formed, and in 1900 there were at least three dozen throughout the United States.

The Hamiltons sold their Cape May property, and in late May of 1900, Charles and Ida purchased an upstate farm in western New York. The retreat was located along the western shore of Conesus Lake on West Lake Road in the village of Groveland within Livingston County. The farm home would serve as a diversion from city life and as a wonderful hideaway to relax and at times exert energy. Although the Hamiltons' regular residence remained in the District of Columbia, their legal residence was now listed as their Conesus Lake farm.

Conesus Lake, one of the smaller north and south lakes in the chain of Finger Lakes, is roughly 9 miles long, 1.5 miles wide and 65 feet deep. The property encompassed 80 acres of beautiful woods, fields and creeks along with a quarter of a mile lake frontage. Their well built two-story house, complete with four bedrooms, a basement and indoor plumbing, was elevated on a 30-foot slope above the lake. To the right of the house and about 50 feet higher in elevation was a free standing garage. There were also several scattered cottages nearby, and Charles named two of them Bide-a-wee and Rest-a-while. A barn and a carriage shed were behind the house on the left at roughly an elevation of 130 feet above the lake. Additional outbuildings included a wood and tool shed, an ice house and a pigpen shed.[9] Drinking water came from the well, but lake water was pumped for washing.

Hamilton spent most of his youthful summers at Conesus Lake, along with his mother, brother and sisters. His father tended to his journalistic duties but got away as often as he could to join the family. Hamilton loved nature and making the dash up and down the hillside soon became second nature, giving him plenty of stamina. If he wished to swim, the lake was all his.

The train was certainly the predominant method of transportation and getting to the local train station from their Capital City home was not a problem. At the turn of the century, the North Central Railroad along with the Erie Railroad and Conesus Branch should have gotten them to their destination, over 300 miles away, in about 15 hours. Shortly after purchasing the property, Charles Hamilton realized that the Erie Railroad Company only operated from May 30 to September 30, so he filed a formal complaint.[10] As might be expected, there was a clause stating the railroad operated during winter months as they wished.

In 1900 Buffalo was the eighth largest city in the United States with a population around 352,000. Washington, D.C., had about 75,000 fewer citizens and was ranked 15th. Buffalo was selected to host the 1901 Pan-American Exposition, which was a worldwide event and served as a prelude to the 1904 St. Louis World's Fair. The host city was chosen because of its electrical power and good railroad transportation.

The exposition was open to the public from May 1 to November 2, highlighting the world's latest innovations and technology with a theme of electric power. Featured attractions were the nearly 400-foot-tall Electric Tower, with an illuminated "Goddess of Light" on top, and the Temple of Music. The fair contained numerous displays and cultural exhibits, such as Eskimo,

Indian, Mexican and African villages. There were athletic events and many side attractions, including a Wild West show and a booth with Geronimo. Additionally there was a detachment of U.S. Marines exhibiting daily drills.

Conesus Lake was only about 90 miles away, and Hamilton, roughly nine years old, likely spent time viewing the show. This was possibly his first observation of a true Marine demonstration.

On September 6 President William McKinley was visiting the featured Temple of Music, and as the special $15,000 organ was playing light music, he was shot twice by a lone gunman. While Secret Servicemen and Buffalo detectives contained the assassin, a squad of city police and the Marine Corps detachment from the fair formed a security line, and the command was given to "Load rifles!"[11] McKinley died several days later on September 14, the third President to be assassinated. Hamilton's father was said to be the last news correspondent to see the President alive.

Vice President Theodore Roosevelt, who was hunting in the Adirondacks, received news that the President's health had turned worse and headed at once to Buffalo by means of stagecoach and train. Roosevelt arrived in Buffalo on Sept. 14, 1901, several hours after the president had passed away. After viewing the dead President, he desired to walk a few streets to clear his head and declared that he did not want protective service. He then went to the home of Ansley Wilcox and at 3:36 P.M., he was administered the oath of office. At 42 years old, he was the youngest President to date. The 43 witnesses in the room included several Cabinet members and two dozen invited newspaper correspondents. As a Capitol Hill correspondent to Buffalo's major newspaper, Hamilton's father witnessed it all.

On September 16 McKinley's body was sent back to the District of Columbia. Since Hamilton's home was only about three and a half miles from the United States Capitol, it would have been only natural for him to join the crowd and view as much as possible.[12] A loud gun boomed every five minutes signaling the arrival of the train at 8:38 P.M. The casket was taken by hearse to the East Room of the White House and the following day to the U.S. Capitol Rotunda to lie in state. On the evening of the 17th, McKinley's body was escorted back to the train station to be transported to Canton, Ohio, for final services and burial. Among those riding in the procession of trains along with the McKinley family were President Roosevelt, his Cabinet, many dignitaries, and numerous military personnel, including Marine Corps Commandant Charles Heywood and 40 journalists and correspondents.

Washington leaders wanted the city to become a vibrant showcase to the world with a focal park similar to Boston Common and New York's Central Park.[13] The planned grounds would be rectangular in shape and encompass the existing Washington Monument. The one major obstacle required moving the current downtown railroad station that was used by many, including the Hamilton family.

It did not take long for Roosevelt to shake things up. On October 16, 1901, after only one month in office, he had dinner with Booker T. Washington. As this was the first time an American of African decent was invited to dinner at the White House, the encounter was kept as secret as possible. Still, word leaked out and the historical event was quickly national news, with Washington correspondents scrambling for details as to who attended.[14]

In February 1902 the President appointed Elliott Woods as architect of the Capitol, and he would assist with two major projects that had already been approved. Members of the House and Senate needed additional space, and over the next several years he would oversee construction of what would later be named the Cannon House Office Building and the Russell Senate Office Building, complete with an automobile tunnel connecting the two buildings.

Roosevelt believed in the rule that "children should be seen and not heard," and with six children, ages four to 17, it was difficult for him to concentrate in his study on his second floor residence. Although several children were off attending various schools, a few like Quentin, the youngest, roamed the house. During his first full year in office, Roosevelt hired some New York architects to design and construct a temporary addition to the White House so he would be able to have some quiet office space. The offices, known as Temporary Executive Offices, would in future years, be fully remodeled and termed the West Wing, which includes the Oval Office.

The presence of the Roosevelt children at the White House was fully evident later in 1903 with the children's Christmas party, which included 400 junior guests. The White House had never hosted such an event of this magnitude with entertainment from 4:00 to 6:30 P.M., including the Marine Corps Band.[15] Hamilton, at 11 years old, would have been able to relate to the excitement surrounding the prominent White House children, just a few miles away.

The hot topic of conversation likely centered upon the major historic event that had occurred a few days earlier. On December 17, 1903, the first successful aviation flight was made by Orville and Wilbur Wright on the sand dunes of Kill Devil Hill at Kitty Hawk, North Carolina. Each took turns flying solo. Orville flew first, going 120 feet in 20 seconds, and before the day was over Wilbur flew the farthest at 852 feet in just less than a minute.[16]

In 1904 President Roosevelt was instrumental in beginning construction on the Panama Canal. It took about two months for a cargo ship to sail from California around the southern tip of South America to get to New York City, and the canal would offer a much quicker and safer route. As America was becoming a world power, the canal would also serve as a valuable asset for the nation's military.

In 1907 the park construction and architectural renovation project surrounding the nation's capital was nearing completion. In future years there would be individual projects on a lesser scale, including additional national monuments. On October 27, 1907, Washington's new railroad station, Union Station, opened with the 6:56 A.M. arrival of the Pittsburg Express over the B&O.[17] Architecturally, the grand new station was a masterpiece with high vaulted ceilings and arches. The massive concourse was 760 feet long and 130 feet wide, with 44-foot ceilings and many windows for extra light. The station was given a prime location directly facing the Capitol five blocks away, and as one of the city's largest private employers, it now served as a prominent hub for the both the United States government and local citizens.

In the spring of 1908, Hamilton was completing his last year of middle school, while his brother was finishing at Central High and preparing to head off to George Washington University.

Miles away in Detroit, the low priced, simply designed, rugged and functional four-cylinder 20-horsepower Ford Model T was being made available to many in American society.

2. Central High

In 1908, as autumn was approaching, Hamilton walked through the doors of Central High, which had a student population of roughly 1,000. At 16 years old he was starting his high school education a little late, and he would be one of the older students in his class. Although George was three years younger than Burley, they were separated in school by four years, so their days at Central High did not overlap. The reason for his late start in high school is unknown.

Hamilton had some close relatives who were also talented scholastic achievers. His first cousin Carlton Herbert Wright was only one month older, and at 16 he was appointed to the United States Naval Academy. Carlton's young age was not totally out of the ordinary for the Naval Academy, as the U.S. Navy was considered to be in a transitional period and there were at least two other 16-year-olds at the Academy. Carlton's mother, the former Mary Jane Hamilton, was Charles A. Hamilton's sister, who was married to George C. Wright.[1] With his cousin now in his backyard, Hamilton would not only be competing in all aspects of life against his brother Burley, but against his cousin Carlton too.

Later in the fall of Hamilton's freshman year, incumbent president Theodore Roosevelt was promoting fellow Republican William Howard Taft to succeed him. His support proved successful, and Taft was elected the 27th President of the United States, taking office early in 1909. At roughly six feet tall and 300 pounds he was the largest President to date. President Roosevelt, the man from Harvard, looked forward to another stage of his life and turning the reins over to his friend from Yale.[2]

In the fall of 1909, Norfolk, Virginia, hosted the second annual convention of the Atlantic Deeper Waterways Association. President Taft and his wife traveled by water on the presidential yacht *Mayflower*, along with other dignitaries, including Mr. and Mrs. Andrew Carnegie. Seventy reporters, including Hamilton's father, followed on the steamer *Norfolk*.

Hamilton ended up being a multi-sport athlete at Central High School. Proudly wearing the schools colors, he truly excelled in football along with track and field events. He was extremely self-motivated, and he put every hour of the day to good use. His efforts paid off, as he regularly broke long-standing school records.

In the early years, the game of football was centered primarily on a good running back, a few good linemen and a kicking game. Whether running through a cloud of dust or a pile of mud, the game plan was usually to grind it out and see which opponent would wear down first. Hamilton was a hard nosed fullback and a good punter whose proficiency in the kicking game often won ballgames.

True competitors are constantly striving to learn and find new ways and means to improve. Hamilton was this type of constant competitor throughout his life. A good example was in December 1909, following his sophomore year as captain of the football team, when he went to New York to witness firsthand the game of English rugby. The *Washington Post* high school section stated, "Hamilton is one of those men who does everything that will in any way better the chances of victory for his team."[3]

Keep this profound statement in mind when in later years this football captain becomes a Marine Corps captain and does everything in his power to achieve objectives and victory for his men. Finesse, peripheral vision, speed, endurance, open field tackling, camaraderie, quick thinking while on the move, team communication and a kicking game are important aspects of rugby. With very few interruptions the free-flowing game has moments of mass confusion and tension, and times to settle down. The "pitch," as the field is called, is like a battlefield. Attacking the opponent through a vulnerable lane at their weakest link is good strategy. Hamilton likely picked up numerous ideas that he would recall in the future.

Hamilton's younger sister Margaret excelled in her eighth grade class at Hubbard School, and in January 1910, she, along with a few hundred other middle school students within the school system, received an early diploma and immediately began high school studies.[4] She entered Central High where the "Hamilton" name had an established reputation.

In 1910, with the backing of President Taft's administration, Congress gave approval for funding construction of a national monument in the District of Columbia to honor Abraham Lincoln. The designer, Henry Bacon, would model the structure after the ancient Greek temples, while sculptor Daniel Chester French was selected to carve the seated Lincoln.[5] The project would not begin for a few years, but Hamilton would often take notice of the progression over its roughly nine years of construction.

This summer, Hamilton, the rising Central High junior was going to be away from the Conesus Lake region for an extended period of time. He was expanding his firsthand view of America's natural beauty by traveling by train across many states to "Big Sky Country" and the state of Montana. His temporary summer job was with the Geological Survey in the Field Corps as an assistant performing topographic survey.[6]

In 1910 Charles A. Hamilton was able to secure a correspondent's position at the *Washington Post* for his nephew James L. Wright, a brother of Carlton Wright. Charles became a mentor to the young man and introduced him to all of his key contacts in the profession.

For the summer of 1911, young Hamilton tried another venture by working for the U.S. Forest Service. The daily duties undoubtedly further strengthened his body for his final senior year of athletics. Hamilton presided as the football captain at Central High for a record three years, from his sophomore year through senior year in the fall of 1911, and during that span Central High won the high school championship all three years.[7] He received recognition by the *Washington Post* as an all-star and member of the "all-high eleven" for all three years.

In track and field Hamilton excelled in a number of events, although his specialty was 440- and 880-yard dashes roughly equivalent to a quarter-mile and half-mile. He was also accomplished at shot put, throwing the hammer, and the broad jump. In his junior year he broke the local high school shot-put record by throwing the weighted ball more than 42 feet.[8]

In the spring of 1912, Hamilton was enjoying his final months at Central High School. April 7 was Easter Sunday and chiming church bells broke the silence in his Le Droit Park neighborhood. For many, life in America was quite peaceful. On the following Sunday, April 14 at around midnight, the White Star liner *Titanic*, on its maiden voyage from England to America, hit an iceberg and sank to the bottom of the ocean. The world mourned the loss of more than 1,500 souls. Ramifications were felt on Capitol Hill, as some of America's most prominent businessmen were among the deceased. Likely Charles Hamilton took time from reporting to recall his own unique rustic voyage from England when his ship skirted many icebergs.

As his high school senior year was winding down, Hamilton was finalizing his plans for the next chapter of his life. Many colleges and universities were trying to recruit him. The University of Virginia was putting forth "strenuous efforts" to try and secure him along with his football and track partner Reuter. A newspaper article mentioned that in the past, the most notable athletes "want to get as far away from their home city as possible while going to school. Then, too, to be a star athlete at Yale, Harvard, Princeton, Pennsylvania, Michigan, or Cornell is a much harder proposition than at either Georgetown or Virginia."[9] It was noted that it was doubtful UVA could land Hamilton, as he would probably go to a Big Four school. However, if the two Central High boys went to the state university, "Virginia would get two corking athletes."[10]

Hamilton continued his exploits in spring track at the important annual M.A.C. Games where he showed his mettle. The interscholastic games between schools in neighboring states were held at the Maryland Agricultural College, and the results made front page sporting news. Central High's big trio of Hamilton, Blackstone and Reuter scored 39 points among them for a team total of 48 points. Baltimore Polytechnic Institute finished second with a total of 16 points. Hamilton won the tournament individual trophy, placing first overall in the half-mile run, shot put, and hammer throw, while taking third overall in the broad jump.[11]

At 19 years old, Hamilton was one of the smartest students among the Central High graduating class of 1912, and the entire student body and faculty knew that he was destined for future success. The commencement exercise for the 141 seniors was held on June 18, 1912, in Memorial Continental Hall, with the girls seated upon the stage and the boys divided on both sides of the room. Methodist Bishop Wilbur P. Thirkield was the keynote speaker, and a section of the Marine Corps Band was present to play a few songs.[12]

Not too far away, his first cousin Carlton H. Wright, at the same age, was blazing his own trail after placing 16th out of a class of 156 graduates at the United States Naval Academy. President Taft was delighted to be on hand to personally hand out the diplomas to each individual.[13] Carlton was off to a fast start; however, Hamilton the track star knew the saying, "It's not how you start, but how you finish."

The Washington Athletic Association decided to become a permanent organization with an overall desire to promote amateur athletics in the Amateur Athletic Union. Their mission was to network nationally with the goal of having the Washington Athletic Association represent the Capital City in national events. The association president selected five fellows, including Hamilton, to serve on the initial membership committee to recruit new qualified members.[14]

During the summer of 1912, the major sports story across the nation concerned American's greatest multi-talented athlete, 24-year-old Jim Thorpe, who was performing at the Olympic Games in Stockholm, Sweden. Thorpe, a Native American, gained recognition through a strong performance in the pentathlon and decathlon, bringing home two gold metals.[15] Hamilton was consumed with following local, national and world record accomplishments in the track and field arena, and Thorpe was the best in the world.

America was struggling with citizenship issues, and many Native Americans, including Thorpe, were not currently considered citizens of the United States. When Thorpe competed in the Olympics he represented the Sac and Fox Nation and the United States. For many with Indians, it would be several more years before full citizenship would be granted.

3. Off to College

Would Hamilton attend the University of Virginia or head away from home to attend an Ivy League school? He had many options. Finally he decided to enter Georgetown University's law school department and also play football.[1] He was trading in his blue and white colors for blue and gray. George Van Dyne, a Central High halfback and teammate of Hamilton's, was following the exact same path.

Chances are that Hamilton's Central High track coach, William "Bill" Foley, prompted his decision to attend the local college. Foley was an exceptional individual and valuable member of the Central High faculty. Prior to coaching at the high school level, he was the track coach at Georgetown University. His own style of physical preparation was so unique and successful that some of his pupils became national champions and world-record holders. In 1900 the American Olympic track team did not have a designated coach, so Foley traveled to Paris as a formal advisor to several of the team members. He switched to coaching at the high school level to follow his passion and ended up being a strong mentor in Hamilton's life. When Coach Foley reminisced about the notable track stars that he assisted through the years, he usually included the name George Hamilton.[2]

Due to Georgetown's proximity to Capitol Hill, politics were always a source of conversation. This was another presidential election year, and during the fall of 1912, extraordinary election campaigns were in full swing. Many Americans were noticeably disenchanted with the platforms put forth by both the Republican and Democratic Parties and wanted an alternative to what they were offering. The third option was the new Progressive Party and its candidate, the man who carried the "Big Stick," former Republican president Theodore Roosevelt. The Progressive platform noted:

> The people of the United States without regard to past political differences, who, through repeated betrayals, realize that to-day the power of the crooked political bosses and of the privileged classes behind them is so strong in the two old party organizations that no helpful movement in the real interest of our country can come out of either; who believe that a nation-wide progressive movement on

non-sectional lines is desirable; and who believe in the right and capacity of the people to rule themselves.³

The Progressive Party, also known as the "Bull Moose Party," had some visionary beliefs included in their platform, such as support "for equal suffrage for women; limitation and publicity of campaign funds; registration of lobbyists; [and] publicity of committee hearings."⁴

The fall of 1912 was a busy time for Hamilton as he juggled college courses and football. Keeping physically in shape was very important to him, so he also remained active with the Washington Athletic Association, competing in a number of regional track meets. As an all-around athlete he continued with the 880-yard run, the broad jump, shot put, discus throw and hammer throw.

Football was usually referred to as the "eleven," because teams generally played the eleven starters for the entire game, both on offense and defense, unless there was a valid reason for a substitution. For the upcoming 1912 season major changes were made to the rules of football. Instead of three downs, each team would now be given four downs. The field was decreased from 110 yards to 100 yards and points for a touchdown increased from five to six.

The GU eleven had all three starting running backs returning along with nine additional very talented fellows, including Hamilton and Van Dyne, competing for the positions.⁵ Jim Dunn, a rugged 185-pound junior fullback, weighed 15 pounds more than Hamilton and won the starting position as the workhorse. In mid-season Dunn was noted as most likely the best line-smashing running back in GU history.⁶ The quarterback, Harry Costello, was also a junior and pound for pound one of the most athletic players in the nation. At only 138 pounds he could not only run and pass, but also handle the all important talent of drop-kicking the pigskin through the goal.

The team was divided into two squads, and both Hamilton and Van Dyne made the team, ending up on the second squad. The tandem, which played together in high school, was as fast as ever. Hamilton, as a combination fullback, halfback, punter and drop-kicker, would have to bide his time, which was something he was not accustomed to. It appears that as a freshman, he would find his enjoyment through each physical practice.

Georgetown was building their football program to rival the traditional national powerhouse teams.⁷ Their current nine-game schedule included rivals such as the University of North Carolina and University of Virginia.

One exceptionally formidable team that stood out on the schedule was the Carlisle Indian Industrial School, an independent school in Carlisle, Pennsylvania, with an amazing history and heritage. As far as football is concerned, however, when the Carlisle team traveled to away games they "took the show on the road." Their coach, who was extremely innovative, was the 40-year-old legendary Glenn Scobey Warner, known by many as simply "Pop" Warner. The team's star halfback was none other than the multi-talented Olympic star Jim Thorpe.

On October 26 Carlisle showed up undefeated at 6–0–1 to play Georgetown, who was also undefeated at 4–0. With the presidential election just a couple of weeks away this Saturday's game was the place for folks in Washington society to be. Many U.S. congressmen and senators were a part of the more than 5,000 folks jammed into the bleachers to catch a firsthand glimpse of the Olympian in action. Before the game, senior senator Boies Penrose of Pennsylvania half-heartedly mentioned to the Carlisle players that citizenship might be forthcoming for those with outstanding performances on the field. One Indian player named "Big Bear" was not overjoyed and stated in a matter of fact manner, "They tell me if I become a citizen, I will have to pay taxes."[8]

Hamilton, who traveled all the way to New York to study a rugby game, would have paid plenty to just watch Jim Thorpe run and perform on the field. Thorpe was extremely muscular yet agile, and at 6'1" and 190 pounds he was one of the larger players on the Carlisle team. The versatile athlete also handled the kicking duties. Hamilton did not play; however, as a member of the Georgetown squad, he had a standing sideline front row view. Georgetown lost its only game of the season to Carlisle 34–20 and went on to finish the schedule with a final record of 8–1.

On Tuesday, November 5, American citizens cast their votes, and when the election results were finally tallied, the new Democrat on the scene, Woodrow Wilson, was elected as the 28th President of the United States. Roosevelt the Progressive candidate came in second, and the incumbent Republican, President Taft, finished a distant third.

On the following Saturday, November 9, two weeks after the Georgetown game, Carlisle, still undefeated, visited the West Point Military Academy. Army's halfback was Dwight David Eisenhower, who at 5'10" and 180 pounds was a powerful running back. The game did not need any extra buildup as a team consisting of American Indians was pitted against a U.S. Army team. Coach Warner of Carlisle knew exactly how to motivate his team by finishing his pre-game sermon stating: "Remember Wounded Knee. Remember all of this on every play. Let's go."[9]

Towards the end of the game, the versatile Eisenhower playing linebacker injured his knee as he closed upon Thorpe. Carlisle decisively beat the Army Cadets 27–6 and went on to contend for the Collegiate National Championship, finishing at 12–1–1. Their only defeat was to the University of Pennsylvania by a score of 34–26.

For reasons unknown Hamilton up and left Georgetown University in November during his first semester. Vincent Dailey, the athletic director and twice captain of the football team, left the school in January 1913 for personal family reasons.[10] Perhaps there was a strong bond between Dailey and Hamilton as a football recruit. His teammate Van Dyne was a potential starter on next season's varsity squad; however, he planned to forgo football to devote extra time to studies.[11]

Had Hamilton stayed at Georgetown he eventually would likely have been the collegiate national star many envisioned. As a law student he might have become a prominent Washington lawyer and more.

Hamilton appears to have been very frustrated, but like his father, he had full confidence in his own abilities that he could succeed on his own in whatever career path he chose. He was quickly hired on November 20, 1912, as a real estate clerk in the National Savings and Trust Company in Washington, D.C. While in this position he continued to search for his path in life. By the spring of 1913, he had a clear vision for his future.

Growing up in the Capital City atmosphere certainly exposed a young man to many professions. One thing that is very clear is that Hamilton never shied away from a competitive challenge or a pressure situation as further evidenced by his next major decision; he set his sights on the Marine Corps!

4. Becoming a Marine

On April 1, 1913, Hamilton left his position at the National Savings and Trust Company to devote time towards studying and preparing for examinations to obtain a commission in the Marine Corps.[1] Likely his reasons for attempting to become a Marine Corps officer were similar to those of other individuals at the time. The world was basically at peace, but the opportunity for adventurous travel to distant parts of the world enticed many. Through the Marine Corps he would be able to expand his education and there might also be a chance to test one's courage in action. Finally, protecting and serving his country were always important to Hamilton.

Marines spent a lot of time on board ships as "soldiers of the sea" and were therefore cross-trained for both duty on board ships as well as light infantry combat. This service obviously required more extensive training than other branches of the armed services. In general there was not much action aboard the ships, and if a Marine wanted to be thrust into a unique experience, it would be on land, quelling disturbances, fighting bandits or other insurgents, usually on uncivilized islands in warm water locations.

No one can contest the fact that Hamilton seemed to have all the qualities that the Marine Corps was looking for. He was an ambitious, honest, highly intelligent, very athletic young man, who was looking for a challenge. He enrolled in the local Dowd Army and Navy Preparatory School, also known as the Dowd Military Academy, which basically consisted of tutoring classes from Michael Dowd, the principal of the school. He even did some studying back at his old Central High location. Certificates from the accredited school were also honored by George Washington University.

He stood very erect and appeared to be much taller than he really was. As part of his preparations to enter military service, he took a preliminary physical on April 14, 1913. This physical noted his stripped height at 5'11", weight 170 pounds, along with a 38-inch chest.[2]

He secured written recommendations from the president of the National Savings and Trust Company, the chairman of the United States Senate Committee on the Geological Survey, and Congressman Henry G. Danforth from his Groveland, New York, district that served as testimony to his character.

Another recommendation came from his principal at Central High. The letter addressed to the Honorable Josephus Daniels, secretary of the navy, mentioned:

> Young Hamilton is a graduate of this school and for four years came under my daily observation. By reason of his prominence in school athletics I came to know him perhaps more intimately even than I do most of the boys. I feel that I can speak of him with absolute certainty. He is a young man of unusual mental ability and, although interested in many school activities, he never permitted them to interfere with his work but always took high rank in his classes. He has an attractive personality and has very strongly those elements which are bound to make him a leader of men. I know of no recent graduate of this school whom I would consider better material for the government military service. His habits are good and I have absolute confidence that he is a young man of sterling character. I recommend him strongly.[3]

In the midst of his studies, a controversy erupted that had direct implications for his future. In the past, roughly 90 percent of officer candidate vacancies were filled from civilians outside of the military service. In the latter part of May, Josephus Daniels publicly stated that he planned to fill the current ten vacancies from within the enlisted ranks, or at least give them the first option. Although Dowd felt that at best only 1 percent of the current enlisted men could pass the required exam, it appeared that the actions of Secretary Daniels were not only discriminatory against civilians but illegal. Dowd complained, stating:

> At the time this statement of Secretary Daniels appeared there were in Washington, to my knowledge, fifteen young men who had been studying several months at a very heavy expense preparing themselves for this examination, which was to have been held early in June. They had also received letters from Mr. Daniels stating that they would be designated to take the examination when it was held. You can imagine the effect this statement had upon these young men, who had spent several hundred dollars, given up good positions, and had been studying for months for this examination.[4]

In the end, Secretary Daniels backed off his stance and kept an open policy towards qualified civilian applicants. Hamilton remained focused on his education, and the examinations were pushed back. Following the exams, he went to the Conesus Lake farm to spend the summer days awaiting the test results. All of his diligence paid off, as internal Navy Department paperwork made reference to Hamilton being appointed a second lieutenant in the Marine Corps on August 20, 1913. On August 29 he sent a brief handwritten letter to USMC commandant Major General William P. Biddle acknowledging that he had received notification of passing the exam and that he was now headed home to 1032 Lamont Street in Washington, D.C., where he could be contacted.

4. Becoming a Marine

A 1913 USMC Recruiting Poster, painted by S. H. Reisenberg (courtesy National Archives).

Hamilton spent the next couple of months preparing mentally and physically for the official day. On November 13, 1913, Josephus Daniels issued a list of a little more than a dozen officer candidates to the United States Senate, and after brief discussion the list was confirmed. On the list was George W. Hamilton of New York.[5] New York stands out as being odd, but then again, this was his legal residence. It is interesting to review the names of his contemporaries who also joined at this moment. Two men were noted with a home address in the District of Columbia, one of whom was William H. Rupertus, who would become a Marine Corps legend.

Hamilton accepted the appointment on November 14 in Washington, D.C., when he took the oath of office. He spent a few days at the Marine Corps headquarters, and on November 29 he reported for duty at the Marine Officers' School at Marine Barracks in Norfolk, Virginia. This location would serve as his home base for the next year and a half.

On December 3 he had an official officer's physical, and most of the information was close to his spring physical. He had light brown hair and his grey eyes, noted in April, were now noticed to be blue with 20/20 vision.[6]

He would receive a full complement of training in areas including drill regulation, small arms firing, administration, U.S. Naval and military law, signals, fire discipline, field engineering, topography and certain tactics. It seems that he would enjoy all aspects of his education; however, it is quite apparent that he got his greatest pleasure from rifle shooting.

Although Lieutenant Rupertus was not selected to join Hamilton and others in the future fighting on the Western Front, he later rose through the ranks to become a major general and a legendary name to all Marines. While a brigadier general commanding the Marine Corps Base at San Diego, California, he authored the creed "My Rifle," also known as "The Rifleman's Creed," "The Creed of the United States Marine," or simply "The Creed." Today it is a part of all Marine Corps basic training.

"MY RIFLE"
The creed of a United States Marine

1. This is my rifle. There are many like it, but this one is mine.
2. My rifle is my best friend. It is my life. I must master it as I master my life.
3. My rifle, without me, is useless. Without my rifle, I am useless. I must fire my rifle true. I must shoot straighter than any enemy who is trying to kill me. I must shoot him before he shoots me. I will...
4. My rifle and myself know that what counts in this war is not the rounds we fire, the noise of our burst, nor the smoke we make. We know that it is the hits that count. We will hit...
5. My rifle is human, even as I, because it is my life. Thus, I will learn it as a brother. I will learn its weakness, its strength, its parts, its accessories, its sights

and its barrel. I will keep my rifle clean and ready, even as I am clean and ready. We will become part of each other. We will…

6. Before God I swear this creed. My rifle and myself are the defenders of my country. We are the masters of our enemy. We are the saviors of my life.
7. So be it, until victory is America's and there is no enemy, but peace!⁷

The rife of choice was the .30 caliber M1903 Springfield bolt action, with a five round internal box. The history of the rifle stems from the German Mauser Company. The Germans were known to make a good quality rifle and when it comes to rifles, quality counts. During the Spanish-American War, the Spanish used the latest 1893 model, commonly known as the "Spanish Mauser," to great success. In that war the Americans, including the Rough Riders, used a Krag rifle, which was much older technology. At the turn of the century, when all segments of America were gearing up manufacturing, the Springfield, Massachusetts, Armory tested making adaptations of the German Mauser.⁸ Production began when an improved model was fully agreed upon, and hence the year 1903 and Springfield were incorporated into the name. As the best rifle around, it became the favorite of the Marine Corps and other branches of the military for years to come.

Lieutenant Hamilton arrived at the Winthrop, Maryland, rifle range on May 2, 1914, a range that could be used later not only by Marines at Quantico, but also those stationed at the Philadelphia and Norfolk Barracks. In training camp the Marine Corps designated the three top classifications in rifle shooting: "marksman"; the higher classification "sharpshooter," which was very good; and "expert." Few were categorized as elite top-tier shooters. The training instructors were fully capable of teaching the necessary advanced skills to the recruits, and it was up to each individual to apply the knowledge to perfect his technique. Under constant guidance, supervision, intense practice, and competition, men shot from 200 to

2nd Lt. Hamilton, March 25, 1914, during officer training (courtesy National Archives).

600 yards using a variety of positions. Some shots were slow and deliberate, while at other times the training involved rapid fire shooting under specific time constraints. The weeks of practice culminated with an individual shooting test and comparative final score. If a man was proficient enough on the range he could earn extra pay for his skills as well as a medal of recognition. Marksman was an extra $2.00, sharpshooter $3.00 and expert $5.00 per month. After 15 days of education and training, Hamilton achieved the highest classification "expert." His thoughts regarding the value of a rife would be similar to those of Lieutenant Rupertus. A few years later, as a commanding officer in the World War, Hamilton said, "I carried a rifle on the whole trip and I used it to good advantage."[9]

Rifle competition became a new passion for Hamilton. The best knew all the tricks of the trade, such as blackening the gun sights with smoke or shoe polish to avoid unnecessary glare. The sport involved not only calm hand-eye coordination, but also much analytical thought, taking into account critical factors such as distance, sun and wind conditions, and even mathematic calculation tables.

On Tuesday, June 16, Charles and Ida Hamilton's youngest child Margaret received her high school diploma from Central High following a ceremony held at the National Theater. Central High, with its proximity to Capitol Hill, often received special recognition in the city, and this was clearly evident in this years' commencement speaker, President Wilson's secretary of state, Robert Lansing.[10]

The previous summer it took on average twelve and a half hours to make a Ford Model T; however, by the summer of 1914, thanks to the assembly line, it now took only one and a half hours to make the same basic black automobile.[11] American engineers were creating advanced technology, and a dedicated manufacturing workforce had the country on a roll.

This summer it would be difficult for Lieutenant Hamilton to get to Conesus Lake. The Hamilton family was becoming better known in the Capital City, and occasionally the *Washington Post* social section made a small notation. It was noted that Hamilton's mother, Ida, and sisters, Mary and Margaret, were heading to Conesus Lake on June 1 and, furthermore, that his mother was staying on until November.

The Marines often used a summer camp in Gettysburg, Pennsylvania, for month-long exercises. This year Hamilton attended the camp from July 18 to August 28, and the large gathering of Marines shared knowledge and worked on their skills. Following the camp maneuvers, he headed back to the Norfolk for continued education and training.

While away at camp, several major news stories broke, keeping national correspondents busy. One involved the Panama Canal, which was now officially open for traffic, including U.S. Naval ships. Word also spread acknowledging that parts of Europe, including Russia, had begun a war; however, they did not realize that this action would be the start of the Great War.

On June 28 Archduke Franz Ferdinand, heir to the Hapsburg throne of Austria-Hungary, was assassinated by a Serbian nationalist. One month later, on July 28, Austria-Hungary declared war on Serbia. Germany joined the fold on the side of Austria-Hungary, creating what was to be called the "Central Powers." On August 1 the Central Powers declared war against Russia; two days later, against France; and the following day, against Belgium. The countries opposing the Central Powers were known as the Allied Powers, or Allied Forces. Some Allied Power countries would technically take a month or much longer to declare war against the Central Power aggressors. France, however, declared war on August 3, 1914, the same day war was declared upon them. England did not wait for war to be thrust upon them, and in support of France, they voluntarily declared war against the Central Powers on August 4, 1914.[12] It appeared that the unsettled world was like a volcano preparing to fully erupt like never before (see Appendix A).

Major General Charles Heywood the ninth Marine Corps commandant, who was serving when Hamilton was born, passed away on February 26, 1915. In his earlier days he had served in the Civil War as a major and lieutenant colonel. In his honor an order was issued directing all officers in the Marine Corps to wear a designated badge of mourning on their sword hilts for a period of two weeks.

Saturday, May 1, 1915, was a notable day as 2nd Lieutenant Hamilton's officer training classes were finally over. He received his "Certificate of Proficiency" and graduated at the top of his class.[13] He was now granted a one month leave of absence.

On the same Saturday, Hamilton could notice from the newspaper interesting developments. The war across the Atlantic had been going on for months, and the intensity was now being felt in America. Charles P. Sumner, the agent for the Cunard Line, received what appeared to be an official threat pertaining to the upcoming voyage of the *Lusitania*, and on May 1, the following notice was carried by most of America's leading newspapers:

NOTICE!

Travelers intending to embark on the Atlantic voyage are reminded that a state of war exists between Germany and her allies and Great Britain and her allies; that the zone of war includes the waters adjacent to the British Isles: that, in accordance with formal notice given by the Imperial German Government, vessels flying the flag of Great Britain, or any of her allies, are liable to destruction in those waters and that travelers sailing in the war zone on ships of Great Britain or her allies do so at their own risk.

IMPERIAL GERMAN EMBASSY,
Washington, D.C., April 22, 1915.

Sumner issued a rebuttal describing beefed up security precautions and current travel conditions on the Cunard vessels:

> No passenger is permitted aboard them unless he can identify himself. No express matter of any sort is taken. Every passenger must identify his baggage before it is placed aboard. There are now no German cruisers in the Atlantic, and the "danger zone" does not begin until we reach the British Channel and the Irish Sea. Then one may say there is a general system of convoying British ships. The British Navy is responsible for all British ships, and especially for Cunarders.[14]

On the next day, May 2, following a two and a half hour delay, the *Lusitania* set sail for Liverpool, England. Among the 1,388 passengers were the famous playwright Charles Klein, Alfred G. Vanderbilt, and Mr. and Mrs. Elbert Hubbard, who were nationally known free-thinking philosophers and founders of the Roycrofter Society of East Aurora, New York. With no bookings cancelled, the crew of 600 increased the total number of people traveling on the steamship to just shy of 2,000, which was the largest group that year. The vast majority were English citizens.

Initially the highly controversial facts regarding the cargo on the *Lusitania* were not fully disclosed. The large ship was apparently carrying loads of munitions. American statutes prohibited passengers from boarding trains or vessels carrying such dangerous explosives.

Five days later President Wilson had just finished lunch and was looking forward to playing a round of golf when news arrived that the Lusitania had been sunk by a German submarine eight miles off Ireland. Germany felt that it had appropriately warned England and America of the consequences. Only three years had passed since the sinking of the *Titanic*, and the tragic news brought back vivid, sad memories that further bonded the English, Irish and Americans. President Wilson remained at the White House checking the updated bulletins as they came in. Initial reports hinted that there were many survivors, but in the end it appears that 1,195 lost their lives.

The Central High Alumni Association held a special evening on Saturday, May 15, with a series of short plays. Margaret Hamilton, along with other alumni and students, assisted with the production "How the Vote Was Won." For those who could attend, the play served as a welcome distraction from all the recent bad news around the world. If Hamilton had not been away relaxing at Conesus Lake, he probably would have enjoyed seeing his sister and faculty at the Central High event.

On June 1, following his one month leave, Hamilton was notified that he was being detached from the Norfolk base and would be afforded another few days off before reporting to the Philadelphia Marine Barracks. He reported for duty on June 5 to the 20th Company, First Brigade. Hamilton spent the month in Philadelphia, except when the brigade went to a camp in West Chester, Pennsylvania, for a few days.

Starting July 6, the day after he turned 23, he was detached from Philadelphia to compete with other Marines in rifle competition at the Winthrop, Maryland, training facility. First Lieutenant Calvin B. Matthews was chosen to select the rifle team to represent the Marine Corps and participate in the National Rifle Matches for several months. The competition between Marines of all ranks would be extremely tough, as many of the rough and tumble privates, corporals and sergeants took pride in their profession. Hamilton was one of the few officers to make the cut, and as a member of the 1915 team, he now understood that if he kept his edge he could look forward to competition in future years.

Historically the National Rifle Association started holding United States Government sanctioned annual National Matches in the mid–1870s. These matches encompassed a variety of events to test the rifle and pistol skills of the best shooters in military organizations.[15] Practice rounds started each summer and led to official competition in early fall. The best shooters from the final matches would have a chance to represent America on the U.S. Olympic Team.

At the turn of the 20th century, the Marine Corps started to become active in the National Matches. However, they did not fare well in competition, and the top chain of command was not pleased. The Corps quickly realized that through competition, they could absorb an abundance of information and eventually master the shooting technique. Their serious approach to shooting, under the guidance of Major C. H. Lauchheimer, showed signs of progress, and in 1910 over a third of all enlisted Marines were classified as marksmen or higher.

In 1915 there were divisional matches in a four locations, which led up to the National Matches at Black Point Military Reservation near Jacksonville, Florida. The assistant executive officer for the National Matches was William Curry Harllee, who had been instrumental as an instructor to Hamilton and others at the Marine Corps Winthrop rifle range. To many, Harllee was known simply as "Bo."

In early August, Hamilton received a notice stating that he had not acknowledged orders issued to him through the company to which he was attached. The situation was quickly cleared up, as he reminded all parties that he was away from his unit and on active duty with the rifle matches. The fact that his assigned company was en route to Haiti must have given him mixed emotions. He was currently excited about the rifle competition, but he certainly did not want to miss out on any real action and adventure.

On August 5, Hamilton, Rupertus and other members of the team went to Wakefield, Massachusetts, to prepare for the upcoming New England Military Rifle Association matches. During the matches, Hamilton took second place in the individual competition of the Clapp Match.

To further prepare for the Divisional National Match, Hamilton and the other team members proceeded to Sea Grit, New Jersey, on September 4. Sea Grit, a host to the National Matches in prior years, was celebrating their 25th annual rifle tournament. Eight men were chosen to be on the official "Marine Team," where shooting scores would be tallied as a group. A team victory along with a trophy would not only provide bragging rites throughout the military, but also serve as great national press coverage for Marine Corps recruiting efforts. Hamilton competed in individual events, but he was not a member of the eight-man team.

One featured event was the long distance Remington Match 1,000-yard shoot out, in which three men tied with a score of 73. A fellow from the 71st Infantry Regiment, New York State Guard, took first place based upon shot location. Marine Sergeant George Jones took second place, 2nd Lieutenant Rupertus third place, while 2nd Lieutenant Hamilton tied for fourth place with a score of 71.[16] A few days later Hamilton competed in an All-Comers' Expert Match in which a contestant had ten minutes and ten shots at a target 600 yards away. Scoring was not tallied until all ten shots had been fired. It was noted that Hamilton placed high enough in this event to win some prize money.[17]

Following the September district event, Hamilton and the rest of the rifle team headed to Jacksonville, Florida, for the National Rifle Association Match. It does not appear that Hamilton placed in the Nationals. November 5 was his last day of duty with the NRA Matches, and he now prepared for his next assignment.

5. A Soldier of the Sea

With the National Rifle Matches over, Hamilton was now officially assigned duty to a ship. On November 8, 1915, 2nd Lieutenant Hamilton joined the USS *Arkansas* (BB-33), as a junior Marine officer. He would now receive his "sea legs," as he would be assigned to this battleship for about one and a half years, up until April 20, 1917. Currently, the *Arkansas* was positioned at the New York Navy Yard receiving minor repairs in preparation for taking to the waters in January. During the intervening time he got accustomed to his men as well as the layout of the ship.

Like a true Marine he hoped to travel in search of action and adventure, but unfortunately this was not the time or place. During years past, the Marines had been called to duty to serve around the world in places such as China, Korea, Cuba, Panama, Nicaragua, Vera Cruz, Haiti, Santo Domingo and the Philippines. Now, however, the raging war in Europe seemed to have a calming effect on other distant areas of the world. With an escalating war across the Atlantic, this period of time was perfect for extended practice sessions, while also providing the country with important national security. He would have to be patient and wait for his day to come.

The United States Navy consisted of three fleets: the Atlantic, Pacific and Asiatic. The Atlantic Fleet was by far the largest and had the primary responsibility of protecting the entire East Coast of the United States.

The Atlantic Fleet had four main divisions: battleships, a torpedo flotilla, submarines and auxiliary boats. The battleship division was divided into an additional four segmented divisions. The first division was composed of dreadnoughts with 12-inch guns and the slightly heavier super dreadnoughts with either 12- or 14-inch guns. The second division was made up of lighter weight dreadnoughts with fewer guns. Older pre-dreadnought ships made up the third and fourth divisions.

The flagship of the Atlantic Fleet was the USS *Wyoming* (BB-32) with a dozen 12-inch guns and displacing about 27,000 tons. The sister ship was the USS *Arkansas*. The *Arkansas*, built by the New York Shipbuilding Corporation, was commissioned on September 17, 1912, and was therefore in very good shape.[1] It was classified as a Wyoming-class battleship, of which two were built, the first being the *Wyoming* itself. The *Arkansas* had a length of 562 feet, a beam of 93.1 feet and drafted 28.5 feet of water. The ship was noted for its overall size, which was about 20 percent longer than the preceding battleships of other classes and was equipped with center turrets and thick side armor.

The repairs on the *Arkansas* were tested on December 22, and following a successful trial, the battleship was pulled back into the New York yard. As a part of the Atlantic Fleet protecting the nation's east coast, it was important to be familiar with the New York harbor and the surrounding area.[2]

On January 5, 1916, Hamilton and others on the ship headed out of New York and down the east coast to Hampton Roads, Virginia. From there they proceeded on to warmer waters in the Caribbean for practice sessions and winter maneuvers, touching base ports in the West Indies and Guantanamo.

In mid–March, while off Mobile Bay, Hamilton instructed his men in fine tuning their skills, with torpedo practice and long-range target practice using guns aimed at objects eight miles away. It would be reasonable that the ship's guns did not come close to giving Hamilton the enjoyment and personal satisfaction that he received from individual target practice with his Springfield rifle. Following the very successful practices, the USS *Arkansas* maneuvered back to Guantanamo where it maintained a presence from March 20 through early April.

On April 15 the battleship was once again back in New York joining four other super-dreadnoughts, including the battleships *Wyoming, Texas, Nevada* and *New York* of the Atlantic Fleet, one pre-dreadnaught, one armored cruiser, three flotillas of destroyers, a division of submarines and other vessels.[3] With war across the Atlantic and the nation's mightiest vessels in port, extra security and lock down precautions were tested for the first time ever at the Naval Yard. At night the ships used their intense spotlights to scour the surrounding waters. Six hundred bluejackets and Marines served guard duty at all gates and selected areas over three shifts with 200 men per shift. Relatives were not permitted visitation, and only people with credentials signed by Rear Admiral Nathaniel R. Usher, the commandant of the yard, were allowed. Even officers were at times subjected to identification checks. German cargo ships docking in New York City were also scrutinized. On Friday, April 21, Assistant Secretary of the Navy Franklin D. Roosevelt visited the Navy Yard to check on procedures and meet with selected officials.

Passes were granted on April 25 to attend the first showing of a motion picture film involving the Marines in action in Haiti.[4] The small country, consisting of more than 10,000 square miles of mountainous terrain, was also full of bands of bandits, who played havoc on the local citizens. In years past, Marines had been called to quell the disruptive aggressors and establish some order. More than 100 officers had requested seating, and they marched from the 23rd Street Pier to the Chandler Theater. Some of the officers who had fought in Haiti would have the opportunity to view themselves under fire. Understandably, Hamilton would wish to be first in line to attend, as, if he could not get in the real action, this would keep him on the edge of his chair.

Even the thought of the movie must have had a big impact upon Hamilton, as just a few weeks later paperwork was sent to USMC Commandant George Barnett requesting permission for him to join the Haitian gendarmerie.[5] The forthcoming decision determined that he was too new of a recruit for the action and that he needed to continue with his presence on the *Arkansas* and wait for a vacancy. Hamilton wished to be active, and he constantly had the Caribbean islands on his mind. Roughly six years later he would once again request duty on the islands.

Weddings often take place in the springtime, and Hamilton received a leave pass to attend a friend's wedding at Annapolis, Maryland. He proudly served as an usher for the wedding of Miss Mary Tolley Ligon and U.S. Navy Ensign Fredrick Gore Richards, who was also assigned to the USS *Arkansas*. Miss Ligon's grandfather was the late governor Thomas Watkins Ligon of Maryland. The formal service included the military tradition of the bride and groom passing beneath the ushers' crossed swords.[6]

On May 31 the British and German naval fleets fought in the North Sea off Denmark's Jutland peninsula. The battle would end up being the single most significant naval battle of World War I with both battered sides claiming victory and vowing to be more vigilant at war.

A top promotion was in order, and on June 19 Vice Admiral Henry T. Mayo became a full admiral. In the process he departed from the *Arkansas* and joined the sister flagship *Wyoming* as commander of the Atlantic Fleet. The ceremony at the New York Naval Yard was quite simple, yet formal. The battleships *Arkansas*, *Texas*, and *Oklahoma* were in their berths next to the flagship, and all men stood at full attention until cheers went forth with the firing of the *Wyoming*'s seventeen guns.[7] Hamilton now had Vice Admiral De Witt Coffman as his new commander.

Navy Secretary Josephus Daniels issued a report on July 7 pertaining to the overall target shooting efficiency of the Atlantic Fleet. Of the seventeen ships that were graded, four, including the *Arkansas*, were classified as "Excellent"; four, including the flagship *Wyoming*, received a "Good" grade; while two were "Fair," three "Unsatisfactory" and four "Poor."[8] The officers on the *Arkansas*, including 2nd Lieutenant Hamilton, were commended for their fine training and supervision of their men.

In mid-summer of 1916, the *Arkansas* and other ships moved up the

The 1916 wedding party photograph of Miss Mary Tolley Ligon and U.S. Navy Ensign Fredrick Gore Richards. Hamilton is the second man on the right. The bride's brother Thomas Watkins Ligon is standing behind the groom wearing a U.S. Army uniform (courtesy John Thorpe Richards Jr.).

northeast coast to be based out of Newport, Rhode Island, where the Naval War College is located. As the details from the recent naval Battle of Jutland were being complied, the officers in the Atlantic Fleet gathered to tend classes in preparation for simulated war games. On July 10 the *Arkansas* along with 42 other ships headed out of the Newport's Narragansett Bay territory to participate in tactical manuevers.[9] Later, back in port with beautiful summer weather at hand, a number of ships took turns serving as host locations for formal evening dinners and dances for commanders, their wives and selected guests. July 31 was one evening that the formal entertainment took place on the *Arkansas*. Certainly Hamilton had his men focused with all of the necessary preparation and details. In late August additional war games played out.

At the end of the summer, Hamilton and the men aboard the *Arkansas* departed from Newport. Several weeks later there was a very notable incident in Newport. On October 7, 1916, a German war submarine was spotted for the first time in an American harbor. During that afternoon the 213-foot German *U-53* with 36 men appeared for about three hours before departing for the shoals off Nantucket to intercept international vessels.[10]

At 4 P.M. on October 17 a new super dreadnought, named the USS *Arizona*, was commissioned, becoming the grandest battleship in the Atlantic Fleet, with 12 14-inch guns.[11] Before long, Hamilton got a view of the magnificent ship, but for some reason, it appears that he was not overly taken by naval ships and the seas. As a member of the Marine Corps, he wished to jump off the ship and fight rebels.

The annual National Rifle Association competitive rifle events took place again this fall, but at the same time, there was an Atlantic Fleet battleship football league to consider, culminating with playoffs. It's uncertain if Hamilton had a choice in which avenue to take, but he ended up as a member of the *Arkansas* football team, once again testing his physical and athletic skills, playing fullback and handling the kicking duties. There was the old adage about becoming a Marine and seeing the world, but for now Hamilton could add sports competition to his agenda.

In late October the *Arkansas* beat their rival sister ship *Wyoming* in a second round championship game by a score of 12–6 with Hamilton scoring one of his squad's two touchdowns. The win was promotional front-page sporting news for the *New York Times*.[12] To prepare for the championship game, the *Arkansas* team played a practice game against Columbia University. During the first week of November, Hamilton made the headlines within the *New York Times* sports section under the title "Hamilton Wins for Tars," as his *Arkansas* team beat the USS *Texas* team 12–0 to win the Atlantic Fleet Championship. The article compared Hamilton's athleticism to John Dewitt, a well-rounded athlete, who had won the silver medal for the hammer throw in the 1904 Olympics. In the hard fought game neither team crossed the goal line, but Hamilton was successful on four of five field goal attempts, thus scoring all his team's points.[13]

The following Tuesday, November 7, was Election Day, and the national contest was between incumbent President Woodrow Wilson and Republican Charles Evans Hughes. Across the nation's 48 states, women were now allowed to vote in 12 states, and in Montana a woman was running for Congress. The day after the election some national papers proclaimed Hughes was victorious, but after several days of additional counting, President Wilson's reelection was confirmed.

In late November the *Arkansas* was again stationed at the New York Navy Yard for minor repairs. On Saturday, November 25, the annual Army/Navy football game was held at the famous Polo Grounds in New York City, and among the 50,000 in attendance were 10,000 military men from local battleships.[14] On this occasion Army was victorious 15–7.

Just as in 1916, Hamilton began 1917 on the *Arkansas* stationed in New York. On Thursday, January 4, a fire broke out in a coal bunker on the hospital ship *Solace* docked in the yard in close proximity to much of the Atlantic Fleet. A general alarm was sounded, and men from the dreadnaughts *Arkansas, Wyoming, New York, Pennsylvania, Texas,* and *Arizona* assisted in putting out the blaze. Fifteen men were treated for smoke inhalation.[15]

Admiral George Dewey passed away on January 16. In 1899 Congress had created the rank of admiral of the Navy under the condition that Dewey be the only officer ever commissioned to such a position. On Saturday the 20th all businesses in Washington, D.C., were ordered closed during the period of the funeral. Mounted police led the path to Arlington Cemetery followed by many dignitaries and official units, including a battalion of bluejackets carrying arms from the *Arkansas* and six Marine companies.[16] Following the service at Arlington Cemetery, the men from the *Arkansas* returned to their ship.

Woodrow Wilson was reelected to the presidency in 1916 with the notion of keeping America out of the war; however, certain events were changing his mind as well as the opinion of most Americans. One incident involved a note from German Foreign Secretary Arthur Zimmermann to the German Minister in Mexico:

> Berlin, Jan.19, 1917
>
> On the 1st of February we intend to begin submarine warfare unrestricted. In spite of this, it is our intention to endeavor to keep neutral the United States of America.
>
> If this attempt is not successful, we propose an alliance on the following basis with Mexico: That we shall make war together and together make peace. We shall give general financial support, and it is understood that Mexico is to reconquer [sic] the lost territory in New Mexico, Texas, and Arizona. The details are left to you for settlement.
>
> You are instructed to inform the President of Mexico of the above in the greatest confidence as soon as it is certain that there will be an outbreak of war with the United States, and suggest that the President of Mexico, on his own initiative, should communicate with Japan suggesting adherence at once to his plan. At the same time offer to mediate between Germany and Japan.
>
> Please call to the attention of the President of Mexico that the employment of ruthless submarine warfare now promises to compel England to make peace in a few months.
>
> ZIMMERMANN[17]

In February many ships in the Atlantic Fleet headed to warm waters again for maneuvers around Haiti and Cuba, but with ever present rumblings of United States intervention into the war, some ships were left behind to protect strategic ports. The *Arizona* remained in New York, while Hamilton, aboard the *Arkansas*, remained stationed at Norfolk.

Although war had not been declared, on February 4, 1917, the U.S. Navy captured their first enemy ships, not in the vicinity of the Atlantic Fleet, but rather far off America's West Coast. The German gunboat *Geier* and tender *Locksun* were captured at a location known as Pearl Harbor. Later Secretary Daniels stated: "Hawaii, situated as it is at the "crossroads of the Pacific," whether in the piping times of peace or in the midst of war's alarms, will always demand our attention and consideration."[18]

Hamilton had been stationed with the *Arkansas* for 17 months when he was awarded with his first promotion: a commission to first lieutenant, accomplished on March 16, 1917, with consent of the Senate.[19] The timing was twofold. He had proved himself worthy of the extra responsibility, but additionally the military establishment knew they had to make preparations for the likelihood of war.

The historic moment finally came during a special session of Congress on April 2, 1917, when President Woodrow Wilson asked Congress to declare war. A few days later the U.S. Senate cast their vote, and the House of Representatives followed on April 5 with a vote of 373 "YEAS," 50 "NEAS" and 9 "NOT VOTING" to enter into war.[20] On April 6, 1917, President Wilson followed up the votes and declared that a state of war existed between the United States and the Imperial German Government, making war official.

Congress was watching the nation's expenditures very closely, and in order to fund the gigantic new war effort, additional revenues were needed at once to keep the budget balanced. The House of Representatives immediately increased tariff duties on imports, while all items that had been listed as "duty free" now carried a duty of 10 percent across the board.[21]

America's most talented and brightest youths and top collegiate athletes now bailed from academics to enlist with different military organizations. Other patriotic men quit work with the hope of experiencing the adventure.

Meanwhile, with war declared Hamilton was thinking about his future as a Marine officer. What role would he play? A few weeks later, on April 20, 1st Lieutenant Hamilton's days aboard the USS *Arkansas* came to an end. He was now granted four days leave prior to reporting back to the Marine Barracks at Norfolk, Virginia. He remained at the barracks for a few days awaiting his next assignment.

On April 28 he was officially assigned to the USS *New Hampshire* (BB-25), but the eleven-year-old ship was currently docked at the base being overhauled. Hamilton's cousin Carlton Wright would be quite familiar with the, ship as he had served aboard it back in 1915.[22] Lieutenant Hamilton was the only commissioned Marine officer assigned to the *New Hampshire* containing, among others, 67 enlisted Marines.[23] Over the next few weeks the war atmosphere around the barracks quickened. For Hamilton and the men around him there was a sense of urgency along with days filled with unanswered questions.

Hamilton did not want to miss out on this major opportunity to serve his country, and he was methodically searching his mind to find his best avenue to the adventure. Finally on May 14 he seized the moment by sending a quick telegram to General John A. Lejeune stating: "Am especially anxious for training at Quantico request that I be sent with first troops to france [sic] am scheduled to go aboard New Hampshire this afternoon but understand that deRoode doesn't want Quantico and prefers sea."[24]

One week later, on May 21, a dispatch was issued at 4:21 P.M. calling for Hamilton and his Marine detachment to "transfer immediately" to the Marine Barracks at Quantico along with camping equipment.[25] He was officially detached from the *New Hampshire* on the 21st, after less than a month of association with the ship in dry dock.

He looked forward to trading in his "sea legs" for a position on land where his strong legs were more accustomed. The nation's war plans were coming together and Hamilton's questions were being answered. He would soon be heading across the Atlantic to war.

6. America Enters the Great War

A brief primer concerning basic war preparations and terminology is necessary to understand the new adventure into which Hamilton's life was thrust.

The U.S. Army currently consisted of about 133,000 troops and the National Guard 67,000 troops, for a total of 200,000 men.[1] The Marine Corps consisted of only 511 officers and 13, 214 men.[2] Congressional approval was quickly given to increase the Corps to 1,197 officers and 30,000 men. Military aviation was in its infancy, containing a combined total of no more than 1,185 officers and men with very few airplanes.[3] The Americans from all branches of service heading overseas to war would be known as the American Expeditionary Forces.

On May 7 President Wilson and Secretary of War Newton D. Baker agreed to select 56-year-old U.S. Army General John J. Pershing to be the commander of the AEF. Although neither man had previously met Pershing, their final decision was based upon high recommendations from Theodore Roosevelt. At West Point, Pershing was an average student, but he was noted for his strong leadership skills and service as class president. As he prepared to head overseas to war, one tragic incident still weighed heavily on his mind. His wife, the former Helen Frances Warren, daughter of Wyoming Senator Frances Warren, chairman of the Senate Military Affairs Committee, had died in a house fire less than two years earlier, along with three of his four children. Only his six-year-old son Warren survived.[4] Organizing America's military force for the Great War now occupied General Pershing's mind.

The Marine Corps, through their connection with the U.S. Navy, was not currently considered a stand-alone land-force fighting unit, but the Marines wanted to play a significant role on land and be part of the action. The situation became a political tug-of-war as Secretary of War Baker was in favor of letting the Marine Corps send a fighting unit, while newly appointed AEF Commander Pershing wanted only the U.S. Army to fight on land.

On May 16, Secretary Baker requested from President Wilson the authority to have the Marine Corps organize an infantry regiment. Shortly thereafter, President Wilson formalized the process by issuing an order for one regiment of Marines to be sent to France with the very first American Expeditionary Forces, pleasing Secretary Baker and USMC Commandant Barnett. Pershing was overruled and not enthusiastic about the decision.

Initial approval called for a division of about 25,000 U.S. Army personnel and one regiment of U.S. Marines consisting of roughly 2,600 men to be deployed to France. The Marine Corps, with four current active regiments, created a new regiment for overseas duty, known as the Fifth Regiment.[5]

The expanding Marine Corps was in desperate need of more land with water access in the Washington, D.C., area, and they settled on leasing 5,300 acres beside the town of Quantico, Virginia.[6] This property was acquired and quickly designed with plans for barracks, offices, training facilities, airfields and much more. Besides the Fifth Regiment, a future Sixth Regiment would also be approved to form a full Marine Brigade, known as the Fourth Brigade. Authority however, was not given for the Corps to have their own full separate division.

Naturally, most every person in the Marine Corps wanted to be among the first 2,600. Commandant Barnett was to remain stateside, while Colonel Charles A. Doyen was chosen to begin as the commander of the regiment and serve as the highest ranking Marine officer overseas. Doyen was a good friend of General Barnett, as both had graduated from the U.S. Naval Academy in 1881. A colonel since 1909, he had been stationed in Washington since January 1915, most recently as commander of the Marine Barracks.

Every Marine enlisted by choice, as you could not be drafted into the Marine Corps. The new recruits generally volunteered for the duration of the war and teamed up with the career veterans known as "leathernecks."[7] The recruits first had to make the all important cut, as the Corps had very high standards. Of the 239,274 men who attempted to become Marines, only 60,189 were accepted, resulting in 75 percent of all applicants being rejected.[8] Basic requirements were that one had to be between the ages of 18 and 36, from 5'5" to 6'2" and between 130 and 245 pounds.[9] A Marine had to be born in America or a naturalized citizen, unmarried, able to read and write, with no addictions, and display high moral character with mental fitness.[10]

The demand for quality recruits remained consistently high, and 67 percent of those who became Marines scored as marksmen or higher on the rifle range.[11] The Corps' goal was to have every fighting Marine selected for service overseas to be proficient with a rifle and classified as a marksman, sharpshooter or expert. Of the total accepted to become Marines, only 31,315 were shipped overseas to France, and only slightly more than half of that lot saw action on the Western Front.[12]

When the fighting began, the Marine Corps ground troops were associated under the umbrella of the Second Division, a unique hybrid division of brotherhood services composed of two brigades, one Regular Army and enlisted men, and one U.S. Marines. The Fourth Brigade of Marines had the utmost respect for their counterparts in the Army Third Infantry Brigade. As neither brigade contained their own individual artillery, both were assisted by the Second Field Artillery Brigade. Along with other support units, the division had about 28,000 men, of which 1,000 were officers. This figure is true for each of the other AEF divisions. If necessary, future plans called for a total of 80 AEF divisions in France by July 1, 1919[13] (see Appendix B).

Bonds also evolved with the Second Engineers known as "Pershing's Veteran Engineers" in the division, who often spent their days repairing and constructing new roads and bridges so that logistical travel could flow freely. Other engineers performed necessary duties, such as searching ahead for good water sources and cutting barbed wire, which was everywhere. They trained for situations they knew they would encounter but were also challenged with new obstacles and projects that arose constantly. Their vital assistance allowed Hamilton and others to concentrate on battle plans and fighting.

In simplistic numbers the Fourth Brigade was composed of the following: each company contained 250 Marines, and a battalion consisted of four companies and therefore at least 1,000 men. A regiment was three battalions or well over 3,000 Marines, and a brigade was made up of two regiments plus the machine gun battalion and other support personnel. Specifically, the total composition of the Fourth Brigade at full strength was 258 officers and 8,211 enlisted men.[14]

The First Battalion, Fifth Regiment, was commonly identified as 1/5 and correspondingly the Third Battalion, Sixth Regiment, was classified as 3/6. During World War I each Marine company was identified by a number, but after the war numbers were replaced by alphabetical letters.

Hamilton was always associated with the Fifth Regiment. To give you a clear picture before we move ahead, he was first a captain of the 49th Company, then the battalion commander of 1/5, and later the commander over both 1/5 and 2/5. In following his path, the focus is more on the units in which he had responsibility. The uncanny fact is that this trail happens to be associated with locations where most of the grand action on the Western Front took place.

America possessed many of the greatest minds in the world, and these folks were working with manufacturing companies to produce the latest innovative ideas. All types of new technology would be introduced for the first time on the world stage. Still, as in previous wars, the Great War would be dominated by the overall training and willpower of warriors.

New to this war was motorized transportation. Trucks, referred to as camions in Europe, were the best means to rush reserve battalions to the front lines, and more than 30,000 trucks were sent to France from America. Five- and ten-ton tractors were used to haul large guns across rough terrain. Motorized ambulances provided a quicker response time, transporting wounded men away from the front lines with added comfort. Basic autos were accessible to certain high commanders, and motorcycles could traverse the crowded roads and varying landscape for special errands.

Aviation was still in its infancy, but technology and pilot flying skills were improving every day. There were many different production models of biplanes; some were agile and could maneuver easily, while others had increased speed and horsepower. Naturally, quality and reliability were important factors. Many young pilots often found that the type of plane that they had been trained to fly was different from the one they were assigned to fly during the war. A critical factor was how quickly the pilot adapted and became comfortable in handling his new warplane.

General Pershing determined in the beginning that aviation was to be a support group and not the focal part of the action. The plane's biggest contribution to the cause was its use as a means for important observation and surveillance of enemy ground troops. Fighter planes were generally called upon to protect the observation planes. Additionally planes were used for bombing raids, searching over land for prime targets, such as storage ammunition and rail cars, and over water for submarines and their home-bases. The planes carried mounted machine guns, and the pilots were fully trained in their use.

Balloons were an integral part of observation, and pilots were also cross-trained for this job. The balloonist was placed in a basket below the large inflated object, which was attached to a winch cable and commonly secured to the rear of a flatbed three-ton truck. Using a telescope along with radio or telephone communication, the observer provided detailed intelligence to the men in the truck below. The information was relayed to assist heavy ground artillery with focal points to fine tune their accuracy as well as to assist Allied troops with enemy troop movement. If weather conditions were favorable, the balloons were deployed at sunrise to a height of 2,000 feet along both sides of the Western Front. For added safety they were placed at least two miles behind the front lines and spaced about 15 miles apart. With common dimensions of 200 feet in length and a diameter of 50 feet, they were noticeable targets for enemy planes and served as featured backdrop scenery for ground troops throughout their adventure.[15]

With planes and balloons in the air there came along another new weapon known as anti-aircraft guns to be used against enemy planes. The weapons were also strategically placed to protect the defenseless balloon pilots.

Radio and telephone communication on the battlefield was a new concept. When war was declared the Signal Corps of the Regular Army had 55 officers and 1,570 men.[16] The Signal Corps expanded quickly, taking talented men from leading companies like American Telephone & Telegraph and Western Union Telegraph. Over time in France, they installed over 100,000 miles of telephone and telegraph lines. Having temporary telephone lines strung was one thing, but having a secure private conversation was another. One report mentioned "party lines," and therefore basic human "runners" were the most common reliable method of communication for fast moving troops along the Western Front.

The war brought about another new motorized vehicle, the tank. The armored equipment was used for a variety of purposes, but the main use was to search and destroy machine guns in heavily fortified positions. Tanks were not an abundant commodity, and the French and British generally kept the larger tanks to support their own troops. There were not a lot of small tanks either, but those which were available to the American Forces were generally deployed in groups.

Chemical warfare was one of the most feared weapons, consisting of a variety of chemical mixtures to form a poisonous gas. This new type of warfare was used extensively by the Germans and to a limited extent by the French and English. Although gas attacks did not kill men in large numbers, it caused many casualties and created panic which ultimately disengaged troops for a period of time. It was therefore considered a psychological weapon as well.

Some gasses were chlorine based, some phosgene, and others were combinations. Canisters of gas were sent towards the enemy via exploding shells, with the hope that a light prevailing wind would carry the mixture throughout the opposing troops. Mustard gas (Dichlorethylsulphide) used by the Germans was the most feared and essentially not a true gas, but more of an agent that caused skin blisters, or even worse, internal blisters on lungs. As the gasses were attracted to moisture through the nose or mouth, one often started sneezing and soon realized that his lungs were full of the toxic poison, followed by vomiting. In such cases the gas caused lingering, increasing pain over a period of days to weeks followed by potential death. The heavy mustard gas also differed from other gasses in that it did not take effect right away, but rather lasted for longer periods of time in areas lower to the ground around fox holes. To overcome the colorless gasses troops would immediately put on their personal gas masks and evacuate the low areas, where they had sought shelter. The uncomfortable mask severely hampered visibility and communication, but it was essential equipment.

The machine gun was definitely one of the most lethal weapons. It was, by itself, not a new invention, but the latest technology made it an advanced piece of equipment. Hiram Maxim came up with a simple design, and the Germans took his concept, producing the feared Maxim machine gun. Although small, the Maxim, which weighed about 135 pounds, usually remained in one spot as a major defensive weapon. In a losing scenario men usually kept the machine gun operational, firing up to 600 bullets per minute until their death.

The Americans liked their own Lewis Gun, which was capable of firing over 500 rounds of ammunition a minute and was highly mobile, weighing only about 26 pounds. Manufacturing conditions in the United States limited the production of these preferred lightweight guns, which soon found their way to the Air Corps. The AEF ground troops ended up with the less favorable lightweight French Chauchat and the heavier Hotchkiss. The Chauchat automatic rifle, which the men called "sho-sho," was the most mass produced automatic weapon of the war. Due to its specifications and raw material components, it was not a high quality gun, and many comments were made concerning the guns comprehensive reliability under constant use.

The French supplied the Americans with much of the heavy artillery equipment, including the reliable workhorse French 75 model. It fired a shell weighing 13 pounds a little more than five miles, while the 155mm howitzer shot a projectile weighing 117 pounds roughly seven miles.[17] Although not abundant, the French had a huge gun dubbed the "Mosquito," which, supported by a railway truck, was capable of handling an 1,800 pound bomb.[18]

For Americans, the Springfield M1903 rifle provided reliability and quality. Rifle scopes were new technology and in limited supply. There were a few different types, but the Winchester A5 telescope was the most dominant. One historian sums up the issue by stating:

> A number of the rifle team '03s fitted with A5 scopes accompanied the Marine contingent when it deployed to France. Little has been written regarding the performance of these weapons, but they were undoubtedly put to good use in the hands of skilled Marine marksmen. However, the number on hand was quite small, and virtually all Marines were armed with standard '03s without scopes.[19]

For Hamilton, an expert rifleman and past member of the Marine Corps rifle team, it would be very reasonable that he secured a scope for his Springfield rifle.

It should be noted that in 1918, when America started fighting in the war, there was another very catastrophic event going on. Throughout the world well over thirty million people died from the Spanish flu epidemic, which roughly lasted two and a half years from 1918 to mid–1920. Some death estimates even approached a figure of fifty million. This flu was not the common illness, which attacked weaker elderly or infant immune systems, but rather it often took the lives of healthy individuals. Overall there were close to 70,000 cases of the flu in the AEF resulting in about 24,000 deaths.[20]

To keep deaths in perspective, roughly sixteen million people died worldwide in World War I, which lasted more than four years, from 1914 to the end in 1918. Of the more than sixteen million deaths, about 9.5 million men across the world died fighting, while an astonishing 6.5 million civilians died.[21]

It was a war involving opposing forces that wore identifiable uniforms. When America entered the war the stalemate was broken, and when you were on defense you were making preparations for defense. When on offense, one side marched forward with their best attempt to annihilate the enemy, and in their quest, most everything in their path created by God was obliterated. There was no safe haven along the shifting lines of the entire Western Front.

Finally most citizens today do not realize the determination that the fighting Americans brought with them when they hit the battlefield. The highly intense period from June 6, 1918, to November 11, 1918, Armistice Day, was but a brief 159 days, but it was packed with everything imaginable. What George W. Hamilton faced could not be chronicled by seconds, minutes, hours and days. Some days the fighting seemed to last forever, and the day could not end soon enough. Conversely for those who found it to be their last day of life, the day could not last long enough.

With this basic information we now follow Hamilton off to war.

7. To France and a Time on Land

Hamilton went at once to the Marine Corps Barracks at Quantico, Virginia. One legendary Marine officer, Leroy P. Hunt, described Quantico as a "slumbering little village," which would be forever changed.[1]

On May 24, 1917, Lieutenant Hamilton was assigned to the 49th Company. The following day the first piece of the Fifth Regiment was being formed at Quantico with the initial organization of the First Battalion, Fifth Regiment, along with its four individual companies. The 49th Company, which originated in October 1916 with certain members from the USS *Nebraska*, was now being readjusted for war preparations with a mix of men. First Lieutenant Hamilton quickly replaced Captain Henry P. Torrey as the commanding officer of the company.[2] He would be called by the informal title of "skipper," which was given to all company commanders at the time.

Lieutenant Hamilton would be introduced to his new battalion commander, Major Julius Spear Turrill. Besides the 49th, there were three other companies under the umbrella of Turrill's 1/5. The initial companies were the 15th under Captain Andrew B. Drum, the 67th under Captain Edmond H. Morse and the 66th under the command of Captain George K. Shuler.

It appears that Shuler was already a good personal friend of Hamilton, and therefore the two men would not need any introduction. Shuler had worked for the *Washington Post* during the same period of time as Hamilton's cousin James Wright. Like Hamilton, Shuler also received personal tutoring from Michael Dowd to pass Marine Corps entrance exams.[3] Additionally, Shuler was from northwestern New York, and the two fellows could reminisce about the rural countryside of the northern state.

Hamilton was now focused and committed to organizing his land-based Marines for future fighting. His first project was to get to know the handful of officers reporting to him, along with the roughly 250 noncommissioned men serving under his command. The many leathernecks with abundant tales of past encounters were as anxious as Hamilton to play an early role in the upcoming adventure. Sergeant Robert "Chuck" Conner, a leatherneck and original member of the 49th Company, became an initial nucleus within the company and a friend to all. The youngest sergeant in the group was a fellow named Arthur Elliott Lyng, who was eager to learn from the professionals. The 49th Company had a unique slogan: "We tame the tough ones, and toughen the tame ones." This motto functioned as a great building block and fit right into Hamilton's training plans. Qualified men from all parts of the country were soon salted into the 49th to bring the company up to full strength.[4]

Many other Marines, from across America, were now gathering at Quantico, anxious to serve their country in a time of need. One fellow noted:

2nd Lt. George K. Shuler in 1913 (courtesy National Archives).

> There was no greater incentive to patriotism than our frequent trips from Quantico, Va., to Washington, D.C., our nation's capital. We, who had lived at great distance from the seat of government, were greatly impressed by its splendid Federal buildings, its departments and their activities. Its many historic spots and statutes, its magnificent piles of marble and granite masterpieces of architecture, the Capitol, White House, Congressional Library, all seemed to be ours by heritage, for it was this and a distant spot called "Home" that we were about to defend.[5]

On Monday, May 28, Hamilton was ordered to go to Washington, D.C., to report to Colonel Ben H. Fuller, president of the Marine Examining Board. He was to appear along with several other first lieutenants for preliminary examination prior to a possible future promotion.

Meanwhile, on June 1 two additional battalions were being organized in Philadelphia. The sister battalions, known as 2/5 and 3/5, would complement 1/5, finalizing the Fifth Regiment. Colonel Doyen chose Lt. Colonel Logan Feland to be his second in command of the regiment.

Sometime prior to leaving the States, Hamilton said farewell to his family, and they would pray for his safety. Back at the base there was a pleasant memo dated June 4, waiting for him. The brief wording stated that he had qualified for a promotion to the next grade.[6]

On June 7, the Fifth Regiment was considered officially organized and on the following day, June 8, 1917, Hamilton and his 49th Company were designated for Foreign Service with the American Expeditionary Forces. This transitional date is important to acknowledge and understand as it meant that Hamilton and his men were now fully separated from both the U.S. Marine Corps and the U.S. Navy and officially under the command of General Pershing and the U.S. Army.

Come June 9, Major Turrill, Lieutenant Hamilton and the roughly 800 men of 1/5, left Quantico by train and headed to Philadelphia.[7] The Fifth Regiment's sister battalions of 2/5 and 3/5 had already left Philadelphia for New York. On the 11th of June, Hamilton and members of 1/5 boarded the USS *DeKalb* (No. 3010), a steamship that had been confiscated from the Germans. After getting situated they took to the waters the following day, leaving Philadelphia and heading for New York.

General Pershing and an assorted staff of 150 were already across the Atlantic waiting for the military forces to arrive. Two men in his entourage, who had sailed with him on this secret voyage, were USMC Lt. Colonel Feland, as a brief temporary member of his staff, and famous national race car driver Edward V. "Eddie" Rickenbacker, who had recently enlisted in the Signal Corps but had agreed to be Pershing's staff driver.[8] They arrived first in England and after spending a few days departed without creating a lot of attention. On June 13 they landed on French soil at Boulogne where French General Dumas was present to welcome the senior American commander. As General Pershing stood at attention, Dumas declared: "Your coming opens a new era in the history of the world. The United States of America is now taking its part with the United States of Europe. Together they are about to found the United States of the World, which will definitely and finally end the war and give a peace which will be enduring and fruitful for humanity."[9]

Following the brief ceremony, Pershing boarded a train heading inland for Paris. The villages between Boulogne and Paris had been notified of this historic event, prompting local citizens and Allied soldiers to line train stations along the way, waving American flags and cheering. The reception in Paris for the American general was set to be the largest promotional event in France since the start of the war three years prior. Colors of red, white and blue were displayed throughout the romantic city and along the parade route; bystanders threw flowers into the general's chauffeured automobile. Later in the day, when Pershing was at the opera, the audience turned and gave him a standing ovation. His American troops would soon be on their way to rescue the citizens of France.

The next day, June 14, 1917, America's first fighting troops sailed from Stapleton, New York, as part of a convoy. In the mix of the first transport group were Hamilton's 49th Company, and the rest of 1/5, on board the *DeKalb*, totaling 20 officers and 790 men. As the *DeKalb* sailed away, some on the boat would be afforded time to catch one last glimpse of the American shoreline before it faded away. The "soldiers of the sea" had sailed out of many ports; however, during this special brief emotional moment, many onboard would naturally have private thoughts, wondering if they would ever see the American shores again. Before long, land was fully out of sight, and everyone was focused on the great adventure, which was now underway.

Colonel Doyen, the members of 2/5, 3/5, and the regimental band, soon headed out to sea, trailing in a separate convoy. They traveled on the USS *Henderson*, while the Headquarters Company boarded the USS *Hancock*. The other boats in the convoys were filled with U.S. Army personnel and soldiers affiliated with General Pershing's proud First Division under the command of Major General William L. Sibert.

Along the voyage the *DeKalb*'s piano in the forward quarter was the favorite location for men to mingle and get to know each other. Undoubtedly Hamilton often met Shuler and others for some laughter and a bit of constructive conversation about future planning. Hamilton had paid for his own piano lessons and could have played a few songs, if he wished to entertain the men.[10]

As the Marines were experienced "soldiers of the sea," they also lent assistance on the transport ship as needed. In an attempt to avoid the constant threat of submarines, the voyage was not a direct route. Each day Hamilton and his men wearing life preservers practiced "Abandon Ship," by following a specific path to their lifeboat. Observers kept a constant watch for any enemy disturbance on the water's surface, and on the night of June 22, the crew's keen vision paid off, as a couple of German U-boats were sighted at 2230. The torpedoes just missed the *DeKalb*'s bow and stern. A gunnery sergeant in Hamilton's command named William Nice was in charge of the ship's guns numbered 5, 7 and 9, which fired away at the submarine as the *DeKalb* sped away.[11]

On the night of June 26 the *DeKalb* and other AEF boats in the first transport group came to port at Saint-Nazaire, France, a location that for security reasons had been kept a secret until the very last moment. The following day, June 27, 1917, was a momentous day as Hamilton and the men of 1/5 disembarked and the U.S. Marines landed! Hamilton and his 49th Company were now "over there" and were a historic part of the very first group of Americans to set foot on French soil. The remainder of the Fifth Regiment in the trailing transport groups would arrive over the following days.

Due to the lack of stevedores, Hamilton had his men help unload the ships, which gave them more physical exercise than they had anticipated.

Since most of the members of the American Expeditionary Forces had never been to France, as part of their early adventure they were checking out the French. Likewise the French were wondering what the American warriors were like. The mayor and citizens all put forth a joyous welcome for the new arrivals, who they hoped would take back their country.

On June 29 Hamilton got his men to erect canvas tents in the outskirts of the port village of Saint-Nazaire. By July 3 Colonel Doyen's entire Fifth Regiment was united and getting acclimated. Lt. Colonel Feland was now relegated back to assisting Doyen and the twelve skippers in the Fifth Regiment.[12] Over time Feland, who had a degree in architecture from the Massachusetts Institute of Technology, would become one of Hamilton's most ardent supporters.

Feland instructed Hamilton to select a delegation from his 49th Company to join others, as representatives of the AEF, to march in the special American Independence Day parade on July 4, 1917, in Paris. The procession would serve as a method to showcase a few American soldiers and Marines to the French public. He selected Gunnery Sergeant Nice and a few others.

Huge crowds, waving assorted U.S. flags, lined the streets to catch a glimpse of the Americans. A leading band was followed by French military personnel, and further down the line, American officers, wearing their prominent Sam Browne belts, rode in automobiles, then additional bands, followed by representative warriors of the United States. The procession marched to the private Picpus Cemetery to honor the grave of Marquis de Lafayette, where General Pershing received credit for saying, "LaFayette we are here."[13]

Following the moment of recognition, the procession traversed over the Solferino Bridge into other parts of Paris. One AEF correspondent on the scene, reporting for the *New York Tribune*, noted:

> The marines were the pick of the lot, for size and behavior too. The sense of being something special was with the marines from the first. They marched that way. And, set apart by their olive drab as well as by their size and comportment, they gave that First Division's first march in France a quality of real distinction.[14]

On July 5 Hamilton turned 25 and was now actively drilling and training his men on a daily basis. For now the Fifth Regiment was assigned to the First Division, which at this point was the only division in France, totaling about 13,000 troops.[15] With troops in France and with relationships being established, General Pershing issued his first general order:

> For the first time in history an American Army finds itself in European territory. The good name of the United States of America and the maintenance of cordial relations require the perfect deportment of each member of this command. It is of the gravest importance that the soldiers of the American Army shall at all times

Marines in the Fifth Regiment packed 40 per cattle car heading to the Gondrecourt area for training by Alpine Chasseurs, July 15, 1917 (courtesy Marine Corps History Division).

treat the French people, and especially the women, with the greatest courtesy and consideration. The valiant deeds of the French Army and the Allies, by which together they have successfully maintained the common cause for three years, and the sacrifices of the civil population of France in support of their armies, command our profound respect. This can best be expressed on the part of our forces by uniform courtesies to all the French people, and by the faithful observance of their laws and customs. The intense cultivation of the soil in France, under conditions caused by the war, makes it necessary that extreme care should be taken to do no damage to private property. The entire French manhood capable of bearing arms is in the field fighting the enemy, and it should, therefore be a point of honor to each member of the American Army to avoid doing the least damage to any property in France.[16]

It took awhile for the French government to secure and designate an expansive piece of land for a practice ground facility because some of their upcoming training would involve simulated exercises with live artillery traveling long distances. Hamilton and his company broke camp on July 15, along with other members of 1/5 and 2/5, and headed by rail aboard open boxcars to the Gondrecourt training area. The two day journey with comfortable summer weather was more of a pleasure ride, giving the men a partial glimpse of the countryside. Members of 2/5 would billet in a village called Menaucourt, while Hamilton and the Marines in 1/5 proceeded on to the next town, located well behind the front lines, called Naix-aux-Forges. The men of 3/5 would arrive later. Upon arrival, the village residents turned out for a festive greeting complete with a welcome banner. The war had been going on for several years, and other than sending men off to fight, the residents were accustomed to living, as best could be, a rather normal life.

Around July 21, the 30th Battalion of the experienced French Alpine Chasseurs, whom the Americans called "chasers," arrived on the scene, to cross-train the Marines with their favorite fighting tactics. The distinguished mountain warriors, who were regarded to be as good as the French Foreign Legion, were separate from the regular French Army, as noted by their dark blue uniforms, complete with blue Tam O'Shanter caps, and their moniker "Blue Devils."[17] From day one, they were preparing Hamilton's 49th Company and others in the Fifth Regiment to go against the Kaiser's best, who were known as shock troops and storm troopers and included the relentless Prussians.

All men wore combat equipment, including two-pound steel helmets, during the drills. Many of the Marines later fastened the eagle, globe and anchor insignia clasp of the Corps on the front of their helmet directly over the bold painted divisional logo. This prominent identification proudly set them apart from other military personnel.

More than a week was devoted to exhaustive work in the art and practice of digging trenches, which were dug every 450 yards. Bayonet practice on dummies and maneuvering through the trenches with barbed wire soon became second nature to the men, so that when the real moment came, all actions would be instinctive. General Pershing did not wish for his forces to fight from trenches as Allied armies had in the past, but rather fight in open warfare. Upon completion of this training, the troops under Pershing's command were in line with his open warfare philosophy, as they would rather fight and die in the open land than hide or be killed in a ditch.

There were moments when the professionally trained Marines questioned some of the advice given by the Chasseurs. One example involved the Chasseurs slowly step-by-step demonstrating the art of throwing a hand grenade using dummy bombs. The Chasseurs' straight-arm movement, which resulted in an arched toss, reminded the Marines of a girl's throw or that of a substitute Little Leaguer. The Marines then lined up to show the "chasers" their fast ball pitches. The French instructors were not amused, and one noted, "You must land your bomb in the trenches — they do no more harm than the wind when the fly straight — and you must save your arm so that you can throw all afternoon."[18]

Camions loaded with Marines arriving at Menaucourt near the Gondrecourt training area in July 1917 (courtesy Marine Corps History Division).

Eventually the practice evolved into competition between the French and Americans, followed in later weeks by the use of real explosive grenades. Other exercises included acquiring a working knowledge of small artillery, including machine guns and mortars. Each of Hamilton's men also became proficient in properly using their gas mask within six seconds of an alarm. In general these training events were held in the morning.

Following lunch Hamilton personally enjoyed training his men in rifle shooting. As competitive as he was, he likely challenged anyone, including the Alpine Chasseurs, to outperform him. By 1600 the men were given free time to swim, walk, write letters or tend to other personal choices.

Additional fresh American troops were constantly arriving at Brest, France. As the Americans were not to be thrust into immediate fighting, General Pershing and his staff took precious time to plan, sort and align the composition of each future division.

After being in France for roughly a month, the days of August were to include many inspections. This would give the top commanders a direct reference point relating to how the new warriors were progressing. On August 1 General Pershing made his first inspection of Doyen's Fifth Regiment at their camp, and all reports were favorable.

More than a week after Pershing's visit, Maj. General William L. Sibert reviewed his entire First Division, and again, Hamilton and his 49th Company performed well. Because the Marine base camp was in a more remote area than the other American camps, the members of the Fifth Regiment were required to hike roughly 12 miles to the divisional inspection site. They all took it in stride, knowing full well this would serve to make them tougher in the long run.

About a week later, on August 19, 1917, General Pershing came with the French Forces Commander, General Henri Philippe Pétain, to inspect the division, and while there Pétain also took time to inspect his Alpine Chasseurs. Pershing and Pétain were both so impressed with the Marine contingent that general staff praised the Marines as "the finest body of men under our command."[19] It was not easy for Pershing to overtly recognize the fine stature of the Marines, as it was well known he favored his Army brethren. If the Marines appeared this good prior to the fighting, one could only imagine what the future might bring.

The Marine warriors were tough, rugged and disciplined, but most of the individuals also had a softer human side, which was displayed through an overall appreciation for animals. Some animals became individual mascots, while others were accepted by the entire company. As long as the men performed and the mascots did not interfere, all commanders generally did not mind the intrusion. The Marines did perform, so the mascots were a part of an informal reward system. Along the way, Hamilton's men had taken a liking to a black and tan dog with a permanent limp, who became one of the featured company mascots. During the formal inspections, including the one on August 19 by Pershing and Pétain, the mascot, known by all as "Parade Rest," was in attendance and lined up in proper formation.[20]

From September 23 through the 25th, the Marines moved to a new training facility in Bourmont, Haute-Marne. This more permanent location would serve as their base camp until March 14, 1918. It took a couple of villages to billet all the men, and Hamilton and his 49th Company settled into the nearby village of Breuvannes. During this time period, the companies within the Fifth Regiment were split up temporarily to partake in different aspects of specialized schooling, training and logistics. Lt. Colonel Feland temporarily replaced Major Turrill as commander of 1/5.

Hamilton drilled his men often with their standard non-combat backpacks, which weighed about 45 pounds. Each pack contained a couple of blankets, extra wool clothing, socks, a cap, and emergency food, such as hard tack and the famous canned "monkey meat" that no one cared for, which was basically corn beef mixed with a vegetable or two, such as carrots, imported from Madagascar and Argentina.[21] Health care items, such as a toothbrush, razor, soap and towel, were also placed in the pack. Essential war equipment that was carried outside the pack for easy access consisted of a gas mask, wire cutters, a canteen, small shovel, trench knife, bayonet, along with their most important Springfield rifle and a belt with 100 rounds of ammunition. The men also found a safe place to carry a standard French issued pull-type five-second-fuse hand grenade. With all of this extra equipment, each individual carried a load exceeding 60 pounds. Every man also wore two light identification tags around his neck. If needed, one would remain on the body, while the second one would mark the grave.

During these days Hamilton received several letters from family and friends, and he also found time to send a few letters of his own. On October 1, 1917, he sent a letter to his older sister, Mary, whom he called "Flax" because of her striking blond hair. He noted that the summer had flown by, and therefore, he was not mailing this letter to the Conesus Lake address:

> Your letter arrived Friday, and helped to make that particular mail the best one I've received since I've been over here — 10 fine letters. I was surprised to see you were back in Spokane, which brought me to the realization that the summer certainly has [emphasis] passed quickly.
>
> This morning a new lieutenant reported to my company, making a total of 5. His name is McClellan and comes from Richmond, via V.M.I. He is a good kid and will be given a job immediately, as I had to recommend that two of my officers be "canned," because they didn't come up to snuff. Oh, I'm a hard old captain these days Mary!
>
> Saturday afternoon Galliford — a 2nd lieut. — and I took a horseback ride down to "— les Bains" and stayed over-night, returning yesterday. The trip was fine, and the town was one of the largest I've been in yet, although the summer season is about over, and most of the hotels closed up. We were the first Americans to visit this town, and everywhere were followed by a gang of kids yelling "vive l'Americaine." Old ladies stopped us to ask if we were "Americaine," and we always gave them a strong "Wei wei." It was a funny trip, but a delightful one, as we covered about 50 kilometers of very pretty French scenery.
>
> We are now comfortably located in barracks, except the officers who have rooms in town. Our mess is the best yet, and we live like kings. Next Friday I am going up to Paris and expect to have some [double emphasis] time. George Shuler just got back and reports everything o.k.
>
> I'll write again when I have more.[22]

Hamilton mentioned he was a captain. Two days after writing the letter to his sister, the first lieutenant was officially promoted to captain, with the consent of the U.S. Senate, on October 3, 1917. Hamilton was now blazing a path, as the youngest captain in the Fifth Regiment.

During this month of October, there were other promotions and organizational maneuverings, above Hamilton. In a war environment not much stays constant, and when one large change takes place, it often creates a domino effect for others. Since much of the juggling did not directly affect Captain Hamilton, it will therefore not be mentioned. However, as confusing as it may be, some facts are pertinent.

In late summer, President Wilson had authorized the Sixth Regiment of U.S. Marines to be sent to France to partner with the Fifth Regiment, forming a full Marine Brigade. By October segments of the Sixth Regiment were in France, and the scattered pieces were starting to come together. Colonel Doyen, who was promoted to brigadier general, took over the Fourth Brigade, and just a few days later on October 26, 1917, he became the commander of the newly formed AEF Second Division. However, several days later on November 8, U.S. Army Maj. General Omar Bundy took command of the Second Division, and Doyen reverted back to commanding the Fourth Brigade of Marines. Captain Hamilton and all other Marines departed the First Division and were now aligned with the new mighty Second Division, which was readily establishing its own identity.

Meanwhile, on October 25, 1917, Captain Hamilton took command of the First Battalion, Fifth Regiment, from Lt. Colonel Feland. Recently the commander presiding over the battalion had gone from a major to a lieutenant colonel to now a captain. His appointment would be temporary in nature, lasting a few months, as the baton to reign over 1/5 was passed back and forth several times before the actual fighting. Part of this transition was for cross-training, but also because the officers needed time away from normal duties for extra class work, instruction and training too.

During October 1917 American forces began limited fighting on the front lines. The First Division, having arrived first and being fully trained, was given this honor. The fighting consisted of filling gaps and giving the French assistance where necessary.

While Captain Hamilton was over the First Battalion his commanding officer over the Fifth Regiment from November 1 until New Year's Day was Lt. Colonel Hiram I. Bearss. Some men in the Marine Corps, notably drill sergeants, have a reputation for receiving proper attention from subordinates upon demand, but Bearss was a lieutenant colonel moving up the ranks. He often used this trait to his advantage when making first impressions. Certainly Hamilton and the other two battalion officers in the regiment would recall throughout their lifetimes the first day Bearss officially introduced himself.

He was also known for being hardnosed and demanding, yet fair, which are not bad qualities for a Marine Corps officer. To date the regiment had received many well deserved accolades upon review, but as the fighting was still months away, a little "dressing down" along with intense conditioning "Marine style" by one of the Corps' legends would be just right. Knowing Hamilton, he took a positive approach to the situation and viewed Bearss as the best personal trainer around, for both physical and educational needs. Gunner Nice, who had played a role in firing at the submarine from the *DeKalb* on the voyage over, gave Bearss the ultimate compliment after the war: "I lay the success of the Second [Division] to the training it received from him."[23]

Bearss was also known as "Hiking Hiram" because of his penchant for hiking. Hamilton, a noted track star with powerful legs and plenty of stamina, was one of the few who also enjoyed hiking. Between the two officers, the thousands of other Marines would now have more than their fill of 16- to 26-mile hikes with full packs and gear.

In December the Fourth Brigade was faced with cold harsh winter training that served to prepare everyone for the full war, which was projected to possibly last a few more winters.

For the past three years French children had been deprived of many things due to war conditions. Hamilton instructed his men to follow the general AEF plan to assist in giving the French children their best Christmas possible. Prior to Christmas Day, the children looked forward to the appearance of the bearded, red-suited man called Papa Noel. Instead of stockings, wooden shoes were left by the fireplace to be filled with candy and small items.

It would be natural for Hamilton to reminisce about his own past Christmas gatherings. Charles and Ida would be at home in Washington, D.C., on Lamont Avenue. His older sister, Mary, at age 33, was now a woman on her own with a professional career. Margaret had just turned 22 and was still residing in the Capital City. His older brother, Burley, was known to have been in the military, but only time would tell his location and status. In France, although Hamilton was still in command of 1/5, he was close to his "Boys," who were his immediate family now.

On New Year's Day 1918, Colonel Wendell Neville appeared on the scene replacing Lt. Colonel Bearss as commander of the Fifth Regiment. Colonel "Buck" Neville, known for his leadership skills and booming voice, had just arrived in France on December 28, on board the reliable *DeKalb* transport ship.[24]

It's never too early to start a peace process, and President Wilson was doing just that. Back in America on January 8, President Wilson mentioned to Congress for the first time certain terms and conditions that Germany needed to agree upon for peace to occur. The terms were quite similar to his eventual specific Fourteen Points. Although the speech centered on a peace proposal, it was noted that the United States was fully prepared to fight to the end.

On January 19 Captain Hamilton relinquished his temporary duties as commander of 1/5 and handed the responsibilities over to Major Edward A. Greene. He had done a fine job and now reverted back to being the skipper of his 49th Company.

In early February, Major Thomas Holcomb appeared on the scene along with his Second Battalion, Sixth Regiment, to complete the Marine Brigade. Therefore, on February 10, 1918, the Fourth Brigade, consisting of the Fifth Regiment, Sixth Regiment, Sixth Machine Gun battalion and all support units, was now considered finalized. With just a little more preparation they would be ready to serve on the front lines.

During February, American aviators in France received the first De Havilland planes from the United States. They did not like the quality of the DH-4 planes, preferring rather to fly planes made in Europe. For reasons that may not be apparent now, it is very important to continue to follow and acknowledge the progression of aviation.

There was no holding back Rickenbacker, who was now an aviator. He had parted ways as Pershing's chauffer and was quickly absorbing aeronautical education. The noted national race-car idol figured that he could use his same aggressive competitive talents to become the best Allied pilot in the war. Flying came very natural to Rickenbacker, and the day came when he was selected among the men in the 94th Squadron to join Major Raoul Lufbery and another fellow to make the group's first flight into German occupied territory. Of all the geographic locations along the Western Front, it is very interesting that the Champagne sector was the chosen location to observe on their spy mission for soon Hamilton and his men would be engaged in fierce fighting there. Their French Nieuport planes were scheduled to take off from the Epiez aerodrome base, southwest of Toul, at 0815 on March 6. As Lieutenant Rickenbacker noted:

> I left the hangar and looked down the road for the Major. Campbell was already in his flying clothes. I wanted to be ready on the exact minute, but not too soon. So I lit a cigarette and kept an eye on the Major's door. All the boy's came sauntering up, trying to look as though they were not half mad with envy over my chance to get my head blown off first. They wished me well, they said, but they would like to know what to do with my personal effects.[25]

Rickenbacker's observations during his first adventurous scouting mission would stay with him forever. Within months that exact same location at ground level would be ingrained in Hamilton's mind, with thoughts he would often try to forget. The reason would be the bloody battle of Blanc Mont in the Champagne sector.

In the middle of March 1918, Captain Hamilton and the entire Fourth Brigade left Bourmont to assist other Allied Forces in a sector known as Ver-

The Marines pause in a French village on their journey. Their expressions portray confidence and uncertainty regarding their looming adventure (courtesy Marine Corps History Division).

dun. Major Julius Turrill, who started out commanding 1/5, was now back, replacing Major Green as the battalion commander. Hamilton and his company spent a few days behind the front lines at a location known as Camp Douzaine. The guns on the Western Front could be heard in the distance, and on St. Patrick's Day his men and others in the Fifth Regiment got their first wake-up call, as incoming artillery hit a portion of the Regimental Band's equipment, destroying the bass drum and a few other pieces.

On March 20 Secretary Baker, while in France, took time to review the Second Division. As this was his third and last AEF division to inspect, he was able to make a good and fair comparison, and his review appeared to be quite favorable.[26]

Hamilton's men were now fully trained and prepared to fight when the calling came. Around the camp he noticed that his men were a little edgy, so he instinctively decided to loosen them up by implementing a unique company-wide spelling contest with all 250 men participating.[27] The captain was a creative leader with a lighter side, quite similar to his father.

The future fighting around Verdun was actually skirmishes involving much intelligence gathering by patrols, along with continued probing of the enemy. These encounters with limited action were similar to what the First Division had been performing over the past months.

On April 1, the French Army pulled back from the front lines and 1/5 took over. At night in "No Man's Land," the Germans often crawled forward with wire cutters and military backup. Once their ploy was detected, the Americans would shoot a rocket into the sky, creating several off-shoot stars, as a signal for an Allied artillery barrage to take place. An additional multi-star rocket burst might be a signal to prompt Allied machine guns to commence fire.

One letter that either George or his brother, Burley, wrote home made an interesting story that was told in the *Washington Post* newspaper under the title "Two Long-Separated Washington Brothers Meet in German Trench." The last time that the brothers saw each other had been in the United States, before war preparations were under way. A portion of the article mentioned the following:

> The American forces in Toul sector were staging one of their daring raids on enemy positions. The Yankees were greeted with an outburst of machine gun and rifle bullets as they made their way through the barbed wire. Two officers were the first to reach the boche's line. They bumped into each other in the dark.
>
> A star shell lighted the ground around them as they cast a glance at each other. "It's Burwell!" one cried.
>
> "George!" replied the other, as they grasped hands for an instant and then proceeded with their task of clearing out the Huns.
>
> When the raid was over and the men once more settled in their positions the two officers sought out each other.[28]

The setting was quite different from when they played around the pigpen shed and ran the hills at Conesus Lake, but they cherished the moment. Burley had risen in rank on the U.S. Army side to also being a captain.

This skirmish had given Hamilton and his 49th Company a small taste of what a major battle might be like. They would remain in this sector for roughly six weeks, witnessing, to a limited degree, death and destruction. Overall, however, Hamilton's company and the entire Second Division remained in very good shape.

The Great War had been going on for nearly four years; however, there still was not a firm united command in place and America's commitment to the fight was an additional new element. A conference was held among Allied nations to try and put some structure into their chain of command. The meeting ended in agreement by all parties that the French would retain authority and control over the troops from all Allied countries. President Wilson gave the final approval as the commander-in-chief of the United States. The terms were issued with the following statement:

Beauvais, April 8, 1918

General Foch is charged by the British, French and American Governments with the co-ordination on the action of the allied armies on the western front;

to this end there is conferred on him all the powers necessary for its effective realization. To the same end, the British, French and American Governments confide in General Foch the strategic direction of military operations.

The Commander in Chief of the British, French and American Armies will exercise to the fullest extent the tactical direction of their armies. Each Commander in Chief will have the right to appeal to his government if in his opinion his army is placed in danger by the instructions received from General Foch.

(Signed.)   G. CLEMENCEAU
PETAIN
F. FOCH
LLOYD GEORGE
D. HAIG. F. M.
HENRY WILSON
    General 3.4.18.
TASKER H. BLISS
    General and Chief of Staff
JOHN J. PERSHING
    General, U.S.A.[29]

On April 21 the German flying "Ace of Aces," Manfred von Richthofen, known by many as the "Red Baron" for flying his vibrant red triplane, was shot and killed by Allied Forces. The 25-year-old pilot, born exactly two months before Hamilton, had been feared and respected by all the Allied pilots for his 80 victories in the air. Realizing this, the Allied aviation officers gave the "Red Baron" a full military funeral. His death was a blow to German morale both in the air and on the ground.

During this period Hamilton's 58-year-old mother, Ida, was ill and spending her last days of life at the Conesus Lake home surrounded by nature's beauty. Under the care of Mary and Margaret, she passed away on April 23. The *Washington Post* listed a brief notice: "Mrs. C. A. Hamilton Dead — Wife of Washington Correspondent Passes Away in New York."[30] Charles Hamilton waited in Washington, D.C., for Ida's body to be brought back for funeral services.

It appears that it did not take long for Hamilton to be informed of his mother's death. Upon entering the military, he had listed his mother as his sole beneficiary. On April 25 he updated his paperwork, designating his youngest sister, Margaret Dorothy Hamilton, as his sole beneficiary.

Around this time Charles Hamilton's older sister, Mary Jane Hamilton Wright, also passed away.[31] The Wrights had resided in New Hampton, Iowa, but the passing of Mrs. Wright propelled George Wright and his youngest son, George C. Wright, to consider moving. With Carlton Wright in the U.S. Navy on the East Coast and James Wright in Washington, D.C., the East Coast seemed to be the place to relocate. They decided to gravitate to the

Hamilton's district in the Capital City where George C. Wright would be enrolled at Central High with the class of 1921.

In early May, before America entered the intense fighting, General Pershing decided to exercise his authority by making a structural change. Brigadier General Doyen, the top Marine Corps officer in France, commanding the Marine Brigade, failed an officer's physical examination and was thus relieved of command, heading back to the States on May 7. Doyen was understandably upset as he had proudly prepared his brigade for war and had been looking forward to guiding them through battles.

Pershing selected his chief of staff, Lt. Colonel James G. Harbord, to fill Doyen's vacancy. Harbord was not a West Point graduate but had rather risen through the ranks, starting as a private, accumulating his expertise in administration. Many Marine officers and others within the ranks were as upset as Doyen with this unusual maneuver. Their new brigade commander was not only from the U.S. Army, but he had never commanded many more than one hundred men, and furthermore, as a U.S. Army lieutenant colonel he was replacing a Marine Corps brigadier general. Reporting to Harbord were two full colonels, who had both received the Medal of Honor: Colonel Neville of the Fifth Regiment and Colonel Albertus Catlin of the Sixth Regiment.

To his advantage, Harbord knew his limitations, and he was fully aware of how qualified the Marines appeared to be. The transitional ceremony was kept very simple with Harbord and Doyen each stating a few sentences. Harbord tried his best to be accepted, and before long his efforts paid off, as he soon acquired the full respect of the Marines. In the process he was quickly elevated to a brigadier general.

The Fifth Regiment departed from the Toulon sector on May 14 and headed to the village of Vitry-en-Perthois for a week-long stay. Following this period of rest and exercises, Hamilton and other Marines remained in the vicinity, north of Paris, enjoying springtime in France with high spirits. During this time Hamilton wrote another insightful letter to his father revealing his feelings: "It is a wonderful country, and one can well realize why France should fight to the finish for it. One of the towns in which we camped is a model of cleanliness. The French are the most hospitable people in the world."

Hamilton was still enjoying the brighter side of life, as his adventure was not yet fully tainted by the horror of war. He then revealed a glimpse of his humor and lighter side by saying:

> Gen. Pershing was up to watch us entrain, and I showed him the fine art of putting a company aboard cattle cars. It took about ten minutes to load 250 men in the little "cheveaux 8, hommes 40 cars," which means 8 horses or 40 men. Sardines had nothing on them.
>
> We are in a beautiful little town many kilometers back of the line. For seven

days in 1914 the Germans occupied the village, but on account of a hurried exit they didn't do much damage. They stripped the mill of all the machinery, and the drawer of a wardrobe in my room shows the effects of a boche attempt at invasion with a bayonet, which was successful, but beyond this there is not much to show that they stopped here.

Like most French villages, this place is marvelously clean. The trash piles which sometimes decorate French front yards are either carefully obscured or have been moved into the back yards or to the fields. The contrast between this town and the trenches is certainly pleasant. My bed is unequaled in all France.[32]

For the Americans, May 30 was a day of rest and reflection in observance of Decoration Day, known also as Memorial Day. The division at this time was located at Chaumont-en-Vexin, and some of Hamilton's men obtained day passes, but most apparently spent the day attending religious services, writing letters and playing a few relaxing games. As astute as Hamilton was, he could sense that something on a grand scale was ready to take place.

The Germans were not being stopped by the current Allied Forces on the front lines, and the enemy's confidence was growing every day as they quickly headed towards Paris. In fact the Central Powers were now within a three-day march of the French capital. For the Germans, success was a "take it while you can" mentality. Their movement was so quick that their support artillery, food and ammunition were lagging behind. Because of this the enemy slowed their pace as they neared the town of Château-Thierry, a village about 40 miles northeast of Paris that was not a particularly strategic location.

The French had a very weak defense, and with no particular plan to stop the enemy, there was much confusion. One obvious observation was that reinforcements were needed immediately to keep the Germans from crossing the bridge over the Marne River towards Paris. The Marne at this location was not as much a river as it was a winding canal, but for strategic purposes the enemy needed to be kept from crossing the water. An American machine-gun battalion assisted the French, and the resistance was enough to temporarily halt the enemy's forward progression and cause the Germans to ponder their next strategy.

French General Pétain requested that General Pershing assist with two American divisions to stop the Germans from taking Paris; for if Paris was lost, most likely the entire French Army would give up fighting. The best battle-ready division available was Maj. General Bundy's Second Division. The nearby fully trained Third Division was also called upon. At 1700 on May 30, the French officially notified the Second Division Headquarters that the division was to move out early on the morning of May 31.[33]

They were headed to stop the Germans' most dangerous offensive momentum, and the American involvement would be known as the Aisne defensive. Without diminishing any prior AEF fighting along the Western Front, the Second Division would soon be honored with recognition as the first division to be engaged in a major American battle. For now there were no details, as to what lay ahead, as Bundy himself said: "So the great adventure began. We knew that we were going to Meaux, but what would happen after our arrival there was a sealed book."[34]

Logistics were in full motion as artillery and horses were jammed into railroad cars. Hamilton and the rest of the Marines ate a healthy breakfast, and at 0600 they left the area in camions heading east towards the little town of Meaux, about 25 miles northeast of Paris. Each camion, loaded with about 18 to 24 men, was destined for the front lines. Because of the many potholes in the road and a lack of support springs on the camions, the motorized ride was extremely bumpy and uncomfortable. If your camion happened to break down, you were basically out of luck, and you'd have to try to hitch a ride or hike much of the distance on your own. The trucks were followed by supply camions making the caravan trail close to 16 miles long.[35] The course over the congested road took up to 30 hours. Along the way Hamilton and his 49th Company passed through several quaint villages where the locals waved and threw flowers into the trucks.

The most striking sight was a constant stream of French citizens, consisting mainly of women and children of all ages, heading in the opposite direction. They were abandoning their villages as fast as possible, carrying all the possessions they could manage. The residents were now refugees. Carts, wheelbarrows, and assorted farm animals were a part of the motley flow. Women were clutching their babies, while the elderly often rode in farm wagons.

The camions proceeded past Meaux to the small town of May-en-Multien. At midnight Bundy received a change in orders; he was now to direct his division towards Château-Thierry. Captain Hamilton, along with others in the division, unloaded from the camions and began a hike to the front lines. As they approached the front on Saturday, June 1, the disorganized French were still trying to figure out what to do with the arriving American forces. The unloaded trucks quickly headed back away from the battle zone, picking up helpless refugees on the way.

With the main bridge across the Marne at Château-Thierry blocked, the Germans now looked for other avenues to Paris. As the Germans were putting the pieces of their plan together, one focal piece involved taking the nearby town of Belleau and its surrounding territory. Lately, the Germans had gotten what they wanted.

Just as Hamilton and his men arrived, they noticed lots of planes in the distant air. One group in particular, which was known to bear distinctive bold colors, was the famous enemy "Flying Circus," which used to include the "Red Baron." Each Fokker plane also displayed the large black German cross. Some were the biplanes, while others were the less common triplanes, but all were known to be a mighty force against the Allied planes. The action adventure was evolving.

When Hamilton's company was on the move, his responsibilities grew in direct proportion to the needs of the men under him. With his men healthy, his current concerns were food, shelter and ammunition. Food was much scarcer than it should have been because many of the rolling kitchens were still stuck in traffic on the incoming road.

Hamilton collected his men and spent the first night of June camping in soft fields of wheat.[36] Some laid on their back looking up at the stars, while others used their arm as a pillow. Their lives would soon be changed forever.

Before dawn on the following morning of June 2, Hamilton was notified by Turrill of plans to move right away as 1/5 was needed to assist the French in holding back the enemy. He got his company together and lined up in darkness with the rest of the battalion. They headed out for a six mile hike northwest through several eerie deserted villages, ending at the small town of Bois de Veuilly. Along the way, his men were using up their emergency energy rations consisting of bread and a hard tack form of bacon.

Finally in the early daylight they filled a gap in the French line and began taking selected aimed shots at the enemy. The Germans did not realize that Americans had entered the fight, and furthermore, they where perplexed as to how their men were getting shot and killed up to 800 yards from the front. This was unlike anything they had ever witnessed. The Marines would continue with their exemplary accurate shooting until the war's end. They were putting their entire rifle training to work, and even the French nearby were amazed at their counterpart's success. The French had not put much emphasis towards rifle practice or supported funding for practice ammunition, and therefore, they were poorer marksmen than the Marines. French training relied on trench warfare tactics with hand grenades, as they generally waited for the Germans to come within 100 yards before reacting.

Although Turrell's 1/5 had closed the gap, he was requested to further expand his thin front line. Brigadier General Harbord mended the precarious situation with his full brigade by issuing orders for Colonel Neville's other two battalions in the Fifth Regiment, along with Colonel Catlin's Sixth Regiment, to fill the voids. The event was basically a mixed scramble aided by a lack of precise communication. Still the Allied Forces were holding due to the fact that the opposing Germans were continuing to ponder their next move.

By mid-afternoon Hamilton's company and the rest of 1/5 were called into reserve. Overall, his men did not see a lot of action; however, they did participate and the Germans took notice. Others in the Fourth Brigade continued to fight and spar with the Germans on a limited basis. The Marines liked the action, but the French were not as enthusiastic and generally growing tired.

The sky overhead contained some enemy stationary "sausage" observation balloons along with a few airplanes engaged in a dogfight. Each side continued to test each other, but this was not yet the time or place for the big battle. Late at night Hamilton and his men were transported to nearby Pyramid Farm, where they remained in the vicinity of Bois de Veuilly for the next few days. Upon daylight they remained in wooded terrain to be hidden from enemy observation. This mode of hide and seek involved having Hamilton and his men sleeping during the day while working at night with preparations.

The French were continuing to pull back from the front lines. On the following day, June 3, Marine Captain Lloyd W. Williams of the 51st Company of 2/5 arrived at the front with his men physically and mentally determined to fight, when a French officer ordered him to fall back too. The Marines were taking orders not only from the U.S. Army chain of command but also from French authority too. Many Marines were currently at wit's end and primed to see some real action. William's now famous words to the French officer, "Retreat, hell! We just got here," were not only inspirational to members of the Marine Corps but also to others in the Second Division.[37]

On June 4 the Second Division took full control of the area, as the French completed their demoralized withdrawal. While the Germans continued with unsuccessful, mild counterattacks in the Château-Thierry region, some additional enemy movement was observed heading into Bois de Belleau.

The following day, June 5, Bundy was afforded time to make organizational plans and assess the present conditions of his division. He relayed his strategy to Harbord who later reflected upon the absence of vital key information: "The French had informed us that Belleau Wood was not occupied except by a very short line across the northeast corner which was entrenched. Little or no reconnaissance or scouting appears to have been done by the companies in front of their positions between June 4th and 6th, the responsibility having been ours since the withdrawal of the French on the 4th."[38]

Colonel Catlin later looked back upon this time and recalled the following, which indirectly paid tribute to Captain Hamilton and others in the Fifth Regiment:

> All through June 5th we waited, with nothing of moment occurring save increasing artillery fire on both sides. The sound of it was deafening. To this day I do not know why the Germans did not attempt a sortie — whether they felt so secure

in their position that they could afford to wait for overwhelming reinforcements, or whether the resistance and then the offensive dash of the Fifth Marines had frightened them into caution.

As a matter of history, they never did come out, for on the following day the Marines went in.[39]

The summertime picturesque landscape with rolling hillsides found Hamilton and his men in woods on an elevated area known as Hill 176, and from that vantage point he could look down upon Hill 142. The Germans continued testing the Americans and searching for weak spots with long-range high explosives, which the Americans called "sea bags." The incessant sound of the incoming nine-inch shells tested the nerves of all.

With the rolling kitchens stationed five miles to the rear, Hamilton's men had eaten very little over the past days, and with a lack of food and incoming artillery, they were becoming very agitated. Finally their overall temperament elevated to a boiling point with news that 2nd Lieutenant Walter D. Frazier in their 49th Company had been killed. If there was any thus positive about their situation, it was that Hamilton knew that their current mood was a good attitude for warriors.

8. Belleau Wood

Château-Thierry Sector
June 6–26 — Paris Is Saved

The village of Belleau was known for its pristine water, and the name of the area, Bois de Belleau, meant "Wood of the Beautiful Waters." Consequently, the Americans called the area, including land south of town where a Parisian aristocrat had a game preserve and a large château, simply Belleau Wood.[1] The preserve's domain was an irregular shape roughly a mile in length and 1,000 to 2,000 yards wide.

The scattered wheat of early summer was roughly thigh high, lush green and intermingled with occasional clusters of vibrant blood-red poppies. Beyond the open territory were elevated dense woods with many conifer trees that had been well maintained with selective cutting. There was very little distance between each tree, and one could only see about 15 to 20 feet ahead. The timber itself was exceptionally tall, as each tree sought its own airspace and sunlight, creating darkness at ground level. In contrast to the manicured woods, there were a lot of thickets, hollows and underbrush around the woods to enhance the natural habitat. Among the hills and ridges were a few large boulders and woodpiles that were just the kind of places to hide machine guns. In a few days the landscape would look much different. Who would have thought such a major battle would be fought over a hunting lodge and accompanying land? Hamilton and his men would not be hunting deer or pheasant, but rather, as noted by Captain Leroy P. Hunt, leader of the 17th Company: "The Marines would be attacking some of the best fighting units Germany had to offer. The highly respected proven warriors maintained profession pride and instilled fear in anyone who opposed them. The enemy forces within the German Imperial Army, would be identified as the 28th, also called the 'The Kaiser's Own,' the 362nd and others."[2]

Keeping track of the many smaller mobile enemy divisions was not an easy task. It appears that the German forces surrounding the Belleau Wood also included the Royal Prussian 237th Infantry Division, the 10th and 197th

Divisions, the 460th, 461st and 462nd Regiments and portions of the 87th Division and 5th Prussian Guards Division.[3]

There was a definite absence of French intelligence and a lack of maps of the area. The maps that were available included several inaccuracies, such as streams being ravines. After having spent an entire summer working with the Geological Survey team, along with officer training, Hamilton was quite proficient in topography. However, in the midst of a battle, even an expert would have difficulty identifying a specific location with a poor map. This situation regarding maps would persist through the coming months.

The plan was for the Fourth Brigade to take the area north of the Paris-Metz highway, which included Hill 142, about two-thirds of a mile southwest of Torcy, along with Belleau Wood and the rail junction and village of Bouresches. The hill contained several slopes, ridges and many Germans. Hamilton was used to hills from his fun loving days at the Conesus Lake house, but he soon found out that the hills he faced in France were all too often occupied by the enemy and these elevated works of nature were not friendly places.

As the football captain at Central High, he huddled up his teammates, gave them the plan and then carried out the objective to the best of his ability, gaining yards and protecting the football at all times. As an athlete, he likely experienced a few stomach butterflies before the whistle to kick off the start of a big game, or prior to the sound of a gun signaling the start of a major track meet. Although he was now facing a totally different situation on irregular turf, as a Marine captain, he was fully prepared to accomplish his mission and protect his men.

Many commanding officers carried a swagger stick, which was a small cane and used at times as a symbol of authority. To start a battle one often pointed the cane in the direction forward and blew a whistle. As an expert rifleman, Hamilton was a different breed. There was no way he was going to trade his Springfield '03 rifle in for a cane, but he kept his whistle.

New orders were issued from Harbord to Neville down to Turrill shortly before midnight on June 5. The plans called for Major Turrill's 1/5 and Major Benjamin S. Berry's 3/5 to commence on June 6 at 0345 and take Hill 142. Due to short notice and poor communication, the entire 3/5 was unprepared to enter the fight and the same was true for two companies of 1/5. Captain Hamilton's 49th Company and First Lieutenant Orlando C. Crowther, skipper of the 67th Company, were in place and fully prepared to jump off at the appropriate time. This critical factor meant sending 500 men into unknown territory versus 2,000 men from two full battalions along with a small battalion of French.

Still, Hamilton was elated to put his training to use and serve his country.

After the battle he wrote to a friend stating his excitement: "On June 5th, Old Jule Turrill, our battalion commander, got word that we were going to participate in an honest-to-God attack the next morning and selected my depleted company and the Sixty-seventh to start things for his battalion."[4]

Hamilton looked over the objective plans while his men tried to sleep. What he did not know was that since the area ahead had not been fully scouted, he would be among the first to identify the conditions he was heading into. The top commanders and generals were aware of the burden ahead. For Hamilton it was an awesome responsibility to view his men resting knowing full well many would die in a few hours when the big adventure started.

On June 6, 1918, the captain woke his men with the phrase "up and at 'em," or some similar call, to ready them for battle. The men were apprised of the plan and then notified to secure their lighter 20-pound combat packs, check their rifles, fix bayonets, add an extra bandoleer of ammunition, and get their minds set straight.

For a few brief moments there was light artillery fire in advance of the jump-off, which was not very effective other than causing a commotion. The load of work ahead would be shared by many, but the responsibility, starting with the first step forward, rested squarely on the shoulders of the two skippers venturing out. Hamilton and Crowther were now ready with their companies at their proper starting location. One could always count on Hamilton to be prepared, and he was often noted to be "Johnny-on-the-spot." The 49th Company would head north taking the right side of the ridge, while the 67th Company would take the western edge and lower slopes. The other two 1/5 companies, the 17th and the 66th, along with the Eighth Machine Gun Company, were back at Les Mares Farm waiting on the French.[5] They hoped they would catch up and engage in the fight before too much time elapsed.

The French had been fighting for years and were pretty much spent; however, this did not relieve them of their important support roles that were an integral part of the overall plan. When the H-hour came, as Hamilton described the situation, "we were to have Americans on our right and French on our left, and were to make our get-away at 3:45 A.M.... I was supposed to guide left and keep in "liaison" with the French. I couldn't see them and knew that at 3:45 they had not started. At 3:50 I started things by myself, and we were off."[6]

The new moon for the month of June would fall on the 8th, and the official sunrise for these long summer days was about 0530. Still at 0345 there were hints of light, and any movement or even a shadow in the vast open territory was noticed by well trained eyes, triggering a reaction. Along the Western Front scouts were always watching. There would be no protection crossing the open areas.

8. *Belleau Wood*

The terrain at Belleau Wood with an open field and wooded hill (courtesy Marine Corps History Division).

The Germans thought the Americans might put up some sort of fresh defense in place of the weary French. However, the word "amazed" is not powerful enough to describe the German frenzy when they soon realized that they were facing U.S. Marines and that these warriors were raring to go on a major offensive rather than play defense.

The plan given to Captain Hamilton called for his men to set off in ranked straight line formation, as in military battles of long years ago. The line formation in waves was used in the Civil War and recently taught to a limited degree by the French Chasseurs. Still the dash was on. Hamilton recalled, "We hadn't moved fifty yards when they cut loose at us from the woods ahead — more machine guns than I ever heard before. Our men had been trained on a special method of getting out machine guns, and, according to their training, all immediately lay down flat — some Jell."[7]

Hamilton's platoon leaders, wearing their Sam Browne belts, were leading the way. This prominent identification along with their forward movement was a special target for German snipers, as well as machine gun operators, and therefore they were the first to fall as casualties. One of the very first to fall, by machine gun fire, was 2nd Lieutenant William Chandler Peterson, an architect by trade and a graduate of the University of Illinois.[8] Peterson gladly joined the 49th Company on May 26 as a fill-in for one of the officers who had become ill. Hamilton was just getting familiarized with him, and now he needed yet another replacement.

The men hugging the earth could feel their light backpacks being hit. The Germans in the woods with camouflaged Maxims had a distinct advantage and continued to fire low. Their machine guns were everywhere, in trees, behind boulders, woodpiles and in trenches. The Marines were spaced out in an unprotected open line and could only be expected to lie low for so long.

Hamilton was witnessing his officers and men being shot and killed all around him. Everything was happening so quickly that action needed to be taken to find safety fast. The time came when the captain rose and ran through the field encouraging each of his men to get up and rush forward to the woods. The unprotected open area was bad enough, but the straight line formation had taken its toll on his men. Maybe he recalled the unregimented flow of the rugby game that he had witnessed in New York, or possibly his natural instinct took over, but the rapid dash deployment to the woods was a good call by the skipper. One current historian wrote, "It seemed to Major Turrill, who was directing the action from his post of command in the jump-off trench, that his entire force would be annihilated in the field. And indeed but for one man [Capt. Hamilton], the attack might well have been stopped in its tracks."[9]

Crowther, skipper of the 67th, was facing a situation similar to what Hamilton faced in the fields. He made it to the first woods and wiped out one machine gun crew, but as he continued on to the next crew, he was killed by a bullet to the throat and one of his available lieutenants stepped up and took over command.

German observation balloons were deployed in the sky, watching and reporting every move by the Allied Forces. Because the French aviators were assisting in other regions and the smaller groups of American flyers were just getting situated, there was no air support from Allied Forces to shoot down the enemy observers.[10]

It was safer in the woods, but they were much closer to the enemy. Hamilton and his men rushed around the many trees like a band of wild Indians. His men were not equipped with grenades or mortars on this mission, so the best option was to continue with the adrenaline rush and capture the enemy by surprise. When contact was made with the enemy there appeared to be all sorts of mass confusion, but in reality his men were prepared for this combat. A few Germans ran, and those that did were usually fired upon. Some manned their Maxims at very close range to their eventual death. Others instantly gave up by throwing their hands in the air and stating, "Kamarad!" As prisoners they were sent to the back lines under guard.

The German elite forces also entered the rugged combat where natural instincts and survival of the fittest took control of the fight. It was every man for himself, kill or be killed. There is no better example of this than Captain Hamilton killing four Germans in hand-to-hand combat in one wild rush.[11] He was leading from the front.

The Marines' continuous charge was unlike anything the Germans had ever faced or imagined. Their determination to advance under horrific conditions, using all means available including bayonets and hand-to-hand combat, gave the Germans reason to call the Marines "Teufel Hunden," translated to "Devil Dog."[12] The nickname quickly stuck to members of the Fourth Brigade, and it became an honored recruiting tool for the U.S. Marine Corps back in the United States through posters and other promotions.

Hamilton's men performed admirably in the woods and once the area was in control, it was time for the 49th Company to continue pursuing their objective. They now had to venture out of the trees once again and make their way across another clearing to enter another wooded area on Hill 142. His men had been through one initial experience with an open field, and this next crossing called for an immediate quick rush from the start. Hamilton recalled what they found upon reaching the woods:

> Afterwards we found why it was they made it so hot for us — three machine-gun companies were holding down these woods and the infantry were farther back. Besides several of the heavy Maxims we later found several empty belts and a dead gunner sitting on the seat lying near by. It was only because we rushed the positions that we were able to take them, as there were too many guns to take in any other way.
>
> After going through this second wood we were really at our objective, but I was looking for an unimproved road which showed up on the map. We now had the Germans pretty well on the run except a few machine-gun nests. I was anxious to get to that road, so pushed forward with the men I had with me — one platoon (I knew the rest were coming, but thought they were closer). We went right down over' the nose of a hill and on across an open field between two hills. What saved me from getting hit I don't know — the Maxims on both sides cut loose at us unmercifully — but although I lost heavily here I came out unscratched. I was pushing ahead with an automatic rifle team and didn't notice that most of the platoon had swerved off to the left to rout out the machine guns. All I knew was that there was a road ahead and that the bank gave good protection to the front. It happened however, that there was a town just a few hundred yards to the left, and while most of the Germans had left, about one company was forming for a counter attack. I realized that I had gone too far — that the nose of the hill I had come over was our objective, and that it was up to me to get back, reorganize and

dig in. It was a case of every man for himself. I crawled back through a drainage ditch filled with cold water and shiny reeds. Machine-gun bullets were just grazing my back and our artillery was dropping close (I was six hundred yards too far to the front). Finally I got back, and started getting the two companies together, and I sent out parties to the right and left to try to hook up with our French and American friends, but it wasn't until the next day that we got a satisfactory liaison.

And now came the counter-attacks—five nasty ones that came near driving us back off our hill—but—we hung on. One especially came near getting me. There were heavy bushes all over the hill, and the first thing I knew hand grenades began dropping near. One grenade threw a rock which caught me behind the ear and made me dizzy for a few minutes. But I quickly recovered my senses when I saw one of my gunnery sergeants [Hoffman] jump toward the bushes with a yell and start shooting to beat the devil. Not twenty feet from us, was a line of about fifteen German helmets and five light machine guns just coming into action. It was hand-to-hand work for several strenuous minutes, and then all was over. We hauled the guns in the later and buried most Germans.

After the counter-attacks we settled down to the work of digging in. Gee, but it was a long day! The night proved to be worse, and on account of my flanks I was more worried than I cared to admit. If the Boches went up the valleys to our right and left and from their flares I thought we were all but surrounded. Two more companies had come up, however, and the fire from the rifles and auto-rifles of several hundred men must have made the Germans nervous, too, for about dawn they went back and only left several machine guns to worry us during the next day.

I'm tired of telling about fighting and I'm going to knock off. We held the positions; the lines came up on the right and left, and we now have satisfied the Germans that they haven't a chance as long as they are up against Marines.[13]

It's interesting to note his words, "I realized that I had gone too far." It's a minor point, but if one could ever find a fault with Hamilton, it was that at times he went a bit too far. His long legs, which had helped him achieve great accomplishments in track and field events, combined with his determination found him constantly on the move. In his defense, the much needed flank support would have been missing even at a slower pace, and the available maps were terrible. Most importantly, in all instances through the war, one of Hamilton's greatest attributes was the fact that he was always prepared with his men at the start of a battle. He would complete his given objectives, and finally, he would always end up in the proper location. When the war ended, few military officers were able to make that claim, as evidenced by the start of this battle alone.

He had overrun his objective by about 600 yards and was heading towards the main road to Torcy. A group of his men were caught up in the action and continued on to the town where they encountered many Germans. The action was similar to that experienced near Hill 142, and some casualties, including deaths, occurred.

By mid-morning on the 6th, the summer sun was beaming down, foretelling that it was going to be one hot June day. Thanks to intensive training and drills, the boys of the 49th had now reached the objective they were given. They performed just as Hamilton knew they would, displaying courage and determination with many heroic deeds on the first day of America's major entry into warfare. Hamilton took a moment to assess his own personal issues, noticing he had been nicked up a bit, and although he experienced many close calls, he was physically all right. The captain was very concerned about the status of his men.

Lieutenant Peterson was dead, and all of his other commissioned officers were wounded, except for Lieutenant Francis S. Kieren. Additionally, he had lost most of his non-commissioned officers and half of his total company.[14] The 67th Company was in a similar situation, and without their "skipper" Crowther, they were down to one lieutenant and in need of a proven leader. Hamilton took temporary control of the situation by commanding both companies as one unit. With so many causalities on the battlefield, word soon filtered back to the Fourth Brigade's reserve units that "Hamilton is gone and all his men."[15]

Two runners were immediately dispersed to establish verification of the statement. The messengers had difficulty making their way through the open areas and thickets, but finally one courier named Brady made it through and noticed that the captain was, in fact, alive. With a messenger at his side, Hamilton put him to good use and dispersed a return message: "Who said I was dead. Send me the mortars and a thousand hand grenades."[16]

Hamilton could not have been more proud of his men for how they carried on the fight. One platoon leader, 2nd Lieutenant James B. Garvey, was wounded and disoriented. Another top officer, 1st Lieutenant Jonas Henry Platt, received a serious leg injury early in the morning but continued to direct his platoon and assist another in driving the enemy away from a specific machine-gun nest. He then made certain his men were dug in and positioned properly for a counterattack. Due to loss of blood, he finally had to be relieved of command. He later received the Distinguished Service Cross for his conduct.

On the north ridge of Hill 142, Gunnery Sergeant Charles F. Hoffman spotted 12 Germans crawling towards him. The Germans had five light machine guns and were planning a surprise counterattack. Hoffman alerted Hamilton, as he rushed towards the enemy. He bayoneted two while the others fled, leaving their weapons behind. For his bravery in this early engagement with the enemy, Hoffman was the first person in the entire American Expeditionary Forces to be awarded with the Medal of Honor, which he received from both the U.S. Army and the U.S. Navy.[17]

Gunner Nice was busy firing away taking out German Maxims. He later noted: "One of the worst nests was in a wooded depression and death came spurting out of there in a constant stream. Shell fire was poured into it and then the boys went into the mess and Floyd Gibbons, the newspaper correspondent, was with them. The Germans had pulled off a clever trick. They were operating their guns with lanyards stretching to the top of the depressions. Strings of ammunition containing 1,000 cartridges were operated by weights."[18]

Another trick of the Germans, which the Marines noticed, involved enemy first-aid personnel carrying stretchers of wounded and dead away from the battlefield. This practice was undertaken in what was thought to be a mutual safety zone for both sides. A few German stretcher-bearers were carrying away what appeared to be a large wounded man curled up and covered with a blanket. The Marines thought he might have taken a stomach wound when a gust of wind blew the blanket revealing a machine gun with ammunition. Word of that story quickly spread throughout the troops, and from that point on the Americans did not concede any trust to their enemy, and, in fact, the Marines were now determined to be even more aggressive. The Germans now believed the "Devil Dogs" would shoot at anything that moved.

In the middle of more action, Nice went further forward to assist wounded 2nd Lieutenant Vernon L. Somers, whose wounds appeared to be quite serious. Somers needed first aid at once, so Gunner Nice stepped up to carry him to the rear, but in the process he was himself shot in the back. When he arrived at the first aid station the positive news was that the bullet in his back appeared to be in a good location. The unfortunate news concerned Somers's wounds, which were so severe that he later died.

Nice remained under the care of the first aid station overnight and then escaped back to his company the following day with the bullet still lodged in his back. For the proud leatherneck, this would not be the last time he would escape from a medical station. Men were often known to escape from hospitals and aid stations to get back to their company. There were several reasons for this. The main reason was the Marines truly enjoyed being beside their comrades, and they wanted to participate in protecting each other as much as they could. The second reason was that they were concerned that as time progressed they might get transferred to another company. This type of loyal bonding remained exceptionally strong throughout the entire war.

Hamilton also recalled how his first sergeant, Murl Corbett, stepped up to fill the leadership void of downed officers. Late in the morning he was able to hold a strategic defensive position against counterattacks. As the war progressed, Hamilton developed a special relationship with the non-commissioned officer, who was always reliable in times of need.

A number of brave sergeants who had gallantly led the way were dead, including Sergeant Raymond P. Cronin, Sergeant Peter Conway, Sergeant Charles A. O'Connor, Sergeant Arthur F. Ware and 39-year-old Gunnery Sergeant Arthur Russell. Russell, a former lumberjack from Oshkosh, Wisconsin, had been in and out of the Marine Corps since 1906, serving in various roles as a leatherneck on board different ships, and prior to joining the 49th Company, he was a drill instructor at Quantico. Like his captain, the rugged sergeant had perfected his shooting skills over the years to be classified as an expert; however, even with all his acquired talents he would not escape death on this day.[19]

Among the dead was friendly Gunnery Sergeant Gerald R. Finnegan, the sponsor of the company dog "Parade Rest." Shortly before jump-off he was positioning his bayonet as best he could to open a can of salmon when a lieutenant summoned him to properly mount his bayonet and get moving. He made it through the open area but was killed in the process of bayoneting a German.[20]

A few of Hamilton's dead sergeants were awarded the Distinguished Service Cross, and the same recognition was given to some who survived. Sergeant John Casey, who was born in Ireland and now called Massachusetts his home, received a serious leg wound, yet remained calm through a counterattack and created a safety zone for his men before retiring. Another, Sergeant John H. Culnan from New Orleans, Louisiana was in the process of assisting a wounded man to the rear when he received a wound to the head. He completed his mission but was unable to continue with the action.

The majority of men in Hamilton's company were dedicated Marines who reported to the commissioned and non-commissioned officers. Often they did not seek or receive recognition for performing their duty, but rather found gratification through camaraderie and pride as members of a successful unit.

One fellow that did stand out on the first day was Russian-born Private John Kukoski, who now called Buffalo, New York, his home. He charged a machine-gun nest and single-handily captured its crew along with an officer. Another member, Corporal Eugene W. Wear, entered an open field to assist a wounded comrade to safety. Both would be awarded the Distinguished Service Cross for their bravery.

The accomplishments on June 6 came at the expense of much personal sacrifice against a tenacious enemy. At the onset there was poor advance scouting, combined with little artillery assistance, a lack of troop support at jump off, initial absence of hand grenades and mortars, followed by the lack of French flank support.

At 1210 Captain Hamilton sent a message to Turrill:

Think it important that artillery have our position and get busy to the front in order to stop constant enemy activity and save our ammunition. Ammunition is now the big point and we need as much as can be gotten up. Several hospital apprentices should come forward to *dress* wounds. We could evacuate later.
Need water badly...
Need Very pistols and illuminating rockets.[21]

In the heat of the battle, a lot of officers were issuing statements to entice their men on. One special incident involved a hardened 44-year-old leatherneck gunnery sergeant named Dan Daly assigned to 3/6 under Major Berton Sibley. Prior to setting foot on French soil, the role-model sergeant had already received two Medals of Honor. When a lieutenant went down, he stepped up in command and rose to rally the men around him, shouting, "Come on you sons of bitches! Do you want to live forever?"[22] Reporter Floyd Gibbons, the war correspondent for the *Chicago Tribune* newspaper, heard the story and spread the word of Daly's comments.

Turrill's battalion had maintained their ground throughout the counterattacks, but they were depleted and needed immediate replacements. First Lieutenant Robert Blake of the 17th Company in 1/5 received recognition and awards for keeping in liaison with Hamilton's company. Towards the end of the war, Blake would serve under Hamilton, providing further valuable assistance. Hamilton's friend Shuler was currently the adjutant of the Fifth Marine Regiment and involved with lots of information. Meanwhile, the other five battalion commanders in the Fourth Brigade were keeping an eye on their captains and assessing objectives.

When the day of June 6, 1918, was over and Hill 142 had been secured to a degree, the casualty count consisting of wounded and killed was 31 officers and 1,056 men for a total of 1,087.[23] This figure was more than the total of all Marine casualties over their past 143-year history. Through all the tragic details there was good news in that the Marines, in true fashion, had carried the day. Their message was clear to the Germans, and the news reverberated back home to America. A lot of credit for the day's success was given to the basic training of each Marine with his Springfield rifle.

The Germans had lost control of the elevated ridge, but they were not about to retreat or give up the thought of retaking the hill. It would take several more days of action before Hill 142 would be finally secured. Claiming ultimate control of the Belleau Wood territory was another separate issue. Over the next 20 days the battle for rights to the entire Belleau Wood landscape was ceded back and forth several times. Men from other battalions and companies within the Marine Brigade were performing admirably. German planes dropped bombs at the worst moments, and there was to be little relaxation or sleep at night in trenches until the total mission was fully accomplished.

The success of the Marine Brigade could not have come at a better time. Allied Forces had been retreating towards Paris, and the news of the initial German defeat gave renewed hope, optimism and inspiration to the French and English.

Hamilton and his company were regrouping to get back to full strength, while they maintained their gains and continued their progress. A few like Nice had wounds that allowed them to return, while others returned to their comrades as quickly as they could.

On June 7 several new replacements arrived and introduced themselves to Captain Hamilton. First Lieutenant John W. Thomason Jr. would soon prove to be an excellent reliable officer in the 49th Company under the skipper. Thomason had come from a prominent Texas family; his maternal grandfather, Major Tom Goree, had been a member of Civil War General Longstreet's staff. He was the first of nine children, and his father wanted him to follow his path and become a medical doctor. The young man, however, had many gifts and interests.[24] Thomason would later become nationally famous through writing memorable stories, including "Fix Bayonets." Throughout the war, during periods of rest, Hamilton often found Thomason drawing in a sketch pad. Thomason noted right away that the German opposition had a "confident look [about] them, with a touch of Berlin swank, they were Prussians of a very good division; and there were no better soldiers in the world."[25]

Communication was always difficult on the front lines. One voluntary job was that of runner, whose task was to run messages back and forth, often between the officers on the front lines and the commanders stationed back in a sheltered area. Many runners quickly became casualties, and therefore the duty was commonly labeled a continuous suicide mission. Hamilton received a new runner in the 67th Company that he was temporarily watching over. Initial small talk usually centered on where one was from, and the new replacement, Private Elton Mackin, was from Lewiston, New York, a small town in Niagara County just on the other side of Buffalo near Niagara Falls.

Correspondent Gibbons was just beginning his coverage of the Fourth Brigade's action in America's first big engagement on the Western Front. General Pershing had instituted strict rules pertaining to restrictions and censorship of information. All letters sent by AEF personnel were checked and censored. The press was also instructed to avoid mentioning specific units involved with current activity. Bundy's Second Division was large enough to mention; however, Harbord's Fourth Brigade was another issue. Technically the Fourth Brigade, composed of just 8,000 fighting U.S. Marines, was considered by some to be a unique unit.

Gibbons highlighted the U.S. Marines in an article featuring the exploits of the initial assault at Belleau Wood, and his press release was forwarded through the proper channels to the U.S. Army censors in Paris. The correspondent was quite personable and no stranger to the Army personnel and journalists in the French capital city. While a couple of other factors were in play, the bottom line was that a censorship decision had to be made, and right or wrong, the ultimate decision was to allow mention of the Marines. His stories hit the *Chicago Tribune*, and instantly the media floodgates were open, and U.S. Marines were being praised on front pages across the entire nation.

One example appeared on June 8, within the *New York Times* article "Marines Win Name of 'Devil Hounds,'" followed by "Valor of Marines Stirs All America," and a day later "Flock to the Marines."[26] The Army personnel did not appreciate the attention given to the Marines, and they instantly labeled Gibbons as a press agent for the Marine Corps. The Marines had full reason to be proud, but they were also very complimentary of the Army soldiers that made up the major portion of their Second Division. Harbord, a rather physically large man with mixed emotions, was caught in an awkward predicament. He was proud of his Fourth Brigade and had grown attached to the Marine Corps lore, but he was firmly affiliated with the U.S. Army, and to further compound his identity, for some unexplained reason he often wore a French helmet.[27]

Back in the States, many patriotic men were caught up in the emotional wave rolling across the nation. On June 9, 1918, the Marine Corps was flooded with an overwhelming record number of applicants. One volunteer in the mix was a single

Brig. General James G. Harbord shown while commanding the Fourth Brigade wearing his French helmet (courtesy Marine Corps History Division).

athletic 28 year old named Ove Emanuel Mortensen. The proud American was willing to put his established career as a purchasing agent on hold, and after checking in at the recruiting station in Boston, Massachusetts, he proceeded on to the USMC Parris Island, South Carolina, training facility, where he officially enlisted on June 9 with the hope of making the grade. Hamilton and his fellow skippers would need even more qualified fighting men in the not too distant future. As Colonel Catlin, commanding the Sixth Regiment, described:

> It is still possible to become a Marine — if you're man enough.
>
> Our standards have always been high in the matter of physique, intelligence and character. We have sought for men above average in physical strength and agility. We have sought intelligent, educated men, for we have learned that they have sense enough to realize the necessity for obedience. They get the idea of the discipline quicker than the other sort and it stands by them in a pinch.
>
> The recruits we took in for the overseas service were even higher quality than the average in previous years.[28]

On the battlefield the counterattacks continued, although less frequently and not with the casualty rate of June 6, day one. Hamilton was back in action issuing orders, and at one point the captain found himself firing away next to a 20-year-old private, who noted:

> On the second day of our advance my captain and two others besides myself were lying prone and cracking away at 'em. I was second in line. Before I knew what had happened a machine gun got me in the right arm just at the elbow. Five shots hit in succession. The elbow was torn into shreds but the hits didn't hurt. It seemed just like getting five stings with electricity.
>
> The captain ordered two men to help me back. I said I could make it alone. I picked up the part of my arm that was hanging loosely and walked.[29]

Meanwhile, the rest of the Fourth Brigade was involved with much action. Besides Major Turrill's 1/5, the other battalions involved were Major Frederick Wise's 2/5, Major Benjamin Berry's 3/5, Major John A. Hughes's 1/6, Major Thomas Holcomb's 2/6 and Major Berton Sibley's 3/6. They were all unified traversing the fields and forests tracking down the enemy and achieving objectives in critical areas away from Hill 142.

On June 12 Sergeant Corbett, who had made it through the 6th without a scratch, took three men on patrol through "No Man's Land." He secured valuable information, but during a skirmish he was wounded in one eye. Before leaving enemy territory he assisted other more seriously wounded men back to safety. Corbett was sent to the hospital, but like other loyal Marines, he, too, escaped without permission and came back to the front lines.

Eventually Hamilton and his men completed their final assignment and were afforded time away from the front, while others in the brigade finalized the security of Belleau Wood. On June 21 Hamilton found time to write to his sister Mary revealing his innermost feelings after his first major battle. He also sent his pay home hoping that "Flax" would follow up on the deposits. The letter continued:

> I don't believe our rest period is going to be long. We are do for a healthy rest and it will come within a month, but dope has it that we will get another crack at the Boche first. Gee but I wish I could have ten days to lie around Nice or Brittany right now. A trip to the States is too much to be hoped for, but you know what it is that "springs eternal in the human heart!" Every time I think about that attack I have to pray a little, and thank God I'm here today. There were both Germans + Americans falling on all sides, and later when both took up the heavy shelling, things were awful. I have seen men cut in two by machine guns and have seen shells wipe out platoons and knock down villages. Our first night up near the lines airplanes bombarded us severely for a while and long range guns tried to find us. German snipers were bad, but I believe ours did more damage. I had one man who sniped off about three machine guns when we could get them in no other way.[30]

The letter went on to portray a very humanistic and personal side of him, as he mentioned one German in particular whom he wished he had not had to kill. The man was being taken captive but then, unfortunately, became overly aggressive.[31] He finished by writing:

> A bandolier of cartridges I was carrying was struck by a rifle bullet and on two different occasions stones hit me in the head when shells exploded nearby, but beyond that, I came out without a scratch. I ducked down once to go into a dugout, and as I did so, four high explosive shells went over my back + wounded a bugler right near me.—One thing which hurt—I ran into the grave of an old friend of mine in the woods, never knowing before that time that he had been killed. I'm thankful to say however, that most of my old friends are alive + in good spirits. Matt Kingman got a "blighty" in the shoulder, but is getting along nicely.

On June 26, five days after his letter, the Belleau Wood territory was finally secured for the last time. Major Maurice Shearer, the battalion commander of 3/5 in place of Major Berry, issued the proud words in a message to Brig. General Harbord: "Belleau Woods now U.S. Marine Corps entirely."[32]

The total Marine casualties for Belleau Wood amounted to 4,598 and close to 25 percent of those were on the first day, June 6, when Hamilton's company took the charge and faced the initial fire.[33] The big news was that the Fourth Brigade had played a leading role in stopping the German offensive movement, and Paris was saved!

Colonel Catlin led a life that Hamilton could easily relate to. The colonel, who attended the U.S. Naval Academy, graduating two years before Hamilton was born, also had a love for football, and while at the Academy he was the starting tailback for three years and served as a team captain. Describing the action at Belleau Wood, he said:

> It was like many a football match you have attended, with the game going dead against your side in the second half. The opposing team has recently made a touchdown and the score is in their favour [*sic*]. The ball is in their possession and they are forcing it steadily down the field, five ten, fifteen yards at a rush. The defense seems to have crumpled. Your team, beaten by superior weight, appears to be all in and there is small hope of regaining the offensive before another score is tallied.
>
> Nearer, nearer to the goal the scrimmage line is pressed. You sit on the bleachers with clenched fists and groan inwardly — perhaps aloud. The game seems lost.
>
> Suddenly from the sidelines, at the command of coach or captain, a substitute back field jumps in to take the places of the worn-out plungers.[34]

Captain Hamilton was not sitting but was a very active "substitute" who assisted in turning the action and holding the line. Catlin finished by mentioning the American forces: "They were untried, inexperienced, green in the grim business of fighting; they were substitutes, if you will; but when they went in it made all the difference in the world to the losing side. For it was then that the French took heart of hope, and with their new allies at their elbows, they held the baffled Hun for downs on their five yard line."[35]

The beautiful nature preserve that was so lush on June 5 had been destroyed. Nature over time has its own way of healing, but it was severely tested and the landscape had a long way to recover, as evidenced by post-battle remarks from Lieutenant Thomason:

> It was gassed and shelled and shot into the semblance of nothing earthly. The great trees were all down; the leaves were blasted off, or hung sere and blackened. It was pockmarked with shell-craters and shallow dugouts and hasty trenches. It was strewn with all the debris of war, Mauser rifles and Springfield's, helmets, German and American, unexploded grenades, letters, knapsacks, packs, blankets, boots; a year later, it is said, they were still finding unburied dead in the depths of it.[36]

The Germans had been on the offensive since the start of the war in 1914. When the battle of Belleau Wood was over, the Germans fell back. Germany did not yet realize it, but in essence they had fought their last major offensive battle and had lost.

Pershing issued a telegram to Bundy praising the Second Division for their effort: "Please accept for the division and convey to General Harbord and the officers and men under him my sincere congratulations for the splendid conduct of the attack on the German lines north of Château-Thierry. It was a magnificent example of American courage and dash."[37]

The entire Fourth Brigade was recognized with the very prestigious Croix de Guerre award from the French Government. To further honor the Americans for their successful battle and saving Paris, the French renamed Bois de

Belleau. Many of the Marines heard the official news when they were lined up in formation:

> VI Armée
> Etat Major
> 6930/2
>
> Au QGA le 30 Juin, 1918.
>
> In view of the brilliant conduct of the 4th Brigade of the 2nd U.S. Division, which in a spirited fight took Bouresches and the important strong point of Bois de Belleau, stubbornly defended by a large enemy force, the General commanding the VIth Army orders that, henceforth, in all official papers, the Bois de Belleau shall be named "Bois de la Brigade de Marine."
>
> The General of Division Degoutte
> Commanding VIth Army
> (Signed) Degoutte.[38]

Geographical maps were quickly revised to reflect the new name. A few years later Marshal Foch visited a little cemetery where many of the Second Division were buried and said: "Glorious dead, you can sleep in peace on this soil which was the cradle of Victory. La Fayette in America built the first span of Franco-American friendship; you have built the second."[39]

For his bravery at Belleau Wood, Captain Hamilton would later receive the Distinguished Service Cross, as well as the Navy Cross, America's second highest awards. Additionally, he was honored with an individual Croix de Guerre award of recognition by the French Government.

Of great importance was the fact that, while the battle of Belleau Wood was still raging and thoughts were fresh in his mind, Colonel Neville took precious time from commanding the Fifth Regiment to officially recommend Hamilton for the Medal of Honor. Neville, the future 14th commandant of the Marine Corps, knew firsthand what was required to receive such an honor, as he had been awarded the Medal of Honor in 1914. His memo stated:

> UNITED STATES MARINE CORPS
> HEADQUARTERS, 5th REGIMENT,
> EXPEDITIONARY FORCES
>
> France, June 10, 1918
>
> From: Commanding Officer
> To: Commanding General, 4th Brigade, Marine Corps, American E.F. [Harbord]
> Subject: Recommendations for Distinguished Conduct in face of the enemy
>
> 1. The following named officers and enlisted men are recommended for award for gallantry in action of exceptionally meritorious service during the operation against the enemy northwest of CHATEAU-THIERRY on the morning of June 6th 1918.
>
> X X X

Captain George W. Hamilton, U. S. M. C., 49th Company, during the attack on the enemy near hill 142, showed exceptionally brilliant leadership. He advanced his company a kilometer to his final objective against an enemy in trenches and equipped with machine guns. He and his company passed through several zones of Machine Gun fire. When it is known that this company lost approximately 90% of the officers and non-commissioned officers and 50% of company casualties, Captain Hamilton's rare quality of leadership is apparent. During latter stages of the attack, after men had lost their leaders, he ran up and down his line under severe fire, leading his men forward and urging them on by cheering and similar efforts. In view of the fact that this was done at great personal exposure Captain Hamilton displayed a quality of extraordinary heroism which in the opinion of the undersigned warrants recommending him for a Medal of Honor.[40]

The request was issued to U.S. Army Brig. General Harbord, and from there the channels flowed towards U.S. Army General Pershing. As the commander of the AEF, Pershing and his staff had the final say in the military ranks for approving medals associated with the Fourth Brigade, before the U.S. Congress took up the matter. Pershing was definitely not pleased with correspondent Gibbons' very recent public promotion of Marines in the American media, and the bottom line was that there was no way the commander was going to approve issuing a Medal of Honor to George W. Hamilton, or any other commissioned officer in the Marine Corps anytime in France. That bold fact remained true.

Entering the war, the Marine Corps organization was still trying to solidify their own identity and prove their worth and existence as a branch in the United States military. General Pershing's staff member and historian Lt. Colonel Frederick Palmer echoed how those on the outside perceived the Marine Corps at the time: "Its honor and future were at stake there before Bouresches and Belleau Wood. If it were to get more recruits as a small organization, which is hardly accepted by the army and not, perhaps, altogether by the navy as a little brother, it must be worthy of those recruiting posters at home."[41]

The Marines were earning their reputation one day at a time, and with Belleau Wood now behind them, they were off to a great start. Ask anyone about World War I, and if they know anything concerning the Marine Corps, they generally mention Belleau Wood. Relationships and rivalries between the U.S. Army, U.S. Navy and the U.S. Marine Corps continued to flicker, but following Belleau Wood there was no doubt about the future of the Corps.

Although the general public would not always be briefed and understand the encounters to follow, there would be just as much unbelievable action and adventure to follow. For Hamilton, two future events would rival his personal contribution at Belleau Wood.

9. Soissons
July 18–22—The Long March

Following intense fighting men are usually given down time to recuperate, reorganize and assess conditions. The Germans were retreating to some degree, while Foch and Pershing worked at putting together a plan of attack to keep the Germans from having any additional thoughts of taking Paris. The next battle plan called for attacking the enemy further away from Château-Thierry and towards the direction of Soissons.

During the month of June, the Fourth Brigade had lost over half of its men as casualties at Belleau Wood. By July, the brigade was back to a little less than full strength. Captain Hamilton did not let up and kept working with all the members of his company to have them unified as a solid group once again. Those who experienced Belleau Wood now had a very good understanding as to the effort required to take on the Kaiser's forces.

The 4th of July appeared once again, providing Hamilton and others with many thoughts, including the fact that they had been in France for a year. With a little downtime, the Marine Brigade was again requested to participate in the Paris parade honoring American independence. Every company selected roughly three members from each platoon. Overall Hamilton chose a good dozen men from his 49th to complement the roughly 50 Marines representing 1/5. There were no hard feelings by the majority left behind; in fact, the chosen representatives were sent off with plenty of good cheer.

Prior to the festivities, the men on leave made certain they first devoted time to visit with some of their severely wounded comrades in the Paris hospitals. In many respects this served to be the highlight of their trip. The common fact was that all of the wounded men wanted to get back to the adventure to support their friends as quickly as possible. It was then on to the parade, and along the route, crowds of people threw flowers into the middle of the street, honoring the warriors who saved Paris. The glorious event included many spectacles, including biplanes flying overhead performing aerobatic stunts and dives towards the large crowd.

The men who were not attending the show in Paris spent the day relaxing

Typical countryside destruction. This photograph was taken near Belleau Wood (courtesy Marine Corps History Division).

and tending to personal hygiene. Later in the day they received a good meal and a small portion of canned peaches and pears from the Red Cross.

On July 5, Captain Hamilton was yet another year older at 26. It was coincidental, but on his birthday official paperwork was documented to issue a personal citation to Hamilton for his heroic deeds at Belleau Wood. Behind the scenes this was a "good news, bad news" situation. The good news was that this was his first personal citation. The bad news, which he might not have realized at the moment, was that his recommendation for the Medal of Honor, which began with Neville, was to be denied by the U.S. Army chain of command. Who issued the citation? It's very interesting, as two separate pieces of paperwork, both dated July 5, under the title General Orders, No. 40, appear in records. One paper is signed by Maj. General Omar Bundy of the Second Division.[1] The second document is signed by the command of Maj. General Lejeune through the chief of staff, Brig. General Preston Brown.[2]

Lejeune had been in America working with Commandant Barnett, requesting permission to go overseas. With Doyen back in the States, the

Corps wished to fill the vacancy with another proven officer, and Lejeune was granted his wish, arriving in France on June 8, 1918, when the battle of Belleau Wood was going strong. Over the past several weeks he had been working with the U.S. Army, commanding the 64th Brigade of the 32nd Division on the front line of the Swiss border. In time he would be aligned back with the Marines.

On July 8 Hamilton received notification that he was selected for increased authority. He would continue as skipper of the 49th Company, but he would additionally serve as second in command to Major Turrill of 1/5. The young captain's leadership skills were being noticed, and he was continuing to advance.

The courageous fighting and superior marksmanship by the "Devil Dogs" had caught the Germans by surprise, and the top Allied commanders were now thinking of the next way to surprise the Kaiser's troops. In general the overall plan called for Allied Forces to be on the offense from now until the end of the war. Specifically, the next element called for divisions to travel as much as possible under the cover of darkness to the front lines. The Allied Forces would attempt to keep the Germans from identifying when and where the next major strike would take place. If successful, the enemy would not have time to bring in reserve ground troops, aviators and other support units to assist in fighting.

Starting July 9 Hamilton and his men were in the vicinity of the village of Crouttes for a week's stay, where they continued to recuperate and train. To prepare for the next phase, officers in the Fourth Brigade performed some nighttime logistical maneuvers with their men. They were still in Crouttes on the French Independence Day known as Bastille Day. To honor France and its citizens, General Pershing made the following declaration in advance of the national holiday:

> July 14 is herby declared a holiday for all troops in this command not actually engaged with the enemy. It will be their duty and privilege to celebrate the French Independence Day, which appeals alike to every citizen and soldier in France and America, with all the sympathetic interest and purpose that the French celebrated our Independence Day. Living among the French people and sharing the comradeship in arms of their soldiers, we have the deeper consciousness that the two anniversaries are linked together in common principles and common cause.
> By Command of
> General Pershing[3]

All four sons of former President Theodore Roosevelt were serving in various roles on the Western Front. They were not in the Marine Corps, but they were proudly serving their nation on the front lines in other vital areas of support.

His youngest son, Quentin, enjoyed being a regular person. As a youngster, he often threw his book bag over his shoulder and rode his bicycle from the White House to the public Force School unattended by service agents.[4] During his first day at the school, his teacher questioned him about his last name Roosevelt, wondering if there could possibly be a connection. Quentin was proud of his father, but he did not want to go through life on his father's coattails, so he politely answered the question in a roundabout way.

He was currently the most popular pilot in the 95th Squadron, and although he did not feel worthy, he was quickly made a flight commander before he was tested in battle. As a true Roosevelt he wished to earn his reputation and way in life through action and responsible leadership rather than have it handed to him. Therefore he initiated a secret pact where by his three fellow aviators with more experience would take turns in the air as the in-flight commander. He was like many young men who took to the air, as noted by Rickenbacker: "He was reckless to such a degree that his commanding officers had to caution him repeatedly about the senselessness of his lack of caution. His bravery was so notorious that we all knew he would either achieve some great spectacular success or be killed in the attempt.... But Quentin would merely laugh away all serious advice."[5]

When Sunday, July 14, arrived, those serving on the front lines were not able to take Bastille Day off. U.S. Army biplanes from the 95th Squadron were over enemy territory fighting German aircraft when Lieutenant Roosevelt's Nieuport 28 became separated from the pack, and he was killed.[6] The Germans realized Roosevelt's status from his identification and knew the impact his death would have on the American nation. They kept his belongings for family members and took time to properly bury him with full military honors at the location where he perished.[7]

A couple of days later Quentin's death was confirmed, and on the third day the news reached Theodore Roosevelt at his Oyster Bay residence on Long Island, New York. The fatal news took the joy of life out of him, and he himself would die about six months later at the age of 60. Before his own death the former President revealed some of his intimate feelings upon life and death, saying: "Only those are fit to live who do not fear to die; and none are fit to die who have shrunk from the joy of life and the duty of life. Both life and death are parts of the same Great Adventure."[8]

From his training days through the recent battle of Belleau Wood, Hamilton had been getting to know the medical personnel attached to the Second Division, and he was further establishing close personal relationships with a few of the doctors. One doctor was extremely grief-stricken upon hearing the news of Roosevelt's death, as Quentin was his brother-in-law. Surgeon Richard

Derby was married to Quentin's sister, former President Roosevelt's youngest daughter and fourth child, Ethel Carow Roosevelt.[9]

Meanwhile, with the Château-Thierry Sector secure and Belleau Wood behind them, several promotions and organizational changes were made to fine tune the Second Division. Harbord was now a major general and took over the division, replacing Bundy. In conjunction with the move, Neville was promoted to brigadier general and took full command of the Fourth Brigade, while Colonel Feland assumed control of the Fifth Regiment.[10]

Foch's latest plans called for putting a major force against the German right flank for an offensive movement known as the Aisne-Marne offensive. He had at his disposal the French, English, American, Italian, and Belgian armies totaling millions of men. Having settled on the time and location for the attack, what he needed now was the selection of what he considered to be his three very best Allied Force divisions to do the fighting.

He first chose his own First French Moroccan Division under General Dogan from his French Army. The Moroccan Division was composed of a First Brigade with the famous French Foreign Legion, consisting of professional warriors representing most countries throughout the world, and three battalions of Senegalese from northwest Africa, along with a Second Brigade of fighters from Morocco. Aside from the French Foreign Legion, all the men in the Moroccan Division were Moslems. To complete the selection, Foch then chose the American First Division, under Maj. General Charles P. Summerall, and the American 2nd Division, now under the command of Maj. General Harbord.

On July 15 Hamilton's men became a bit uneasy as long-range enemy shells were exploding too close for comfort and there was little sleep during the night. On the 16th his men figured something was up as their lunch was earlier than normal and the rolling kitchens skirted away. At this point Hamilton did not have much information to share with his men other than there was an indication that they were headed to the front again. Official word came later on the afternoon of July 16, noting only for Hamilton to get his 49th Company in line, as the full brigade was to march out. The situation slowly evolved into a "let's see where the adventure takes us" scenario. The mass movement of the three divisions to the front involved roughly 67,000 men, 5,000 animals and 3,000 vehicles.[11]

Others within the Second Division were also following brief orders directing them to head in the same direction. The division's Second Engineers had been alerted at 0100 on the 16th to be ready to head out. They quickly packed up and stood in the dark, waiting until 0400 when finally word came that they had a little extra time. A brief snapshot as to what their commander, Colonel W.A. Mitchell, encountered will fill in the broad picture of what the forward movement was like outside the Fourth Brigade, but within the division, under "hurry up" conditions.

At 1800 on July 16, Colonel Mitchell was able to secure an automobile and remain ahead of what would soon be massive road congestion and gridlock. Along the road through the night, French guides assisted him with directions at each road crossing. The closer he got to the front lines the vaguer the directions became, but at around 0500 on the 17th, he came to a stop and was able to locate definitive orders stating that the Second Division was to be a part of the Army Third Corps and that fighting was to commence on the following day, July 18. He was to command the division reserve consisting of the Second Engineers and the Fourth Machine Gun Battalion. In the final hours leading up to the battle of Soissons, Mitchell could find only four maps to share with all of his reserve units.

A great part of Hamilton's pending adventure involved getting to the jump-off location at the front lines. His men did not know what the trail ahead would involve, but aside from some individual heroic moments, the general group of survivors from the upcoming battle would forever remember the seemingly endless journey to the front lines more than the battle itself. There would be no singing to pass the time. At the end of the trail, the men would be drained and fatigued to the point of exhaustion. They could hardly stand when the whistle blew at H-hour to go forward and attack.

Water is always a necessity and all canteens were filled before departing, as it was sometimes difficult for the engineers to identify in advance where one might find good available water next. Hamilton gave the word to head out, and his physically fit men started the march, as usual, with one foot first and then the other. As the assistant battalion commander, he was also keeping an eye on the entire group of 1/5. After hiking awhile they came across other groups of men, and someone asked where they were headed, to which the reply was "Dunno — don' care — But you see the ole 1st Battalion is leadin' as usual!"[12]

Finally the Fourth Brigade came to a town with lots of camions, and they instantly realized this could only mean one thing. The men who had boarded camions before knew their purpose was not for pleasure. They were needed at once on the front lines.

To add an additional element to the overall world war, most of the drivers were gaunt looking Annamites, who had come from the mountainous ranges on the outskirts of China.

Hamilton's men had plenty of questions. Where were they headed? Were their rolling kitchens or galleys, as the "soldiers of the sea" called them, in fact in front of them? Regardless, his men were now carefully holding on to their emergency rations for as long as possible. Where were their light artillery and machine gun companies? Just as important was the needed supply of all sorts of ammunition.

When darkness came, few men were able to sleep during the bumpy ride. It was not just the ruts and potholes, but the fact that some of the trucks had steel rims without tires. Through the clear night they could view the stars, and when the sun appeared on the 17th, the men unloaded from the camions. There was no breakfast available; instead the men were issued additional emergency rations with notification not to eat them. On this day a note was issued from the AEF, which filtered down to Harbord's division, stating:

> *Headquarters Third Army Corps American Expeditionary Forces,*
> *France, July 17, 1918*
>
> *Memorandum:*
>
> The Third Corps of the American Expeditionary Forces has been created and consists of the 1st and 2nd, Divisions, two divisions that are known throughout France.
>
> Officers and men of the Third Corps, you have been deemed worthy to be placed beside the best veteran French troops. See that you prove worthy. Remember that in what is now coming you represent the whole American nation.
>
> R. L. BULLARD
> Major General
> Commanding 3rd. Corps.[13]

It was time to begin marching again, and the path forward now involved two columns. The Fourth Brigade took the right side, with a contingent of Senegalese from the French First Moroccan Division on the left. First Lieutenant Thomason noted: "On the left of the road, abreast of the Marines, plodded another column of foot — strange black men, in the blue greatcoats of the French infantry and mustard-yellow uniforms under them. Their helmets were khaki-colored, and bore a crescent instead of the bursting bomb of the French line. But they marched like veterans, and the Marines eyed them approvingly."[14]

Hamilton had trained his men with abundant practice hikes, which hardened them for rugged endurance, but with the heat of one of the hottest summer days now upon them, along with extreme drowsiness, his men were feeling the effects. Many had empty canteens and parched throats as the dust from the roads rose and circulated around them.

By late afternoon they had hiked into the small village of Villers-Cotterets, which was surrounded by forest. The shade was a great blessing and water was available. The stop with tree cover was also part of the overall plan to avoid being detected by observation planes and balloons as they approached the front lines. Most of Hamilton's men shed their packs, drank water, and collapsed on the ground until the time came to move on. After two to three hours, Hamilton once again called his men to rise and form a line. They donned their heavy packs, tightened the straps and adjusted their equipment. The long line then continued forward once again in the direction towards the sound of artillery shells.

They now proceeded to hike through a dense forest known as Bois de Retz. The humid day brought forth an abundance of dark clouds, followed by rain, and in short order the trail was a muddy mess and getting worse. When evening approached, the increasing clouds created a thunderstorm full of wild lightning, wind gusts and constant loud thunder that masked the sound of bombs bursting in the distance. France does not have a lot of electric storms, so these weather conditions were quite uncharacteristic. Any enemy observation planes that were scouring the area were now taking protective cover. The black clouds remained through the night, but even without the clouds, the forest was so dense there would be total darkness everywhere. Occasionally a large cloud burst really opened up fully drenching everything, making the continuous deep ruts in the road sloshing mud pits.

Hiking in total darkness is not easy, but when combined with a lack of sleep, wet slushy conditions and soaked backpacks, which increased the overall load, the venture was now extremely difficult. Along their path was a constant procession of horses pulling pieces of artillery. There was not supposed to be any movement in the opposite direction, but at times there was a row heading back, away from the front lines, containing mules, wagons and equipment, making the trail very narrow. Rolling equipment often sank in the mud up to its axles and needed pushing to continue on.

It was so dark that one could not see the man in front of him, and when the line movement slowed, one's face usually hit the backpack or trenching tool of the man in front, and a domino effect soon started down the line. One considered himself lucky if he stayed on his feet. To avoid falling down, most men tried to hold onto the shoulder of the man in front to keep pace. At other times they tried to grab hold of anything they could but often didn't have much strength to hold on to maintain balance.

With the grueling march and sleep deprivation, some men literally passed out and were left by the wayside, while others fell off the side of the slightly elevated road into ditches and swamps breaking an arm or leg. The men who were not recent replacements might certainly think back to their training days of the past November and December, when "Hiking Hiram" reiterated that he was just preparing them for future events.

While the Second Division was plodding ahead, the path of the First Division was noticeably easier. They also were traveling to the front through darkness, but their path took them through open flat fields, which were much more conducive to travel.

An exhausted runner from the front lines backtracked through the night with impending news, finally catching up with Neville's brigade. The messenger stated that the timing of the battle was fixed and that the jump-off might begin without the Second Division in its proper position. With time passing, top officials were very concerned because this scenario could certainly be catastrophic. The Sixth Regiment received welcome news, as the plans called for them to spend the day in reserve. However, Hamilton and the other weary men in Feland's Fifth Regiment were notified that they were heading straight into battle to support the Second Division's left flank. All other men quickly stepped aside to let the Fifth through.

Hamilton would have scant time to get his men together to coordinate plans with his officers and men, as they now ran towards the front with "double time" instructions. Incoming artillery shells were landing nearby, and at 0430 the Second Division opened with their own artillery. Upon arrival he immediately instructed his men to shed their heavy equipment and get down to their combat packs. Through constant motion they were instantly preparing to fight and shove off at 0435. During all the chaos, it should be noted that Hamilton was present and prepared to lead his men at the proper time and location, just as he had done at Belleau Wood.

Gibbons, the heralded journalist who reported from the front at Belleau Wood, had recovered from his own wounds and sporting a black patch over one eye. He reported:

> It was 4:35. It would have been hell if the Germans had found out there were 70,000 men in the forest. Poisonous gases would have knocked out thousands of them, the place would have been filled with shrapnel — and that would have been the end of that movement!
>
> The Marines had plainly the furthest distance to move to get into line, and they had to hurry to get there by zero hour. Yet — would you believe it — after those poor fellows had been on the march all day long, they moved forward on the double time in order to get there on time.
>
> ...The marching was awful. I talked with one chap who was sitting down to rest. When I asked him what was the matter, he said his feet were all in, and he could not run any further.
>
> "I enlisted in the Marines to kill Germans," he said, "but I did not think we had to run them to death. I recommended that they give us lassoes."[15]

Hamilton, serving as second in command of the battalion, got his own 49th Company grouped into patrols and headed out along with Hunt's 17th Company, the 66th under Captain William Crabbe, and the 67th commanded by Captain Frank Whitehead. The men who were left by the wayside on the final march would catch up at some point.

The rush was a part of the plan to surprise the Germans, but the Second

Division and Hamilton's men were to some degree surprised by the immediate call to action too. Had their support units along the trail also arrived? Captain Hamilton and others in the Fifth Regiment took the lead, followed by tank support. They were to be assisted by two machine gun companies, but due to the congested roads, the machine guns units had not yet arrived, so his men were entering the fight without their assistance. Although the Germans were a bit disorganized and in partial retreat, they would assuredly have their Maxims ready and loaded.

The rain finally subsided and the sun was starting to rise to introduce July 18. The Second Engineers in reserve started straggling in around 0530, but they would not be organized as a unit until 0900. At 0600 a division staff officer arrived at the camp and acknowledged that Hamilton and the other three skippers were missing their necessary machine gun support. New orders requested Colonel Mitchell to put his reserve Fourth Machine Gun Battalion into action, but unfortunately they were also missing. Hamilton and his company, which had been fighting for three hours, finally received their needed machine gun support when the Fourth Machine Gun Battalion kicked off at 0732.[16]

Unlike the battle of Belleau Wood, this event had an initial five-minute artillery barrage, which was followed by continuous artillery firing, delivering shells about 100 yards ahead of the ground troops to clear the way. The initial battle was into woods containing conifers and lofty deciduous trees in their full summer bloom with plenty of leaves. However, with the intense artillery, the forest was now being shredded and looked much different.

The Marines had some French tank support this time, and Hamilton's men were in awe of the equipment, as this was their first encounter with such reinforcement. One member of his company joked that the large ones were males and the small ones females.

With clearing weather, observation balloons were rapidly deployed across the skyline. German aircraft flew low, not so much for observation, but to fire their machine guns upon ground troops, while also searching for ammunition dumps to bomb.

The battle soon spread across wheat fields followed by fields of oats, which offered very little shelter, and then on into several villages and towns. The adventurous fighting at Soissons therefore contained some aspects of war not witnessed at Belleau Wood. Shrapnel explosions accounted for many of the deaths.

The 49th Company was on the far left side, and patrol leader 2nd Lieutenant Corbett was given the duty of hooking up with the French Moroccans, which he accomplished. First Lieutenant Thomason was now in his first full battle from the start, and before long his platoon destroyed several machine gun nests, killing more than a dozen Germans. In the process he was nicked with a bullet and in need of medical attention.

The Senegalese were noted to be very vicious fighters who enjoyed killing and showed no mercy. Hamilton's company had captured a contingent of Germans, and while the prisoners were being escorted to the rear a wandering detachment of Senegalese tried to lure the captured men away from the Marine guards. The Germans immediately stated in broken English that they would fully obey the Americans, as long as they were kept away from the Senegalese. The confrontation was eventually broken up, and the French West Africans withdrew.

The ten French aircraft assigned to the division as support had their hands full, as the Germans controlled the air space all day long. Allied antiaircraft fire was caught off guard, and the enemy planes successfully attacked a couple of observation balloons. In the afternoon the German bombers roamed freely and dropped some well placed bombs.[17]

Major Shearer commanding 3/5 had his men assisting Major Ralph Keyser over 2/5 and Turrill with 1/5. Although Hamilton's men were fatigued, they had achieved a lot of success throughout the day. They now found themselves a little behind with their latest objective, which was to take the village of Vierzy by late afternoon. Finally the Eighth Machine Gun Company, originally assigned to the Fifth Regiment, arrived to provide assistance. In the evening around 2000, Turrill got portions of Hamilton's company and others in the battalion to support the division's Third Infantry Brigade in capturing Vierzy. Fighting around buildings in the village was quite different, but the Marines were trained for this type of warfare too.

Gunner Nice was in the action and before long he was wounded again, this time with a flesh wound in his right forearm. He recalled: "While there I was sent out on patrol one night to locate the enemy. We found them all right and they found us. We had 56 men. The Germans cut us off from our battalion and there was a lively scrap in which we sustained 37 casualties. The rest of us managed to fight our way back. We were cited in both French and American orders for that scrap and the days work in general."[18]

The retreating Germans had several ammunition supply dumps full of shells and powder in the area. Rather than leave them for the Allied Forces, they blew them up, creating huge explosions. The bright glowing flames were visible for miles in the nighttime sky. A green rocket flare was also noticed in the air. This Allied signal often indicated the need to put on gas masks, but then again, the Germans were known to try to confuse the Allied Forces with flares of their own. Such was a portion of the adventure and eventually everything settled down.

When the full day of July 18 came to a close, Hamilton and his men were just south of Chaudin with their objectives met. They had entered the fray with no sleep and were now devoid of any adrenaline, desperately needing rest. All the members in the regiment now collapsed for the night. Their accomplishments under strain were later noted in the French Army Order of the Day: "Unexpectedly engaged in the offensive of July 18th, 1918 in the middle of the night, on unknown and very difficult ground, displayed remarkable ardor and tenacity, in spite of exhaustion and revictualling difficulties both for food and water, advanced 6½ miles, capturing 2,700 prisoners, 12 guns and several hundred machine-guns."[19]

The good news for Hamilton and others in the Fifth Regiment was that the rested Sixth Regiment was to take the lead on the following day. The fighting on the 19th proved to be even more intense, and the Sixth Regiment had their hands full. As the fighting became more heated, areas of weakness started to appear. The First French Moroccan Division on the left was lagging behind the Second Division's Third Brigade, creating a gap. Colonel Mitchell realized the potential disaster and immediately ordered his reserve engineers to support the brigade's Ninth and 23rd Infantry on the front lines by digging trenches and supporting the soldiers in any way possible. Their heavy trenching tools proved to be so effective that every member of the Second Engineers carried these tools with them until the end of the war.

Mitchell had sent his reserve engineers into battle without instructions from Harbord, the division commander. Officers in a critical moment were sometimes tested by having to make a judgment call of their own, and it was not until afterwards that possible repercussions were sorted out. As the colonel explained, "It was a rule in the 2nd Division that initiative and independence in action were required and that proper results justified the use of initiative, whereas improper results resulted in sending the officer to a reclassification depot."[20] Before the war would end, Hamilton would himself be called upon to make a very testing judgment call of his own.

Starting on Saturday the 20th, the entire Fourth Brigade began maintaining their positions. The brigade was officially relieved from duty on July 25 as the battle of Soissons came to a close with another victory. The casualty figures appeared to be close to 1,300 for the Sixth Regiment, while the Fifth Regiment sustained about 500 dead, wounded and missing.

Some officials regarded Soissons as a turning point in the war, because it was now proven that the Germans were continuing to retreat. For their overall contribution, the Fourth Brigade was recognized by the French Government with a second Croix de Guerre unit award. Maj. General Harbord, in his first major battle as a division commander, issued a statement revealing his thoughts:

> It is with keen pride that the division commander transmits to the command the congratulations and affectionate personal greetings of Gen. Pershing who vis-

ited the division headquarters last night. His praise of the gallant work of the division on the 18th and 19th is echoed by the French high command, the Third Corps commander, American Expeditionary Forces, and in a telegram from the former division commander. In spite of two sleepless nights, long marches through rain and mud, and long discomforts of hunger and thirst, the division attacked side by side with the gallant First Moroccan Division and maintained itself with credit. You advanced over 6 miles, captured over 3,000 prisoners 11 batteries of artillery, over 100 machine guns, minnenwerfers, and supplies. The Second Division has sustained the best traditions of the Regular Army and the Marine Corps. The story of your achievements will be told in millions of homes in all Allied lands to-night.[21]

German Chancellor Georg von Hertling summed up the impact of Soissons through a simple brief statement: "On the 18th even the most optimistic among us understood that all was lost. The History of the World was played out in three days."[22] The Germans had lost much optimism and morale, yet everyone knew that they were excellent fighters, who were not about to quit. Most certainly they would regroup and identify a future location to make a more memorable defensive stand and, if successful, turn the tide and momentum their way.

Captain Hamilton and members of the brigade were now billeted in an area around Nanteuil-le-Haudouin for several days. While stationed here the command of the Second Division was shaken up once again, and when the dust settled, the structure of the top leadership was basically solidified for the duration of the war. Following Pershing's wishes, Harbord departed as division commander on July 26, with very little ceremony, to take charge of the Services of Supply. The SOS was in need of leadership; however, it was apparent to all that this was not a promotion for Harbord. The departing U.S. Army officer noted that the Marines had lived up to their reputation by never failing him, and he later reflected back with the following sincere words: "I look back upon my service with the Marine Brigade with more pride and satisfaction than any other equal period of my long career."[23]

The new officer appearing on the scene was another legend, Maj. General John A. Lejeune. Upon taking command of the Second Division, he immediately began working closely with all his officers.[24] The prevailing thought was for the division to rest and recuperate after having been through two battles. Over the final two days of July, battalions within the Marine Brigade traveled by railroad boxcars to the vicinity of Nancy, in the Marbache Sector, where they remained until August 9. Hamilton's men enjoyed this downtime, as it was truly a period to check equipment and supplies with little training and drills.

Later in August, the entire Second Division took up residence at Camp Bois de l'Eveque. The engineers were transitioning the camp's simple and

Maj. General Omar Bundy (left) beside current Second Division Commander Maj. General John A. Lejeune, August 11, 1918, Marbache, Metz Sector (courtesy Marine Corps History Division).

crude French target practice area into a full-scale rifle range, resembling what the Marine Corps was used to training on back in America. After five full days of construction work, the range consisted of 80 well-made targets. During the roughly two weeks that followed, most every member of the division attended target practice. The real bonus was that the training was performed under the direction and guidance of none other than Lt. Colonel Holcomb, the commander of 2/6. Hamilton was very familiar with Holcomb, who had served as the Marine Corps inspector of target practice from October 1914 to August 1917, and had been a member of the Marine Corps Rifle Team for six years.[25] It was believed that the "Indian Head" Division was the only AEF division to undergo such training.

One could surmise that the Allied Forces were going to continue with the offensive push, so a few men from every company in the Third and Fourth Brigades were cross trained in wire-cutting detail. Small squads consisting of four men were involved in timed practice events. The two front men used wire cutters to cut the sharp barbed wire, while the third crew member used an axe to chop down the tangled wire posts in the nearby path, and the trailing fourth member hacked away with his axe clearing a wide path free of debris.

A few more replacements were salted into the battalion, and all the new men were given extra training to get coordinated as a unit. Turrill took his battalion on a two day hike to Govillers. Upon their return Captain Raymond F. Dirksen took over command, but his stint was an extremely brief nine days, lasting only from August 20 to the 28th. Following Dirksen's temporary tenure, Lt. Colonel James O'Leary took over the leadership role of 1/5. The quick changes at the top were not a distraction as Hamilton remained the battalion's second in command. After completion of the training sessions, the division was ready to hit the trail again for a September hike.

10. Saint-Mihiel

September 1918—The World's Most Awesome Bombardment

Across the ocean back in the States, Hamilton's two sisters had spent the summer months at the Conesus Lake home. This summer the family retreat was much different with the absence of Mrs. Hamilton, who had passed away during the past spring and notably with their two brothers away fighting on the Western Front. The sisters, with an eleven-year age difference, had taken this opportunity to get to know each other better. Mary was now headed back to her teaching position in Spokane, Washington, and the younger Margaret was following her to the West Coast with plans to return to Washington, D.C., by winter. Their cross-country trip would take them through different parts of Canada, including Winnipeg, Lake Louise, Victoria and British Columbia.[1] Charles was remaining alone in the Capital City for a few more months. His time would be devoted to further journalism, bonding with his peers, and growing his friendship with his brother-in-law, George Wright, who was also a widower living close by.

For Hamilton and his band of warriors, the month of August had served as a welcomed rest period, and they were now set to go wherever needed. On the second day of September, they began a leisurely march headed for the outskirts of Saint-Mihiel, a town that normally consisted of 10,000 residents, but these were not normal times. The village was located south of Verdun, by a bend in the Meuse River. Hamilton had advised his men not to mention their ultimate destination to outsiders, and as a further precaution, they did not take any rest stops in the villages they hiked through.

Along the trail, when they found a moment of happiness they sang a song or two, possibly to the likes of "Tipperary," "Where Do We Go from Here," "The Long, Long Trail" or "Long Boy." They'd continue on and find another song, maybe "Parley-Vous," for which extra lyrics were known to be added along the way.[2] Back in the fall of 1917, when three of the 1/5 companies were in training in France, the 67th Company was in England for a brief period and brought this last song back with them. As some of the lyrics were rather crude and rotten, Hamilton challenged members of his 49th Company to come up with new verses. The men might also sing "The Marine's Hymn," which was very much alive and well back then.[3]

September 6, 1918, was a very special day in Hamilton's life, as he was given a temporary field promotion to the rank of major, with consent of the U.S. Senate, to rank from July 1. Numerous other captains also rose temporarily in rank, including Shuler. For the time being his duties remained the same, serving as "skipper" of the 49th Company and assisting Lt. Colonel O'Leary as second in command of the battalion. Major Hamilton would quickly get used to his new title.

The roadways were once again full of all types of refugees heading in the opposite direction. One particular gorgeous aristocratic woman, who was leading a group of children, stood out from the rest and caught the eye of the many members of the battalion. Private Mackin noticed the very special moment when the lovely lady and Major Hamilton crossed paths:

> Our major was a huge Apollo of a man. Time had been when the fellows spoke of him as "our motion picture captain." That was before he bayoneted four men in one swift hour, way back in June. Kind spoke to kind, with eyes that knew the strength of gentle blood as heritage.
>
> The major? All six-feet four of him was deference to Her Ladyship. He made a picture there, doffing a battered metal helmet easily, with natural grace, as though his topper had swept to greet a miss at Eastertime. He bowed, as a humble, cultured gentleman does to womanhood.
>
> With quiet, easy confidence, she drew him down, one small hand grasping at his Sam Browne belt. She kissed him soundly, once. That was all for us, or so her merry glance said. We took it so.[4]

As noted Hamilton was 5'11", but Mackin was definitely referring to him. Standing straight, wearing boots and his helmet, he appeared to be much taller.

The Germans were in the process of retreating from areas they had held since 1914. The bulk of the upcoming battle would not take place in the town itself but in the neighboring vicinity. The Allied Forces wished to reconnect with Saint-Mihiel for several reasons, one of which was to open up several of the railroad lines for movement of supplies further into the region. Therefore the current overall objective was to push the Germans back further and capture control of the double and four track railways. Additionally, the Allied Forces wished to recapture coal fields and the all important Briey iron fields, which were essential to steel production for the German aggression. The iron basin was believed to contain roughly 80 percent of all the iron in continental Europe.[5]

Weather conditions factored into the timing of the upcoming attack.

Maj. General John A. Lejeune and his staff planning the St. Mihiel offensive. Left to right: Lt. Col. H. L. Matthews, G-1, Col. Preston Brown, C/S, Maj. Gen. Lejeune, Col. James C. Rhea, AC/S, and Lt. Col. Herbst, G-3 (courtesy Marine Corps History Division).

Fall in France can be quite rainy, and since the Saint-Mihiel salient was in a rather swampy area, it would be best to make their advance before too much mud became problematic. Artillery caterpillar tractors could only go three miles per hour on good roads, and they often blocked the path of other trucks capable of traveling 10 to 15 miles per hour. Muddy conditions, as witnessed by many, slowed all troop movements.

Allied Commander Foch and Sir Douglas Haig, commander of the British Expeditionary Forces, both thought that the American Forces should be divided among other Allied military units. Pershing continued to insist that his American troops fight as one unified group. Back on August 9, during an important planning meeting, Foch had reluctantly relinquished control of the upcoming battle of Saint-Mihiel to Pershing. With approval, Pershing laid out his detailed plans, which he shared later in the day with French General Pétain.[6]

The plan of attack called for the use of predominantly American forces, as Pershing planned to show the Allied Forces, once again, what the American troops were made of. The prior fighting at Belleau Wood displayed some aspects of offense and Soissons proved even more so, but this battle from the very start would feature an awesome offense. The initial artillery barrage was scheduled to be unlike anything ever displayed before at any time or place in the world.[7]

Pershing committed seven divisions, the 1st, 42nd and 89th under the Army Fourth Corps commanded by Maj. General Joseph Dickman and the 2nd, 5th, 82nd and 90th of the Army First Corps directed by Maj. General Hunter Liggett, to be among the roughly 300,000 men in the fight. An additional eight American divisions and four French divisions were ready in the area as reserves.

This time many logistical preparations had been made in advance, as noted by the fact that for communication along the extended front lines 6,000 telephones and 5,000 miles of wire were available.[8] Lejeune prepared for his first battle as a division commander by meeting with his staff to review maps and plans.

When Hamilton's men finally reached their next jump-off location some made large foxholes, while others took advantage of old bunkers nearby. Behind them, heavy artillery was being properly positioned and secured into place. Observation balloon pilots were busy relaying target and distance information to the personnel on the ground to assist the mighty guns.

While taking a break, Private Mackin noticed that his 67th Company commander, Captain Whitehead, was sitting comfortably hidden from the enemy, but well advanced in front of his own men. He expressed high respect for his skipper as well as Major Hamilton:

> What? Yeah, that was a damn funny place for a captain to be, but we had a lot of officers like that. Our major [Hamilton] was like that.
> Sure, I know. Plenty of officers wouldn't have the guts to get out in front of their own men. We had plenty of guys along that line that could hit an eighteen-inch target nine times out of ten at six hundred yards. It was different with our skipper [Whitehead], though. Our whole bunch would go to hell headfirst for him. He wasn't in any danger — except from the Germans.[9]

In the early hours of September 11 many new recruits were added to 1/5, bringing the battalion to its proper full strength. The battalion, with over 1,000 men, consisted of many of America's best with representation from every state in America.[10] The replacements' path to the front lines was not as leisurely as the hike in by Major Hamilton and the others in the battalion. After being jammed into boxcars for two days and three nights, they had spent the past night hiking, rushing to the front lines. Upon arrival they were very tired and agitated, which as we have noticed, seemed to be a relatively good temperament prior to fighting. They would use this full day prior to "H-hour" to recuperate and meld into their newly designated companies.

One new replacement was Private Mortensen. He had breezed through basic training at Parris Island, qualifying as a sharpshooter, and within just three months of leaving home, he was ready to participate in the adventure. Besides rifle instruction, the camp gave him training and education in boxing, swimming, wall scaling, bayonet practice, first aid, individual cooking, patrolling, guard duty, message carrying, packing knapsacks, personal care and much more. One of the most important qualities that a new recruit had to possess was overall discipline. It all started with the military courtesies of saluting an officer and then faithfully following and carrying out all orders. Like all the other new recruits he displayed confidence but respect had to be earned.

It would not take long for him to recognize his assistant battalion commander, Major Hamilton, and to get to know the other Marines in the outfit. The proud American, who was born in Denmark, was placed in the 66th Company of 1/5, joining several legendary leatherneck veterans. Many of his fellow Marines were also born in various other countries and had become American citizens too. Most could therefore speak a few languages.

Among the 250 men in the 66th Company, it would be hard to find an older fighting Marine than 51-year-old 1st Lieutenant Henry Lewis Hulbert. The platoon leader, who was born in England, had already received the Medal of Honor for service in the Philippines back in 1899. When America declared war he had a desk job serving on the personal staff of Commandant Barnett, but after receiving a sterling physical and promotion to the new grade of Marine gunner, he finally acquired firsthand permission from Barnett to join the action. At Belleau Wood he was slightly wounded and cited for acts of bravery. There was no keeping the astute seasoned veteran down.

There were also two notable sergeants in the 66th Company, Louis Cukela and Mataj Kocak. To date, within the Fourth Brigade, just three Marines were in line to receive the Medal of Honor. All three — Gunnery Sergeant Hoffman of the 49th Company for his service at Belleau Wood and Gunnery Sergeant Cukela and Sergeant Kocak for heroism during the recent July battle at Soissons — just happened to belong to the First Battalion, Fifth Regiment.[11] Cukela was from Serbia, while Kocak was from Hungary, both unsettled turbulent areas of the Balkan region where the seeds of the world war originated.

Word quickly spread that the battle around Saint-Mihiel was to start shortly after midnight, so final preparations were now being made. Everyone remained on alert, listening for orders and performing necessary details. The Germans could not help but notice some of the AEF preparations, indicating what would soon fall upon them. However there was currently a light rain, and with the terrain quite muddy, the Germans figured the Allied battle would be postponed for another day with fairer weather conditions.

Brig. General Wendell C. Neville in 1918 (courtesy Marine Corps History Division).

Major Hamilton's men had witnessed the transition from summer to early autumn. Many of the recent replacements had shown up wearing their lighter combat backpacks ready to fight, and therefore they were missing many of the cooler weather items, such as blankets and overcoats. Although damp, their movement and wool clothing kept them warm, and assuming they made it through the battle unscratched, they should later be able to find all the necessary items they wanted.

The drizzle continued and with darkness the waiting period was upon them. The men stayed huddled in their sheltered areas, catching what rest they could.

It was during this evening that an unusual event occurred behind the front lines. Brig. General Neville's wife had given him a new overcoat complete with braids, and the soaked coat was hung on a fence railing outside the division headquarters. A U.S. Army soldier, who was passing by, hauling a machine gun cart, noticed the fine coat and instinctively pulled a stupid stunt. The situation is colorfully described by the following sentence: "With a couple of slashes of his trench knife the sleeves were off, and by means of curses, varied with exhortations, he clothed the anterior members of his faithful charge."[12] While proudly admiring his accomplishment, the soldier was soon caught by a low level officer. Initially Neville was totally irate, but his counterpart in the division, Brig. General Hanson Ely over the Third Brigade, thought it was hilarious. Word of the incident soon spread, and before long Thomason, now a captain, had sketched the incident as told to him for posterity. Neville eventually calmed down, as he had much more pressing issues at hand.

The American divisions had set up French 75mm Field Guns and other pieces of heavy artillery, totaling just under 3,000 large guns, across the front lines. At Belleau Wood there was initially brief sporadic light artillery fire and at Soissons there was a five-minute leading artillery assault before the warriors rushed to battle. For Saint-Mihiel the big guns would blast away for four full hours with over 1,000,000 shell bursts, making it the greatest artillery bombardment in world history.[13]

At 0100 on September 12, 1918, the Allied Forces opened up with an artillery barrage against the Kaiser's Forces that shook the earth. With constant reloading and rapid firing, the overwhelming noise was deafening, and the men, who were waiting to fight, could not even hear their own voices. Even the salty leathernecks could not catch an extra moment of sleep; as one officer mentioned, the "man-made aurora-borealis shot out of the wall of darkness."[14] Private Clarence L. Richmond, who had left the University of Tennessee to become a Marine, was waiting with 2/5 taking in the spectacular show and stated: "No Fourth of July display ever equaled this deadly display."[15]

The blasts lit up the air as well as the distant ground, and the concussions from the continuous explosions could be felt ten miles away. Through the nighttime glow, some noticed the advanced wire cutting team, working on clearing a forward path through the tangled maze of barbed wire. A distance away, at the local air base, Lieutenant Rickenbacker was awakened by the loud explosions:

> I was awakened by the thundering of thousands of colossal guns. It was September 12, 1918. The St. Mihiel Drive was on!
> Leaping out of bed I put my head outside the tent. We had received orders to be over the lines at daybreak in large formations. It was an exciting moment in my life as I realized that the great American attack upon which so many hopes had been fastened was actually on. I suppose every American in the world wanted to be in that great attack. The very sound of the guns thrilled one and filled one with excitement. The good reputation of America seemed bound up in the outcome of that attack.[16]

Lejeune's men in the trenches were fully prepared and ready to go. There would be no "up and at 'em" this time, as the alarm had already sounded loud and clear. Finally at 0500, Hamilton and the other officers blew their whistles and everyone proceeded forward. The jump-off was easy and the Marines dashed off on the adventure within their company and platoons, with a good comrade on either side. As this was not a surprise attack, there were a few shouts and "whoops" from the energetic men.

Secretary Baker was with General Pershing on a safe distant hill witnessing the results. With daylight appearing, Hamilton and others were able to see some of the enemy on the run more than a mile away. The retreating Germans did not have their artillery positioned in place to offer an effective counterattack. Of course not all Germans were on the run, and for those hunkered down in the least expected places, great caution had to be taken.

Although the rain was diminishing a low cloud cover remained restricting aviation. The few pilots who flew biplanes under the clouds could also feel the concussions on the ground. Eventually 14 observation balloons rose along the front. In the early afternoon aggressive German aviators appeared on the scene, but this time there were a lot more Allied planes overhead. In fact Pershing had the assistance of the largest Allied air force ever. Over one-third were Americans, with the balance made up of French, British, and Italian pilots. Before long the 12 Allied pursuit squadrons, three bombing squadrons and 11n observation squadrons controlled the skies.[17] Specifically there was noted to be a total of 1,480 Allied aircraft.[18] One plane successfully bombarded a German supply train heading east.

The wooded areas showed the effects of the constant bombing. Many large trees were fully uprooted, while others were splintered to pieces. A few shells were stuck in trees waiting to fall and detonate at any moment.

Everything was proceeding exceptionally well, and by 1450, Hamilton and his men had already achieved the objectives of the second day and were ready to receive additional orders. Their travels took them across valleys and over a stone bridge crossing a river known as the Rupt de Mad and into Thiacourt. The Second Division soon took control of a strategic railroad station along with important rail lines, capturing locomotives and boxcars along with an abundance of valuable warehouse supplies. Under these conditions it took only three days for the Allied Forces to further hasten the German retreat.

Still, the Germans were a good a fighting force, and there were many casualties on each side. Overall the Allied Forces suffered about 7,000 casualties. In Lejeune's Second Division roughly 134 men were dead and 1,000 wounded. The division captured 80 German officers and 3,200 other prisoners, as well as 90 large guns. Some of the German prisoners were put to work immediately as stretcher-bearers for the American wounded.

When this battle was over French President Raymond Poincaré sent a message to President Wilson: "I congratulate you, Mr. President, on a victory which has been completed so brilliantly. General Pershing's magnificent divisions have just liberated with admirable dash, cities and villages of Lorraine which have been groaning for years under the yoke of the enemy. I express the warmest thanks of France to the people of the United States."[19]

Due to excellent preparation and execution the Marines did not have a great challenge this time. The term "walk-away" was a common part of the inner AEF language and after his first battle Private Mortensen wrote:

> This was where the Boche learned something about an American barrage and American efficiency. The 5th and 6th Reg. of Marines, the 9th and 23rd infantry make up the 2nd Division, all regulars and enlisted men. A Division that has been cited more than any other American Division in France. We were backed by the famous Rainbow Div., the 42nd, the 89th and several others.
> At the dawn of day we started over. We expected a lot of resistance, but I guess Heinie thought all hell had broken loose when our barrage opened up and those that were captured were very happy. They were standing with arms uplifted, officers and men alike ready to be taken captive. It all proved to be a walk-away.[20]

Private Mackin, who had become seasoned from previous battles, described the response of the newcomers:

> Our replacements had been shot at in anger, which was all to the good. But they had not been shot at enough. They had not learned. They thought they had been in battle. The guys from Belleau Wood and Soissons knew better. This had been a walk-away affair, with Germans carefully and craftily withdrawing on pre-arranged plans; just holding strong points long enough to get the bulk of their men and guns away.
> That was the first and last time I ever saw horseplay and swaggering cockiness when coming away from the front. We had been rebuilt after Soissons, full-up with green replacements. Now, after an imitation scrap, the kids were poorer risks than before. They thought they were veterans.
> Replacement? Hell, I had been one myself back in June, but that was now two

real fights and that Pont-a-Mousson thing behind me. In three months, I had become one of the "old" ones, a surviving bastard called "Lucky," so named by the battalion. Now the kids would be harder than ever to soldier with. They had all the answers.[21]

The new replacements who did not have cold weather gear now had their choice of ample supplies. One fellow found a warm German overcoat to his liking, but before long he was naturally ordered to take it off. Sweaters, blankets and good socks were fair game and taken from the scattered backpacks. With the rainy season upon them, some men were susceptible to trench foot, which came from hiking for days through mud and sleeping in damp areas. Living in the same clothes for days on end also brought on an infestation of "cooties." Life on the front lines was uncomfortable enough without this extra element. Clean socks and other undergarments were great items to have.

Other personal souvenirs were taken basically on a first come, first serve, basis, and the art of this practice was quite widespread and accepted to a degree. This should not be taken as a sign that the fighting men on both sides were ruthless barbarians and void of emotions, as they certainly had many inner feelings, which they so often kept to themselves.

In the early morning of September 16, Major Hamilton and others in the division marched about seven and a half miles north of Toul to an area known as Ansauville-Royaumeix.

Hamilton had performed exceptionally well again, and as a reward, on September 20, he was now given full command of 1/5 from Lt. Colonel O'Leary. Many months ago he had commanded the battalion briefly before the fighting, being relieved back in January, but this was much different, as the First Battalion, Fifth Regiment, with a motto today of "Make Peace, Or Die," was now actively under his full control. Having command of more than 1,000 men and yet still being able to fight alongside each and every comrade was just the position of responsibility he wanted to have.

On September 20 and 21 the Second Division hiked once again. Billeting at Mon-Le-Vignoble, where they received replacement clothing, equipment and a few extra articles for the fast approaching cold weather season.

The Allied high commanders knew full well that the Germans were not about to quit. Unknown to Hamilton and his men was the fact that what lay ahead could potentially be their toughest assignment yet. Hamilton further trained and drilled his battalion to remove any cockiness. Following a couple of weeks of intensive drills, all four of his companies were in shape to his liking. Private Mackin now said, "Our replacement men were now well knit into our combat outfits."[22]

The French Government had been pressuring General Pershing to temporarily transfer some divisions from under the umbrella of the American

Expeditionary Forces to being the total control of the French military. On September 23 Pershing acquiesced, as he struck a deal with Foch and other French authorities. For one upcoming battle only, Pershing officially relinquished control of the 2nd and 36th Divisions. They were now designated to be loaned to Pétain and the French to use as they wished.

The Thirty-Sixth Division was new to France and primarily made up of National Guardsmen from Texas and Oklahoma. A unique factor was that the division contained more Native Americans than any other AEF division. In fact, the majority of members of one company, called the "Indian Company" within the 142nd Regiment, was made up of representatives from fourteen different tribes.[23]

No sooner had Pétain been given the two divisions, when he handed both over to his youngest top general, Henri Gouraud of the French Fourth Army. The red-bearded General Gouraud had lost one arm at Gallipoli and maintained a ferocious reputation. He hated the Germans and was extremely glad to have immediate access to American troops. Lejeune wanted to know further details and met with his new authoritative commander.

The example below reveals the determination of General Gouraud. Back on July 17, when Hamilton and his sleepless men were trudging through the rain and mud to arrive at Soissons on time for H-hour, Gouraud issued the following statement:

> "*To the French and American Soldiers of the Army*"
> We may be attacked from one moment to another. You all feel that a defensive battle was never engaged under more favorable conditions. We are warned, and we are on guard. We have received strong reinforcements of infantry and artillery. You will fight on ground, which, by your assiduous labour, you have transformed into a formidable fortress, into a fortress which is invincible if the passages are well guarded.
> The bombardment will be terrible. You will endure it without weakness. The attack in a cloud of dust and gas will be fierce but your positions and your armament are formidable.

The strong and brave hearts of free men beat in your breast. None will look behind, none will give way. Every man will have but one thought — "Kill them, kill them in abundance, until they have had enough. And therefore your General tells you it will be a glorious day."[24]

On September 25 the Fourth Brigade traveled by rail car with 48 men packed into a boxcar instead of the regular 40. Upon exiting the train they regrouped and hiked around the perimeter of several villages. Along the hike, the men noticed many Allied support airplanes overhead traveling in the same direction. At times there appeared to be more than 100 in the sky at all different levels. Major Hamilton and his battalion ended up at a small village called

Courtesols, uncertain as to what their next mission would entail, but they were ready.

On September 27 Lejeune met once again with Gouraud at the Fourth French Army headquarters. He was most concerned about a rumor that his division was going to be divided among several French forces. A compromise was worked out where by Gouraud kept control of the two American divisions, while Lejeune received assurance that his Second Division would not be divided. Between the two full American divisions, close to 56,000 men were transferred to the French and history was made.

Back in 1914 the Germans captured the French territory in the Champagne sector, and Gouraud doubted the French currently had the stamina to be successful in a second attempt to overtake the enemy. If there was any military force capable of defeating the Germans in this fortified location, both commanders knew it was the mighty Second Division with the "Devil Dogs." Gouraud then pointed directly to Blanc Mont Ridge on a relief map and challenged Lejeune: "General this position is the key of all the German defenses of this sector including the whole Rheims Massif. If this ridge [Blanc Mont] can be taken the Germans will be obliged to retreat along the whole front 30 kilometers to the river Aisne. Do you think your division could effect its capture?"[25]

Lejeune, like all Marines, loved a challenge, and the answer to Gouraud's question was an obvious positive response. Although Hamilton's battalion and the other members of the division would be fighting under the ultimate command of the French, the plan of attack was to be drawn up by Lejeune.

Historians generally regard September 26, 1918, as the starting date of the Meuse-Argonne Offensive. The Great War was still far from over, and the offensive push by Allied Forces into the Argonne region would last until the end of the war.

Major Derby was now officially appointed as Lejeune's chief division surgeon. His first act was to choose a qualified assistant: "I chose one of the most valiant men I have ever known, Lieutenant-Commander Joel T. Boone.... A descendant of Daniel Boone, he was a slightly-built, fine-featured chap, with deep-set, piercing eyes, that looked at you squarely."[26]

Maybe it was the Daniel Boone side of Joel, his "piercing eyes," or the fact that Boone, like Hamilton himself, had willingly put his life on the line assisting men on the front lines that created so much mutual respect. The relationship between Boone and Hamilton would grow into a lifelong friendship.

On September 29, Germany received news that Bulgaria had signed a separate armistice declaring they were finished fighting the war. The support within the Central Powers was starting to unravel.

Also on this day the Second Division packed up and rode on camions heading once again towards the sound of gunfire. Later Hamilton and his battalion unloaded and marched to a location called Souain-Suippes behind the French Fourth Army, about six miles south of Somme-Py. Everyone could sense that a big announcement was forthcoming.

11. Blanc Mont

*Champagne Sector October 1918—
The Acts of a Former United States President*

We now approach the second major event in Hamilton's war career, which, in its own way, was as filled with action and adventure as what he experienced at the more famous battle of Belleau Wood. One historian, who believed that this was, in fact, Hamilton's greatest contribution to the war effort, summarized the upcoming battle: "In October the 4th Marine Brigade was given its toughest assignment of the Great War, the seizure of Blanc Mont Ridge in the Champagne region. Oct. 4 would be the costliest single day's fighting in the history of the 5th Marines, and Hamilton would render his greatest feats of battle on that day."[1]

The Meuse-Argonne Offensive in the Champagne region, which included Blanc Mont and St. Etienne, was known by many in the AEF, and years later by historians, as the "Forgotten Victory." In reality it should not be titled as such, since most of the American public never heard a word of this event and you can't forget something you were never told. It was a monumental victory, because when the fighting was over, the tide was turned once again, forcing the Germans to retreat quickly, about 18 miles, for some protective cover. Why we have not heard as much about Blanc Mont is not totally clear, but a few historians have come forth with revelations. One stated, "The bloody battle for Blanc Mont has been overshadowed by contemporary battles, and Hamilton's actions were excised, whether by accident or by design, from the official record."[2]

The best explanation of why stories of Blanc Mont never surfaced is put forth by USMC 1st Lieutenant John H. Craige, who served the Corps in France in a multitude of roles, including as a war correspondent. In the year following the Armistice, the journalist wrote:

> Now that America's citizen soldiers have returned to their homes and the correspondents who chronicled their deeds have come back to their desks to turn out war-histories by the score, most of the actions in which American troops had a part down to their minutest details are matters of public knowledge and household

Marine comrades going through the Meuse Argonne (courtesy Marine Corps History Division).

discussion. There are other actions, however, of which little is known, because in them American troops operated under the French or the British, and both of these Allies kept all details and reports of operations dark and secret as the grave in so far as concerns the press and the general public.

Probably foremost of these mute, unsung actions in strategic importance and ultimate result is the battle known as Blanc Mont Ridge, which took place during the Champagne offensive. Fought from October 3 to 9, 1918, it proved one of the most powerful and effective of the sledge-hammer blows struck by Marshall Foch against the retreating Germans, and compelled the abandonment of the whole Rheims Massif and a new German retirement of many kilometers on an extended front.[3]

During this month of October, near Ypres in Belgium, a German corporal named Adolph Hitler was overcome by temporary blindness following a British chlorine gas attack. He was evacuated back to a German hospital where he remained recuperating for the duration of the war.

Two well known events involving Americans should also be mentioned, as they took place in nearby regions of the Meuse Argonne, also within the first eight days of October. One incident involved a platoon of 17 members of the U.S. Army 82nd Infantry Division on October 8. The Germans had the platoon pinned with machine guns, but the American soldiers pushed forward to complete their objective. The very heroic feats of the platoon members allowed some to survive. Special recognition went to Medal of Honor recipient Alvin C. York, a church elder from Pall Mall, Tennessee, for his calm shooting performance and leadership in taking control of the situation. Throughout the ordeal and along the way back to his company, he was able to encourage a total of 132 Germans to surrender.[4]

The other notable situation began around Oct. 2, also in the Argonne Woods. This quagmire involved a mixed group of more than 600 soldiers, from parts of two battalions in the U.S. Army 308th Infantry and fragments of C and D Companies in the 306th Machine Gun Battalion, both affiliated with the 77th Division.[5] After obtaining their objective, they ventured a little further, and although they were technically not lost, they were soon cut off from others in their battalion for several days. The French had failed to supply the needed flank support on one side, and American troops were lacking on the other side, leaving the men surrounded by Germans. There was a little water in the ravine below, which they used, along with their limited supply of food. This allowed them to survive on their own and fight as needed with their ammunition on hand. On October 8, due to casualties, only 252 of the original 679 members were able to walk out.[6] Going forward they always called their deadly location "The Pocket." The commanding officer, Major Charles Whittlesey, also received the Medal of Honor for his courageous deeds and leadership in bringing his soldiers to safety. Keep the accounts of this famous story of the "Lost Battalion" in mind, as we return to preparations within the Fourth Brigade.

There certainly was a lot going on in the extended Meuse-Argonne territory, and before long members of the Fourth Brigade would witness more action and adventure than they had ever hoped to see. Lejeune had been working on his battle plan, and on the first night of October, he stated the following in an official order to his men of the Second Division:

> Headquarters Second Division (Regulars)
> American Expeditionary Forces,
> France, Oct. 1st, 1918.

Order:

1. The greatest battles in the world's history are now being fought. The Allies are attacking successfully on all fronts. The valiant Belgian Army has surprised and defeated the enemy in Flanders; the English, who have been attacking the enemy without ceasing since August eighth, have advanced beyond the Hindenburg Line, between Cambrai and St. Quentin, capturing thousands of prisoners and hundreds of cannon; the heroic Allied army of the Orient has

decisively defeated the Bulgars; the British have captured over fifty thousand prisoners in Palestine and have inflicted a mortal blow on the Turk; and our own First Army and the Fourth French Army have already gained much success in the preliminary stages of their attack between the Meuse and Suippe Rivers.

2. Owing to its world-wide reputation for skill and valor, the Second Division was selected by the Commander in Chief of the Allied armies as his special reserve, and has been held in readiness to strike a swift and powerful blow at the vital point of the enemy's line. The hour to move forward has now come, and I am confidant that our division will pierce the enemy's line, and once more gloriously defeat the Hun.

John A. Lejeune,
Major-General, U.S.M.C., Commanding.[7]

Official.

On the night of October 1, Major Hamilton and his battalion, along with the rest of the brigade, marched north. They skirted the ruins of the village of Somme-Py and continued on to the front lines where they relieved the French Infantry. This adventure was shaping up to be quite different from that of Belleau Wood, as the terrain did not involve gentle wheat fields and a pristine forest, but rather ridges and soil consisting of white clay and part white chalk-limestone. Any form or resemblance of organic topsoil had been blasted away during the past years. The one common denominator was an

A view of the chalky soil and scrub pine tree landscape looking north from Blanc Mont (courtesy Marine Corps History Division).

elevated piece of land where the enemy was waiting with open territory in front. The enemy had been waiting in this location for a long time.

Blanc Mont, known as the "White Mountain," contained slopes and ridges that rose to a height of 250 feet and extended a few miles east to west. Hill 142 was not a particular vantage point in the region around the Château-Thierry sector, but Blanc Mont was the focal point for the Champagne region. The nomans land in the front of the elevation consisted of a mile-wide downward open slope, which afforded no place to hide.

In this battle, the conquest of Blanc Mont Ridge was a main part of the objective, but conquering the surrounding area, containing trenches known as Essen Trench and Essen Hook and the village of St. Etienne, was considered just as ominous and every bit as challenging. Some of the structures in the area consisted merely of blown-out buildings resembling piles of white stones left from destruction years prior.

Essen Hook was full of elaborate mazes with elevated trenches, making it one of the greatest obstacles of all. Within the domain were concrete pillboxes with narrow slits and the home to many machine guns. To take control of this death trap would require never ending brute force and determination.

Back in March when aviator Rickenbacker flew over the Champagne sector in his very first spy mission over enemy territory, he observed: "The trenches in this sector were quite old and had remained in practically the same position for three years of warfare. To my inexperienced view there appeared to be nothing below me but old battered trenches, trench works and billions of shell holes which had dug up the whole surface of the earth for four or five miles on either side of me. Not a tree, not a fence, no sign of any familiar occupation of mankind, nothing but a chaos of ruin and desolation. The awfulness of the thing was appalling."[8]

Rickenbacker was, in fact, fired upon by anti-aircraft fire, and the desolate area was, in fact, teeming with hidden Germans. In the early part of the war, many lives were lost in the surrounding area, and during that long battle the French had held the Blanc Mont Ridge for a brief 15 minutes.[9] The Germans not only occupied Blanc Mont, but over the past four years they had fortified it to their liking and now considered it home territory. Some underground dugouts and dwellings in the Argonne had running water, feather beds and even some pictures, furniture and other items stolen from the French.[10]

Many miles of tangled barbed wire were strewn everywhere and even placed among trees at heights no man could get over. Huge ditches were created to trap tanks, and large cement barricades were strategically placed as additional obstacles.

The landscape was not totally devoid of trees. In certain locations there were mixed groups of cedar, hemlock and scrub pine trees with a few willows

A German dugout entrance at Blanc Mont (courtesy Marine Corps History Division).

at lower elevations. Some veterans could easily recall the abundant spring and summer flowers, including vibrant red poppies, that had been scattered around France, but at this time and place there were no flowers. Huge craters still remained in the soft white soil along with scorched and felled trees. Grave sites were scattered around the terrain identifying the dead of just a few years past and serving as a constant reminder of death. The area had a definite appearance of death and destruction, with a touch of hell, and the upcoming battle had not even begun.

Lejeune's division was placed under the XXI French Corps. He was relying on his two top officers, U.S. Army Brig. General Hanson Ely of the Third Brigade and USMC Brig. General Neville of the Fourth Brigade. Neville coordinated with his two main officers, Colonel Harry Lee of the Sixth Regiment and Colonel Feland of the Fifth Regiment. Major Hamilton assessed the situation with his four skippers: Captain Hunt of the 17th Company, Captain Percy Duryea Cornell over his old 49th Company, Captain Raymond F. Dirksen of the 66th Company and Captain Whitehead of the 67th Company.

The plan called for the division's Third Brigade, composed of the Ninth and 23rd Infantry, along with Third Battalion French tanks, to line up on the right side. Their objective was to control the eastern side before Médéah Farm. On their immediate left Lejeune's plan called for an intentional gap of middle ground consisting of several hundred yards. The far left side was to contain the Fourth Brigade with Second Battalion French tanks. The general objective was for each battalion to move forward in their designated lane. The two brigades planned to meet sometime in the future on the crest of Blanc Mont Ridge as a united force.

The unknown critical factor was how their crucial French support units would perform. Recently they did not have a good track record, and without support Lejeune's best laid plans could unravel. The French 170th Division was to be on their far right, supporting the Third Infantry Brigade, while the French 21st Division, commanded by General Stanislas Naulin, was assigned to protect the left side of the Fourth Brigade.

Within the Marine Brigade each of the six individual battalions was to be assisted by a designated company offering machine gun support. The battalion of 1/6 was assigned the Sixth Regimental 73rd Machine Gun Company, 2/6 the 81st, and Major Shuler's 3/6 the 15th. Major Hamilton's 1/5 was given the Fifth Regiment, 8th Machine Gun Company, 2/5 the 23rd and 3/5 the 77th Machine Gun Company.

Lejeune's division would be going up against the German 200th and 213th Divisions plus remnants of many others. Captured prisoners later indicated that there could have been portions of six additional German divisions with a mix of Prussians involved in the action. The Germans had made good use of the prior years by reinforcing the area, stocking it with ammunition and selecting the best locations in which to hide. They had used an immense amount of concrete to fortify the defensive positions. Pillboxes held two to four men in bunkers generally five feet deep and two feet above ground with concrete walls two feet thick.

The initial shove-off was scheduled for October 2, but because of constant confusion this did not happen. A few patrols performed some initial investigative work, but the day was primarily spent waiting for final plans to arrive. During the evening a few trenches north of Somme-Py were cleared of some Germans. The Essen Hook area was where the French 21st was to concentrate their efforts, but they were absent. Realizing this, the Sixth Regiment started their own preliminary work at Essen Trench, and in doing so, they received a few casualties. These measures were taken to help alleviate resistance during the future jump-off.

Hamilton got his battalion together to go over the details before H-hour. The men once again adjusted and tightened their combat packs and put on an extra bandolier of ammunition. Bayonets were fixed and gas masks double checked. The men tucked an extra hand grenade inside their shirt for ready use, as their destination was predicted to require lots of hand-to-hand combat and explosives. This battle would pit will power against will power as the enemy's strategy was simply "bring it on, come and get us."

The new recruits who had fought at Saint-Mihiel could feel that this situation was going to be much different, as the atmosphere before the jump-off had a different feeling in the air. The silent ones had a certain look in their eyes, while others opened up with a bit more conversation than in the past.

Major Hamilton, now with responsibilities for the full battalion, checked to see how preparations for necessary medical assistance were coming along. Naval medical officers also wore the Marine uniform, and he located Boone, who was now in charge of medical duties pertaining to the entire Marine Brigade. Boone assigned medic lieutenants D. Dickinson Jr. and P. A. McLendon to Hamilton's battalion.[11]

Everything was in good order with an initial dressing station set up about a half mile south of Somme-Py. From there, the Sanitary Train, consisting of Ford ambulances and additional larger smoother-riding GMC trucks, was positioned ready to transport the wounded. They would be taken on a twenty minute ride to the main dressing station at Souain, a village totally destroyed, but now considered a safe location.

On October 3 at 0440, written orders were received at the Fourth Brigade Headquarters detailing instructions for the upcoming battle. The H-hour for the brigade was set at 0630, but for certain reasons it was quickly adjusted to 0550. At 0545 the Second Field Artillery Brigade woke up the Champagne region with an opening barrage signaling the start of the battle of Blanc Mont. The guns were not the full force that was displayed back at Saint-Mihiel but rather, for a few moments, similar to the performance at Soissons.

Future artillery shelling was to continually be placed in front of the advancing troops at coordinated times. The men were to proceed forward covering a distance of a little more than a football field every four minutes. Initial shelling was planned to involve a creeping bombardment of 300 yards beyond the set objective, followed later by a half hour standing barrage. Watches were synchronized and runners stood ready to assist with communication of the timed events. Of course all this depended upon meeting objectives on time.

When the jump-off was issued, the Fourth Brigade headed out on the misty morning led by the Sixth Regiment with the Fifth Regiment following. The regiments headed away in a northwest direction, brimming at full strength at well over 1,000 men each. The battalions following each other were spaced roughly 1,000 yards apart. The men of 2/6 headed off with 12 light tanks and their machine gun company. At Belleau Wood, when the Americans entered the first major battle, jumping off first was quite exciting and a privileged honor for Hamilton and his 49th Company. On this day, Hamilton's 1/5 started out trailing 3/5 and taking the all important rear position of the Fourth Brigade. From that vantage point, he expected to be in contact with the French left flank and to a limited degree the tail of the Second Divisions, Third Brigade. The greatest adventure in this battle, for those who survived, would be viewed by the men in Major Hamilton's battalion, the last to step away.

While leading the way, 2/6 received heavy flank machine-gun fire from Essen Hook but continued forward with their mission. Two men, Corporal John Henry Pruitt and Private John J. Kelly, both from the 78th Company of 2/6, would each later receive the Medal of Honor for their action during this day.

The Fourth Brigade's front five battalions were past the hot zone of the Essen Hook curved trenches, but General Naulin's French 21st Division was still absent from their flank position. The duty to clear out this thorn fell upon Hamilton's trailing 1/5. The major instructed members from Captain Hunt's 17th Company, aided by a few light French tanks and men from the Eighth Machine Gun Company, to gain control of the trenches. This was accomplished prior to 1100, and in the process about 100 prisoners were taken. Following the successful assault the trenches were turned over to the French as this was their objective from the beginning. Unfortunately the French lost control early in the afternoon when the Germans made a counterattack.

During the afternoon new orders called for the Fifth Regiment to take the lead on the left side with the Sixth Regiment to follow. Major Robert Eugene Messersmith was to lead with his 2/5, but because of disorganization within his companies, he could not get aligned to move ahead.[12] The entire Fifth Regiment was caught fighting the Germans to their front and at the same time still trying to eliminate the continuous incoming fire from their left flank. The French 21st had not kept pace, and the status of the vulnerable

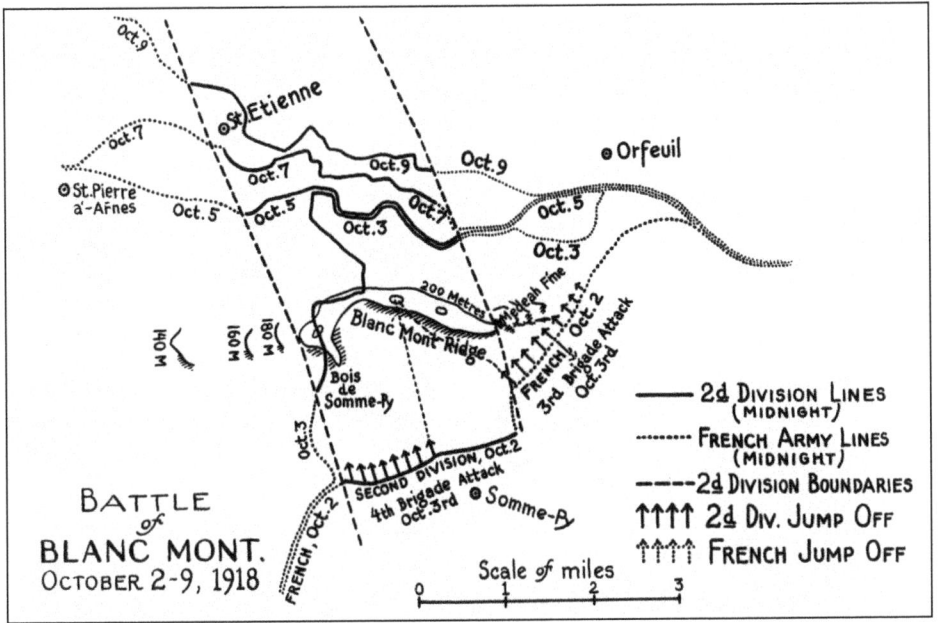

Battle of Blanc Mont Ridge Map.

left flank remained a constant irritation throughout the afternoon. In the course of events, Major Hamilton located the skipper and members of the 55th Company and reconnected the group with their proper battalion in 2/5.

While Hamilton led his battalion forward, shells were landing extremely close, at times making 30-foot craters in the chalky soil. A direct hit could kill close to two dozen men. To further add to the chaotic atmosphere, somewhere in the surrounding area a land mine, or more likely an ammunition dump, with at least 1,000 pounds of explosives went off, knocking some men down a half mile away and creating a 150-foot-wide crater.[13]

Small French tanks were in the mix with barrels flaming, but to some extent they were hindering the Marines, as tanks were a notorious magnet for drawing incoming fire. Finally, some members of the Second Division made it to the top of the ridge, but companies were split apart fighting numerous counterattacks.

As darkness approached, the fighting subsided and both sides remained stationary. Major Hamilton's men were aware of the precarious situation they were in, and some might have viewed the autumn sunset, wondering if it would be the last one they'd ever see. Hamilton and his battalion would spend the night in large dugouts beside a road north of Blanc Mont Ridge. During the day his battalion had witnessed a lot of action, but casualties were not severe. The Second Division had worked together and gained good ground, but they were now in a very unsettling situation. Both opposing sides were thoroughly stirred up, and the Marines knew the approaching day possessed all the elements of an ultimate showdown unlike anything they had ventured into. With the lull in fighting, Major Hamilton took a moment and got his four skippers together to review maps and assess the current conditions. He told them:

> The 6th took Blanc Mont, and they are holding it against heavy counter-attacks. Prisoners say they were ordered to hold here at any costs — they're fighting damned well, too! The infantry regiments piped down the Bois de Vipre, just as we did the Essen Hook. The division is grouping around the Ridge, but we're pretty well isolated from the French. Tonight we are going on up and take the front line, and attack toward St. Etienne-à-Arnes — town north of the Ridge and a little west. Get up on to Blanc Mont with your companies — P.C. will be there, along the road that runs across the Ridge.[14]

The absent French had left a gap on one flank of close to two miles and a little over a three mile void on the other. Naulin's 21st Division was being relieved by the French 22nd Division, which would hopefully perform better. Hamilton could only worry so much about circumstances that were out of his control. After hours of discussion and map surveillance, he was extremely frustrated with present conditions, saying, "Well, orders are to attack, and by God, we'll attack."[15]

Totally exhausted, Hamilton then asked one of his men to wake him at 0530. The morning of October 4 came, and all his men were once again securing their bayonets and performing the crucial routine checks of their personal equipment.

Over in his old 49th Company, 2nd Lieutenant Robert E. Conner, known by all as "Chuck," was sizing up the battle before the whistle blew. The leatherneck and original member of the 49th, who was in the company when Hamilton joined, did not like the looks of what lay ahead. Like Conner, Gunner Nice was also from Pennsylvania, and he considered him one of his best friends. Conner mentioned to Nice that he had a vision about death, and said, "I've got a hunch I'm not coming back."[16] Nice responded with some words of encouragement to one of the most courageous Marines he knew.

The volunteers exchanged more than glances with the veteran leathernecks. Lieutenant platoon leaders and front line sergeants notably made straight eye contact with each individual to be certain everyone was totally focused. They were now all in sync, ready and prepared to go forward.

At 0600 Colonel Feland's Fifth Regiment, with 3,000 plus men, headed out leading the Fourth Brigade. Without initial artillery fire they headed up a road towards St. Etienne with Major Henry Louis Larsen's 3/5 going first, followed 500 yards back by Hamilton and 1/5, and then Messersmith with 2/5 another 500 yards in the rear. St. Etienne was a village about a half mile northwest of Blanc Mont with even fewer trees than Blanc Mont.

On this day Colonel Lee's Sixth Regiment was selected to follow in support. They had achieved much success on October 3, but Blanc Mont was officially not in control, as the western slope remained full of Germans and counterattacks were expected in other areas. Just as the Fifth Regiment had to cover the left flank on the prior day, the Sixth Regiment was now called upon to perform the same task.

Before long several of Hamilton's leathernecks noticed that their location was awfully quiet, and the veterans sensed that the silence was a bad omen, reminiscent of past eerie encounters. The stillness was then broken by an incoming artillery shell with shrapnel scattering everywhere. This was not a random explosion, but rather a defining statement issued by the Germans to let all members of 1/5 know that the Kaiser's Forces maintained control.

By the middle of the morning, 3/5 had moved forward into a dangerous position receiving heavy machine gun fire, and they requested immediate support from the other two battalions in the Fifth Regiment. Hamilton's men were now preoccupied with their own precarious situation. Messersmith's battalion was able to break free and move into position to support Larsen as the aggressive action moved into the nearby wooded pines. Hamilton and his men eventually moved up while continuing to cover the exposed left side.

The French 22nd Division was no better than the 21st Division they replaced, as they were nowhere in sight and the void of flank coverage was now an extremely serious issue.[17] The Sixth Regiment in reserve was not able to advance and relieve the pressure, as they were caught up with fighting similar to what the Fifth Regiment faced on the prior day. Without backup the Fifth Regiment now had to handle on their own whatever came their way.

There was now a constant procession of wounded Marines filling the makeshift dressing station, and Division Surgeon Derby decided to query one individual about his injury and what was transpiring on the front lines. Like a true Marine the wounded warrior knew exactly what the problem was, and he further enjoyed answering the officer's direct question without mincing words. He bluntly replied: "I got mine, sir, because those d----d 'Frogs' [French] never came up on our left, and we ran into cross fire. It's a habit with 'em. They're never there when you need their support"[18]

Derby later reflected upon his early days of training in France, before America began fighting. Casualties in the Second Division had certainly been extensive at Belleau Wood, followed by Soissons and Saint-Mihiel, but it is quite interesting to note the fashion in which he mentions the onslaught of Blanc Mont: "It was in such surroundings as these that our men were to receive those finishing touches from their French instructors which came to the fore in the storming of Blanc Mont Ridge in October."[19]

At around noon Major Hamilton and 1/5 were under extensive pressure and covering the exposed left flank. The battle intensified as heavy shelling increased, and the German Maxim bullets began buzzing everywhere, from two sides, then three. The incessant noise from machine guns all around was overwhelming. Over time, the rapid fire guns overheated forcing the enemy to struggle to cool them down.

As if this was not enough, the German airplanes owned the skies above and roamed freely dropping bombs in selected locations. The French 252d Aviation Squadron was designated to assist Lejeune's division, but today the Allied pilots were nowhere in the vicinity to engage in dogfights or assist offensively.

From their vantage point on a ridgeline known as "Ludwig's Rucken" and an area called "Petersburg," the Germans knew they had the Americans in a tight spot. Using an assortment of weapons, the enemy was throwing everything they had towards the Fifth Regiment, including gas. There is never a good time to don gas masks, but it had to be done quickly, as this was the worst gas attack they had faced. With gas masks on, artillery shells exploding and machine guns firing across the entire terrain, one envisioned being on the threshold of hell. It was pure survival time.

Major Hamilton was watching over his battalion and at the same time shooting away, shoulder to shoulder with his men. It was around this time when he was faced with a very unexpected and troubling situation involving some of his peers in another battalion. He took care of the confrontation first and then sent a note back to his commanding officer, Colonel Feland at Fifth Regiment Headquarters, detailing what had transpired, as well as his current predicament:

From: C.O. 1stBn.
At: P.C. 266.5-281.8.
To: C.O. 5thRegt.Oct. 4, 1918

At about 1:30 P.M. the regt. started to advance with 1st Bn. in support of 3d Bn. and the 2d Bn. in reserve. Immediately a heavy machine gunfire was laid down from the left flank. The woods which the companies had entered was heavily shelled and about 2 P.M. there were numbers of men seen running to the rear. In some instances officers were leading in what appeared to be a grand rout. Among those whom I noticed particularly was Capt.— —[omited], Capt. — —[omited] and Major— —[omited]. There were also several lieutenants whom I did not recognize. Major— —[omited] explained that he had lost all his officers, but didn't show any initiative or leadership. Capt.— —[omited] was hopeless. When it became evident that the retirement had become a rout, Lieut. Nelms ran out and endeavored to turn the men back. His task was a hard one and attempted at great personal exposure to machine gun fire and a violent artillery bombardment. *We then were forced to draw pistols, and it was only by this method that we were able to stop the retreat.* Then, as best we could we disposed the men along the edge of the woods and made them dig in. The position is a bad one and the machine gun fire from both flanks & from our left rear is causing much damage. I don't believe the French have advanced on our left and this leaves our whole flank exposed. The ground that the 3d Brigade passed over has not been cleaned of machine guns. I suggest that the 6th Regt. be requested to put out a strong flank guard. From the number of wounded seen I estimate the regiment's casualties between 35 and 45 percent. Will report later. Hunt sends word that the Germans were seen massing an hour or so ago on the left flank. He gives our left front as shown on attached sketch. Do not know where leading elements are on right. [sgd] Hamilton.[20]

Hamilton did what was necessary to keep the entire encounter under control by literally taking a page out of the handbook of a past U.S. president. Lt. Colonel Theodore Roosevelt was faced with the same type of circumstance during the Spanish-American War. Documenting the event in his own words, Roosevelt stated:

> This I could not allow, as it was depleting my line, so I jumped up, and walking a few yards to the rear, drew my revolver, halted the retreating soldiers, and called out to them that I appreciated the gallantry with which they had fought and would be sorry to hurt them, but that I should shoot the first man who, on any pretence whatever, went to the rear. My own men had all sat up and were watching my movements with the utmost interest; so was Captain Howze. I ended my statement ... by saying "Now, I shall be very sorry to hurt you and you don't know whether or not I will keep my word, but my men can tell you that I always do."[21]

Chances are Hamilton read this passage in the book *The Rough Riders* as a boy. Even with that knowledge, however, his natural human instinct would have taken over in such a situation, and his actions could have been classified under the philosophical saying "Great minds think alike." Derby could probably recite his father-in-law's action words verbatim. The bottom line is Hamilton reacted swiftly and properly to maintain control of a critical situation.

By close to 1430, the men of 3/5 and 2/5 had formed a line, while 1/5 was further away trying to once again seal off the group's left flank. Hamilton's battalion was under intense fire and searching for any type of protective cover. Few options were available, and tough decisions had to be made right away. With incoming fire from at least three sides, the major decided the best way to break up the continuous attack was to take it head on by charging up a hill into direct fire to secure a potentially better vantage point. Captain Hunt, commanding the 17th Company, who months later would succeed Major Hamilton as the battalion commander, stated: "No one but those present will ever know or fully appreciate what the battalion went through during the charge up this hill. The rate of casualties was far above anything we had experienced, but the men kept on."²²

Once the battalion was on top of the ridge, Hamilton's men captured about 100 prisoners as well as several machine guns. They then gathered their many casualties and regrouped. The wounds of some were horrendous. They were all in need of rest, but within 15 minutes all sorts of fire was once again being sent their way. In the near distance there was another ridge, full of Germans, which looked down upon them. The enemy was now giving the battalion everything they had from the high ridge and the exposed rear flank behind them.

It was time to move again, and the major got his men to advance forward towards St. Etienne. Initially the fire seemed to be reduced, but after making a gain of about 200 yards they faced intensive fire from head on. Hamilton's battalion was now boxed in on the slope of a hill enduring extremely hot incoming fire. A magnitude of enemy machine guns were firing up to 600 rounds a minute. The battalion was facing total annihilation.

Private Mortensen was bruised on his left side by a piece of casing and took a little gas, but as his gas mask was now working properly, the sharpshooter continued to fire away with the ammunition on hand. He would not need medical attention. As he recalled, "For the first moments I thought I passed into eternity, but only the good die young. Seemed as though the machine gun bullets had a happy faculty of buzzing all around me and the fellows have often told me that in the heat of battle one hardly feels when he is hit, but to make sure I some times felt myself over and looked for blood marks until I could be convinced that I was still intact."²³

His skipper, Captain Dirksen, however, did not fair as well. With his left foot wounded and having been overcome by gas fumes earlier in the day, he was evacuated at once. Someone else in the 66th Company had to come forward and take over the command.

At the time, Medal of Honor recipient 1st Lieutenant Hulbert of the 66th was a likely candidate to take command from Dirksen. He was firing away, but in an exposed area with Maxim bullets flying all around, he was struck by one or more of the bullets. Captain Thomason of the 49th Company and other comrades saw him fall to the ground. It was said that Hulbert had a peaceful look as he passed away.²⁴

Hulbert had faced many tough encounters over the years. He had performed admirably as a platoon leader in the war, but it was the end of the line for the 51-year-old elder statesman of the "Old Breed." Lieutenant Walter T. Galliford, of the 49th Company, who had ridden to town on horseback with Hamilton before Belleau Wood began, had previously stated, "If the

Fifth Regiment goes over the top, I want to go with Mister Hulbert."[25] Major Shuler also had earlier given a tribute to Hulbert by saying, "I should be most glad to have Gunner Hulbert under me in any capacity, and should he through good fortune be promoted over me I should be most happy to serve under his command."[26] The Corps had lost one of its best.

Also in the 66th Company, future Medal of Honor recipient Sergeant Kocak was doing all he could to keep the situation under control. The ever courageous sergeant had continued to inspire and motivate his men, but before long he also lay dead. His friend and counterpart in the company, 2nd Lieutenant Cukela, had recently received his field promotion and would soon receive the Medal of Honor too. Cukela was now wounded and although not seriously, he could not step up in command.

Within just the 66th Company two Medal of Honor recipients lay dead, a third was injured, and the day of October 4 was not over. Other front line sergeants within the company were proudly displaying great acts of bravery, but unfortunately they would not be able to hold on forever. Sergeant Guy M. Yeaton came from one of the most remote locations in America, the beautiful little island town of Isleboro, Maine. The rugged coastal man performed admirably, serving his country and protecting his comrades all the way to his death. So too did Sergeant John C. McGabe, who died on October 4, and Gunnery Sgt. William Von Lumm, who died of wounds the following day.

Over in Hamilton's old 49th Company, Gunner Nice was wounded once again and sent to a hospital. His leatherneck friend Sergeant Conner's premonition about death came true, and Nice later recalled: "He had command of the first platoon and I had the second, about 40 paces away. There wasn't any cover on the slope we charged. The ground shook with the thunder of the guns and the hills were lousy with Germans. And then a one-pounder got him; tore him all up. I tried to give him first aid but there was nothing that anybody could have done for him. He just smiled, patted me on the arm and died. He had seen 30 years of service and he was a prince."[27]

Murl Corbett was now a battalion intelligence officer for Hamilton and had positioned himself on Blanc Mont Ridge to gain important information. While stationed there, an artillery shell wounded him, and along with this, he was overcome by gas. He refused immediate medical attention in order that the plan of attack could proceed without delay.

Runner Private Thomas A. O. Miller of the 49th volunteered to carry an important message for his major through all the machine gun and artillery fire. He was hit by shell fragments and lost a leg.

Captain Hunt's 17th Company was barely holding together and facing conditions similar to the other companies under Hamilton's command. Like all units in the Marine Brigade, his men represented many different areas of the United States. Two second lieutenants, Everette E. Lindgren from Adrian, Minnesota, and Gillis A. Johnson from Fort Worth, Texas, were severely wounded but continued displaying acts of heroism. They led others in cleaning out selected enemy machine gun nests, while another second lieutenant, Fred J. Zinner of Columbus, Ohio, was doing the same type of work.

Hunt desperately needed new couriers to step forward to carry messages from his company's platoon leaders to other segments of men cut off from communication. The daring runners also needed to make the all-important return trip through areas of bombardment and machine gun fire. Two sergeants, Robert Van Duesen from Vineland, New Jersey, and Daniel R. Fox from Pottstown, Pennsylvania, quickly volunteered. Both were successful in their missions but were wounded in the process. Sergeant Van Duessen's injuries proved to be so critical that he later died from his wounds. Another noncommissioned officer, Gunnery Sergeant Milton R. Scott of Lamonte, Missouri, was also severely wounded but kept moving forward to obtain a better sniping position.

In the 67th Company, Captain Whitehead was wounded in one of the latest assaults. His second in command, Captain Francis S. Kieren, no sooner took command when he, too, became a casualty. Felix Beauchamp, another captain, was a long way from his home in Sitka, Alaska. He took control of the company, but before long he, too, was wounded and someone else had to take control. Still, all four companies had Major Hamilton close by at the helm, leading from the front lines, displaying willpower and continuing to offer encouragement.

Companies primarily consisted of a large percentage of dedicated patriotic privates, who had their own special stories to tell, yet outside of immediate family, they tended to get lost in history. Private Michael T. O'Donoghue, a Princeton University graduate from the class of 1911, was like many physically fit youthful men who were full of emotion and following their heart. With war at hand he felt the duty to serve his country. He put his career on hold, but before heading off to war, he wished to marry his true love. Married on December 28, 1917, he enlisted five days later as a Marine Corps volunteer, becoming a private in the 67th Company. He died along with some of his comrades on October 4.

The crews of the 8th Machine Gun Company assisting the battalion also had their crews decimated. Marine Corporal Jack Jordan was one of the few left in his company to manage the operation of his machine gun. He would find willing assistance from another comrade, but finding more ammunition was a greater problem. He stayed with the gun until it was empty of bullets.

The Kaiser's Forces were gaining confidence, but you could never count

Hamilton out of any type of contest. As one historian wrote, "In George Hamilton, though, the Germans had a tiger by the tail. As combative a man as ever drew breath, Hamilton led his men toward the slopes before St. Etienne under a rain of high explosive and gas."[28]

Now surrounded, the major prepared to fight until his last breath, and his men were devoted to doing the same. There finally came a time when 1st Lieutenant Francis J. Kelly Jr. found himself to be the only walking officer in the 66th Company. Realizing that the Germans were set for a tremendous counterattack, Hamilton wanted Kelly to find a more secure location. The temporary skipper's adrenaline was flowing, and although outnumbered three to one, he ordered the few men left in the 66th Company to advance.[29] The attack was successful, and the enemy counterattack was broken up.

With action everywhere, Sergeant Lyng of the 49th Company moved further forward and soon spotted the enemy bringing in machine guns for still another ambush. Thinking and moving quickly at the same time, Lyng retraced his steps and gathered a few Marines. The small contingent of "Indian Head" Division members raced forward screaming like a band of wild Indians. Although heavily outnumbered, they too broke up the German advance. The small force was later referred to as "Lyng's Comanches."[30]

At 1800 in the early evening of October 4, Major Hamilton had his members of 1/5 move off the slope and back towards the road for some cover. With dusk at hand, his active battalion that had started the day with four full companies now consisted of much less than a company of men. This road-

Major Leroy P. Hunt shown after taking command of 1/5 from Major Hamilton in 1919 (courtesy Marine Corps History Division).

side spot was better, but not the proper place to stay for long. Hamilton sent a runner asking for additional men, ammunition and food.

The major asked Hunt to issue an assessment concerning the current status of the First Battalion, Fifth Regiment. Captain Hunt, the senior ranking captain in the battalion and the officer who in future years would become a USMC four star general, recorded the following:

17th Company	2 officers	35 men
49th Company	2 officers	29 men
66th Company	1 officer	22 men
67th Company	2 officers	40 men
Bn. Hdqs. Group	5 officers	30 men
Total	12 officers	156 men[31]

Due to casualties the battalion was reduced from well over 1,000 officers and men to 168. With good reason, the survivors of the First Battalion, Fifth Regiment, forever referred to their deadly location as "The Box." Hamilton miraculously managed to avoid being killed or wounded and was with his "Boys" the whole way.

On the night of the 4th, the gunfire and attacks did not fully subside, as the Germans were still clustered in several locations and not ready to fully concede defeat. Lieutenant Benjamin of the Second Engineers, along with his platoon, were hastily transported by truck to support the Marines with the notion that they needed wire cutting assistance at once. Fortunately they brought their own rifles, as upon entering the scene they quickly realized they were needed to fight. They experienced their own intense confrontation, which is detailed in the unit's *Official History*: "While disposing his men for the attack, Lieutenant Benjamin decided that one of his sergeants was inefficient because of cowardice, inexperience, or lack of energy or intelligence. Any one of these defects was sufficient to disqualify him to hold the rank of sergeant of the 2nd Engineers, so Lieutenant Benjamin cut off his chevrons and reduced him to the ranks. In such a manner, were we able to maintain the high standard of the 2nd Engineers."[32]

Hamilton determined the time was right to connect with others in the regiment, so his small battalion ventured off. When the day of October 4 finally came to a close, he and others in the regiment were situated at Blanc Mont Médéah Farm Ridge, close to the intersection of the Somme Py-St. Etienne Road.[33]

With all the casualties in his battalion, it's also interesting to note how the medical personnel performed throughout the day. They were fully prepared for this event; however, with so many wounded in such a short span of time, the decision was made to advance the dressing stations and ambulance units closer to the action. It's no coincidence that the medics on the front line assigned to Hamilton had their own difficulties, as noted by Surgeon Derby:

> On the morning of October fourth, we again followed the advance and established our dressing station in a small forest about one half of a kilometer beyond the summit of Blanc Mont. Here we were within range of the machine-gun snipers and under constant shelling.
>
> Hardly had we gotten settled before the wounded started to appear. Not now and then, but in a steady stream, increasing as the day wore on, and filling the shack which we had chosen for our dressing station.
>
> Out in the open, exposed to machine-gun and shell fire, lay many wounded who were being dressed by medical officers and hospital corps men. The ambulance stretcher bearers bore them to the ambulances on the main road, sticking to their job with superhuman tenacity, and utterly disregarding the heavy shelling.
>
> Our dressing station consisted of a small shack with a room about 15 × 15 in front and a narrow passage to two small rooms in the rear. All openings were camouflaged from light by blankets.
>
> About midnight the fourth of October a shell struck the station and exploded in one of the small rooms in the rear, killing two hospital corpsmen and two patients, wounding several other corps men, and re-wounding many patients who had been dressed and placed in these rooms awaiting evacuation.
>
> The concussion of the shell knocked our camouflage down and blew out our candles, so that for a time we had to take care of the wounded groping in the darkness.[34]

In the heat of battle Hamilton was a no-nonsense leader, who did not mince words, preferring to get to the point quickly. In the early hours of October 5, the major was able to secure a courier to carry a message to Colonel Feland: "Large portion of left not cleaned of machine guns ... which are working hard and fast at all times from both flanks and rear. We are in a precarious position ... and unless we can make our last night's objective pretty quick, it is very probable that no advance can be made as *last night's advance was a fiasco*. [Emphasis added.] We need artillery and we need it badly. Also food and water. [Sgd] Hamilton."[35]

Word came that the French were four miles behind and should finally be in their proper location by noontime. Hamilton replied to Feland with the following message: "This battalion will go, or attempt to go, where you order it. You should understand though that your regiment is now much depleted, very disorganized, and not in condition to advance as a front line regiment even though the enemy forces in front are found to be small. It is hard to say 'can't,' but the Division Commander *should thoroughly understand the situation and realize that this regiment 'can't' advance as an attacking force. Such advance would sacrifice the regiment.* Hamilton. [Italics added, but underlining in the original]."[36]

Lejeune knew that for all intents and purposes the battle was over. On the 5th of October, as he assessed the situation, members of his division waited for orders. Finally at 0905 Lejeune telephoned Brig. General Ely commanding his Third Brigade and stated, "H hour will not be given," and instructions for both divisional brigades called for no further formal attacks.[37]

In the process of reaching their objective, the Marine Corps had lost more of their devoted men, and although other Marines would soon fill the ranks, things would never be the same. Many of the survivors stated they had now seen their fill of war.

Some authorities list the battle of Blanc Mont as being from October 1 to October 10 and others from October 2 to October 9; however, the intense fighting played out in a couple of days. The Central Powers no longer had any thoughts of winning the Western Front and knew that a favorable treaty was their best option and exit. Their current retreat was so quick that some AEF patrols even lost contact with them. In showing their force and willpower, Lejeune's Second Division suffered the following casualties:

	Officers	*Enlisted*
Killed	41	685
Missing	6	579
Severely Wounded	48	926
Slightly Wounded	102	2,367
Gassed	12	207
Total	209	4,771 [4764][38]

Of the total figure, Neville's Fourth Brigade suffered a total of 2,185 casualties.[39] October 4 ended up being the worst single day of fighting for the mighty Fifth Regiment in the entire war.[40] That statement alone should be enough cause for Americans to recall the "Forgotten Victory."

Private Mackin of the 67th Company received the Distinguished Service Award for running messages on October 4 and managed to be among the 168 men who survived "The Box." Later in life he made reference to the experience in his book *Suddenly We Did Not Want to Die.*

Survivor Captain John W. Thomason Jr., the second in command of the 49th Company, summed up his view of life in a letter to his mother: "A man is born, gets married and dies. These are the three greatest events in life. If he can add going to war to those three, he can add a great adventure, for that's what war is." He further added: "War is certainly the greatest adventure. It is horrible beyond all words and so hideously and hatefully wasteful and wanton — and yet — you never know what getting down to realities means until you go to war.... Life becomes unbelievably simple and direct. You stand it or you break under it.... There isn't any middle ground."[41]

When time allowed, Thomason continued making remarkable sketches

"5th Marines at Champagne," ink with watercolor wash painting by Capt. John W. Thomason Jr. depicts Blanc Mont encounter (courtesy the George C. Marshall Foundation, Lexington, Virginia).

that included his vivid memories of Blanc Mont, and when the war was over he created a 15" × 19" ink with watercolor wash drawing depicting the battle scene. His formal artistic skills were developed starting in May 1914, when he left Texas and entered school at the Art Students League in New York City for a year of instruction. Private Mortensen, one of 23 Marines in the 66th Company who was not killed or wounded, currently had a brother-in-law, artist Hans Peter Hansen, who had been a full professor at the Art Students League from 1912 to 1917.[42]

On October 5, after exiting "The Box," Major Hamilton received a poignant letter from his commander, Colonel Feland:

> I am very happy to tell you that General Lejeune called me up this morning to ask me about our conditions and to assure you of his appreciation of your good work yesterday and last night.
> He says that General Gouraud had called to assure him that it was the pushing out of this salient and especially our work of holding on last night that made the Boche take up the big retreat now going on in all this RHEIMS sector. General Gouraud told General Lejeune that if we had given an inch the Boche would have

forced us on, that he was giving us all he had to force us back and so prevent the necessity of his general retreat.

General Lejeune is proud of you and sincerely sympathizes with us in our losses. I was so happy when I learned that the good work and devotion of you and your men are properly appreciated that I broke down. Let as many as possible of the officers and men know that the higher-ups know the great results gained by their holding last night, and give them full credit for it.[43]

For meeting General Gouraud's challenge, Major General Lejeune was credited with putting forth a masterful battle plan, which the division carried out faithfully with success.

Lejeune issued his own statement on October 11 to the officers and men of his Second Division:

> It is beyond my power of expression to describe fitly my admiration for your heroism. You attacked magnificently and you seized Blanc Mont Ridge, the keystone of the arch constituting the enemy's main position. You advanced beyond the ridge, breaking the enemy's lines, and you held the ground gained with a tenacity which is unsurpassed in the annals of war.
>
> As a direct result of your victory, the German armies east and west of Rheims are in full retreat, and by drawing on yourselves several German divisions from other parts of the front you greatly assisted the victorious advance of the allied armies between Cambrai and St. Quentin.
>
> Your heroism and the heroism of our comrades who died on the battlefield will live in history forever, and will be emulated by the young men of our country for generations to come.
>
> To be able to say when this war is finished, "I belonged to the 2d Division; I fought with it at the battle of Blanc Mont Ridge," will be the highest honor that can come to any man.[44]

General Pershing knew full well that the Second Division was going to be successful in their dominant role, and in a report he sent forward the following praises: "The Second conquered the complicated defense works on their front against a persistent defense worthy of the grimmest period of trench warfare and attacked the strongly held wooded hill of Blanc Mont, which they captured in a second assault, sweeping over it with consummate dash and skill. This division then repulsed strong counterattacks before the village and cemetery of St. Etienne and took the town, forcing the Germans to fall back from before Rheims and yield positions they had held since September 1914."[45]

Of the four captains who reported to Hamilton, three received the Distinguished Service Cross for their duty in such trying circumstances on October 4. The three were Hunt, Cornell and Whitehead. This personal recognition would be their pinnacle accomplishment of the war. The fourth skipper, Captain Dirksen, was just getting into the thick of the battle when he was gassed and evacuated.[46]

You can't be any more in the center of the action than Major Hamilton was in "The Box." In his first battle as a battalion commander, he displayed firm leadership under the most trying conditions, with personal contributions as significant as those he displayed at Belleau Wood, but the United States government did not recognize him with an award. His actions did not go unnoticed, however, as his superiors in the Marine Corps would once again expand his leadership role with extra responsibilities in the near future. The French government, who had control of the division, stepped forward and acknowledged Hamilton's service at Blanc Mont, as General Pétain later presented him with his second individual Croix de Guerre award.

For actions at Blanc Mont, the French issued an unprecedented third Croix de Guerre award to the Fourth Brigade. No other unit in the entire American Expeditionary Forces received such recognition. Every member of the Marine Brigade was now entitled to wear the French Fourragere, which is a green and red braided rope worn around the left shoulder.[47]

On October 6, while the battle of Blanc Mont Ridge was in its final phase, the Marine Corps lost another great legend. This fellow did not die on the battlefield in France, but back in the United States. The man was Brigadier General Charles A. Doyen, who had commanded the Marines in the early days in France until May 7, 1918, when he was relieved of the Fourth Brigade and sent back to the States. Recently he had been commanding once again, this time the men at the Quantico Marine Barracks and the Overseas Training Station. He was believed to have died of influenza, commonly known as the Spanish Flu.

The Allied victories throughout the Argonne were decisive blows to Germany and the Central Powers. On the night of October 4, following the bloody full day at Blanc Mont, Germany's new chancellor, Prince Maximilian of Baden, offered a proposal for an armistice. The statement was first issued to leaders of Switzerland as mediators and upon translation the wording was forwarded to President Wilson on October 6. It read:

> The German Government requests the President of the United States of America to take steps for the restoration of peace, to notify all belligerents of this request, and to invite them to delegate plenipotentiaries for the purpose of taking up negotiations. The German Government accepts, as a basis for the peace negotiations, the program laid down by the President of the United States in his message to Congress of January 8, 1918, and in his subsequent pronouncements, particularly in his address of September 27, 1918. In order to avoid further bloodshed the German Government requests to bring about the immediate conclusion of a general armistice on land, on water, and in the air.[48]

There was a definite need for troop replacements again, as well as replenishment of equipment. Aside from one's rifle and helmet, a pair of boots was a very special piece of personal equipment. Neville, commanding the Fourth Brigade, issued an operations report to the division covering this time period, and within the body of the report, he noted: "Remarkably few men (reported, not over 50) were evacuated with foot trouble but on the last day about 20 percent of the command marched with difficulty and conditions were beginning to grow serious. The trouble was mainly due to English shoes which had been issued just before leaving the BOUY area on the 20th October. The replacements (about 1,500) recently joined, stood the marches very well considering conditions."[49]

On October 19 some men wrote letters home. They did not realize it at the time, but because of future constant movement along the front lines, it would be close to a month before they could write letters home again.

During this month it appears that Pershing may have caught wind of the confrontations at Blanc Mont on October 4, or another similar incident, for on October 24 he wrote: "When men run away in front of the enemy, officers should take summary action to stop it, even to the point of shooting men down who are caught in such disgraceful conduct."[50]

By October 25 Hamilton and his battalion, along with the rest of the brigade, had moved to the Les Islettes area and then marched to Exermont, where they remained camped in the woods until the very early morning of October 31.

It seemed apparent that Germany's fighting days were numbered, but no one was quite certain what the number would be. Could it be possible that the fighting would finally end by Christmas? Many Allied Force commanders, including General Pershing, hoped the war would not end until Germany was thoroughly defeated.

The number of replacements designated to level the battalion back to a fighting combat force was an indication that maybe the war was truly coming to an end. Every battalion in the brigade was downsized from the normal 1,000 men to a total of around 850 men. The four captains now reporting to Major Hamilton were Hunt over the 17th Company, Fisk over the 49th Company, Blake over the 66th Company and Cochran over the 67th Company.

Blake, who was cited for bravery at Belleau Wood, was now a captain with his own company. Like Hunt he had also enlisted from Berkley, California, having graduated from the University of California a year before Hunt. He had missed the battle of Blanc Mont due to an extended stay in the hospital but was now ready to serve again. Hamilton recognized the character strengths within Captain Robert Blake, and he would rely upon the well-educated true gentleman to provide many men with a steady calming influence.

Gunner Nice escaped once again from a hospital, but the trail back without paperwork was more difficult than his escape from the Château-Thierry sector. Somehow he was able to talk his way through the military police to rejoin his fellow Marines.

It was around this time that some French officials started to clash under the pressure of war, and French Prime Minister Georges Clemenceau, "The Tiger," tried to use his authority. For some reason he felt that the French were doing all the fighting and that the many American divisions were not doing their fair share. He even suggested to General Foch in writing that he could, and in fact should, replace General Pershing. The letter read, in part:

> One does not have to be a technician in order to understand that the immobility of your right wing cannot possibly be a part of your plan and that we have lost — no matter how favorably other things may have turned out — the benefit of movements which, through lack of organization, have not been effected. I am aware of all the efforts you have made to overcome the resistance of General Pershing; indeed, it is because you have omitted nothing in the way of persuasion that I cannot shirk the duty of asking myself whether, after the failure of fruitless conversations, the time has not come for changing methods.
>
> When General Pershing refused to obey your orders, you could have appealed to President Wilson. For reasons which you considered more important, you put off this solution of the conflict, fearing that it would bring reactions of a magnitude which you thought difficult to gauge.
>
> I took the liberty of differing with you. You had a right to think that I was resorting too hastily to a radical solution of the problem. You wished to prolong the experience.
>
> Now that I have learned, however, that you have taken in hand the direct command of General Pershing's troops, I cannot refrain from feeling that this trial should be the last of those we have been compelled to undergo. I ardently wish you success, and it may come, provided it is possible for you, through some miracle, to combine the separate direction of one army with the general conduct along comprehensive lines of the Allied armies as a whole.
>
> I think that it will take long for you to make up your mind on this subject. If General Pershing finally resigns himself to obedience, if he accepts the advice of capable generals, whose presence at his side he has until now permitted only that he might reject their councils, I shall be wholly delighted.
>
> But if this new attempt to reconcile two contrary points of view should not bring the advantageous results you anticipate, I must say to you that, in my opinion, any further hesitation should be out of the question. For it would then be certainly high time to tell President Wilson the truth and the whole truth concerning the situation of the American troops. Indeed, neither you nor I have the right to conceal it from him.
>
> The President of the United States has frequently declared that he was ready to conform to your judgment in all military questions. He will undoubtedly appraise at their true value, as he ought to do, both the patience you have so long shown and the decision to which you have finally been led.
>
> Whether you share my opinion or form a different one, you will certainly agree

with me in recognizing that this state of affairs cannot continue any longer. For this reason, I would be glad if you could find it possible to send me an early answer.

The reason why I have deemed it my duty to offer you these observations is that, in the present circumstance, the responsibility of the French Government and the positional head of the French armies is no less directly involved than is your own. I feel sure that you cannot misinterpret the sentiment which inspires me and I hope you will do justice to my motives, as I do to yours.

CLÉMENCEAU[51]

Foch, who was admired in France, did not agree. The topic faded away, but nevertheless, the story got back to U.S. Secretary Baker who firmly stated that a foreign leader was never going to have the authority to dismiss an American military commander.

During the late days of October, the Second Division and 89th Division were aligned under the umbrella of the V Corps, and Major General Lejeune had a new officer, U.S. Army Maj. General Charles P. Summerall, to report to. The previous Army Corps commanders had not made a profound impact upon Bundy, Harbord or Lejeune, but then again the past Army Corps commanders were not Summerall. He was a man who always left a lasting impression. Lt. Colonel Palmer, in charge of AEF press relations and an author of several pre- and post-war books, said of the general: "He is a leader compounded of all kinds of fighting qualities, a crusader and a calculating tactician, who, some say, can be as gentle as a sweet-natured chaplain, while others say that he is nothing but brimstone and ruthless determination."[52]

The fighting Marines with the Springfield rifles and bayonets saw the more blunt and brutal side of the U.S. Army general, and they did not warm up to him. Maybe part of the rub was the fact he commanded the First Division during the battles of Soissons and Saint-Mihiel and appeared to still favor Pershing's favorite division known as the "Big Red One."

Before long Pershing released an attack plan to Summerall that called for crossing the Meuse River on the evening of Saturday, November 9. On October 30 members of the Marine Brigade would hear a speech concerning the next phase. Summerall's method to detail the plan called for visiting with each battalion separately so his words would be heard more clearly. Summerall did not need an invitation; he just appeared, escorted by Lejeune, to give the news to Hamilton's battalion. Private Mackin, who had been running messages for Hamilton since early June, observed: "An army general came on a beautiful black horse and lectured us; telling combat men about the lay of the land ahead; telling men about a job to do along a route he'd mapped to reach the Meuse."[53]

His detailed plan called for the battalion, once they were across the Meuse

River on the east bank, to climb and attack three ridges full of enemy guns. In plain talk he told them that while the attack was going on he would be back at headquarters waiting to hear of their success. Hamilton's men could not stand arrogance, but they stood at attention giving proper respect to the two-star general. Sitting high on his horse with his gloves tucked into his Sam Browne belt, he often slapped his black riding crop against his booted leg to make a firm point. Mackin never forgot his final and firm parting words, as they were still ingrained in his memory many decades after the war: "— and now I say, and you remember this, on those three ridges, take no prisoners, nor should you stop to bandage your best friend."[54]

The two generals then went over and visited with the hundreds of Marines in 2/5, and Summerall gave his same speech once again. Private Richmond of the 43rd Company, who, like Mackin, was cited for bravery at Blanc Mont, recorded in his diary: "Maj. Gen. Summerall and Maj. Gen. Lejeune paid us a flying visit while we were at this place. They were only pepping us up for what was to come. Paid us a few compliments, and left before we had the opportunity to tell him what we thought about it."[55]

Summerall knew all the qualities of leadership, but either he did not fully understand the true spirit of the "Devil Dogs," or he knew he was in a position to dictate as he wished knowing that the Marines would faithfully follow all orders as given. After the war he wrote the following in an article titled "Leadership": "The exercise of the qualities that make the leader is almost as varied as the men themselves. Some act by speech and some by silence; some possess bearing or manner that carry conviction, while others, not so gifted, dominate by the force of will and the power of knowledge.... An Officer's deportment, the inflection of his voice and the expression in his face have a determining influence in gaining the confidence and control that are essential to leadership."[56]

On October 31, the day following Summerall's speech, Turkey, a Central Power country aligned with Germany, signed an armistice and dropped out of the war. The resulting impact upon this weakened country would be felt a few years later, culminating with the downfall of the notorious long-reigning Ottoman Empire.

Also on the final day of October, there was a meeting at the V Corps Headquarters with Maj. General Summerall, General Pershing and French General Maestre in attendance. As noted by Lt. Colonel Palmer:

> They were waiting when Summerall, who was hoarse from making talks to his troops, came in. "Will we go through?" both Pershing and Maestre asked Summerall. "Are you ready?"
>
> Summerall answered: "We will go through. Everything is ready. There is nothing to change."[57]

Summerall was looking forward to the hand-to-hand combat upon the ridges, but first there was to be the great push forward across land with many divisions participating. The thrust ahead could potentially break the backs of the Germans for good and end the war. That thought was plenty of motivation for the Second Division and Fourth Brigade to show General Pershing and the American public back home, one final time, what they were made of. They planned to "go through" and drive the Germans to the eastern side of the Meuse River.

The Second Division had picked up another nickname, being called the "Race Horse" Division. Major Hamilton was prepared to lead the way through the hills and valleys. The path ahead would not be smooth, as the ever abundant trenches and clusters of barbed wire were always creating more of an obstacle course. Wire cutters and other support personnel members of the Second Engineers were assigned to Hamilton's battalion in preparation of the upcoming offensive rush.

The evening before jump-off was upon them once again, and as evidenced by recordings in several Marine diaries, it was also All Hallows' Eve, commonly called Halloween.

12. The Meuse River and Armistice
Heroes to the End

The warm summer days of wheat fields and poppies were in the past and so too were the autumn sunsets along with the chalked white soil and gates of hell. As October rolled into November, Hamilton's men felt the transition both physically and psychologically. November is a rather cold month in France, and nighttime freezing temperatures and morning frost were a distinct possibility. On certain days, men could now see their breath. Daylight was getting shorter and winter was not too far away. There was no escape from the brisk, damp conditions, and fires were definitely not permitted in their current location on the Western Front. Often, the distant sun did not afford enough rays to fully dry out one's wool clothing, and everything became very clammy with moisture and mud. Personal hygiene was difficult to maintain, but the men had no alternative but to tough it out.

They were to carry out the final phase of the Meuse-Argonne Offensive, called the "Victory Drive," starting promptly on the first day of November. In the very early hours of Friday, November 1, 1918, the Second Division was located south of Landres-et-St. Georges.

Lejeune's division was given a prime spot for the upcoming attack. The Allied plan called for Summerall's V Corps, with the Second and 89th Divisions, to line up in the middle; with Lt. General Hunter Liggett's I Corps, consisting of the 77th, 78th and 80th Divisions, on the left; and the III Corps, under Major General John L. Hines, with the 5th and 90th Divisions, on the right. The V Corps was to function as the wedge point for the two outside Army Corps groups. Summerall was relishing the personal challenge to show not only Liggett and Hines, but others above what results he could attain with his new divisions.

Within the "Race Horse" Division, the 23rd Infantry was taking the right side, the Sixth Regiment the left side, and the Fifth Regiment the very middle ground, with the Ninth Infantry in reserve. The land ahead, towards two small villages, was full of steep hills and valleys. The initial plan called for a multitude of tank support, but when "H-hour" came only about a dozen-and-a-half small tanks were accounted for as division support.

Brigadier General Neville was ready, awaiting orders to pass on to both Colonel Feland's Fifth Regiment and Colonel Lee's Sixth Regiment. Hamilton's men were damp, cold and numb, yet primed for what lay ahead. The good news was twofold. There would not be a mad rush to the jump-off position, and French flank support was not a part of the plans.

Again the major had his men secure their lighter combat packs. Potentially they might cover many miles in the coming days, and they needed to be very agile. With fixed bayonets, they hoped the dash forward would turn into a rout.

At 0330 the artillery opened up, and the November action was under way. After a couple of hours of shelling, the Marines of 1/5 pushed away at 0530. Following the map, Hamilton and his battalion took the assault role in their designated zone, followed by 2/5 in support and 3/5 in reserve.

The divisional artillery continued to lead the troops with precise bombing, and the initial early morning fighting was progressing favorably. Still, there were scattered machine gun nests that were a constant nuisance, but they were located randomly and not as firmly entrenched as at Blanc Mont. The rapid advancement of the Second Division quickly took care of these elements. It appeared that the faster the rush the quicker the enemy, yelling "Kamerad," threw his hands in the air. The many prisoners were immediately sent to the rear.

With Major Hamilton's battalion leading the point wedge at the start, everyone in the regiment knew what the set pace would be, and, in fact, the entire division might have guessed this one correctly. The rapid movement forward soon turned into a chase as Hamilton and 1/5 were constantly on the heels of the Germans. After two and a half hours of combat, Hamilton noted five officers were casualties. Captain Cochran was severely wounded, and 1st Lieutenant Aaron Ferch was killed. The good news was that at 0800 his battalion had advanced about two miles and accomplished their first objective. At this point 2/5 took the lead, and 1/5 followed in their designated path.

The Sixth Regiment made similar progress that morning. Major Shuler in command of 3/6 was keeping pace and had achieved his objective, but the Sixth Regiment had also lost several officers.

The movement forward soon reached into small villages. In the town of Landreville, the Boche was waiting with machine guns set up in windows, but this situation was soon brought under control. At around noon, 3/5 leap-frogged ahead of 2/5, and Hamilton and 1/5 took up the rear. They were on their way to Bayonville.

12. The Meuse River and Armistice

Lejeune's Third Brigade, with the Ninth and 23rd Infantry, was also having success. Meanwhile Summerall's 89th Division was having a little more difficulty, and some members of the Second Division's Sixth Regiment assisted their movement forward.

The pace continued to elevate for the "Race Horse" Division, and the only serious obstacle the Marines were now facing was that some Allied artillery was not leading the battalions enough. Lejeune's men had been going so fast in achieving objectives and capturing prisoners that they were running into their own shelling. Major Hamilton and all the "Devil Dogs" were on the loose at a brisk clip, and with all their success they certainly did not want to slow down. Instead they quickly passed word back for the Allied artillery to increase the firing distances, before it became a serious issue.

The men of 3/5 met their objective in the early afternoon, and Hamilton and 1/5 quickly leapfrogged into the lead again. Within an hour and a half they had attained an additional objective with a couple of hours of sunlight still remaining. They had rushed for more than six miles through the terrain containing hills, edges of forest, valleys with barbed wire, streams and villages.

With everything now going their way, Hamilton and the many other warriors finally called the day complete and wound down for a well deserved rest. Lejeune spent the evening in a house that had not been demolished in the village of Landres-et-St. Georges sharing his room with medical officers Derby and Boone.[1]

Credit for the long successful day was given to the many men and officers involved, from the top military commanders planning the offense to those carrying out the mission. Within the Second Division it was once again a team effort, from the assigned artillery group to the engineers to the fighting men, who in the center of the Meuse-Argonne action broke through the Hindenburg Line. U.S. Army Lt. Colonel Palmer interestingly noted that the events on this day were among his most memorable moments of the entire war. "We knew by the morning of Nov. 2 that the war was won," he said.[2]

When it came to the Second Division, they were reliable and success was predictable, yet nothing could be finer for Summerall than to hear of their job well done. To show his appreciation he issued an official memo:

> Headquarters Fifth Army Corps,
> Army Expeditionary Forces.
> France, 2d November, 1918
>
> From: Commanding General, Fifth Army Corps.
> To: Commanding General, Second Division.
> Subject: Commendation.
>
> I desire to add to my telephone message the assurance of my deep apprecia-

tion and profound admiration for the manner in which the Second Division executed the mission allotted to it on November first.

The Division's brilliant advance of more than nine kilometers, destroying the last stronghold on the Hindenburg Line, capturing the Freya Stellung, and going more than nine kilometers against not only the permanent but relieving forces in their front, may justly be regarded as one of the most remarkable achievements made by any troops in this war. For the first time, perhaps, in our experience the losses inflicted by your division upon the enemy in the offensive greatly exceeded the casualties of the Division. The reports indicate, moreover that in a single day the Division has captured more artillery and machine guns than usually falls to the lot of a command during several days of hard fighting. These results must be attributed to the great dash and speed of the troops, and to the irresistible force with which they struck and overcame the enemy.

The Division has more than justified the distinguished confidence placed in it by the Commander-in-Chief when it was selected to take the lead in advance from which such great results are expected. It is an honor to command such troops, and they have richly deserved a place in history and the affection of their countrymen, which is not exceeded, or perhaps paralleled, in the life of our nation.

I desire that you convey these sentiments to the officers and soldiers of the Second Division and that you assure them of my abiding wishes for their continued success in the campaign that lies before it."

C. P. Summerall,
Major General, Commanding.

John A. Lejeune
Major General U. S. M. C. Commanding.[3]

The terrific gains from the first day by Major Hamilton's men and others in the brigade set a benchmark for others to follow, creating friendly internal competition within their own division. The Third Brigade's Ninth and 23rd Infantry Regiments wanted to continue to show everyone what they were capable of achieving.

Throughout Saturday, November 2, a cold rain poured down, and the men were once again on the move, sinking about three inches with each soggy step. Random enemy artillery shells burst along with shrapnel bombs, exploding about 20 feet in the air over the men's heads. In the air a few enemy sausage-shaped observation balloons appeared, and at times German planes dropped bombs and even hand grenades. When it got too intense, Hamilton and other commanders got their men into the woods for added protection.

It appeared that for the first time on the Western Front, the overall advancements of the second day would be greater than that of the first day. The Germans were retreating so fast that the Second Division and other divisions in the area were noted to be using trucks to catch up with the enemy. There was pride within the Second Division to avoid having any other division beat them to the Meuse River. With the dash on, it seemed as though everyone in the AEF wanted a piece of the action. The officers and men in support divisions were filtered in behind the front line divisions. All were moving in the same eastward direction.

Back before Belleau Wood, it was mighty coincidental that George and his brother, Burley, met in battle and had a chance to talk with each other. Other rare instances happened, as witnessed by Division Surgeon Derby. On November 3, after visiting several hospitals, he was traveling behind the lines and ran into his brother-in-law Captain Kermit Roosevelt of the Seventh Field Artillery, First Division. They had not seen each other for several months, and while catching up on Quentin's death and other issues, another brother-in-law, Lt. Colonel Theodore Roosevelt, the commander of the 26th Infantry Regiment, also of the "Big Red One" Division, passed by and enthusiastically joined in on the conversation.[4]

Rather than rest on the evening of November 3, Lejeune and the commander of the Ninth Infantry devised an unusual nighttime plan to keep moving forward. Members of the Ninth Infantry simply headed down the road through darkness, while the soldiers in the regiment who spoke German engaged in loud conversation. The Germans were unaware the Americans were so close and simply ignored the regiment as they passed through capturing several officers. One U.S. Army historian stated: "The Second Division on the left of the 89th accomplished one of the most remarkable feats of the war. On the night of November 3rd after the Marine Brigade had broken through the enemy's positions the 9th and 23rd Infantry Regts. were formed in column on the road leading north to Beaumont ... while at La Tuilerie Farm the advance guards found the place occupied by German officers sitting around tables with lights burning. They were thrown into dismay by the appearance of American troops whom they thought were many kilometers to the south."[5]

During the night of November 4 and the early hours of November 5, Lejeune's division had the towns of Beaumont and Letanne under control and forced the enemy into a retreat across the Meuse River. The rapid advancement by Hamilton's battalion and others in the division had created some communication problems. The Germans had their own issues and were retreating so fast that they decided to cause further destruction. Roads, railways and bridges were demolished, and land mines were placed in selected locations in an attempt to slow the progression of the American Expeditionary Forces.

By November 5 and 6 the Second Division was on the heights overlooking the Meuse River. Protecting their southern right side was the 89th Division, which was maintaining a position where they could view the French village of Pouilly situated across the river. Within the 89th Division a small patrol of 314th Engineers led by U.S. Army Lt. Colonel Brehon B. Somervell was scouting and probing around a damaged bridge crossing the river. After surveying the bridge, the lieutenant colonel and two of his engineers were able to cross the Meuse and advance more than 500 yards, while keeping track of the enemy. For his action Lt. Colonel Somervell was issued the Distinguished Service Cross. Somervell was only two months older than Hamilton, but when Hamilton entered high school as a freshman, Somervell was already a senior, graduating with the Central High class of 1909.[6]

The forward progression and fighting of Hamilton's battalion had subsided for the time being. The pause would give them time to assess their situation. During the afternoon Hamilton's 17th and 66th Companies sent a combined patrol of about 40 men to scout the Meuse River bank to identify enemy positions. They returned eight hours later with information that many Germans were dug in directly ahead on the east bank and that a crossing at this current location was not the best avenue.

Captain Whitehead, who had been injured at Blanc Mont, had recovered enough to make it back to serve his men once again as skipper of the 67th Company. He replaced the injured Captain Cochran and was ready to assist and follow orders from Major Hamilton.

November 7 was yet another rainy, bone-chilling day. Captain John W. Thomason Jr. of the 49th Company had been along side Hamilton since the early days of Belleau Wood and survived "The Box" at Blanc Mont. It was reassuring to Hamilton knowing that the officer was still along fighting and sketching as he went. The incessant cold rain however had taken its toll on Thomason's immune system, and with a 104 degree temperature, he had to temporarily fall out and receive medical assistance.[7]

There was a constant trail of others like Thomason, who became weak with severe cold symptoms. During this week, the Second Division, which was already less than full strength, was losing about 500 men a day, 100 of which were battle casualties and 400 due to illness. Each battalion in the Fourth Brigade was now drastically reduced in size and losing more men each day. Most of these illnesses did not display symptoms of the Spanish Flu epidemic, which was killing many in Europe and America. It was exceptionally rare for the men in the open outdoors on the Western Front to get the flu. Military personnel who contracted the flu were usually well behind the front lines and indoors. Bronchitis and other cold symptoms were more common side effects from constant exposure to dampness and temperature fluctuations.

The wooden bridges crossing the Meuse River had been strategically destroyed by the enemy and had to be rebuilt. It was the responsibility of the Second Engineers to build the bridges, as without the structures troops could not advance forward. But at this moment, what type of bridges should they construct? The division's engineers were at a local sawmill in Beaumont, about three and a half miles from the river, hastily constructing many bridges with different specifications depending upon their intended use. Their priorities constantly changed as new plans unfolded revealing different needs and circumstances. Word came that the focus was now to be centered upon four temporary floating raft footbridges, so other construction plans were immediately pushed aside. They had practiced making this type of bridge many times, and therefore they were fully prepared to meet this new challenge.

The footbridges were to be constructed in 12-foot sections using available scrap wood taken from old German barracks as well as lumber from destroyed buildings in the villages of Beaumont and Letanne. The boardwalk itself was constructed by lashing six-foot-wide support boards as a bottom layer. Footboards were constructed by lashing three 2" × 12" × 12' wooden planks together. The top layer planks, upon which the men were to walk, would therefore be a total of only three feet wide. Once the top planks were placed perpendicular on top of the six-foot-wide support boards, they were all securely lashed together.[8]

The rain and cold continued to linger all day on November 8. Hamilton's men tried to find deep holes to crawl into for protection from the wind and other elements; however, a deep hole also gathered much rainwater. Wool blankets and overcoats were soaked, but on the positive side, the metal helmets served as small umbrellas with constant droplets falling from the rim. Still optimism prevailed through the old adage and obvious assessment that there is always someone worse off.

As fires were not an option, hiking was one way to warm up, but the men were in a waiting mode without a destination to hike to. On November 9 the limited marching was through ankle deep mud, as Hamilton and others in the Marine Brigade headed towards the rail lines at the Meuse River. It readily became apparent that the original plan to cross the Meuse River on this day was not going to happen. The bridges were just not ready to be deployed, and the crossing was now designated for the following day, Sunday the 10th. The current conditions were hurry up and wait.

Foch was another official who was not overly pleased with the war winding down. Back on November 3, 1914, in the early days of the war, he lost a son in battle and this further fueled his determination. As the top commander he intended to use his authority to stress his views. On November 9, General Pershing received a telegram at 2045 from Foch with orders stating: "The enemy, disorganized by our repeated attacks, is withdrawing along the whole front. It is important to maintain and hasten our action. I appeal to the energy and the initiative of the commanders in chief and their armies to secure decisive results."[9]

Due to Hamilton's illustrious track record of taking on the toughest assignments with overwhelming success, he was now given the additional responsibility of commanding not just one, but two battalions and even more. Along with the 17th, 49th, 66th and 67th Companies of 1/5, he was now given command of the four companies in 2/5, consisting of the 18th, 43rd, 51st and 55th Companies. The plan called for Captain Hunt to oversee 1/5, while Captain Dunbeck was to monitor 2/5, with both officers reporting to Major Hamilton. Being in command of two small battalions, the major was definitely performing the normal duties of a lieutenant colonel.

The Marine Brigade was now called upon to represent and serve the Second Division with one final charge of their own by executing Summerall's directives. The U.S. Marines, known as "The First to Fight," were now to follow orders that potentially called for the comrades to be the last to fight. On the east bank of the Meuse River, the Germans were securely positioned on ridges with plenty of ammunition, just as Summerall had envisioned. The west bank was clear and would serve as the staging area. Crossing the river would require additional readiness along with superb efforts by all members executing the plan.

Come Sunday, November 10, word was spreading from the ground up that the war might be ending the following day. One can never underestimate the astute abilities of the many volunteer privates, who over time had acquired their own means and sources for gathering facts. As a group they had a definite knack of often finding out in advance what was going on, and quite often their information was exceptionally accurate. When a fellow returned to his company from a hospital stay, he frequently brought the latest scoop with him. Numerous men had returned to the brigade recently, bringing with them fresh exciting news, but talk of peace remained a rumor.

Did the fighting Germans at this point have a feeling that the Armistice was forthcoming the next day? There is no concrete evidence; however, as their country was also in the negotiations it is quite likely that word leaked out to them too.

There was noticeable tempered joy and mixed emotions among the troops. They were joyful about the possibility of war ending the next day, but they also vividly remembered the words from Summerall foretelling of the dangerous work ahead. For the time being it was hard to get too excited.

On what would end up being the eve of the Armistice, thoughts of a possible night's sleep quickly vanished when word spread down the line for the Marines to be quiet and to prepare for a hasty assault in the coming hours. Through the early evening darkness, Hamilton and his two battalions now headed off through the woods towards the river.

Two of the four pontoon bridges were to be erected to the north, near

12. The Meuse River and Armistice

Mouzon, where the Sixth Regiment along with 3/5 were to cross. Major Shuler, commanding 3/6, would be in charge of this entire northern crossing and coordinate with the other battalion leaders: Major George A. Stowell over 1/6, Major Clyde H. Metcalf over 2/6 and Major Larsen with 3/5. The plan called for troops to cross both bridges simultaneously.

The engineers' other two temporary bridges were designated for a location a few miles south of Mouzon, but north of Letanne, at Villemontry. Major Hamilton was given full control of the southern crossing, and he would also command a third battalion comprised of the U.S. Army Second Battalion of the 356th Infantry in the 89th Division, under the leadership of Major Mark Hanna. This location called for the battalion from the 89th Division along with 2/5 from the Marine Brigade, to make the crossing, while Hamilton's original 1/5 Marines would be in reserve. Once across the river, Hamilton's battalions would support Shuler's northern battalions.

Meanwhile, the Germans who were once again comfortably settled on the high ground, started using machine guns, trench mortars and artillery, unloading everything they had at random towards the west bank. At around 1630 the Second Division Artillery, assisted by others along the Western Front, started firing back with their own artillery barrage. It was as if the fine-tuned orchestra was elevating the pitch of bombardment and explosions to a final dominating crescendo. Why save the ammunition? If the war was possibly to end, just lob away.

The Second Engineers headed out in different directions to the two distant locations. The engineers destined for Hamilton's southern river location consisted of 200 men from Company A and 150 men from Company B. They loaded four individual 12-foot sections onto each wagon for transport. Once eight wagons were full with a total of 32 sections, they departed Beaumont around 1900. Although the November full moon would not appear until the 18th, the half moon this evening appeared bright. The plan called for removing the sections from the wagons 900 yards from the river to avoid alerting the Germans; however, as they approached the river they could not help but notice a massive fog bank that obscured the entire river. Under these conditions the wagons were able to descend about an additional 500 yards down a second road towards the river unnoticed.

The men then unloaded the sections and dragged them 125 yards to an elevated double railroad track. Once over the tracks they descended 250 yards down the bank to the river's edge. The slope to the river was quite steep, and due to gravel, loose soil and underbrush, the footing was extremely difficult.

Meanwhile, up the river to the north, the other contingent of engineers using their trade were quickly lashing their sections together. With artillery fire everywhere, erecting these pontoon bridges was obviously one of their most difficult tasks in the entire war. The river banks were extremely muddy, and it was easy to sink and be temporarily stuck in the mud. This was certainly not a good location to stand stationary for an extended period of time. While the first northern bridge was being erected, the Germans identified the plot and immediately increased their artillery and machine gun fire. This action prevented a second bridge from being constructed, and with only one partial bridge and explosions everywhere, it soon became evident to Shuler and the engineers that the crossing was not going to take place in this northern location. Shuler then instructed the Marines in the Sixth Regiment and 3/5 to head to sheltered dugouts for protective cover for the remainder of the night. Efforts to cross could still be made up to 0400 on November 11, but after that hour, hints of daylight would start to appear and likely the fog would recede.

Without a northern crossing the success of the overall mission now rested one more time on the shoulders of Hamilton. As long as he was alive, he planned to execute the orders just as they were given to him. That was a part of his duty that he faithfully agreed to perform at his initial swearing-in ceremony as a U.S. Marine Corps officer.

For certain reasons the battalion from the 89th Division was not going to be able to meet their obligation to be in place for the scheduled H-hour crossing. It was imperative that Hamilton have two battalions at his service, so he immediately notified his 1/5 Marines currently in reserve that they needed to step up and fill the void. Captain Hunt's men in 1/5 were now making a profound last-minute mental transition and preparing for battle.

Hamilton and both battalions traversed through woods towards the river at a fast pace and finally located the proper path down the sloped bank to the ravine at the rivers edge. As they descended to the river, they too entered the heavy, damp mystic fog. This natural asset was certainly a blessing, as the thick cover kept them from facing total annihilation. Was the air colder than the water or was it the other way around?

At the southern location where the bridges were being erected the river was generally 60 yards wide with a varying depth from five to 25 feet.[10] The water was frigid and the recent rains had nourished the river, providing a very strong current.

In the valley of the west river bank, the Second Engineers were hastily lashing the footbridge together. While engineers from A Company worked on both sides of one bridge, the B Company group toiled on the second bridge about 400 yards away. The fog bank was so thick that the muted colors of the abundant flares in the sky could hardly be seen less than a football field away. With such poor visibility, most of the random German machine gun fire was directed over their heads towards the railroad tracks and roads, but some engineers were hit by errant flares descending through the heavy mist.

Once complete, the footbridge to the western bank was secured with 30-foot anchor lines. The far end of the bridge was released, and the flow of the river's current took it across to the eastern shore. A few engineers went along for the ride to complete the final details of securing the bridge on the opposite side of the river. The engineers entered the water to assist getting the floating bridge completed. The bridge constructed by the A Company was released and secured on the opposite bank within an amazing seven minutes. The B Company at the other bridge had a little more difficulty, and it took an additional four to six minutes to completely secure the bridge in place.

The Germans finally took notice of the second bridge just as it was completed, and instantly machine guns opened fire all over the area, along with an assortment of artillery and gas. Major Hamilton's men in 2/5 would not be able to cross at this location until the machine gun nests on the east bank were wiped out. One of Hamilton's 2/5 Marines, who had been through the entire war, stated, "The shelling throughout the night was the heaviest that I had been through so far during the war."[11]

The Marines, having been in hot zones like this before, understood danger they were in right away. Even with poor visibility, the river bank was not a place to stay long. The Maxim bullets had an unobstructed path across the river, just as they did back in June before sunrise across the open, lush fields. The Marines did not like their current location, and they wanted to get moving somewhere fast, even if the direction took them straight into enemy fire. As in past battles, forward might eventually be safer, at least for some, and if they were to die, they wanted to die fighting, not standing around.

Under present conditions, Major Hamilton informed his officers that the plan now centered upon Captain Hunt and the First Battalion, Fifth Regiment, crossing on the upper bridge. Summerall's orders called for all six battalions to be across the river, and now only one, less-than-full-size battalion would attempt to execute the initial operation. Once across and settled on the east bank, the battalion was to proceed with the difficult task of wiping out the German machine gun nests and areas of heavy resistance. When the preliminary area was relatively secure, Captain Dunbeck and 2/5 were to venture across. If successful, hopefully other battalions would be able to follow at some point in time.

Hamilton's 1/5 Marines knew the difficult task at hand. Every member had a good reason for being on edge and nervous, but it would be comforting knowing that once again their major was going to be at their side, going every inch of the way, with his '03 Springfield. As one private in the group said, "Men took deep breaths to fortify themselves before walking into hell."[12]

Hamilton had one final dash and what a dash it was to be. The moment for jump-off had come. One member of the group described the scene: "The major came afoot, still talking hurriedly. Seeing him, the fellows scrambled up. Enough of waiting. The major blew a single shortened blast and stepped forward, placing one foot on the floating stuff. He never sent a fellow where he wouldn't go himself."[13]

Major Hamilton was then bumped out of the way and into the mucky river bank. The fellow must have been a very big one, perhaps 6' 4" Private Robert W. Dudley of the 49th Company, or likely just one of many overly aggressive Marines called to action one more time and raring to assist the major with his objective. Hamilton might have been a little stunned at first, but then again these were his men, whom he had trained and molded to act accordingly to his style and methods. Every Marine was extremely unselfish and willing to sacrifice his life for his comrade.

In the mix was 2nd Lieutenant Cukela of the 66th Company. He had fought in every 1/5 battle to date, and after quick recuperation from the battle of Blanc Mont, he was anxious to be back with the men. He had a notorious reputation for knowing only one direction, which was always forward and forward he would go.[14]

Private Mortensen joined Cukela and his skipper, Blake, heading across the pontoon bridge. Who were the other brave warriors trying to make a go of it? Private Michael P. Webber in the 49th Company was moving fast; other last names of other 1/5 privates appear to have been Budde, Naegle, Rutlidge, Marsh, LeBlanc, McCracken, Van Dyke, Frost, Tintera, Oldroyd, Bowers, Gideon, Anselm, Richeson, McCarthy and Musolf. The dash was on, and Major Hamilton got back on his feet and quickly found his place in line.

As the width of the footbridge was only three feet, the Marines, as representatives of the "Indian Head" Division, went single file, Indian style. The path ahead on the flimsy bridge was reminiscent of past individual and team skill obstacle-course relay drills from their basic training days at Quantico and Parris Island. Now they were involved with the real deal. If the over-anxious men got to close to each other and bunched up, the bridge started to sink, so they quickly learned to space themselves 15 to 20 feet apart, leaving them only ankle deep in water. At the halfway point the eastern bank was still not visible, although through the fog one could see the muted hot yellow flashes of the machine guns ahead.

Under the extreme conditions many casualties occurred during the crossing. Men later recalled hearing a "sock" noise that meant only one thing, the sound of a bullet hitting the flesh of a man in front or behind. Some wounded men ended up drowning in the river, while a few jumped into the river, believing it was safer, only to find that the strong current along with their weighted equipment was a lot to handle.

12. The Meuse River and Armistice

At about 2230 the men in 1/5 were finally across. This was not the time to stop and make a lot of assessments. Hamilton had given Captain Hunt and his men proper assignments, and with no time to waste, they were venturing off to complete their first objective.

A famous painting by Fredrick C. Yohn, titled "The Last Night of the War," portrays the final assault by certain members of the Fifth Regiment across the Meuse River on the east bank held by the Germans. Major Hamilton is depicted in the middle of the group holding his helmet under fire. Today the original painting is one of the most prized possessions, among many, in the Marine Corps Art Collection at the Naval Heritage Center.

To their advantage, some Americans had made it across the river without many Germans noticing them. Using the element of surprise to attack, Hamilton, Hunt and 1/5 completed their primary objective of clearing the German machine gun nests. Captain Dunbeck and 2/5 then came across before midnight at around 2330.

Due to continuous explosions, both bridges now needed repairs and new lashings in certain sections. Some crew members in the Eighth Machine Gun Company and one unit of the 23rd Machine Gun Company apparently also made it across, but for the remainder of the night and into the early morning,

"The Last Night of the War," painting by Fredrick C. Yohn, featuring Major Hamilton with his Fifth Marines on the east bank after crossing the Meuse River (courtesy Naval Historical Center).

there was not going to be any additional infantry support. They were now cut off from all communication with headquarters. Major Hamilton and others had recently been subjected to being in "The Box," and as before, they did not panic but continued with their given tasks, applying their training and experience to their advantage. The entire force was on a mission and not looking back.

Hamilton had Dunbeck's four companies in 2/5 head northeast with orders to later split apart and accomplish individual objectives. The major instructed Hunt's 1/5 to proceed towards the elevated enemy positions that Summerall described during his detailed speech on October 30. Once on top of the ridges, the men were then to continue pursuing other planned objectives. Because the current battalion was so small, the four companies were to a certain extent functioning as one mobile unit. Two members of the 17th Company, Corporal William J. Furguson and Private Hans M. Naegle, received recognition for silencing an enemy machine gun.

By dawn on Monday November 11, Hamilton's battalions had the three elevated ridges under control, but there were still many pockets of resistance. With their original objective accomplished, other assisting forces, if designated, could now cross the pontoon bridges without being under serious attack. Communication through runners was also restored. Major Hamilton took a moment to review the action in a message to his brigade commander, Brig. General Neville:

> 1st and 2d Bns. of the 5th Marines did not complete the crossing of the Meuse until 11:30 P.M. last night due to heavy shelling, a break in upper bridge and confusion of moving in dark. The Bn. of the 89th got lost at the start and at 6:00 A.M. this date [11/11] had only gathered together some 300 men. Major Hanna was here but has disappeared now. Crossing made under heavy artillery and machine gun fire. The 1st Bn. on the right, ran into a machine gun nest immediately after crossing and had great trouble keeping the men together. The entire Bn., numbering approximately 100 men, is now combined as a company and under command of Captain Hunt. The 2d Bn. advanced to the north through the Bois des Flaviers but had to hold up movement until daybreak on account of machine gun nests and heavy underbrush. This morning at 6:30 A.M. the 2d Bn. on the left and the Bn. of the 89th on the right advanced toward the objective. Sniping and machine guns overcome and advance going smoothly at present. Enemy artillery fire heavy. On account of the small number of men it is going to be difficult to organize this position in depth. Urge that another battalion be sent across the river to reinforce us. Message just received from captain Dunbeck states that advance progressing satisfactory and that he is taking many machine guns.[15]

Hamilton's 1/5, which had traversed the pontoon bridge first, suffered the worst casualties, but 2/5 was also hit hard. Private George W. Budde of 1/5 made it across the bridge, but was killed on the final day of the war while on a scouting mission. He was posthumously issued the Distinguished Service Award. Casualties continued up until 11 A.M. on November 11, 1918, when the Armistice took effect. There is no evidence that casualties occurred within the Marine Corps after 1100.[16]

With daylight, and the Armistice, members of the Fourth Brigade, who remained on the western bank, were out and moving along the river bank. Through the entire war Cpl. Henry Kindig had witnessed many awful sights. The Marine attached to the Sixth Regiment that was unable to cross the river at the northern location, mentioned in his diary: "Took a walk to Meuse and saw one of the most horrible sights I ever witnessed. Fifth reg. boys were laying dead along the roads in columns."[17]

Private Clarence Richmond, who made it across with 2/5, saw the same loss of life and stated:

> It could be seen that the hillside or bluff along the river was lined with machine guns and trench mortars. From their elevated position, they commanded a full sweep of the river, and it was very evident that had there not been a heavy fog during the night, which had made the flares of no avail, we would have suffered greater casualties, if not complete annihilation. Near the small bridge, the bank of the river was strewn with our dead. I counted about twenty-five within a distance of a hundred yards. Several shells had hit directly where we had laid along the bank of the river. Nearly all of one platoon of one of the other companies had been either killed or wounded. All the dead still lay where they had fallen.
>
> On the opposite side of the river, the dead were more numerous. Here wad [*sic*] had suffered our greatest casualties. As many as four and five dead could be seen around many single shell holes, and in two or three instances, I saw as many as eight lying around a single shell hole.[18]

On the last day of the war, headquarters in all locations worked frantically to pass the official word of the Armistice to all chains of command further down the line. Messages were sent by all appropriate means available, through telegraph, telephone, as well as runners, to the Western Front. Because Major Hamilton and the battalions under his command played distinguished roles on this historic day, it is worthwhile to look at the official documents, starting from the top down. First was the official signing of the Armistice as noted by Ferdinand Foch:

> The present Armistice was signed on the 11th day of November, 1918, at 5 o'clock A.M. (French time).
>
> *Signed*
>
> F. FOCH   ERZBERGER
> R. E. WEMYSS OBERNDORFF
>   WINTERFELDT
>   VANSELOW[19]

Second, from the Allied Commander Foch to his numerous commanders-in-chief, including Pershing of the American Expeditionary Forces, came:

> Headquarters Second Division (Regular)
> American Expeditionary Forces,
> *France, 11 November, 1918, at 10 hours.*
>
> Secret.Field orders No. 62.
> 1. The following messages have been received:
> 6:01 A.M., November 11, 1918: Official radio from Paris:
> Marshal Foch to the commanders in chief:
> 1. Hostilities will be stopped on the entire front beginning at 11 o'clock November 11 (French hour)
> 2. The Allied troops will not go beyond the line reached at that hour on that date until further orders.
>
> Mars'hal Foch
> (5:45 A.M.)[20]

General Pershing then notified his commanders in the First, Second and Third Armies. They all sent forth word to their commanders beneath them in the various army corps. Major General Charles P. Summerall, commander of the Fifth Corps, received his message and issued a telephone message to Maj. General Lejeune as well as other divisional commanders.

> Headquarters Fifth Army Corps,
> American Expeditionary Forces,
> *France, November 11, 1818, 8:30 hours.*
>
> {Second Division.
> Commanding General {Thirty-ninth Division
> {Seventy-seventh Division
>
> Armistice signed and takes effect at 11 o'clock this morning. Accurate map, showing location of the front line elements, patrols, and detachments, will be sent to these headquarters without delay.
>
> Telephone exact location of front line at 12 noon to-day to G-3, Fifth Army Corps.
>
> W. B. Burtt,
> *Chief of Staff.*[21]

Brigadier General Wendell Neville, commanding the Fourth Brigade, received word from Lejeune and issued his important memorandum:

> Headquarters 4th Brigade,
> Marines, American E.F.,
> 11th November '18 — 8:40 A.M.
>
> Peace Memorandum No 1.
>
> The following telephone message received from Surprise 1 at 8:35 A.M. this morning forwarded for compliance.
>
> 8:40 A.M. message from 5th Corps: Armistice signed and takes effect at 11 this morning. Accurate map showing locations of front line elements including patrols and detachments, will be sent to those Headquarters without delay.[22]

12. The Meuse River and Armistice

Colonel Feland over the Fifth Regiment soon received Neville's notification. Once acknowledged, he sent forth his own written memo to be sent to Major Hamilton. Feland knew getting the notification to Hamilton on the extreme Western Front was going to be a very daunting task:

Nov. 11, 1918.—9:10 A.M.

To Major Hamilton:
All firing will cease at 11 A.M. today. Hold every inch of ground that you have gained, including that gained by patrols. Send in as soon as possible a sketch showing positions of all until 11 A.M.

(Signed) Feland.[23]

Although the fighting stopped at 1100, Major Hamilton was properly holding his territory and following orders until official notification arrived. His dash had taken his men forward to such a distant and remote location over rugged terrain that inevitably a courier would have difficulty making contact with him. Most assuredly the major was in his proper location, as noted by his strong record of always ending up where he was supposed to be. The eight small Marine companies and the battalion of the 89th under his ultimate command were scattered around the surrounding vicinity. One noted historian stated, "It appears as though the 66th Company had penetrated farthest eastward."[24]

Captain Blake was guarding the area with his 66th Company. The company was down to about 25 active men, and having not "dropped out," Cukela and Mortensen were a part of the active group.

The consensus among the "Devil Dogs" was that Cukela was one of the most colorful characters in the entire Marine Corps, and he had even caught the attention of General Pershing and the entire AEF through an assortment of cartoons. His eccentric hard-nosed personality is best exemplified by his unforgettable saying, "Next time I send a damn fool, I'll go myself."[25] Additionally, it appeared that Cukela would end up as the most decorated U.S. Marine of World War I, having received the Medal of Honor, the French Croix de Guerre twice, the French Legion of Honor and many more awards.[26]

In the early afternoon Captain Blake and his small unit from 1/5 were requested to assist Captain Dunbeck, commanding 2/5, on a search mission. With afternoon fog still present everywhere, they followed a path single file towards the commotion. Blake described the final moments:

And after we got down a ways, I could hear the Germans shouting and wheels moving around. The column stopped. The word came back to send up an interpreter. I thought maybe Captain Dunbeck wanted to send somebody down through the woods to see if he could hear anything, pick up any information. We waited and waited and waited and nothing happened. So I got impatient and walked up to the head of the column, and there at the gates of this village—an old village that had apparently once been walled — Captain Dunbeck was standing with a short of half smile on his face, and across the road were a half a dozen Germans, no helmets, no arms, no anything. I said, "What goes on here?" He said, "These damn fools say the war is over." I said, "What are we going to do?" "Well," he said, "they don't care what we do. We can take them prisoner, do anything we want. They're through."

So we went back up the hill. Major Hamilton, who then was the battalion commander, had just arrived; and as I walked up, a runner handed him a message. I think it was about 1:30 then, and that was the official information that the war was over. So we were informed that the war was over two and a half hours afterwards, and we got our first word from the Germans.[27]

When you think of the title and phrase *All Quiet on the Western Front*, Major Hamilton was the final high-ranking officer in the entire American Expeditionary Forces, and perhaps the entire Western Front, to hear the welcome news that the war was over. As the official notice was received declaring the Great War was over, Major Hamilton and 2nd Lieutenant Cukela were together at the end.

General Pershing later reflected upon what transpired as Hamilton and his Marines crossed the pontoon bridges facing adversity up until the Armistice. In his synopsis he stated:

> In consequence of the foregoing instructions, our Second Army pressed the enemy along its entire front. On the night of the 10th-11th and the morning of the 11th the Fifth Corps, in the First Army, forced a crossing of the Meuse east of Beaumont and gained the commanding heights within the reentrant of the river, thus completing our control of the Meuse River line. At 6 A.M. on the 11th notification was received from Marshall Foch's headquarters that the Armistice had been signed and that hostilities would cease at 11 A.M. Preparatory measures had already been taken to ensure the prompt transmission to the troops of the announcement of an Armistice. However, the advance east of Beaumont on the morning of the 11th had been so rapid and communication across the river was so difficult that there was some fighting on isolated portions of that front after 11 A.M.[28]

The greatest war the world had known, involving many countries, had come to a halt. There were many ongoing celebrations around the globe and in the States back home. Most men in the American Expeditionary Forces joined the cheer and rejoiced. Hamilton's men experienced a much more solemn evening. Their mixed emotions were filled with joy, sorrow and much reflection. The Marines dreamed of going home, but at the same time they were consumed with heavy thoughts of their fellow comrades who had died in the past 24 hours. That thought and sadness would inevitably remain with the survivors for the rest of their lives. Semper Fidelis.

His men camped for the night on a hill beyond the river, and although peace was assured, they remained professional, keeping a distance of about a half mile from the Germans. In their current precarious eastward location, they did not fully let down their guard, but rather continued to remain at a relaxed alert through the night. Many Germans could be heard singing. Their pleasant voices traveled through the peaceful air, and they were said to have sounded like professional quartets.[29] From the heights, a few bands could also be heard.

Folks back in the States would forever remember where they were when the heard the news of the Armistice and how they spent the day. The Great War was over! For some unfortunate ones, the moments of joy and laughter would days later turn to terrible grief with notification of the death of a loved one. Private Richmond took time to record the first night of peace: "After dark, all the hills around resembled a mammoth Fourth of July celebration. There were camp fires everywhere along the front, and the sky was lit up all night with lights of all colors. It was evident that some did not sleep any during the night, or else they worked in relays. There were also a number of explosions during the night in the rear of the German line, doubtless being the setting off of mines, and blowing up ammunition dumps. Outside of this there was a quiet that had not been known for over four years."[30]

The night was very tranquil. Individuals were now able to warm up and dry out their clothes, which for obvious reasons was something they had not been able to do along the Western Front. The hilly countryside along the front lines sparkled with glowing lights resembling a vibrant village.

With all objectives completed, there was praise for the participants in the Marine Brigade and Second Division. Officers devoted much time towards carefully choosing their congratulatory words in writing their personal statements. A general order of appreciation to all the Allied Forces was issued by Foch:

> Officers, Non-commissioned Officers and Soldiers of the Allied Armies:
> After resolutely repulsing the enemy for months, you confidently attacked him with an untiring energy.
> You have won the greatest battle in history and rescued the most sacred of all causes, the Liberty of the World.
> You have full right to be proud, for you have crowned your standards with immortal glory and won the gratitude of posterity.
>
> FOCH
> Marshal of France
> Commander in Chief of the Allied Armies.[31]

From Neville to his Marines in the Fourth Brigade, on November 11, the very day of the Armistice, came the following:

> Upon this, the most momentous hour in the history of the World War, the undersigned wishes to express to his command his sincere appreciation of their

unfailing devotion to duty and their heroic and courageous action during the recent operation.

The time when the results of our efforts during the past year are shown, is here. The hour has arrived when the convulsion which has shaken the foundations of the civilized world has ceased. The enemy is defeated and the principles of freedom and democracy have triumphed over barbarism and autocracy. We may all feel justly proud of the extent of our participation which has forced the enemy to ceassation [sic] of hostilities. It is fitting at this time, to thing of those of our comrades who have fallen on the field of honor and rejoice in the fact that they did not give their lives in vain.

Your display of fortitude, determination, courage and your ability to fight has upon more than one occasion been a determining factor in making history, and your work has had a direct bearing upon the remarkable chain of events which have this day culminated in such a satisfactory manner. Along the fronts of Verdun, the Marne, the Aisne, Lorraine, Champagne, and the Argonne, the units of the Fourth Brigade marines have fought valiantly, bravely and decisively. They have nobly sustained the sacred traditions, and have added glorious pages to the already illustrious history of the United States Marine Corps. It is a record of which you may all be proud.[32]

From Major General Lejeune on the following day came this proclamation:

HEADQUARTERS SECOND DIVISION (REGULARS)
AMERICAN EXPEDITIONARY FORCES
Order

FRANCE, November 12, 1918

On the night of November 10th heroic deeds were done by heroic men. In the face of a heavy artillery and withering machine gun fire, the Second Engineers threw two foot bridges across the Meuse and the First and Second Battalions of the Fifth Marines crossed resolutely and unflinchingly to the east bank and carried out their mission. In the last battle of the war, as in all others in which this division has participated, it enforced its will on the enemy.

(Signed)John A. Lejeune,
Major General, U.S.M.C., Commanding.[33]

Major General Summerall over the V Corps would wait nine days, and on November 20, he issued an official citation under General Orders No. 26:

The Second Division, in line at the launching of the attack, broke through the strong enemy resistance, and, leading the advance, drove forward in a fast and determined pursuit of the enemy, who, despite new divisions hastily thrown in, was driven back everywhere on the front. This division drove the enemy across the Meuse, and under heavy fire against stubborn resistance, built bridges and established itself on the heights. The cessation of hostilities found this division holding strong positions across the Meuse and ready for a continuation of the advance.[34]

As you can see from Summerall's own words, it appears that he did not wish for the war to end and that he wanted to continue the advance. Conversely, Lejeune was quite compassionate, and he expressed his sincere feelings for the loss of his men in a personal letter to his wife: "We fought our last battle ... it was pitiful for men to go to their death on the eve of peace."[35]

Because most top officials wanted to wrap up the war and put it behind them as soon a possible, few awards were issued for heroism shown during the final hours of the war. With this understanding, Hamilton was not recognized with any awards for his accomplishments in crossing the Meuse River on November 10 or his actions on November 11.

13. Assessment of the AEF

When the Great War was over and the Fourth Brigade came home to the United States, Franklin D. Roosevelt, the acting secretary of the navy, stated in his welcome home address: "The Fourth Brigade as a part of the immortal Second Division, has been engaged in all of the principal operations of the war. Their record speaks for itself."[1]

Knowing the Marine Brigade was involved in all the major battles, one must next ask how did the Second Division compare with the rest of the American Expeditionary Forces? A view of the big picture will reveal the accomplishments and results.

Of the 42 AEF divisions, 29 of them participated to some degree in the war, and of all the divisions, the Second Division was the most highly decorated. Over 600 Distinguished Service Crosses were issued to members of the division, which was more than twice the number awarded to the next ranking division. More than half of the division's Distinguished Service Awards were issued to Marines. This speaks volumes and is a good reason why the U.S. Marines were so proud to be associated with their U.S. Army counterparts and support groups within the division.

Comparisons among the different divisions may be drawn from the War Department publication *The Official Record of the United States Part in the Great War*.[2] In the entire AEF, 248 American officers and 3,302 men were captured by the enemy.[3] Throughout the war only 25 Marines were believed to have been captured, prompting Marine Commandant Barnett to state, "It is considered that this constitutes a most remarkable testimonial to the magnificent morale and individual courage of the men."[4]

During the war the AEF captured a total of 63,079 prisoners, and of all the divisions, the Second Division captured the most. They alone captured 288 German officers and 11,738 enlisted men.[5] Listed below are accomplishments of the top five American divisions with regard to captured prisoners.

Rank	Division	Captured Prisoners	Percent of Total
1	2nd	12,026	19.07
2	1st	6,469	10.26

Rank	Division	Captured Prisoners	Percent of Total
3	89th	5,061	8.02
4	33rd	3,987	6.32
5	30th	3,848	6.10

A record was kept detailing the kilometers each division advanced against the Germans. Naturally the figure does not portray the intense fighting in one given location or deal with certain types of terrain, but nevertheless, listed below are the figures.

Rank	Division	Kilometers	Percent of Total
1	77th	71.5	9.14
2	2nd	60	7.67
3	42nd	55	7.03
4	1st	51	6.52
5	89th	48	6.13

The hybrid Second Division was often charged with carrying out the toughest assignments. Realizing this, they paid a high price for their aggressive role in accomplishing their objectives. Certainly no one is proud of deaths; however, this ranking reveals the true intensity under which certain divisions lived. Each AEF member who proudly sacrificed his life for his country or was wounded in battle should never be forgotten. It appears that the Marine Corps deaths within the Second Division were 2,764.[6] Listed below are the casualty figures for the divisions that suffered the greatest losses.

Rank	Division	Deaths	Wounded	Total Casualties	Percent of Total
1	2nd	4,787	17,752	22,230	8.68
2	1st	4,411	17,201	21,612	8.44
3	3rd	3,177	12,940	16,117	6.30
4	28th	2,551	11,429	13,980	5.46
5	42nd	2,644	11,275	13,919	5.44

Division Surgeon Richard Derby noted that the First Division saw more initial action. As the early division to arrive in France, they started assisting the French prior to the Second Division. However, Derby noted: "Of course as our experience became greater we grew to feel, as many another division did, that we were the best American division in France. But in a group of Second Division officers collected round a table, whenever the relative merits of divisions were discussed, the First Division was sure to be the unanimous second choice."[7]

The "Indian Head" or "Race Horse" Division was unofficially tagged with a new motto, "Second to None," which was not just a fancy slogan. They truly were the best American division and even accomplished more than the First Division, known as the "Big Red One" and "Pershing's Own." The Second Division was now considered one of the best divisions in the world.

Finally it would be good to follow the path of the Second Division and review the overall impact each battle had upon their hospital admissions. Hospital One, also known as the First Field Hospital, served as the triage for the division. This hospital was usually located about four miles from the constantly shifting front lines. When ambulances reached the First Field Hospital, patients were checked in for assessment and then often sent to other specialized hospitals located further away. Listed below are figures complied by Alexix P. Minos, MD, sergeant, First Field Hospital:[8]

Battle Sector	*American*	*Allied*	*Prisoners of War*	*Total*
Verdun	1,071	-	-	1,071
Château-Thierry	5,929	224	167	6,320
Soissons	1,589	29	19	1,637
St. Mihiel	726	-	66	792
Blanc Mont	4,345	689	149	5,183
Meuse-Argonne	4,508	-	190	4,698

Château-Thierry, which included Belleau Wood, had the highest admissions followed by Blanc Mont and the Meuse-Argonne. However, Blanc Mont was different, as noted by Frank Tousic, a chief pharmacist's mate in the U.S. Navy. "Many remember Blanc Mont Ridge; it was the Château-Thierry experience again, but packed into a few short hours."[9]

It's interesting to note that hospital admissions did not just involve Americans, but others who were also given medical attention. In some hospitals it was difficult to identify exactly who was who, as the green uniform of the U.S. Marine was similar to the green/grey German uniform. When you add the abundant variety of Allied soldiers, such as French, English, Senegalese, Moroccan and Italian, you have a mix that caused confusion. It was under these conditions that another notable Marine Corps story evolved. The situation occurred in the spring of 1918 before Belleau Wood, and involved a hospitalized man covered with blankets, who was asked by the inquisitive Second Division Consulting Surgeon Major Burton Lee, "Are you an American?" "'No sir,' was the quick response and the smiling face continued by stating, 'I'm a Marine.'"[10]

Finally the words of USMC Major Robert L. Denig might sum up the accomplishments of the Second Division the best. Major Denig was quite different from most U.S. Marines serving in France, as he spent most of his time commanding a battalion within the Second Division, Third Brigade, U.S. Army Ninth Infantry. He said: "The Second Division was the second division to be formed in France, and the name does not imply that it was second in anything else. In fact, it was first in everything. According to the War Department, we captured more cannon, more officers, more men, gained more ground, recaptured more towns than any other division, and we had greater casualties in doing it and got about one hundred and fifty per cent more decorations than any other division."[11]

14. The March to Germany
Belgium, Luxembourg and Christmas Letters

When the Armistice was signed Maj. General Lejeune issued the following proclamation, which summarized the deeds of the Second Division:

Headquarters 2d Division (Regular)
American Expeditionary Forces,
France, Nov. 11, 1918

Order:

1. An armistice between the allied nations and Germany has been signed, and hostilities ceased temporarily at 11A.M. today.
2. It is fitting that the great part played by the 2d Division in bringing about this momentous victory over a redoubtable foe should be recounted at this time.
3. At the end of May, the enemy broke through the allied lines on the wide front west of Rheims and reached the Marne near Château-Thierry. The safety of Paris and of the allied army itself was at stake. At this critical hour the 2d Division was deployed to meet the foe. It stopped his advance; it drove him back, and it demonstrated for all time that the American is second to none in valor, be endurance, and in the grim and unyielding determination to conquer.
4. Again, on July 18, during the last great enemy offensive, the 2d Division, after a night march of unparalleled difficulty, struck, near Soissons, the flank of the enemy's salient, penetrated his lines, and brought his offensive to a standstill. This was the beginning of the allied offensive, which has continued unceasingly and untiringly until today.
5. On Sept. 12 to 15 the American Army fought its first battle in France under American leadership. To the 2d Division was assigned the most difficult and the most important task — the capture of Thiacourt and the Jauiny-Exammes Ridge. It reached its second day's objective on the first day, drove off the enemy's counter-attacks, and clinched the victory.
6. In the Champagne District, Oct. 2 to 10, it fought beside the Fourth French Army. On Oct. 3, it seized the Blanc Mont Ridge, the keystone of the arch of the main German position, advanced beyond the ridge and, although both flanks were unsupported, it held all its gains with the utmost tenacity, inflicting tremendous losses on the enemy. This victory freed Rheims and forced the entire German Army between that city and

the Argonne Forest to retreat to the Aisne, a distance of thirty kilometers.
7. During the latter part of October, the division was ordered to join the First American Army for the great attack of Nov. 1. It was given the post of honor, and the lead advance. It drove through the enemy's fortified lines to a depth of over nine kilometers, seized the heights of Bayonville and destroyed the enemy divisions on its front. On Nov. 3 it advanced to Fosse, and attacked and captured the heights of Vaux. At night, it pressed forward through the Forest of Beival by a single road and occupied the ridge near Beaumont. On the night of the 4th it again attacked and advanced its lines to the Meuse. Finally, on the night of the 10th, it forced its way across the Meuse and seized a commanding position on the eastern bank.
8. This superb division of fighting men in unsurpassed valor, in skill, in endurance, in determination, to conquer, and in service to the cause of the Allies.
9. In the great struggle, many of our comrades have made the supreme sacrifice for our country, but their heroic spirit dwells in the hearts of the officers and men of the 2d Division."

JOHN A. LEJEUNE
Major Gen., U.S.M.C. Commanding[1]

It was difficult for Hamilton's men to get over the loss of their fellow Marines who had died in the final ambush, and the void created by those left behind in fresh graves was huge. Some of the men had fought and survived through the entire war only to perish in the final hours. American casualties on the last day are very difficult to ascertain; however, a couple of years later the *New York Times* reported Congressional information stating there were 3,912 casualties, including 268 deaths.[2] On the final day, November 11, along both sides of the entire Western Front, there were said to have been more casualties than on D-Day during the next world war.[3]

On November 13, two days after the Armistice, Maj. General Summerall paid another visit to Major Hamilton's men. In life one does not often get second chances, but Summerall was afforded such an opportunity. Would he seize the moment, make amends with gracious thanks to all and give a memorable speech? He'd accomplish two of the three.

Likely due to bridge conditions, he did not come this time on his black horse, but rather on foot. Captain Dunbeck escorted the general to his battalion, which now consisted of about 350 Marines. There is no mention of Major Hamilton, but as he was ultimately over both 1/5 and 2/5 he was likely in attendance along with Maj. General Lejeune, Brig. General Neville and Colonel Feland. The Marines formed on three sides, and when Summerall entered the entrance was sealed off making a complete square. Jack Ausland, a member of the 55th Company in 2/5, described the situation: "We waited, wondering what the general would say this time. All his predictions have been fulfilled. He would see us again across the Meuse. Many of us would be killed getting here. Many Germans would bar our way, but we would know how to deal with them. But we have had the point of honor, and he has been depending on us, so I guess that's all that's necessary. When he spoke to us on the thirtieth of October, he received a little applause. We now felt more like killing him than applauding him."[4]

The general congratulated the Marines on accomplishing the set objective on the final day of the war. He was slapping his boot leggings again; only this time, as he was without his horse, he was using his swagger stick. The following three sentences from the general's 15 minute speech remained lodged in Ausland's memory years later: "I am very sorry that the Armistice has been signed. We are fighting men. We don't want to hike to the Rhine, we want to fight our way to the Rhine."[5]

The Devil Dog recalled what happened after the general's speech:

> When finished, the general bowed low and turned, took a few steps on his way out and stopped. Where was the applause? Not a handclap sounded.
>
> He turned around again and looked at us, one by one. We were at parade rest, and looked right back. Not a word was spoken. Even the officers failed to applaud. The general left. The Second Battalion had unanimously decided the general had said nothing for which applause was forthcoming.
>
> He went over to the First Battalion, which had been in the attack, going down the river while we went up. He made the same speech and got the same amount of applause.[6]

The engineers were not getting much rest, as they were now in the process of restoring several permanent bridges across the Meuse River. One major priority called for the men to rebuild a damaged wooden bridge capable of handling heavy wagons and equipment. Working around the clock, they kept their sawmill busy making all sorts of boards, which enabled the projects to be completed within a couple of days.

In France, the refugees, who had fled towards Paris, could now return to their villages. The folks heading back hoped to find their homes intact; they were instructed to be aware of unexploded shells and similar devices. Residents with small children who had elected to stay in their homes and managed to live through the war now had children speaking the German language, as the enemy had occupied some villages for four years.

On November 14, Major Hamilton's battalions were relieved from their position, and in the afternoon they hiked a few miles to the village of Pouilly, where they camped the next three days. Once settled into Pouilly, time was taken for a head count to see exactly who was accounted for and who was missing in action. Following the count all battalions would be filled back to full strength. Over in 2/5, the count revealed the 18th, 51st and 55th Companies were down to fewer than 100 men each, while the 43rd Company, nicknamed "Lucky," was somehow about twice the size of the other companys' average. Hamilton's November 11 memo to Feland noted that 1/5 was down to roughly 100 men. Captain Blake reported that his company had approximately 25 active Marines, which is in line with Hamilton's figures. The battalions were beefed back up with Marines from assorted units, including military police. When they were leveled at full strength, Hamilton reverted back to his regular command over 1/5.

Each of his men received replacement equipment because, even with the ceasefire in place, the battalion still needed to be prepared to fight if called upon at a moment's notice. The Marines had been wearing the same clothing for an extended period of time while exposed to filthy trenches, combined with rain and mud. They were now afforded time to get their apparel disinfected to rid themselves of lice and "cooties," which infested 99 percent of the warriors. The cleaning process was performed by passing clothing through steam chambers set upon the back of a flatbed truck.

The rest stop in Pouilly also gave his men time to write letters, which

This photograph, likely taken after the Armistice in Pouilly, shows (left to right) Chaplain Mokeley, 2nd Lt. Louis Cukela and his skipper, Capt. Robert Blake of 66th Company in 1/5, still displaying a determined look, and an unidentified Marine, who could use extra sleep (courtesy Marine Corps History Division).

was something they had not been able to do since October 19. At this time there was no official word regarding the selection process and the order in which divisions would return to the States. The optimistic men dreamt of being home by Christmas, while the ever realistic ones knew they were likely issued new equipment for a specific purpose. Before the three day rest ended their questions would be answered.

Hamilton wondered how his brother, Burley, had fared during the war following their chance springtime encounter. As it turns out Burley, a captain in the 30th U.S. Infantry Regiment of the Third Division, was wounded by fragments from a 150mm shell burst and was in a French hospital. He was recuperating just fine and was expected to go back home soon. Burley, like his father and brother, had a comical side, as evidenced by the following: "My luggage was in the lorry behind us and was smashed all to pieces by a German shell. I had nothing to wear but a pair of pajamas, no clothes of any sort, and as I had not identified the lorry and was unable to get the number of the shell, recovered nothing for my claim ... as it was incomplete."[7]

On November 15 Lejeune issued formal paperwork to the adjutant general, AEF, recommending that Major Hamilton be promoted to lieutenant colonel. This move was prompted to fill a vacancy left by Lt. Colonel Turrill and justifiably would serve as the right compliment for Hamilton at this point in his career. On the following day Hamilton passed the physical examination, given by United States Navy Surgeon Robert A. Lawler, needed to become a "Lieutenant-Colonel, Army of the United States."[8] However, for reasons unknown, the recommendation was not fulfilled.

Lejeune's Second Division now parted from Summerall's V Corps and became aligned with the III Corps of the Third Army under the command of Major General Joseph Dickman. At 61 years old, Dickman was the elder statesman of the U.S. Army, and he was now responsible for the upcoming adventure known as the "Occupation of Germany."

The American forces in the III Corps, proceeding forward to Germany, were the 1st, 2nd, 3rd, 4th, 32nd, and 42nd Divisions, along with the 66th Field Artillery Brigade. These divisions, accompanied by several from France and Britain, were to stay in Germany until a formal treaty was agreed upon and signed by all parties. The other divisions within the AEF, which were the vast majority, were headed home in an orderly process in conjunction with scheduled transport services crossing the Atlantic.

Hamilton's initial assignment was to take his battalion on a march covering about 60 miles through portions of Belgium and Luxembourg to the German border. They would later cross into Germany and march close to 100 miles towards the Rhine River to remain as a peace keeping force. The basic marching arrangement called for two marching columns, with the Second

Division, Third Infantry Brigade, leading on the right, starting at Stenay, and the Fourth Brigade leading on the left, departing from Pouilly. Some of the men wondered why the plan called for a march rather than a ride in one of the numerous camions.

At 0500 on November 17, Hamilton and his battalion lined up, and the entire brigade left the French villages followed a mile back by other divisional forces. Major Hamilton and his First Battalion, Fifth Regiment, once again led the entire Fourth Brigade, remaining always on guard in the event of a possible uprising. Along the way men noticed strewn German equipment, but also the beautiful French countryside. The Marines in the Fifth Regiment were feeling festive, and when they entered the central square in the village of Montmedy they all began to sing "Hail, Hail, the Gang's All Here." They kept a good pace and when night came they were close to the Belgian border.

On the morning of the 18th, everyone hit the road again, and to their liking, the cool day with overcast skies was just fine for marching. This was a very memorable day for Hamilton and everyone in the brigade, as late in the morning they crossed into Belgium. At this juncture, the regimental bands in the brigade took the lead and began to play. The Belgian citizens were anxiously waiting the arrival of the noble American warriors to give them a rousing welcome. Some village residents constructed large lattice arches made of pine boughs adorned with colorful flowers and the words, "Welcome to our Allies," for the battalion to march under. The streets were so crowded that the warriors generally had to file through two abreast or even single file.

The locals, wishing to honor the brave Americans as best they could, constructed handmade American flags with available material on hand. The unique flags appeared in all sizes without a unified pattern using red, sometimes pink, white and blue colors. The flags contained a variety of stars, from one to many, and the same was true for the number of stripes, of which some were wide and some narrow.

Their country had been occupied by Germans ever since it was bombed back in 1914. The residents, consisting mainly of the elderly and children, but also some pretty women, rejoiced with cheers, while jazz bands played, prompting dancing in the streets. The Marines hiked on and in the villages where Hamilton and his men billeted for the night, grateful citizens offered up their homes and beds for the weary Marines. During German occupation, Belgians were kept inside at night under a curfew, so with renewed freedom the dancing continued into the night with bright torches lighting the streets along with fireworks.

It took his men roughly three days to cross Belgium, and in each village they entered, residents conducted their own special celebration displaying their fervent gratitude. Only the infantry within the division was taking part in the necessary march, but they alone accounted for at least 13,000 men. Often at night the men were spread out in several different local villages in order to accommodate their large numbers.⁹

On the 21st, with the Sixth Regiment in the lead, Hamilton and his battalion departed from Arlon, Belgium, a city of 100,000, and marched into Luxembourg. Different diaries within the Fourth Brigade give a mixed view as to their reception in this tiny country. Some state the reception was similar to that of the Belgians, while others stated the folks remained civil but rather distant. The citizens were certainly inquisitive as to the appearance of the American liberators, who had beaten the Kaiser's mighty forces. The different elevations throughout Luxemburg added to the wonderful scenery, but at the same time made hiking much more difficult. The Marines with their poorly constructed and improper fitting boots were now feeling the effects as noted by Surgeon Derby: "Instead of there being a large number of sick to evacuate, as I had feared, we had mostly to deal with cases of sore feet, caused by the infernal English shoe."¹⁰

Late in the afternoon of November 23, Hamilton's battalion found themselves by the Sauer River at the German border. Here they would not only billet for the night, but stay the remainder of the month. This was because the terms of the Armistice prohibited Allied countries from entering Germany until after December 1. The good news was they could all relax and enjoy the upcoming American holiday of Thanksgiving in the local area on November 28. The men now had several days in advance to scout out the best place to find a warm meal in town consisting of beef or a rare old hen, but there was certainly no turkey. Across the great Atlantic Ocean, President Wilson issued a proclamation for the holiday to be filled with thankful prayers.

The major encouraged his battalion to write Christmas letters home to their families telling of their experiences and adventures. Hamilton often wrote letters to family members and friends, so it would be reasonable that he took time to send a few personal letters home too. *Stars & Stripes* was the official United States military newspaper printed in France for the troops. The Friday, November 22, weekly edition stated the following in a front-page article:

> Lid Off Censorship For Father's Letter — New Rulings Announced Just in Time to Allow Family to Know Whole Story of Your Life in France — Tons of Writing Paper in Sight for Sunday — Postmaster General Promises to Speed Messages at American End — Don't Forget the Inscription: Dad's Xmas Letter.
>
> ...The censor has removed his green whiskers and appears as a pretty harmless individual. You can tell where you've been and what you've done. So thus conveniently applied there won't be any dearth of things to write about. The trouble will be telling it all.

Tell the old gent the battles you were in, whether it was Château-Thierry or Tours.
Tell him how we licked 'em.
Tell him how you helped.
Tell him what you're doing now."[11]

On the day after Thanksgiving, Mortensen wrote his Christmas letter home, mentioning: "I have lots of experiences to tell about 'bon' and 'par bon' places, but this letter is just to give you a little of my three months in France now that the lid is off, the more exciting things will have to wait until I see you personally in order the make the experiences effective. I have to tell things, which the Censor even now would not allow."[12]

In Luxembourg everyone was so rested, they were becoming a bit restless. The men were looking forward to moving onward into Germany, and the month of November could not come to an end soon enough. Hamilton knew how to use his leadership skills to get his Marines in the "Race Horse" Division focused again.

When December 1 arrived, reveille sounded at 0230, and the entire Second Division was up in the pitch dark. A cold, light rain was falling as the men rolled their damp blankets into a firm roll for their backpacks. Soon Hamilton and his battalion were on their way, marching in darkness. At 0700 Hamilton and 1/5 took the advance guard position and headed across the Sauer River at Wallendorf and into Germany. The men did not stop to reflect upon this memorable and historic moment, but rather they

Colonel Logan Feland photographed after the Armistice wearing his Distinguished Service Cross and Croix de Guerre (courtesy Marine Corps History Division).

kept marching along. Around noon the division took about an hour break for coffee and bread. Following the rest period they hit the road again keeping a brisk pace until about 1930. The fellows who were carrying an abundance of souvenirs were fully feeling the effects of the extra weight. The major's well-conditioned men and others in the division were glad to finally halt for the day.

On the following day the hike was more leisurely, covering a distance of only about six miles, with added rest stops throughout the day. Over the next several days the pace varied and so, too, did the weather. On some days a light mix of freezing rain and snow fell. Early in the morning of Friday the 13th, platoon leaders using lanterns corralled the men into a line for roll call. When all were accounted for, the skipper in Hamilton's old 49th Company told the men: "Nice day for a hike. Major [Hamilton] says, goin' to the Rhine to-day. Eighteen or twenty kilomets — don't know exactly. Dam' such a war!"[13]

Maj. General Lejeune (left) and General Pershing meet December 22, 1918, at Heddesdorf, Germany, during review of the Second Division (courtesy Marine Corps History Division).

On this historic day they left Waldorf, Germany, in light rain, and by late morning they had the famous Rhine River within their sights. Around noontime, Colonel Feland's Fifth Regiment led the Marine Brigade across the Rhine River Bridge at Remagen. Since leaving Pouilly, Major Hamilton and the others had marched roughly 150 miles.

Hamilton did not like idle periods of time, and now that he had led his battalion safely into Germany and across the Rhine, he wished to take care of some personal hygiene. A dental surgeon was able to briefly examine him on December 14, and the oral inspection revealed a few problems. The dentist recommended that X-rays be taken at a hospital for a complete checkup.

The major and his men reached Neiderbreitach on the 15th. Due to the size of the Fourth Brigade, each individual company would billet in a different village within the surrounding designated area.[14] The future "Occupation of Germany" was also now referred to as the "Watch on the Rhine."

Realizing that there was not expected to be any action during their stay in Germany, Hamilton decided to proceed with the dentist's advice. On December 15 he took sick leave and headed to a hospital in Paris. In doing so he had to relinquish his duties as commander of the First Battalion, Fifth Regiment. Captain Hunt, the senior captain, who had assisted the battalion crossing the Meuse River on November 10, now officially became the commander of 1/5.

15. Germany and Court Trials
Through Spring 1919

One immediate observation in Germany was the numerous children everywhere, of whom many were illegitimate. Through more than four years of ongoing war, the overall attitude tilted towards "anything goes." This behavior was not discouraged, as the country viewed males as a commodity that needed to be replenished.

Naturally some of the local Germans did not appreciate the Americans in their country. The most vocal objectors tended to be mothers who had lost a son or even more. Generally however, most all citizens tended to be civil and obedient.

On January 6, 1919, former President Theodore Roosevelt passed away. The recent death of his son Quentin had broken his heart. Though he was only 60 years old, he had lived a life full of zest, leaving behind a true lasting legacy. Upon hearing the news, members of the U.S. Senate and House of Representatives paid tribute to the former president and adjourned. Word of Roosevelt's death quickly traveled across the world to President Wilson, who was on official business in Italy. Secretary Daniels issued orders via telegraph, cable and radio, to all officers on naval ships and Marine Corps personnel overseas stating: "Ex-President Roosevelt died this morning. Colors are to be half-masted until sunset this evening."[1]

Major Derby heard the very sad news of his father-in-law's death from a colonel. Back on Christmas Day, the surgeon had been able to gather with his wife's brothers to share festive moments around a Christmas tree followed by a wonderful feast.[2] His thoughts now went back to the recent Christmas letter he had received from the former President, which mentioned: "Of course I am as proud as Punch of what the First and Second Divisions (ought I to transpose their order!?) have done, and as a mere matter of *panche* I am very glad that they are east of the Rhine, on the bridgehead into the heart of Germany. You boys have certainly done everything, in the greatest military achievement our country has ever had to its credit. It is worth while to have lived in such a time, if, and only if, one has risen level to the time."[3]

In Germany staff flags were lowered upon hearing the news. The former President was revered by men in the Corps for his days as Colonel Roosevelt, the leader of his Rough Riders, and many had tried their best to emulate the hero in France.

Back in the States the director of military aeronautics instructed two flight groups, consisting of five army planes each, to fly 24 hours a day over Roosevelt's Sagamore Hill home in Oyster Bay, New York. This was performed until the day of the local funeral as a tribute to former President Roosevelt with a direct connection to Quentin. The biplanes also occasionally dropped wreaths in front of the home.[4]

In Germany many men needed to remain active until a peace treaty was signed and assurance was given that it would be obeyed. The days were devoted to some training; however, much time was also allotted for an assortment of recreational activities, including athletic competition along with a variety of entertainment. Some of the sporting games were oriented towards fun and pleasure, while other events were highly competitive matches between companies, battalions, divisions, branches of service and even one country's best athletes against another. The assortment of sports included football, basketball, baseball, track, and rifle shooting; to name a few. The Fifth Regiment would end up winning the AEF small-arms matches.

In January General Pershing started the Inter-Allied Games through written invitations to twenty-nine Allied Nations. Eighteen nations accepted the challenge to compete in the events to be held at Pershing Stadium in Paris throughout the spring and into early summer. Each participating nation had separate tryouts and final team selection. In a way these games continued to revive the national competition witnessed in the Olympic Games.

The game of basketball originated in 1891 with James Naismith in Springfield, Massachusetts. As other countries were just learning the game, the American team held a strong advantage, and they won the Inter-Allied championship game against France, 93–8. America won many other team events; however, the individual events were more competitive.

During the occupation there was also entertainment to cheer up the men. Mortensen became a member of a select battalion show circuit by playing fiddle music in a raucous theater group. The combined music and entertainment was a welcome relief for the men of 1/5, as they continued to bond through relaxation and laughter, while trying to forget the past battles.

With the war over, the "Watch on the Rhine" served as an appropriate time to review the performance of officers. On January 12, 1919, Colonel Feland officially recommended Hamilton for a promotion to lieutenant colonel. This notice was in conjunction with the November 15, 1918, promotion letter from Lejeune to the AEF adjutant general. Feland's memo stated:

UNITED STATES MARINE CORPS,
HEADQUARTERS, 5th REGIMENT,
EXPEDITIONARY FORCES
Germany, January 12, 1919

From: The Regimental Commander.
To: The Commanding General Second Division. [General Lejeune]
Via: Military channels.
Subject: Promotion of officers.
Reference: (a) Verbal instructions received from Commanding General, Second Division.

1. In compliance with reference (a) the following named officers are recommended for promotions:

X   X   X

Major George W. Hamilton. M. C. to Lieut. Colonel (Temporary).

Service in A.E.F. 18 mos. Participated in actions: Verdun (sub-sector Montgirmont) Pont-au-Mousson (sub-sector Mananville) Chateau-Thierry, Soissons, St. Mihiel, Blanc-Mont Ridge, Argonne Forest and march to Rhine.

Has been awarded Distinguished Service Cross and a Croix de Guerre.

X   X   X

LOGAN FELAND.[5]

This report was followed up with an additional request on January 25 through military channels to the chief of staff, Headquarters, Second Division stating: "Major Hamilton is recommended for promotion to the grade of Lieutenant Colonel on account of his high qualities of leadership and dashing courage, ability to handle and control men and his zeal and efficiency in the performance of all his duties. Major Hamilton has shown these qualities continuously since the formation of the regiment."[6]

On March 8 a dispatch cable was sent from the acting secretary of the navy to Lejeune noting that Pershing was to select four Marine Corps officers to serve as members of a general court-martial. Major Hamilton; Major Metcalf, the commander of 2/6 during the final days of the war; Major George H. Osterhout, who had commanded the Sixth Machine Gun Battalion for a period of time; and Major Alphonse DeCarre were appointed and approved by direction of the president. Osterhout would serve as judge advocate.

Six days later Hamilton received the following order from Lejeune stationed at the Second Division Headquarters in Germany:

From: Force Commander
To: Major George W. Hamilton, U.S. Marine Corps.
Subject: Appointment as member of a general court-martial

1. Having been appointed as a member of a general court-martial ordered to convene at Headquarters, U.S. Naval Forces Operating in European Waters

London, England, at 10 A.M. On Monday March 24, 1919 you will report to Captain Horace W. Harrison, U.S. Navy, the president of the court, at the time and place specified.
2. is in addition to your present duties.[7]

The upcoming affair was not just any court trial, but one with implications as a possible precedent-setting case. The story had already received worldwide publicity. A trial of this magnitude was rare and to be asked to serve was an honor for the four officers and a reflection upon their own personal character. Each major had studied certain aspects of U.S. Naval and military law as a part of their extended officer training. Their expertise, combined with their individual personality traits, such as fairness and astute reasoning, made them excellent role models and select representatives of the Marine Corps.

Hamilton had thrust all his efforts and attention into the war, and it was now time for him to say good-bye to his "Boys" with the hope of seeing them once again before long. It would be reasonable that the First Battalion, Fifth Regiment, entertainment theater group gave the major an uplifting musical performance show as a tribute to the mighty warrior before he departed.

Another memo came on April 30 mentioning that the flagship of the U.S. Naval Forces Operation in European Waters, the USS *Corsair*, was in London, England. A more precise order delivered on May 2 requested Hamilton to report to Commander Archibald D. Turnbull, U.S. Navy, president of the court, at 10 A.M. on Tuesday, May 6.

Knowing Hamilton, this period of inaction away from his men would have been his last choice for duty. If nothing else he could be representing the Marine Corps in the Inter-Allied Games in rifle competition, football or track and testing his skills against some of the best athletes in the world. He would miss mentoring his men, along with the camaraderie of his peers. He had no choice, however, but to follow the orders he was given.

The trial centered on USMC Captain Edmund Gillette Chamberlain, born to a prominent family in San Antonio and educated at Princeton and the University of Texas. Shortly after Congress declared war, he entered the Marine Corps as a 2nd Lieutenant with high hopes of becoming one of the Corps' first aviators. Chamberlain was a fine young man, and like other potential aviators, he was full of spirit and wished to serve his country in the best way possible. Also, like most aviators, he was intelligent, rather wild, very daring and full of energy.

Through studies and constant practice under the guidance of Major Roy S. Geiger he became one of the first members of the Marine First Aviation Force group, receiving recognition as Marine Corps aviator No. 7 and ranked as Naval Aviator No. 96 1/2. In May of 1918 he traveled to France on board the *DeKalb*, the same transport ship that Hamilton had traveled on about 11 months earlier. He soon reported to his new commanding officer, Major Alfred A. Cunningham. Because Marine Corps aviation was just getting started, Lieutenant Chamberlain was assigned to the Day Wing of the Northern Bombing Group and aligned to fly with the bombing group of the Royal Air Force 218 Squadron. Flying in American-made DeHavilland DH-4 planes, he spent his first month performing more than a dozen bombing raids over German-occupied territory in Belgium.

His duty and association with the 218 Squadron was completed on July 26, 1918. Chamberlain then had a few days off to do pretty much as he pleased. This is when events related to the trial began and although there were a few minor variations to the story, in general the tale was basically the same. Rather than relax and see the area's attractions with his fellow aviators, the inquisitive pilot ventured off on his own and soon hooked up with some British aviation officers. In conversation, he expressed how much he would relish the opportunity to experience the sensation of flying a totally different plane during his off days. Knowing full well that he needed proper authorization, he was able to contact Captain J. H. Cone, USN, commander, Aviation Forces, Foreign Service, who apparently stated: "I have no right officially to let you go, but you can go unofficially."[8]

This statement satisfied Chamberlain and gave him enough wiggle room to continue with his personal adventure. Seizing the moment, he then went to the nearby English aviation field at Touquin, and on July 27 he was able to convince a British commander to allow him to borrow a plane and, furthermore, assist a British bombing squadron. Since he had never flown a Sopwith Camel, this new experience was set to be an exciting thrill for him. After the flight on the first day, he was raring to go again, and with another day off he took to the air once again. On this day he was assisting 30 British aviators escorting French bombers over a battlefield.

Lieutenant Chamberlain's July 28 encounter was mentioned in several newspapers across the world. The *New York Times* later covered the story "Chamberlain Tells of His Air Exploit" on September 15, 1918. His detailed account was also mentioned in the book *Soldiers of the Sea*, which went to into publication in 1918 before his trial took place. His story also appeared in the "Recruiters' Bulletin" published by the Marine Corps. The published documents containing Chamberlain's statements could have been entered into testimony as trial evidence. A portion of the episode's pretrial testimony mentioned:

> We left the grounds at 9:08 in formation and joined the bombers at 10 over the Marne. The going was calm, with some machine gun and antiaircraft fire from the ground, but not much, and the bombers had a wonderful time; hit a train

which blew up and raised an awful stew. Then we started home and were attacked by thirty strong. A good fight followed. We lost three machines and the Hun three. He then withdrew and we were a bit scattered, but got together again, having fought our way well eastward.[9]

A few miles further on, in formations of ten each, the Hun came at us again, and this time outnumbered us nearly ten to one. We had an awful dog-fight, and we lost two bombers and four fighters to one Hun. I got several bullets in my plane, and one partly disabled my engine — made it die on me every few minutes or so, and then run fine for a spell — and one gun jammed.[10]

Chamberlain found himself in a small separated group roughly eight miles from friendly territory. He survived another dogfight, but while still over enemy ground his engine failed for good. As the plane lost altitude, he searched for an open field in which to land. The location he chose had a few German troops on the ground, and he scattered them with the remaining bullets in his machine gun. "Then I landed in a sloping depression near a wood," he said, "about an eighth of a mile beyond the enemy outposts, in a wheat field about 100 yards from some thick trees that were being swept by enemy machine guns. The enemy outposts couldn't see anything but the top wings of my machine, but they began to shell it, so I tore out the round iron compass and maps and tried to burn the machine with the maps, but I only set the wheat afire."[11]

Chamberlain did not have a weapon, but when he encountered a group of three Germans he pretended his compass was an explosive devise similar to a hand grenade. Two fled and when the third surrendered, the lieutenant now had not only a prisoner, but a rifle and a pistol. While they walked back towards friendly territory, Chamberlain came across a wounded French officer and offered him water and assistance. The group of three finally arrived at an outpost where the French officer received first aid and the prisoner later gave valuable information to Division Headquarters. As for Chamberlain, he stated: "After a time I succeeded in getting to a phone [French field phone], and reported by phone to my commander."[12] An auto then took the American lieutenant back to the Touquin base where he "then reported 'ready for duty,' asked the major in command of the British airmen [Major O. M. Vancours] not to make any report of the affair and refused to give his name."[13]

Everyone tried to sort out the events of the long day, during which the lieutenant was said to have downed five German planes. The Marine commander in the region, Captain Francis Evans, requested a written statement from Chamberlain and there was also to be a personal testament from British Major Vancours. Could it be possible that portions of the story were elaborated or even a complete hoax? There were many questions to be answered, and Chamberlain was standing trial for violating "the Articles for the Government of the Navy, Article 8, Section 1, 'Falsehood' and 'Scandalous conduct tending to the destruction of good morals.'"[14]

Once charges surfaced, other individuals involved backed away, leaving Chamberlain without support and lacking witnesses. When the trial began, undoubtedly Major Hamilton had mixed emotions. He could easily relate to the personality traits within Chamberlain, as both were highly adventurous men who enjoyed further educational training and relished being active participants in a competitive atmosphere. One other famous aviator had the same character traits, and, in fact, he had performed a similar stunt several weeks before Chamberlain's, yet was able to avoid standing trial.

Back on July 4, 1918, Lieutenant Rickenbacker had obtained a pass to attend the festivities in Paris. While his fellow aviators went ahead, he decided to head off to Orly to check out the new French designed 220-horsepower Spad planes at the American Experimental Aerodrome. The biplanes had recently been flight tested, and a few were even destined for the 94th Squadron. Rickenbacker did not see any reason why he could not take one of the new planes for a personal test flight, so he introduced himself to a mechanic on duty and provided identification showing he was from the 94th. The mechanic, who had very little authority, had no issues with releasing one of the planes. However, Rickenbacker soon realized his actions could have led to a court-martial or more. He wrote:

> Not until I had landed and had begun to answer the questions of my comrades as to how I got possession of the new machine, did I begin to realize the enormity of the offense I had committed. I did not contemplate with any pleasure the questions that the Commanding officer would hurl at me, on this subject.
>
> But to my joy no censure was given to me. On the contrary I was given this first Spad to use as my own![15]

At some point in time, USMC Commandant Barnett had asked Congress to promote Chamberlain to captain, and he was considered for the Medal of Honor. Chamberlain was promoted prior to the trial, but he did not receive the Medal of Honor.

Hamilton was a trained military professional who fully understood that officers had certain responsibilities, and as role models for others, they needed to be held to a high standard. They had to work within the confines of military rules, knowing full well that orders are orders and the law is the law. Had he been captivated by law, he would have stayed at Georgetown and become the law professional he originally set out to be.

Standing straight with square shoulders, Major Hamilton was an imposing figure. When Hamilton entered the courtroom, all cleaned up and in his dress uniform, Captain Chamberlain would certainly have taken special notice of him.

Finally on May 15 the court-martial case of Captain Chamberlain was considered complete. After ten days of testimony, he was found guilty, yet through appeals, the case would continue to remain open for a couple of years.

Rather than head back to Germany to reconnect with his men of 1/5, Major Hamilton was detached from the American Expeditionary Forces with orders to proceed immediately to Washington, D.C., and report to USMC Commandant Barnett. Being detached from the AEF meant that he was now detached from service with the U.S. Army, reverting back under full command of the U.S. Marine Corps. There would be no more family letters to write, as he was now going home. Majors Metcalf, Osterhout and DeCarre were also requested to head back and report to the commandant. In fact the majors were to telegram the USMC Headquarters upon arrival in New York.

When not under combat conditions, Hamilton always devoted extra time and attention to make certain that his appearance, including his dress uniform, was perfect. As a representative of the United States Marine Corps, this was very important to him. Because he did not have advance notice as to when he was to be issued back to the States, he had purchased another uniform from his tailor in America with instructions for it to be sent to France. When he arrived back home he was faced with both a bill and the duty of tracking down the lost uniform in France.

A few other officers were also heading back home to America. Hamilton's commanding officer, Feland, now a brigadier general, left Brest, France, on May 5 traveling on the USS *Von Stuben*. Lejeune and most all of the Fourth Brigade, however, were continuing their stay in Germany.

On May 20 Hamilton sailed on the USS *Louisville* (ID 1644) from Liverpool, England, to Brest, France. The twin-stack transport steamship, formerly known as the S.S. *Saint Louis*, was completed in 1895 and had seen many days upon the waters. At Brest, several squadrons of joyous fighter pilots also boarded the *Louisville* for the ride home. One unit was the 94th "Hat in the Ring" Pursuit Squadron, which was at one time commanded by Captain Rickenbacker. The squadron, which brought down 69 German planes and plenty of observation balloons, had more "aces" than any other. Rickenbacker was personally credited for 26 of the confirmed planes that were shot down.[16]

The ship left France on the May 21, 1919, with 1,897 officers and men. Many passengers on board commonly experienced some seasickness over the ten day voyage, while Hamilton relied upon his sturdy old "sea legs" from his days aboard the USS *Arkansas* to keep him healthy. He had many mixed emotions in his head. With the war over this should have been a very joyous time in his life, but everything points towards much apprehension, as he was experiencing an empty feeling knowing he was not receiving full recognition for

USMC Commandant Major General George Barnett (courtesy Marine Corps History Division).

all that he had accomplished. Maybe it was politics or bureaucracy, but he felt that his personal ambitions had not come to fruition. To some degree he felt alone after leaving his men behind in "Occupied Germany." At least he had Metcalf, Osterhout and DeCarre as confidants.

Would he feel a little out of place amongst a bunch of wild airmen, or would he enjoy food drink and laughter with the pilots? There would be plenty of daring stories of air combat to be heard from bow to stern. Some would be quite true and certainly some would contain recently added embellishment. Overall casualties in the 94th totaled ten dead, five wounded and three taken prisoner.[17] On the ground, Hamilton experienced so much more of the adventure, where the battle was won.

His last full day on board the ship was Friday, May 30, Memorial Day, and those aboard spent the day honoring and reflecting upon those who had died in France as well as in years past. This was the first such observance since the Armistice had been declared, and many cities across the nation, including New York, were having Memorial Day parades.

The *Louisville* arrived in New York City on Saturday, May 31, 1919. Last year, May 31 was the memorable day when Hamilton and his men of the 49th Company, along with the entire Second Division, loaded onto camions for the long ride towards Château-Thierry, followed several days later by the major battle of Belleau Wood. A lot had happened in the past 365 days of his life.

It would be a very busy day for Hamilton, so he gathered his personal belongings and prepared to disembark from the ship. The dock was crammed full, shoulder to shoulder, with happy families with tears in their eyes, welcoming home the lads who had served their country. The adventurous boys who had departed for France were headed down the crowded gangplanks, arriving back as men with changed lives. In fact 65 on board were now married with new brides at their side, and some even had children.[18]

A telegraph was sent to Marine Headquarters stating the officers had arrived in New York. Hamilton then caught the Saturday train and arrived home in Washington, D.C., later in the day.[19] He had made it back safely from the adventure. His stay would be short, as many in the military were requesting his services. It would be reasonable that he would try to find a moment to visit the grave of his mother, Ida, who had passed away while he was gone.

Come Monday morning, June 2, Major Hamilton promptly reported to USMC Major General Barnett. The commandant wanted to hear the major tell of his many exploits in France as well as the recent court trial. Following the discussion, he was officially attached to the Marine Corps Headquarters with orders to report for duty to Lt. Colonel William C. Harllee, the executive officer of the National Rife Matches. There was no annual National Match in 1917, but in 1918, with the war going on, the competitive shooting event drew exceptionally large crowds. This year the NRA National Matches were being held at the U.S. Navy ranges in Caldwell, New Jersey.

Back in 1915 Hamilton participated in rifle matches under "Bo" Harllee, but this time he was to assist him with instruction and coordination of the tournament rather than being personally involved in the competition. As an added bonus his friend Major Shuler, along with Major Metcalf and Major Paul Marmion, were also attending with similar duties.

Barnett's schedule continued to be as full as ever. Three days after meeting with Hamilton, he was on Capitol Hill, accompanied by U.S. Navy Secretary Daniels, to attend Congressional hearings concerning naval budget estimates. With an imminent peace accord, the U.S. government was now looking to save money in the budget anywhere and everywhere. Downsizing the U.S. Navy and the U.S. Marine Corps was open for all discussion and possible action. Many questions were raised pertaining to what size the Corps should be during peace time. Commandant Barnett was even asked to justify why Quantico still needed to exist, as some thought Parris Island could handle all of the duties. After all, Quantico had been established just two years ago, in May 1917, for the war effort, which was now behind them. Barnett's testimony was over, but the issue was to remain open for possible questions and answers at a future date.

Back at the Marine Headquarters one small annoying piece of business was creating quite a trail of paperwork and needed to be addressed. Madame Ruzie's home in Breuvannes, France, had been occupied by the regimental mess of the Fifth Marines from September 27, 1917, to March 16, 1918. During that period of time, she stated, portions of her home had been damaged and correspondingly she had filed a claim for a total 3,198.5 francs. Hamilton, then a captain, was a member of the group and therefore asked to tell his side of the story. He stated that her claim was exaggerated, and furthermore he only stayed in the house for a period of time when Colonel Feland was also residing. Upon departure the colonel inspected the house with Madame Ruzie, and at that time it was declared in good condition with no claims. Hamilton did not have control of other officers, who later stayed in the house.

During his first week home, he was quickly getting acclimated to life back in the States. Before heading off to the NRA National Matches, he was allowed to spend some precious vacation time back at his favorite getaway, Conesus Lake, where he could fully get his mind set straight. The natural setting and home had not changed, and the familiar permanent sign BUR-GEO-MAR on their garage served as an immediate welcome home to his favorite spot.[20] The innocent days of playing around the pigpen shed were over. He was certainly a man.

16. His "Boys" Come Home
1919 Summer and Beyond

The Great War officially ended with the formal signing of the Treaty of Versailles at 3:14 P.M. on June 28, 1919.[1] When the treaty was signed, there were only a handful of American divisions in Germany. All indications were that Germany was going to honor the treaty, so President Wilson instructed General Pershing to send the remaining divisions home. On July 1 Pershing sent a cable stating that Lejeune's Second Division was to start moving to base ports on July 15. The Third Division would be released on August 3 and the First Division on August 15.

In July, Hamilton was able to break away from the National Rifle Competition to attend his older sister Flax's wedding. The wedding of Mary Elizabeth Hamilton and Roger Conant Barnard, a graduate of Harvard University, would take place at the Hamiltons' Conesus Lake home. As the couple was flexible with their wedding plans, it was determined that the service would be held at 3:30 P.M. on Thursday, July 10, to accommodate the major's schedule.[2]

The service would be intimate, yet informal, with about 20 family members attending. Methods of transportation had noticeably improved over the past 20 years, and most guests took a train to Rochester, New York, followed by a one hour trolley ride through the fields to Genesco. Arrangements were made in advance for automobiles to travel the final eight miles to the BUR-GEO-MAR Farm.

Hamilton, still single, had just turned 27 years old, and was in peak physical condition. The Marine Corps major showed up standing tall, wearing his special white full-dress uniform. When asked to describe the numerous medals that adorned his uniform, he replied with plain talk and without boasting. As the groom's mother noted, "He told of none of the deeds, simply explained the decorations to us."[3]

Like so many weddings, the event also served as a family reunion. Missing from the festive occasion was Ida, who had passed away in the home the previous year. Mary shared the common Hamilton traits, of family love and true unselfishness. This was her own special day, yet she chose to share the honor with her brothers, as evidenced by the numerous flowers in tall vases, including wild flowers, white hydrangeas and one with red, white and blue flowers, in recognition of George's and Burley's service to their country.

A little extra love might have been in the air as the major had become attracted to a young lady, and following the wedding service, he immediately headed north to Toronto, Canada, to spend a long weekend with her. Following his visit he traveled back to New Jersey to continue with the ongoing rifle matches.

Major Hamilton's second day back, Tuesday, July 15, 1919, was not a pleasant day. His status as a major had been temporary from the beginning, and on this day his full appointment was revoked and he was reverted back to the rank of captain.[4] He did nothing wrong, and while it would not be any consolation, many of his peers, including Shuler, Metcalf and Marmion who were working at the National Rifle Matches, were in the same situation. In fact 68 majors were now returned to the rank of captain. The basic fact was that with the war over there was no need or justification for so many high ranking officers. These reductions also aided in reducing the country's military budget.

Captain George W. Hamilton back in the United States sometime after the war.

While Captain Hamilton was tending to the rifle matches, his "Boys" in the First Battalion, Fifth Regiment, who were still across the Atlantic were constantly on his mind. The contingent of 1/5 left Niederbreitbach, Germany, on July 17, heading back to Brest, France. On July 24, Lejeune, along with the headquarters staff of the Fourth Brigade, the entire Fifth Regiment and 2/6, boarded the USS *George Washington* and headed for New York.[5] This was not just any common transport ship, but rather the ship that had carried President Wilson on his most recent European voyage. Upon arrival they disembarked on Long Island at Hoboken and proceeded to Camp Mills.

On Friday, August 8, the entire Second Division was scheduled to march in a victory parade in New York City. Since most other divisions had come back to the United States shortly after the Armistice was declared, the Manhattan crowd had seen their share of victory parades and the nostalgia was wearing off, but throngs would come to see the "Indian Head" Division. The

Maj. General John A. Lejeune (left) and Brig. General Wendell C. Neville sailing back to America (courtesy Marine Corps History Division).

members had bonded with much more than their common "Indian Head" shoulder patch and Indian star insignias on their helmets. This parade would serve as their farewell tribute, being the final time they would be together as a group.

Many curious spectators wished to witness the "Devil Dogs" in person.

Would Hamilton, along with Shuler, Metcalf and others, be able to break away from the nearby NRA Matches and see their comrades now back on American soil? Would they take part in the parade?

The Marines arrived in Manhattan by multiple ferries to East 10th Street and from there the parade organized at 9th Street. The five-mile-long parade route started at Washington Square with Major General Lejeune leading the division on horseback, going up Fifth Avenue to 110th Street. Each company marched by platoon, wearing their combat packs and helmets, and carrying their '03 Springfields, with 16 paces between the platoons. The official reviewing stand was situated in front of the New York Public Library at 42nd Street and Fifth Avenue, with many dignitaries in attendance, including Assistant Secretary of the Navy Franklin D. Roosevelt and USMC Commandant Barnett.[6] Some wounded Marines were also in the reviewing stand waiting for their comrades to approach. A loud cheer went up when the Fourth Brigade finally came into view, accompanied by an announcement proclaiming, "Here come the marines!"[7] Spectators threw roses and mentioned how stern and professional the Marines looked.

The colorful Marines had carried across the Atlantic aboard the *George Washington* many mascots, including 56 dogs, four deer, two monkeys, a cat, a fox and a coatimundi named Jimmy. The coatimundi looked like a stretched raccoon and had been with them since Vera Cruz and Haiti in 1916. Not all of the animals were participants; however, the parade did include several fast-stepping fox terriers.[8]

At 110th Street, Lejeune backed his horse to the curb to review the passing Second Division, his division, one last time. Following the parade, the Fourth Brigade marched west on 116th Street to the ferries at 129th Street. At the ferry house the American Red Cross served a dinner of hot dogs and sauerkraut along with milk, cake, pie, ice cream and offered cigarettes. The Marines departed Manhattan on ferryboats and headed to the Jersey City terminal. Here they boarded one of 13 trains arranged to depart every 15 minutes destined for the Marine Barracks at Quantico, Virginia. The final train left the station at 12:10 A.M. on August 9, arriving at Quantico about one o'clock in the afternoon.[9] At the base, all United States Marines were rendered from their service with the U.S. Army and returned to their original alignment with the U.S. Navy. In a few days, on August 12, there was scheduled to be a parade, like never before, in the Capital City to honor just the Marine Brigade.

On Monday, August 11, word spread of the death of one of America's most prominent industrialists, Andrew Carnegie. He had emigrated from Scotland as a youth and lived a life that was to many symbolic of the American dream. Some estimates placed the self-made entrepreneur's wealth at close to a half billion dollars.

The evening of August 11 was the second to the last night the members of the brigade would be together as a unified group. The path for the career regulars would continue on, but for the volunteers who had enlisted for the duration of the war, although they would forever be called Marines and be in the brotherhood of the Marine Corps, their time serving their nation was winding down. On this evening there was a band concert at Quantico, and the Marine Corps Band was at their finest.

BAND CONCERT TODAY

At the Marine Barracks, at 4:30 P.M., by the United States Marine Band, William H. Santelmann, leader.

The program:

March, "The Pathfinder of Panama"	Sousa
Overture, "The Model"	Suppe
Novelle, "In Poppyland"	Albers
Excerpts from "Eileen"	Herbert
"Southern Rhapsody"	Hosmer
Waltz, "The Bachelors"	Santelmann
"Humoresque"	Dvorak
"March, "Regiment Sambro et Meuse"	Rauski
Descriptive fantasia, "A Hunting Scene"	Sullivan

Marines' hymn, "The Halls of Montezuma"
"The Star-Spangled Banner"

At the bandstand, at 6:00 P.M., by the United States Soldiers Home Band, John S. M. Zimmermann, director.

The program:

March, "Royal Australian Navy"	Lithgow
Overture, "The Voice of Nature"	Lortzing
Morceau original, "Slumber and Rest Thee"	Zimmermann
Grand Selection, "La Boheme,"	Puccini
(By Request)	
Fox trot intermezzo, "I'm Always Chasing Rainbows"	Carol
Waltz suite, "Vichha Citizens"	Czibulka
Finale, "The Navy Will Bring Them Back"	Schuster

"The Star-Spangled Banner"[10]

When Tuesday, August 12, arrived, about 8,000 Marines left Quantico by train at 7 A.M. and stormed into the nation's capital at 8:30 A.M. where the atmosphere was most festive. Emotions ran high, not only for the thousands of spectators who arrived early, but for each and every Marine too, as this was the final public appearance of the Fourth Brigade. There were numerous police present to protect the many dignitaries, including President Wilson, but there was no need for extra security, as the "Devil Dogs" had taken over the city.

Poet Isabel Likens Gates, one of the most prominent women in the Capital City, wrote a poem to honor Hamilton, which was carried by the *Washington Post* on this day, under the title "The United States Marines," "Dedicated to Maj. George W. Hamilton, Fifth Marines."[11]

Where were Hamilton, Shuler and Metcalf, three officers who had contributed so much? During the final assault at the Meuse River, the three officers were responsible for almost all of the battalions in the Fourth Brigade. Metcalf commanded 2/6; Shuler was over 3/6, as well as the aborted northern crossing with the Sixth Regiment and 3/5; while Hamilton was ultimately over 1/5 and 2/5. Hamilton was, in fact, in the city, as noted by Sergeant Frank Hunt Garvin, the 49th Company historian:

> On August 12, 1919, Major George Washington [sic] Hamilton, U.S.M.C. reached his hometown. It was the town where he was born; had attended school, and captained the greatest football team his High School had ever cheered. It was the City of Washington, D.C. where, years before, he was the only man to start at scratch and run a race with the national champion, Ted Meridth, [sic] and George came in second of all the entries. But in the greatest foot-race of all time, The World War, that tried men's souls and their courage, George Hamilton had come in first; that is, George and his gang. No other outfit ever equaled it on a hike. No other outfit achieved so many "FIRSTS" in the war. Perhaps nobody pointed out these facts to President Wilson on that 12th day of August, 1919, as he reviewed you as you marched down historic Pennsylvania Avenue, but what other Marine Commander ever brought his own Gang to his Home Town before he said "Adios"?[12]

Hamilton, Shuler and Metcalf were not the only famous Marine officers without a definitive role on this day. Major General Lejeune was also left without a functional duty to perform. He had had his shining moment recently in New York City, leading the Second Division up Fifth Avenue, but the division was now disbanded. Lejeune soon realized that he was not a part of the parade and that Commandant Barnett had not reserved a seat for him in the review stand to join President Wilson and other dignitaries. After a little scurrying around, a back row seat was finally secured and eventually he was able to move closer to the front.[13]

The U.S. Marines stacked their guns on the Capitol grounds and were served refreshments of coffee, buns and ice cream by the Red Cross. Did the men of the First Battalion, Fifth Regiment reflect upon the fact that they were in Hamilton's backyard and within walking distance of his home?

The U.S. House of Representatives and the U.S. Senate met precisely at noon, and following an opening prayer, both adjourned within five minutes for a two-hour recess to observe the parade outside their doors. The parade route was to start at the Peace Monument, go up Pennsylvania Avenue, then turn south on 19th Street and go over to Union Station. The wide avenues were lined with flags, and buildings were adorned with banners along with red, white and blue colors. Just as in Manhattan, the Marines wore their steel helmets, combat packs and carried their rifles with fixed bayonets, which sparkled during the bright summer day. The Quantico band, along with both bands from the Fifth and Sixth Regiments, were part of the parade.

Brigadier General Neville, the commander of the Fourth Brigade, led the parade down Pennsylvania Avenue on horseback. The man who officially recommended Hamilton for the Medal of Honor was having his day in the sunshine. He was followed by staff members also on horseback, then the Sixth Regiment, the Fifth Regiment, the Sixth Machine Gun Battalion and finally about 50 wounded Marines from the local Naval Hospital, driven in ambulances and motor cars.

At 12:40 the parade reached the reviewing stand of President Wilson and other prominent officials. Marching 26 men wide, it took 35 minutes for the entire brigade to pass by the President.[14]

After the parade the U.S. Senate resumed their daily session, and room in the chamber was afforded to the Marines, who wished to listen and view firsthand the American political process. Republican Senate Majority Leader

A USMC Fourth Brigade Color Guard passing in front of the White House reviewing stand with President Wilson and other dignitaries during the Washington, D.C., Victory Parade, August 12, 1919 (courtesy Marine Corps History Division).

Marine warriors back home marching down Pennsylvania Avenue, Washington, D.C., Victory Parade, August 12, 1919 (courtesy Marine Corps History Division).

Henry Cabot Lodge, an opponent of President Wilson, started the session promptly at 2 P.M., with a speech that lasted close to two hours.

It was one of the boldest and most rousing patriotic speeches ever given on the Senate floor. Senator Lodge from Massachusetts was determined that the United States stand on its own and not join the International League of Nations, which he called a "deformed experiment." One reason he gave was that other countries would be able to control America by voting the nation into a future war, bypassing the sole authority of Congress. Many times he stressed the need to obey the Monroe Doctrine. To understand the upheaval surrounding his free flowing emotional speech, a brief portion of his oratory is given below:

> Nobody expects to isolate the United States or make it a hermit Nation, which is a sheer absurdity. But there is a wide difference between taking a suitable part and bearing a due responsibility in world affairs and plunging the United States into every controversy and conflict on the face of the globe. By meddling in all the differences which may arise among any portion or fragment of humankind we simply fritter away our influence and injure ourselves to no good purpose. We shall be of far more value to the world and its peace by occupying, so far as

possible, the situation which we have occupied for the last 20 years and by adhering to the policy of Washington and Hamilton, or Jefferson and Monroe, under which we have risen to our present greatness and prosperity.... I can never be anything else but an American, and I must think of the United States first, and when I think of the United States first in an arrangement like this I am thinking of what is best for the world, for if the United States fails the best hopes of mankind fail with it.[15]

The Marines recognized a good speech when they heard one. Months ago they had heard two speeches from Major General Summerall while they stood at attention. They listened respectfully, but as they did not like what they heard, they did not applaud. This time the Marines were relaxed, sitting patiently for two hours, and they appreciated what they heard. They were chomping at the bit to show their ardent approval, which they were more than capable of doing. What followed the speech was undeniably believed to be the biggest outburst in the history of the U.S. Senate chamber. The Parliament House rules were pushed aside, and all control was lost as pandemonium prevailed in the ruckus galleries with standing applause, whistles and waving of handkerchiefs. The big event was front-page news everywhere, and as the *New York Times* reported: "The cheers that went up from the Marines could be heard through the corridors of the Capital. It sounded very much like the roar that breaks loose at a ballpark game when the home team wins the game in the ninth inning."[16]

The local *Washington Post* was used to reporting stories from the Senate galleries, but not anything close to an event like this: "*Marines Join Outburst:* The outburst was as spontaneous as it was unexpected and any efforts of Vice President Marshall to restore order would have been drowned in the din. Marines in uniform beat down on the seats with shrapnel helmets and war whoops perhaps of the Château-Thierry brand, added to the ensemble. No one recalls a similar occurrence in the staid Senate Chamber."[17]

You couldn't bottle up the assorted group of patriotic Marines and expect them to sit on their hands. Was Hamilton in the galleries with some of his "Boys" to witness a part of Capitol Hill his father knew so well? The *New York Times* further mentioned: "Vice President Marshall, in the chair, made no effort to check the thunder of applause [over three minutes]. Later when the galleries burst out in disapproval of Senator Williams of Mississippi, who accused Mr. Lodge of making a 'show' of himself, the Vice President threatened to clear them in the event of repetition."

This would have been extremely interesting as the Central Powers and the German Imperial Army could not accomplish such. Trying to evict the U.S. Marines, America's finest body of men, would certainly have created even more headlines. The Marines, at least for one more day, refused to give up the adventure and continued to live life to the fullest in service to their country. America's best were home.

Top Marine officers and their wives were invited to a luncheon after the parade hosted by the acting secretary of the navy and Mrs. Roosevelt. The invited guests were: Admiral and Mrs. Benson, Gen. and Mrs. Barnett, Gen. Lejeune, Gen. and Mrs. Feland, Gen. Neville, Gen. Long, Gen. and Mrs. Richards, Gen. and Mrs. Catlin, Col. and Mrs. Lee, Col. Snyder and Miss. Snyder, Col. Haines, Col. and Mrs. Lemly, Col. and Mrs. Dunlap, Col. Porter, Col. Russell, Col. and Mrs. Theall, Col. and Mrs. Holcomb, Col. and Mrs. Rixey, Col. Fay, Col. Evans, Maj. Stowell, Maj. Shearer, Maj. and Mrs. Hunt, Maj. Keyser and Maj. and Mrs. Kilgore.[18]

When Hamilton left Germany for the trial in England, followed by the National Rifle Matches, he left Major Hunt in charge of his old First Battalion, Fifth Regiment. It seemed odd with Hamilton, Shuler and Metcalf not participating, but it was clearly evident that postwar life was quickly moving on.

Late in the afternoon the Marines headed back to Union Station and caught trains for the trip back to Quantico. During the evening Lejeune gave a farewell speech to all the volunteer Marines, who were spending their last night in the Corps, and issued thanks to the leathernecks in the audience who were continuing on with their careers.

Also on this historic day, Secretary of War Baker sent a letter to Secretary of the Navy Daniels praising the service of the Marines. The next day F.D.R., the assistant secretary of the navy, issued the following reply:

> Navy Department. *August 13, 1919*
>
> Hon. Newton D. Baker,
> *Secretary of War, Washington, D.C.*
>
> Dear Mr. Secretary: Your very cordial letter and the tribute it bore to the Fourth Brigade of Marines was received with pleasure and deepest appreciation. The heroism of the Marines and Regulars in the famous Second Division, and their sacrifices, have endeared them to all Americans, and it is with very pardonable pride that we welcome them back to the Navy.
>
> The spirit of cordial cooperation between the Army and the Navy was never better manifested than in the participation of these Marines in the great battles in France under the command of Gen. Pershing as a part of the United States Army, and shoulder to shoulder with units of the Regular Army. It is with extreme gratification that we can look back upon this unbroken cooperation between our two departments that started at the time the first Navy ship carried troops to France and continued uninterruptedly through to the end.
>
> On behalf of Secretary Daniels, the Commandant of the Marine Corps, the officers and men of that organization, I wish to thank you for the sentiments expressed in your letter and convey to you our appreciation of the heroism of the officers and men of the Army who with the Marines made the Second Division one of the greatest fighting organizations the world has ever known.

It is very gratifying in our pride over the achievements of the Marines, to know that the pride is shared by the War Department and your warm approbation of their conduct as a part of the Army will be treasured by the Corps as well as by the individuals.

Sincerely, yours,

Franklin D. Roosevelt
Acting Secretary of the Navy.[19]

Pvt. Ove Mortensen back home in Winchester, Massachusetts. The volunteer in the 66th Company of 1/5 was one of the few "Boys" in Hamilton's battalion who walked out of "The Box" and survived the Meuse River Crossing.

On Wednesday, August 13, the 6,677 Marine Corp volunteers who were in the war for the duration were officially relinquished of their duty under the jurisdiction of the U.S. Navy at Quantico.[20] Under a prearranged coordinated process, the volunteers of the Fifth Regiment were the first to muster out early in the morning, followed by those from the Sixth Regiment. Captain Blake, commanding the 66th Company, who would later rise to become a World War II major general, signed Mortensen's discharge papers, noting "Character Excellent."[21]

Special arrangements were made at Union Station for extra departures to accommodate the overload of Marines heading home. The modern trains, with clean polished passenger compartments, did not come close to resembling the old box cattle cars that they had crammed into in France. While the steam engines hissed and the train bell clanged, the conductor called out the final "all aboard," and the doors were locked, signaling the end of their adventure. In future years there would be reunions consisting mainly of career Marines, but many of the men who bonded so closely together and would have died for each other, would never see or hear from each other again. Mortensen went home to Winchester, Massachusetts, a mid-sized New England town with railroad service outside of Boston.[22]

Army Captain George K. Livermore, who served as an operations officer in the 167th Field Artillery Brigade, 92nd Division, was already at home in Winchester, Massachusetts, living less than a mile from Mortensen's apparent residence.[23] Livermore came from a very prominent family, and the 1914 Yale University graduate had many contacts, including his good friend W. Averill Harriman, a 1913 Yale graduate and member of the Skull and Bones Society. Livermore had personally witnessed what he felt were many needless deaths on the last day of the war, and he wished to have the issue investigated.

Many conversations across the nation followed with the same sentiments, and the consensus seemed to be that if America's politicians and top military officers understood the ramifications of the last day of the war, such an ending would be prevented from happening again. Members of Congress soon followed the nation's urge to address the issue and formed the Congressional House War Investigation Committee No. 3 as a branch of the much larger war expenditure hearings. Several hearing dates were set, but the main testimony would come early in the upcoming year.

Throughout all this, Hamilton remained with the National Rifles Matches, which had been going on for months. Assistant Secretary of the Navy Franklin Roosevelt was a guest at the matches on August 25, and Commandant Barnett attended the final event and closing ceremonies on August 28. The Marine Corps was well represented this year, winning many honors, including the coveted team trophy, known as the National Team Match, against other service branches. There were also many interesting sideshow events, which would have attracted Hamilton's attention. One of the best was a 150-foot miniature French village constructed to portray German occupation, and to the crowd's pleasure, American aviators simulated bombing raids over the town.

Captain Hamilton's duty assisting with the rifle matches was over, but he stayed under the direction of Colonel Harllee until the end of September. Hamilton then headed off to the USMC Headquarters in Washington, D.C. In a parting written review Harllee jotted down the following three tributes to Hamilton:

Performs above duty with unusual skill and ability.
Calm even tempered forceful active bold painstaking
An all round excellent officer of Marines [space] ability especially in command of men. always dependable[24]

Another national event occurred that had national correspondents scrambling for further details. While President Wilson was traveling and maintaining a heavy workload, he suffered a massive apoplectic stroke, which limited the use of his left leg and arm. The President's health was kept private for as long as possible, as he remained confined to the White House.[25]

The Marine Corps, while trying to return to normalcy, faced many dilemmas that had to be addressed. One issue concerned promotions and seniority; a second, how medals of recognition were awarded during the war; and a third, question concerning the deaths on the final day of the war. The first two issues occupied Hamilton's free thoughts day and night. All three issues would be addressed to some extent through upcoming Congressional hearings.

The first issue to be addressed was promotions. Congress had first addressed the question by interviewing U.S. Navy and Marine Corps officials in June; however, politicians wanted to hear more. Hamilton and many others felt that honorable service, action and leadership in France should be factored into the decision-making process, while others wanted to continue the status quo by having promotions based solely on seniority status. Hamilton did not like to be idle in a situation that was out of his control, and the days spent waiting for answers tried his patience to the limits.

On October 16, 1919, Captain Leon Lemar Dye, the assistant paymaster of the U.S. Marine Corps, appeared before a Congressional committee to answer questions regarding the current number of officers at each grade level, as well as payroll concerns within the military budget. Marines were on the lowest pay echelon within the U.S. Navy. Although Hamilton constantly owed money for uniform expenses and other items, he was not as concerned with money as he was with increased responsibility and promotions. Under the

Naval Act of July 11, 1919, more than 50 percent of the permanent officers who were in the Corps at the start of the war were now back at their prewar rank with no extra pay. Dye mentioned that by law the Marine Corps could have 1,096 officers between the grade of second lieutenant and major general and that since Armistice Day 75 captains had resigned.

He presented a few tables including the one below:[26]

	Number	Percentage still holding promotions
Brigadier generals to major generals	2	
Holding these promotions now	2	100
Colonels to brigadier generals	8	
Holding these promotions now	4	50
Lieutenant colonels to colonels	28	
Holding these promotions now	17	61
Majors to lieutenant colonels	52	
Holding these promotions now	37	71
Captains to majors	234	
Holding these promotions now	83	35
First lieutenants to captains	403	
Holding these promotions now	233	57
Second lieutenants to first lieutenants	262	
Holding these promotions now	97	37

At some point, word filtered down serving notice to all Marine Corps officers that the prewar seniority system would be maintained. The writing was now on the wall, and Hamilton was noticeably upset, as the relative youngster was now a junior captain on the status scale. He would have to bide his time through many years to regain his prior rank of major. As if this was not bad enough, it seemed apparent that some of the officers he confronted at Blanc Mont now reverted to having seniority over him.

On October 27 Hamilton was detached from the Marine Barracks in Washington, D.C., and given a couple of days off to tend to personal business before his next assignment. On the last day of October he reported for duty with the First Regiment at the Marine Barracks, Navy Yard, in Philadelphia, Pennsylvania, but nothing much happened there, as he continued to wait about a month for his next official duty.

On November 11, 1919, cities and towns across the nation observed the first anniversary of Armistice Day. Although the day was not a national holiday, each community established their own way to celebrate peace and reflect upon the veterans who had served their country. Many individuals and civic organizations planted memorial trees as an act of remembrance. In Philadelphia a tree was planted at the Pennsylvania Hospital as a tribute to a Red Cross nurse who had died in France. In the nation's capital a Lombardy poplar was planted at the Force School to honor former student Quentin Roosevelt, while a short distance away General Pershing planted a redwood tree opposite the White House in Lafayette Park.

On the following day Livermore sent a letter to his U.S. Representative, Alvan T. Fuller, questioning how the last day of the war played out on the Western Front. Congressman Fuller had received many letters regarding the same subject, but it was Livermore's letter that stood out, prompting him to draft a letter three days later to General Pershing:

House of Representatives
Washington, November 15, 1919

Gen. John J. Pershing,
United States Army, Washington, D.C.

My Dear Gen. Pershing: You will remember at the joint meeting of the Senate and House Military Affairs Committee I asked you the following question: "Were the American troops ordered over the top on the other side on the morning of the day when under the terms of the armistice firing was to cease at 11 o'clock?" You will recall your reply.

I have picked out what seems to me to be a typical letter which I have received on this subject, and it fairly represents other questions which I should have liked to have asked you when you were before the committee. I felt, however, that perhaps you were somewhat handicapped in answering these questions offhand, so I thought perhaps I would write and ask you particularly in regard to the question whether it was true if the French were regardless of the wastage of men with the armistice in sight as we were, and did you not know before 6 o'clock on the morning that firing was to cease that the armistice had been signed?

I would be very grateful to you if you would give me replies to the questions brought up in Mr. Livermore's letter of November 12. As I said to you before, I have been deluged with questions on this subject, and I would like to feel that I had from you a real, frank, full answer to the question as to whether American lives were needlessly wasted because some of our officers were not as considerate of their men as the French were. Will you please return Mr. Livermore's letter with your reply?

With kindest personal regards, please believe me,
Very truly, your,
Alvan T. Fuller.[27]

General Pershing issued a lengthy official response letter to Representative Fuller dated November 21, 1919, in part stating:

The armistice, effective at 11 A.M., November 11, was not signed until 5 A.M., November 11; hence the information which Capt. Livermore states that he received about midnight of November 10 was only a rumor, although that rumor proved to be correct....

...The casualty records show that on November 11 the Ninety-second Division lost 17 killed and 286 wounded, of whom 99 were gassed. The casualty records of the Marines show that their losses on November 11 were 9 killed and 172 wounded.[28]

This number of Marine deaths would appear to be a gross inaccuracy, as the diaries of Marines mention conflicting numbers. However, as most of the deaths would likely have occurred late in the evening on November 10 along the river banks, during the river crossing and in initial combat on the east side, General Pershing's numbers might be correct, although misleading. One recent historian cites a figure that appears to be more reasonable: "The 5th Regiment lost thirty-one killed and 148 wounded while crossing the Meuse in the final hours before the cease-fire."[29] If you add the 31 killed, along with a portion of the 90 members of the Fifth Regiment listed as missing in action during the shortened month of November, you will have a more realistic total figure of deaths.[30]

Meanwhile, Hamilton was upset as to how history was recording the actual facts. For him it was not as much about medals, as it was his own personal honor and the contribution of his comrades. The man, who always stood his ground and never minced words in combat, while witnessing war's worst conditions, had now seen enough of society's pitfalls. His current enemy was the backroom bureaucratic paper pushers, in conjunction with those meddling in behind-the-scenes politics. With Hamilton, right was right and wrong was wrong, and he was determined to fire a shot back at those in his quest for righteousness.

Captain Hamilton decided to take action and document for the sake of history his firsthand account of what had transpired around him at Belleau Wood. His angst, however, was not with the Marine Corps, as would become evident in the months ahead. Still, his best avenue to acknowledge his dissatisfaction was through proper channels of communication within the Corps itself. He set forth and drafted the following lengthy letter, which after all these years, respectfully deserves to see the light of day:

Navy Yard, Philadelphia, Pa.
November 19, 1919

From: Captain George W. Hamilton, U.S.M.C.
To: The Major General Commandant. [Maj. Gen. George Barnett]
Subject: Citation for the Distinguished Service Cross.
Reference: (a) D.S.C. citation, War Dept. G. O. No. 15, dated 1/21/'19

1. Although recommended at various times for the Medal of Honor, the Distinguished Service Cross, and the Distinguished Service Medal, it has been a matter of deep regret to me that the only citation for which a decoration was awarded, Reference (a), so inadequately tells of my participation in that action as to make it appear that I might have been awarded a D.S.C. for simply being "present" in a battle.

2. After much deliberation, I have decided to state the facts, telling in detail

my personal participation in the action of June 6, 1918, and with the request that the entire matter be thoroughly investigated and my statement substantiated.

3. Should it be found that the facts are as stated, I then request that the wording of my citation for the Distinguished Service Cross be changed to include any acts worthy of mention. My statement follows:

Shortly after midnight on the night of June 5-6, 1918, General Wendell C. Neville, Marine Corps, (then a Colonel), came to the basement of the power house in Marigny, France, the Headquarters of Lieut.-Colonel (then Major) Julius S. Turrill, and gave him the orders for an attack which was to take place at 3:45 A.M. June 6, 1918 on Hill 142, in the Chateau Thierry Region. The two companies from the First Battalion selected for the attack, were the 67th, commanded by First Lieutenant Crowther, and the 49th, commanded by me. Both companies were in reserve positions near Marigny at the time, and about two miles from that portion of our front lines which we were to relieve before the attack. A French battalion was to attack on our left and the Third Battalion, Fifth Marines, on our right. We were to base on the French. Due to the great haste necessary, Lieutenant Crowther and I were the only company officers who were told of the attack plans, and were the only ones given maps. We later gave our platoon officers as much information as possible, but as we were rushed for the time, could not satisfactorily do this.

I arrived in the front lines with my company at 2:40 A.M. but could not find the company commander to be relieved until 3:00 A.M. After talking over the matter of relief with him, we decided that it would be impossible in the short time remaining, to make a regular relief, so I had to decide what method I was to use in order to get my company into position. It was now just beginning to get light, and I had about fifteen minutes to complete all arrangements. I gave orders to the company being relieved not to fire at anything in the foreground, or at any suspicious movements, and warned them that a friendly company was occupying a position in front of the woods in which they were entrenched. I then moved my company into the open, and with a prayer that they would not be seen, arranged them for the attack. The enemy were only eighty yards away. At 3:45 A.M. we were ready to advance. I ran over to the left of my company to see if the 67th company [sic] was ready. They had just taken position. There was no sign of the French and no sign of our Third Battalion. At 3:50 A.M. I grabbed Lieutenant Ashley, commanding the right platoon of the 67th company [sic], told him we would have to start regardless of the French, and blew my whistle for the advance. We had not gone twenty yards when a deadly machine gun fie broke out from the woods ahead and both companies dropped to their bellies.

It is here necessary to explain that our French instructors had taught us that in an attack, when a hostile machine gun opened up, all men were to immediately lie down. The automatic rifles were then to concentrate on the nest, the rifle grenadiers were to drop grenades in its vicinity, and hand bombers were to crawl up on the flanks and destroy the nest.

I saw immediately that such tactics would not do in this case. They might work against one nest, or two, but here was a nest broader than our battalion front and containing more machine guns than we had automatics. (No heavy machine guns attacked with us, and none joined us until several hours later.)

I here credit myself with doing the only thing which made that attack possible. As quickly as possible I ran along the entire line, made every man get on his feet and rush across to the cover of the woods. It was necessary in some instances to kick men to their feet. These tactics were demoralizing. Not even the non-commissioned officers knew just what they were to do, and how far they were to advance. Although the machine guns in these first woods have been routed, most men had already lost their sense of direction and stood helpless, working their bolts in a frenzy and firing with absolutely no regard to direction or purpose. They needed noise to distract their thoughts from the horrors of the wheatfield [*sic*] behind them, and it was again "up to me." I could not find an officer, but as quickly as possible gathered five or six non-commissioned officers. My instructions to them were hurried, and about as follows: "Here is our direction. We go about one mile farther. When you come to a road, just over the nose of this hill, halt and dig in. Let's go. Give 'em a yell." Myself yelling at the top of my lungs, I ran along the line telling the men to follow on, assuring them that we "had 'em on the run" and telling them only to fire when they had something to fire at.

About five hundred yards farther on I came across Corporal Fred Myers, 49th Company, who was trying to make two big Germans take off their equipment. He was nervous however, and would frequently stick the larger one with the point of his bayonet. Just as I arrived, the big German found he couldn't quite make the speed required, and decided to close with Myers. He grabbed the bayonet, and although badly outing his hands, managed to wrench it away. The other German ran. By the use of a little fast bayonet work I saved Myers life and made it a perfect score by bagging the other man as he ran.

We were now getting down over the hill and I began looking for the road which was our objective. Picking up an automatic rifle crew of one corporal (?), and three men, I raced down the valley as fast as I could, my object being to locate the road and halt our men as they came up. We came to a road, but the fire from our flanks and *rear*, caused me to ponder. The crew set up their automatic and cleaned out an entire battery which was just limbering up about 100 yards beyond the road. While they were doing this, I studied my map and found we had advanced about a half a mile too far. The fire from both sides of the ravine we had come down was now so hot that I feared that we should be killed or captured. Also, we could see large numbers of Germans forming in the streets of Bussiares, just around the nose of Hill 165, and about 350 yards to our left. I could see Hill 142 and knew we should be on it. I told the automatic crew to go back as best they could and direct any men they saw on their way back, where we were to form our line of resistance. I have since heard that two of the privates were killed on the way back, and one severely wounded. I had been under the impression that the non-commissioned officer was a corporal in the 49th Company named Davis, but have since been told that he was really Sergeant Thomas Dale. Both I believe are still alive.

On the way back to Hill 142, I crawled through a drainage ditch which was filled with reeds and water. The enemy spotted me and machine gun nests located in the sand pits on Hill 165 made my trip rather precarious. On the way I met Corporal Myers once more. He was wounded in several places and half dazed. I told him to go back to the dressing station and gave him the direction, but do not know whether he made it or not. When almost back to the proper objective, I met a group of men, nearly a platoon, under Captain Jonas Platt, Sent [sic] him word to retire to Hill 142, but he directed an attack against several machine gun nests before returning, and broke up a well organized counter-attack.

A number of our men had halted on Hill 142 and among them several good non-commissioned officers. I learned that two of my lieutenants, Somers and Peterson, had been killed, and that all the officers of the 67th Company were either killed or wounded. Lieut. Crowther had been killed. Another of my officers, Lieutenant Frazier, had been killed the night before and Swindler, a platoon commander, had gone to the rear with a nasty leg wound. Lieutenant Garvey had lost direction and was on his way to the rear with one platoon. When Platt returned, he was dragging a badly shot leg after him, and though he was rendering valuable assistance, it was soon necessary to order him to the dressing station. This left me the only officer,—Lieutenant Kierens being the first one to come to my assistance, several hours later.

Telling my non-coms just what there was to be done, we now feverishly began to dig in and organize the very bad position. I sent two of my best sergeants out to the left to try to locate the French, and two out to the right to find the Third battalion. I think their names were Gunnery Sergeant Finnegan and Sergeants O'Connor, Ware and Cronin. They never returned, and all have since been reported killed.

While organizing our position, the fire from the flanks was terrific. From one particular point, a fine view could be obtained of the enemy nests, but to get to it, it was necessary to cross a space about twenty yards wide which was being spattered with machine gun bullets. I sent two snipers out to try to pick off the hostile gunners. One of them, Private Samaritan was badly wounded while crossing the open space, and the other was killed before he had gotten fairly started. Two more men tried to make it and both were killed. It was not until half an hour later that Private Robert Slover, 49th Company, was able to make it, and from this point of vantage his aim was so accurate that nearly all the nests were cleaned out by his deadly work alone. It was reported to me that morning that Private Slover had sniped upwards of twenty men.

The sun by this time had come out strong and the bodies of the dead men were turning black and emitting a horrible stench. Private Samaritan had been lying in the exposed space all this time with a bullet through his lungs, and begging for help. One man tried to reach him and he was wounded. I didn't have the heart to let him lie unattended, but at the same time hated to detail men for a job which there were no volunteers. I could stand his cries no longer however, and finally crawled down to him and gave him first aid. Private Samaritan lay the entire day in those awful surroundings without a murmur. He was carried back to the rear just before dark that night.

Our scattered elements were now beginning to join us and by 8:00 A.M. our strength was nearly one hundred men. The enemy however took every advantage of our condition and position, and during the day, launched five distinct counter attacks at us. One of them was not discovered until the attackers were within twenty yards of us. Gunnery Sergeant Charles Hoffman is the man who should be credited with breaking up this escapade. For the purpose of showing my part however, it is necessary to tell my remembrance of the entire action:

    Gunnery Sergeant Hoffman had been wounded in the arm. I am sitting talking to him in a little patch of scrub pines and much as I regretted it, had just told him that he must go back to the dressing station. Suddenly Hoffman gave a yell and with a "Come on Captain," dashed past me through the pines to the edge of the hill. I turned just in time to see a German raise his rifle and aim at Hoffman. I fired as quickly as possible and missed. Luckily, however, the German also missed, and Hoffman finished him with his bayonet. Hoffman was now tearing into a group of four or five Germans, slashing, jabbing and firing with lightning-like rapidness. I too found myself in a rather bad fix and bayoneted two men who had closed in on me. The others broke and Hoffman and I shot at them as they ran. All told, I think we got some twelve raiders. We later found that they were in the act of setting up five light machine guns when discovered by Hoffman. His wound was not bothering him so much that I ordered him to the rear. Later upon my recommendation, he was awarded the Medal of Honor.

    Soon after this, our machine gun companies reported to me, and with their help and with the aid of a few of those wonderful soldiers — a detachment of the 2nd Division Engineers — our position was soon consolidated, and our absolute control of Hill 142 made possible, that afternoon, the initial attack on Belleau Woods.

    4. I think the following named men, other than these mentioned above, are still alive and will substantiate my statement: Lieutenant Louis Cukela, Sergeants John Stahl, Arthur Lyng, William F. Nice, and Reilly, and Corporals McDonald, Hart and Gresuell [Arthur Geuwell].

George W. Hamilton[31]

On December 7 Captain Hamilton left his Philadelphia post for temporary duty aboard the USS *Delaware* (BB-28), destined for the shores of Santo Domingo in the Dominican Republic and also Haiti. The trip involved transporting a detachment of six companies to the two locations. The Marines were properly delivered to the islands, and the *Delaware* arrived back in port on December 20. Hamilton now had a Christmas break to try and settle his mind.

17. Days of Discontent
1920

During the first week of 1920, the conversation across America involved the public announcement proclaiming the recent trade agreement of George H. Ruth Jr., known as the "Babe," from the Boston Red Sox to the New York Yankees for $125,000. Americans, in their attempt to move forward and put the war behind them, did not have a problem finding new front-page headlines.

The following day, January 6, Captain Hamilton was detached from the Marine Barracks Navy Yard at Philadelphia and was once again associated with the barracks back at Quantico. His brief days with the USS *Delaware* were over, and, in fact, his days on the ocean waters were now behind him forever. He remained in a quandary trying to sort out his current status and envision his future.

Congressional hearings concerning deaths on the last day of the war were back in session, lasting several days, under Chairman Royal C. Johnson. This issue did not concern Hamilton's future, but he would be curious as to what transpired. High ranking military commanders were called to testify before the Congressional board to settle the mess created on the final day of the war. On January 8, U.S. Army Brig. General John H. Sherburne from Boston, Massachusetts, the commander of the 167th Field Artillery Brigade, 92nd Division, testified for close to three hours with Livermore at his side. The letter from Representative Fuller to General Pershing, addressing the concerns of Livermore, was entered into evidence, as was Pershing's letter of reply.

Hamilton, who as a major was given full on-site command of the southern Meuse River crossing and was the final ranking AEF officer to hear the war was over, was not called to testify, and neither were commanders from the Marine Corps. No matter how you look at the terrible events in the final hours before the Armistice, along with the tragic loss of life, you cannot fault the men who were fighting on the front line or the Marine Corps officers, from Maj. General Lejeune on down. Orders were orders, and as always, they had to be followed, as was evidenced at Blanc Mont when Hamilton stated,

"Well, orders are to attack, and by God, we'll attack."[1] The situation involving the Meuse River was no different.

It would have been very interesting if some aviators had been called to testify, as they spent the final 24 hours of the war under conditions extremely different from Hamilton and his battalions. The thought of such testimony probably did not occur to politicians as the air bases were naturally located in safe locations well behind the front lines.

Major Maxwell Kirby of the 94th Squadron wished to experience a combat mission before the war ended, so on Sunday, November 10, he took to the air over Allied territory. At 1000 he was not only credited with a confirmed downed plane, but also what appeared to be the last downed plane of the war. Thereafter, with fog conditions present, all planes remained out of the air, which ended up being for the duration of the war. Coincidentally U.S. Army General Liggett was at the base at 1100 for a formal decorations ceremony to issue awards to the aviators.[2] Later that evening, while Kirby was describing his eventful day, Captain Rickenbacker, commanding the 94th, mentioned:

> While listening to these details that evening [Sunday November 10th] after mess, our spirits bubbling over with excitement and happiness, the telephone sounded and I stepped over and took it up, waving the room to silence. It was a message to bring my husky braves across the 95 Mess to celebrate the beginning of a new era. I demanded of the speaker, (it was Jack Mitchell, Captain of the 95th) what he was talking about.
>
> "Peace has been declared! No more fighting!" he shouted.[3]

At the 95th Squadron the festive atmosphere brought forth a constant flow of liquor along with pandemonium. To celebrate, the aviators used their creative imaginations to come up with methods of making noise. They clanged pots, pans and an assortment of other objects, while musical instruments in a makeshift ragtime band made even more clatter. This jubilation was combined with the celebratory random firing of a machine gun, pistols and colored signal flares in the air. The spontaneous outburst, along with Captain Rickenbacker's words of "spirits bubbling over with excitement and happiness," certainly clash with what Hamilton and his battalions were facing at the same moment on November 10 further to the east. Evidently the aviators had somehow intercepted some preliminary information. Sometime between 7 and 8 P.M. on November 10, the Allied Headquarters received a couple of wireless messages from the German Chancellor stating:

> I. The German Supreme Command to the plenipotentiaries at headquarters of the Allied High Command:
> The German Government accepts the conditions of the Armistice communicated to it on November 8th.
>
> The Imperial Chancellor — 3,084.

II. The German Supreme Command to the plenipotentiaries at headquarters of the Allied High Command:
The Government of the empire transmits to the High Command the following for Under Secretary of State Erzberger:
Your Excellency is authorized to sign the Armistice. You will please, at the same time, have inserted in the record the following:
The German Government will do all in its power to fulfil [sic] the terms agreed upon. However, the undersigned deems it his duty to point out that the execution of some of the conditions will bring famine to the population of that part of the German Empire which is not to be occupied.
If all the provisions which had been accumulated for feeding the troops are left in the regions to be evacuated, and if the limitation (equivalent to complete suppression) of our means of transportation is maintained and the blockade continued, to feed the population and organize a food service will be impossible.
The undersigned requests, therefore, to be authorized to negotiate with a view to modifying certain points, in order that supplies may be assured.
(*signed*) The Chancellor of the Empire[4]

During these days, correspondents continued reporting from the Congressional Press Galleries and hallways. Still, the postwar hearings were kept, as best they could be, on the back burner and away from becoming front-page news.

Back on January 16, 1919, the 18th Amendment to the Constitution was ratified, signaling that prohibition would take effect one year later. On October 28 the House and the Senate voted to override President Wilson's veto of the dry law, and when Friday, January 16, 1920, rolled around, prohibition began across the nation. It was now illegal to manufacture, sell, or transport alcoholic beverages. Technically it was not against the law to purchase alcohol, and therefore the illegal bootleg business immediately surfaced to fill the void.

The way medals were designated to members of the Marine Corps was the final issue to be addressed. Months earlier, the U.S. Navy had established an internal commission, known as the Knight Board, with Rear Admiral Austin M. Knight as president, to try and sort through the numerous problems with awards, but much confusion was still at hand.[5] On prohibition day at 10:30 A.M., the newly formed Subcommittee on Naval Affairs met in room 235 of the Senate Office Building to discuss how medals were issued. Senator Frederick Hale, who presided as chairman, served along with fellow U.S. Senate committee members Key Pittman, J. Medill McCormick, Park Trammell and Truman H. Newberry, who himself had served as secretary of the navy in 1908 and 1909.

USMC Commandant Barnett testified on Wednesday the 21st, producing several official letters noting that Marine Corps ground troops were serving in France under the U.S. Army in the American Expeditionary Forces. The general stated:

> After considering these orders that I have read you here, organizing the different commands, and the order of the President of the United States detaching them [A.E.F. Marines] from the Marine Corps during their service with the Army, I decided that in my recommendations I would not be authorized to recommend awards from the Navy for any man who had been so detached and had served with the Army and had received suitable award according to the decision of the Army board organized and put in force for that purpose. Therefore, in my recommendations I did not recommend any men of the Marine Corps who had been serving in France with the American Expeditionary Forces.[6]

General Barnett mentioned through testimony that he was, however, involved with awards for Marine Corps aviators in France, as they were an exception to the rule: "The only ones who went across the water who were recommended by me were those that I have mentioned as having served in the northern bombing group. That was essentially a naval function. They were never a part of the Army. They were never detached from the Marine Corps and the Navy."[7]

A few officers frustrated by the system continued to pursue medals for individuals whom they strongly felt deserved recognition by going through the Marine Corps chain of command. One letter addressed to Commandant Barnett, sent by Hamilton, was included as evidence. The letter stated:

> It is recommended that Second Lieut. Murl Corbett, United Marine Corps, be awarded either the distinguished service cross [sic] of the Army or the naval distinguished service medal, a citation for which is being forwarded.
>
> The undersigned was of the belief that Lieut. Corbett had been awarded a decoration, else this matter would have been brought to the attention of the headquarters sooner.
>
> Lieut. Corbett was so valuable a man, and so fearless under fire, that

Brig. General Logan Feland wearing his braided French Fourragere (courtesy Marine Corps History Division).

it is believed that a great injustice would be done should he be refused suitable recognition.[8]

The testimony answered many of the outstanding questions; however, the faulty system remained in place for any future appeals. At least all three major issues had been addressed by Congress in relatively short order.

At the age of 27, Hamilton's fast track to success had hit a wall, and there was not much he could do about the bureaucratic system that surrounded him. Although Brig. General Feland was stationed outside the United States, he had become aware that Hamilton was thoroughly disappointed. At one point in the war, Hamilton was an active major, while his commanding officer Feland was a colonel. There was now a vast gap in rank between Hamilton who was currently a captain and Feland who was now a brigadier general. Feland sent a very personal letter to Hamilton stating both praise and recognition on official stationary:

> UNITED STATES MARINE CORPS.
> HEADQUARTERS
> SECOND PROVISIONAL BRIGADE
> SANTO DOMINGO CITY, D. R.
>
> 19 February, 1920
>
> My dear Hamilton:--
> I have learned with the deepest regret that you contemplate resigning from the Marine Corps. I write this not to dissuade you from what you feel to be your best interest, but to tell you fully how much I think your services contributed to the success of the Fifth Regiment of Marines in France.
> In the beginning, during the severe and monotonous period of training, your zeal and cheerful performance of duty were marked and did much to keep up the spirit of the regiment. The same qualities stood out during the equally trying period of service in the trenches east of Verdun.
> In the initial attack in the Bois de Belleau sector on June 6, 1918, your splendid bravery, enthusiasm and dash was the principal cause of the brilliant success of the battalion to which you were attached.
> When the grand offensive of July 18th, 1918 was launched your battalion, after tremendous difficulties in the reaching of the jumping off line in the morning, was the farthest advanced of any in the splendid advance realized that day.
> At St. Mihiel in September, 1918 and in the Champagne in October, 1918, your zealous, untiring and courageous work was repeated. On October 4th, 1918, in the Champagne you, aided by a few others of the same resolution and bravery, saved the regiment from disaster and enabled it to stand against the strongest efforts of the enemy to dislodge it from the position won without support and held without support.
> In the Argonne on the morning of November 1, 1918 we were sent against a position that had been said to be impregnable, the Freya Stellung at LANDERS

ET ST. GEORGES. I selected your battalion to lead the attack; you broke the enemy's lines and advanced over them with a rush.

Finally, on the last night of the war, you made the name of our regiment immortal by the gallant manner in which you carried out the task of forcing the crossing the Meuse river and driving the enemy from the heights on the eastern bank.

A simple recital of your service is all that I can do to show you how highly I appreciate your value as an officer.

I understand that you, for business reasons, are requesting leave of absence for six months. I feel that your record entitles any request you may make to the fullest consideration.

Sincerely your friend,
(Signed) Logan Feland
Brigadier General, U.S. Marine Corps.

Major George W. Hamilton,
U.S. Marine Corps.[9]

During the war Hamilton made plenty of exceptionally difficult decisions. He now decided to part from the Marine Corps. After close to seven honorable and astonishing years of service to his country, he was walking away with his head high knowing he had done his best. On March 8, 1920, the day before his resignation, USMC Commandant Barnett sent a letter to Secretary of the Navy Josephus Daniels, stating his concern of the situation. In closing he said: "He served with distinguished gallantry with the Fifth Regiment of Marines, American Expeditionary Forces and in his separation from the service I feel that the Marine Corp will lose a most efficient and brave young officer."[10]

Captain Hamilton's resignation was accepted, as noted by the direction from President Wilson. Officially he resigned as a commissioned officer of the U.S. Marine Corps on March 9, 1920, taking effect on March 20.

Hamilton headed straight to New York City to fill an executive position as a branch department manager for the Hoff, Kleve Corporation. He would work out of the corporation's lower Manhattan office located at 15 Park Row in the financial district. The international corporation with branches throughout the world was a major importer and exporter with Norway. Exports consisted of paper, machinery, steel, cement, chemicals, dye stuffs, coffee, teas, sugar, grain, canned goods and much more, while imports were predominantly Norwegian fish products, cod-liver oil, furs, hides and wood pulp.[11] The days of wet and muddy clothing were in his past, as pressed suits, starched shirts and polished shoes were a part of the current agenda. Look out corporate America, he was now off to compete in the business world.

In June 1920 his older sister, Mary, gave birth to a baby girl named Margaret, making Hamilton an uncle for the first time. Naturally he would look forward to meeting his niece, and as this was summertime, possibly he could see her at Conesus Lake.

If he had second thoughts of getting back into the military, he would find that the Marine Corps was also changing constantly with the times. On the first day of July, Maj. General John A. Lejeune became the 13th commandant of the Marine Corps, replacing Commandant Barnett.

Two weeks later another big military story came from the U.S. Army. On July 15, four DH-4B biplanes, commanded by Captain St. Clair Street, left Mitchell Field on New York's Long Island for a journey to Nome, Alaska, just 150 miles from the Russian boarder. The trip to Nome and back covered 9,000 miles over 97 days with 112 flight hours at an average speed of 80 miles per hour. They flew at an altitude of a little more than a mile, but when they encountered mountains they soared to over 8,000 feet. The mechanics traveling with the group had little work, as the reliable 400-horsepower twelve-cylinder Liberty engines performed throughout the trip without a flaw. Improvements in engine technology had advanced a long way since the Wright brothers' 1903 first flight with a twelve-horsepower engine.[12] Nome was reached on August 12, and the planes touched down back at Mitchell Field on October 20. The pilots experienced a couple of unique factors during their trip, one of which was temperatures reaching 70 degrees below zero in an open cockpit. Another encounter was on the ground with the native Indians, who had naturally never seen the likes of an airplane. As one elderly Indian stated, "The white man pretty damn smart, but damn fool."[13]

A national historic event with major ramifications took place on August 26, 1920, as the U.S. secretary of state officially signed the 19th Amendment, known as the Suffrage Amendment, allowing women the right to vote. The issue, which had been debated for decades, had passed the resolution process in Congress the previous year and was now finalized.[14] America was changing with the times, and between his time spent in Manhattan and Washington, D.C., Hamilton was personally witnessing much of the activity.

Although New York City offered plenty of excitement, he was beginning to feel grounded in the business world behind a desk. He missed true action, adventure and the camaraderie with men who had similar interests, so he was now plotting for a possible new career. Feland had mentioned a six-month leave of absence in his letter. Could it actually be true that he might consider returning to the Corps? Hamilton's thought process propelled him to send a very brief telegram to the Marine Corps on October 1, 1920, stating:

From: George W. Hamilton, Ex. Capt. USMC, The Hoff, Kleve Corp. 15 Park Row N.Y.
To: M. G. C.
Sub: Request permanent appointment in USMC

Ref: MGC Cir. Let. Apr. 1920
1. Request my name be considered for permanent appointment[15]

Later in the month of October, Hamilton was back in the Capital City for a few fall days, and it would be understandable that he would spend time with his father and sister Margaret who was almost 25 years old. One additional purpose for his visit was political in nature, to assist a loyal friend.

A reporter arranged to meet him at the famous downtown Willard Hotel for an interview. Hamilton mentioned that Republicans had represented the New York 36th Congressional District, which encompassed five of the leading agricultural counties, for more than a generation. He avoided saying what his political affiliation was, but he did feel that it was time to change things. The Democratic Party had laid out a plan to nominate a representative who had three important credentials. The candidate, who needed to have been born in the district, know the territory well and have proven leadership skills, was none other than his good friend Shuler. Hamilton said of his friend:

Captain George K. Shuler (left) and Captain Charles Grimm in 1920, the year Shuler ran for Congress (courtesy National Archives).

George Schuler is something of a leader of forlorn hopes. That's why he was awarded the Cross of the Legion of Honor by the French republic, The American Distinguished Service Cross and the Croix de Guerre with enough palms to thatch a roof.

As soon as he was formerly nominated for Congress in his native district he secured leave of absence and has been running his own campaign. He has gone at it exactly as he went at the task of helping to make the world safe for democracy. Up there in Cayuga, Wayne, Ontario, Yates and Seneca counties the Democrats have awakened from a Rip Van Winkle sleep, and we who served with George K. Shuler in the Marine Corps in France are all rooting for him, in spite of our individual political opinions.[16]

Shuler did not win the election, and, in fact, the Republicans would continue to represent the district for the next 54 years. Hamilton and Shuler continued to keep in contact, while both searched for new ventures.

This year's presidential election was of special interest to Charles Hamilton. Woodrow Wilson had served two terms, and the new Democratic candidate was James M. Cox, an Ohio politician, who had been an editor of several papers and for more than 20 years was the owner and publisher of the *Dayton Daily News*. His Republican opponent was Warren Gamaliel Harding, who, like Cox, was an Ohio politician and for more than 30 years had been owner and publisher of the *Marion Daily Star* in the state. Harding was elected President on his 55th birthday, November 2, 1920. He received 60 percent of the vote, making his election the largest landslide victory to date.

By 1920, the groundswell movement by the veterans of the world war had increased pressure at the local level to observe the second anniversary of Armistice Day. Some mayors of towns and cities declared November 11 a half holiday as a day of remembrance. Years later the day would become a national holiday.[17]

18. Time to Fly
1921

Hamilton's time away from the Marine Corp gave him an opportunity to fully reflect upon life. It was inevitable that whatever his new career was going to be, it would entail yet an even greater personal challenge. Everything slowly started to unfold with the receipt of his next letter, simply labeled as "Sir," and dated January 26, 1921, from Commandant Lejeune, telling him to report in two days to the U.S. Navy senior medical examiner for a physical examination. Following the exam he had to wait the normal time period for the test results.

On the first day of February a letter was sent from the secretary of the navy to Captain Chamberlain stating:

> The GCM [General Court-Martial] before which you were tried at London, England, by order of the Commander, U.S. Naval Forces Operating in European Waters, found you guilty of "Scandalous conduct tending to the destruction of good morals" (2 specifications, one proved) and II. "Falsehood" and adjudged the following sentence: "The court therefore sentences him, Capt. Edmund G. Chamberlain, U.S. Marine Corps, to be dismissed from the United States Marine Corps and from the United States Naval Service."
>
> The President on 31 January 1921, confirmed the sentence of the General Court-martial in your case.
>
> You are hereby dismissed from the naval service of the U.S.[1]

With no more appeals the sad case of a great pilot, in the wrong place at the wrong time, came to a close. Hamilton also put this chapter of his life behind him.

Outside Hamilton's lower Manhattan office on February 5 there was an extremely unusual sight in the air. The U.S. Army had deployed 15 planes to fly over New York City, and at noon they engaged in a mock "bombing raid" using smoke bombs at selected targets across the city and along Fifth Avenue.[2]

There were no problems with Hamilton's physical exam, and he could now go forth with his new career. While serving on the Western Front, Hamilton had viewed firsthand the air combat missions above him. As a World War

I Marine, he had already earned the label "Devil Dog," and he was now proceeding to become a "Devil Dog" daredevil, as a Marine Corps pilot and aviation officer.

What was the key piece of the puzzle that made him make such a career choice? Was it the early feats of different aviators or conversations with the members of the 94th Squadron on the USS *Louisville*, with whom he shared the 11 day voyage from France to the United States? Was it Eddie Rickenbacker's comments that called flying over the Great War the most spectacular free show ever that piqued his interest? The Marine Corps was expanding their own aerial division because they did not want to be dependent upon other military organizations for proper air support in future conflicts. Hamilton wanted to play a future major role and be a part of it all.

He's back! On March 22, 1921, after about a year's sabbatical, Hamilton officially returned back into the fold of the Marine Corps, becoming a Marine captain, subject to confirmation. Four days later he registered for the permanent appointment, and on March 29 he once again took the oath of office at Marine Corps Headquarters, Washington, D.C.

Captain Hamilton was then given a few days off prior to reporting back to the Marine Barracks at the Navy Yard in Washington, D.C., on April 8. He'd spend the following months biding his time as an assistant to the Barracks commanding officer until the next pilot training class opened up for students.

One Marine Corps officer, Captain A. C. Dearing, attached to the USS *New Hampshire* at the Philadelphia Navy Yard, took exception to Hamilton's appointment as a captain. Quite possibly he had learned that Hamilton was now ranked approximately 56th out of 329 captains.[3] Dearing issued a memo to Lejeune saying:

> 1. The feeling among the officers of the Corps is that they can freely take up any matter with their Commandant. While I have the highest regard for Captain Hamilton's ability as a marine officer and desire that he be a member of my Corps, yet I feel that the appointment is unfair to me. Captain Hamilton was given the opportunity to try his luck in the open market for nearly a year. This is something that perhaps many others would like to try, but they have continued in the service, performing the duties assigned to them. It has been a time honored custom that officers, desiring to return to the service, go to the foot of the list or come back as extra numbers. It seems to me that an appointment of this kind directly reflects on our training, if an officer can spend a year in civil life and come back ahead of those having spent a year in the service.
>
> 2. I respectfully request that the Commandant reconsider this appointment, taking into consideration the records, hopes and ambitions of the officers affected.[4]

There was no way Lejeune was going to reverse his decision, and the issue was closed. In his spare time Hamilton studied and reviewed aeronautics. He now had a passion and a direction upon which to focus and learn.

It is recognized that Marine Corps aviation began on May 22, 1912, when Hamilton was finishing his senior year at Central High. On that date USMC Lieutenant Alfred Austell Cunningham reported to the aviation camp at Annapolis to concentrate all his time towards the pursuit of flying. As the first Marine aviator and the fifth in the U.S. Navy he was designated Marine Aviator No. 1 and Naval Aviator No. 5.

On May 2 Hamilton received orders to report to the Marine Barracks at Quantico for a temporary duty assignment with the rifle and pistol competition taking place.

Come Saturday, May 28, folks in the Capital City were looking forward to the upcoming Memorial Day holiday. That evening, at a little after 6 P.M., the nation experienced the worst single air crash to date.[5] A Curtiss-Eagle air ambulance, being used as common transportation for seven prominent individuals, was on a return flight to the city from Langley Field when it ran into turbulent winds 40 miles south of the city. Everyone on board, including five U.S. Army officers, perished. One person was a former member of the U.S. Congress and had served as a major in the Air Service during the war, while another was the chairman of the executive board of the American Automobile Association. French air attaché Captain de Lavergne, flew on the initial trip to Langley Field, but chose alternate transportation on the return trip, as he felt the plane's 400-horsepower was not sufficient to handle the combined weight of the plane and occupants. The pilot was well qualified and not faulted for the accident. Flying was continually dangerous even for well qualified pilots, as they were at the mercy of the plane's structural quality, from overall construction to individual critical parts. Additionally weather conditions were always a critical variable.

Also on May 28, Rickenbacker, the country's premiere pilot, was heading to Washington, D.C., on the last leg of his solo transcontinental flight from California. Having left Chicago earlier in the morning, he also ran into turbulent weather and had to touch his plane down to ride out a violent thunderstorm. Upon arrival in the Capital City, he changed clothes and went to a private dinner hosted by General Pershing at the Metropolitan Club.[6]

With noted demand, the inception of passenger plane service was becoming very apparent. On the following day a trial run between New York City and Atlantic City was successfully performed using the largest commercial plane in the world.[7] The twin-engine plane, with 900 total horsepower and an enclosed luxury cabin, was capable of transporting a pilot, two crew members and twenty passengers. On June 15, passenger service from 97th Street in Manhattan to the Atlantic City Inlet began with the 57-minute flights departing every hour from each location. Future service was planned using the same type of plane for flights between New York City and Philadelphia every two hours, and between New York City and Washington, D.C., every three hours.

Hamilton's younger first cousin, George C. Wright, was now graduating from Central High with the class of 1921. The younger Wright had one brother blazing a trail in journalism and another brother on the fast track in the U.S. Navy. What path would he take? It wasn't too long ago that the Central High principal and a few teachers had written praising recommendations to assist Hamilton in becoming a Marine Corps officer. The Central High faculty might be getting a good case of writer's cramp now because not only was George C. Wright headed off to the U.S. Naval Academy at Annapolis but so were twelve of his classmates.[8]

On June 9, 1921, Captain Hamilton officially learned that he was enrolled in the Student Naval Aviator program. The upcoming six-month course would cover many aspects of aviation, including ground instruction, aircraft construction, engineering, navigation, flight training as pilots and observers, plus tactics and instruction with bombs and other weapons. Some aviators might be selected to later attend advanced courses for one term at the Naval Academy and one year at the Massachusetts Institute of Technology. Hamilton's final day at the barracks in Washington, D.C., was June 28; he would then have a few days off before traveling to Pensacola, Florida.

Hamilton checked into the Pensacola station on Independence Day 1921. Classes would begin the following day, July 5, his 29th birthday. He was embracing this new challenge with all of his attention; if successful, he would soon be given approval for duty that would allow him to fly all sorts of aircraft, including airplanes, balloons and dirigibles.

While he attended the six-month aviator classes, it is good to step back and understand what was going on outside of his personal endeavors, with regard to the nation he was defending. Americans had put the war behind them, and technology, innovation and manufacturing were continuing to fuel the growth of the country. Three giants in this arena — Henry Ford, Harvey Firestone and Thomas Edison — often went camping together. The escape allowed the friends to refresh their minds with creative thinking and futuristic ideas, while discussing thoughts for quality improvements and increased production. They also truly shared a love of getting away outdoors. President Harding also enjoyed camping and mingling with the nation's brightest entrepreneurs. On Saturday, July 23, he joined the three prominent men camping in Maryland. Firestone had brought six of his best horses, and President Harding mounted one and took the lead, followed by Firestone, Ford, a member of the Secret Service and a couple others. The following day included an open-air worship service at the campsite that was open to the public.[9]

This year numerous new world records were set at the National Rifle

Matches. At Wakefield, Massachusetts, USMC Sergeant Theos J. Jones hit a 10-inch bulls-eye 132 straight times at 300 yards, and at Sea Grit, New Jersey, USMC Gunner C. A. Lloyd won the "all-comers" 600-yard expert match by hitting the 20-inch bulls-eye 101 consecutive times. At Camp Perry, Ohio, USMC Sergeant T. B. Crawley won an 800-yard shoot out by hitting the 36-inch five-ring bulls-eye 176 times in succession, and USMC Sergeant J. W. Adkins hit the 1,000-yard bulls-eye 75 times in a row.

For the first time at the rifle matches, several planes were exhibited on the ground with the largest group consisting of four DH-4B planes. Each biplane had a mounted machine gun that was synchronized to fire through the propeller opening, as well as a .30-caliber Lewis gun positioned on flexible mounts. The air competition events involved shooting at moving targets over land and fixed targets on water. The aviation exhibition was such a success that it was scheduled to be a part of future annual matches. Knowing Hamilton, he was looking forward to testing his skills at this new event.

The Marine Corps also continued with their training and exercises at the camp in Gettysburg, Pennsylvania. The facility, now referred to as Camp Harding, was to be the site of featured exercises and events during late September and early October. A mock battle would be performed on the Gettysburg battlefield showing how the Civil War battle would have played out using modern warfare, including airplanes and tanks. The exercises were also a venue to promote the Marines Corp to the public. President Harding arrived on October 1 and drove past long lines of Marines at full attention. He stayed two days viewing more than 4,000 Marines exhibiting maneuvers. Some Civil War veterans attended, wearing their old uniforms, causing the President to proclaim, "Let's blend the Blue and the Gray."[10] Without war there was now an annual pattern of scheduled events for the Marine Corps, which included the National Rifle Matches and the Camp Harding reenactment event.

The Teapot Dome scandal was becoming the biggest national news story of the times. The issue involved public land containing oil reserves, which former President Taft had set aside for use by the U.S. Navy. President Harding had the reserves transferred to the Department of the Interior. His secretary of the interior, Albert Fall, leased the land without competitive bidding, and before long, drilling was started and talk of bribery was all over the news. This story did not go away and was a hot topic of conversation in the Congressional Press Galleries over the next several years.

For America, this year's third anniversary observance of Armistice Day was going to be special. England and France had taken the initiative to honor a dead unknown warrior as a token remembrance of the many lives sacrificed in the Great War. Other European countries followed suit, and America now planned to do the same. In 1921 there were 1,237 AEF bodies that were still not identified. Of this lot, the bodies of four American men, who were known to have died in combat, were selected from four different cemeteries in France, exhumed, and placed into identical caskets. U.S. Army Sergeant Edward F. Younger was chosen to make the final selection by placing one rose on a given casket. He later reflected upon the moment by saying: "I went into the room and walked past the caskets. I walked around them three times. Suddenly I stopped. It was as though something had pulled me. A voice seemed to say: 'This is a pal of yours.'"[11]

On November 9 the casket of the Unknown Soldier was brought to the Capitol rotunda to lie in state for two days. This recognition was very historic as up to this time only the three assassinated presidents — Lincoln, Garfield and McKinley — along with seven additional dignitaries had received this honor. At 8:30 A.M. on the morning of November 11, 1921, the flag-draped casket was carried out and down the rotunda steps as the Marine Band played the familiar tune "Nearer My God to Thee." The casket was then carried by a horse-drawn caisson, as part of a full military procession, to Arlington National Cemetery. The seven-mile route passed by the White House to Georgetown, then across the Potomac River and through the gates of Arlington Cemetery, with more than 100,000 spectators lining the way.

President Harding and Supreme Court Chief Justice Taft led the way on foot. Because of his prior stroke, former President Wilson was very frail and rode in a carriage. The former president, who was so strong during the war, had not appeared in public recently, and he received a warm welcome. Vice President Calvin Coolidge, along with his wife, General Pershing, French General Foch and many other dignitaries from across the world, wearing official dress adorned with medals and sashes, were also present and in the flow. The patriotic atmosphere within the crowd elevated as a procession of Medal of Honor recipients passed by to a constant applause, but the loudest cheer, which turned to a rousing tearful roar, was unquestionably reserved for the Gold Star mothers, who had lost a son during the war.

A loudspeaker system, known as the "Bell Loud Talker," was installed so telephone amplifiers could transmit live recordings to speakers outside Madison Square Garden in New York City and on to further facilities across the nation. Once inside Arlington's gates, President Harding eulogized the fallen. His closing words were:

> Standing today on hallowed ground, conscious that all America has halted to share in the tribute of the heart and mind and soul to this fellow-American, and knowing that the world is noting this expression of the republic's mindfulness, it is fitting to say that his sacrifice, and that of millions of dead, shall not be in vain. There must be, there shall be, the commanding voice of a conscious civilization against armed warfare.

As we return this poor clay to its mother soil, garlanded by love and covered with the decorations that only nations can bestow, I can sense the prayers of our people, of all peoples, that this Armistice Day shall mark the beginning of a new and lasting era, of peace on earth, good-will among men.[12]

At the conclusion of his speech, President Harding asked the huge crowd listening through the speakers to join him in the Lord's Prayer, which he proceeded to recite with his right hand extended into the air. He then pinned the Medal of Honor and the Distinguished Service Cross on the flag covering the coffin, thus issuing America's two highest awards to the Unknown Warrior. Many other foreign leaders followed suit presenting honorable medals from their own countries.

The coffin was lowered, French soil was laid on top, and following "Taps," a 21-gun salute was fired. In part, this national event recalling memories of the Great War took place so that the many sacrifices made along the way would never be forgotten by future generations.

Understandably, Hamilton would have been consumed with thoughts of the ceremony in his home city but also with an event in New York City. On the evening of Armistice Day, more than 800 aviators n from the United States military, Allied countries and Central Power countries attended the third annual Armistice Day dinner at the Hotel Commodore. The event was started in 1918 by the American Flying Club, but as the club was no longer in existence, the Aero Club of America had taken control of the event.[13]

At the Florida base, Captain Hamilton was completing his six-month training course, and in the following month of December, he was deemed a capable Marine aviator and proudly given his certificate. His final graduation mark of 3.3869 placed him 15th in a class of 67.[14] He was now a certified trained pilot with an abundance of independence. There were certainly leadership roles ahead and plenty of challenges to his liking. He was detached from the school in Pensacola on December 22, 1921, with orders to report to the Marine Barracks at Quantico on the 28th. During the transfer he was afforded several days off to be at home with his family for Christmas.

19. Wings and Prayers
1922

Hamilton began 1922 stationed at Quantico assigned to Major Roy S. Geiger's First Aviation Group, Marine Corps East Coast Expeditionary Force. There was no better instructor than Major Geiger, Marine Aviator No. 5 and Naval Aviator No. 49, who several years ago had assisted Edmund Chamberlain. With proven leadership skills Captain Hamilton would soon be given command of an air scout squadron.

Quantico was the primary base for Marine Corps aviator activity and one of five Marine Corps Aviation Stations. The other stations were located at Parris Island, South Carolina; Santo Domingo City, Dominican Republic; Port Au Prince, Haiti; and Sumay, Guam, Marianna Islands.[1] Hamilton liked Quantico, but he had his eyes set on one of the more intriguing distant locations.

The facility at Quantico was growing with the times. Back in 1911 an aviation camp was constructed near Annapolis, complete with a wooden hanger, but it was soon deemed to be an inappropriate location as errant bullets from the nearby U.S. Naval Academy rifle range came too close for comfort.[2] At the new location two steel hangers for planes had recently been erected, along with fourteen temporary 20-by-80-foot barracks for the aviators. The large amusement hall contained a bowling alley and enough space to seat the entire air command for a function.

During the war, flyboys on the Western Front flew assorted aircraft, but the only American made plane was the De Havilland DH-4, nicknamed the "flying coffin" because the pressurized gas tank was situated between the pilot's seat and the observer's seat.[3] In the event of a crash, the pilot was often crushed between the motor and the heavy gas tank. Additionally the rubber fuel hose under the hot exhaust manifold was known to cause fires. By the start of the 1920s, the nation had approximately 3,800 planes in military service, of which 2,800 were DH-4 planes. To correct this serious design error, Congress appropriated funds for major adjustments to the DH-4 at a conversion cost of $1,200 for each plane. The biggest construction change was positioning the pilot behind the gas tank to make the planes safer. This also improved communication between the pilot and the observer. By 1921, 1,000 planes had received alterations and were then designated as DH-4B models.[4] For 1922 modifications were planned for an additional 250 DH-4 planes.

Across the nation "barnstormers" and daring "wing walkers" enticed crowds, along with assorted stunt flying, but it was the more practical side of aviation that industrial entrepreneurs were focused on. Postal air mail delivery had been in service for roughly three and a half years with an excellent track record. The future of America hinged upon aviation, not only for military and national defense, but also for government, private business, commercial and civilian use. Commercial aviation had not yet flourished, and there were only 1,200 civilian aircraft and pilots across the nation. With increasing air traffic, aviation groups were putting forth initial bills to license pilots and regulate flight routes. As an aviator, Hamilton was now afforded a completely different perspective of the District of Columbia.

Flight records were constantly being broken, and in the previous year a new top speed of 197.8 miles an hour had been achieved. During the final week of December 1921, a flight endurance record of 26 hours, 19 minutes, and 35 seconds was set over Long Island.[5] Also, towards the end of 1921, a new parachute record was established from just under five miles high. The adage "records were made to be broken" was never truer.

You can only keep a good multi-talented man hidden behind the scenes for so long. It had been less than three weeks since Hamilton had graduated from aviation school as a qualified pilot, when the athletic 29-year-old stepped fully into another world.

On Monday evening, January 9, 1922, the Aero Club of America held its 14th Annual Banquet at the relatively new Commodore Hotel at 42nd Street and Lexington Avenue in New York City. This was the true aviator annual banquet, and therefore it was even more spectacular than the Armistice Day dinner event held a few months ago at this same location. The function also served as a prominent business meeting to assess the accomplishments of the prior year and kick off the year with visionary goals and objectives.

The "who's who" of aviation was in attendance. Club president Benedict Crowell, the past assistant secretary of war, presided over the gala event, with famous inventor Charles F. Kittering as the toastmaster. The eight honorary guests were Rear Admiral W.F. Fullam, U.S. Navy; Major General Mason M. Patrick, A.S., chief of Air Service; Rear Admiral William A. Moffett, U.S. Navy; Honorable Fred C. Hicks Jr.; Captain Guy de Lavergne, French air attaché; Captain St. Claire Street, A.S.; Captain George W. Hamilton, U.S. Marine Corps; and Captain Eddie Rickenbacker.[6]

Yes, there were many Hamiltons in society, but there was only one USMC

Captain George W. Hamilton. He now had the moment he was now looking for, recognition to put the past behind him and a second chance for new adventures, goals and horizons.

As so often happens, the honorary guests, such as Captain Rickenbacker, did not need much of an introduction. Rear Admiral Moffett was the current chief, Bureau of Aeronautics of the Navy Department. The new position, created on August 10, 1921, controlled all Marine Corps aviation procurement. Rear Admiral W.F. Fullam had retired from the U.S. Navy after serving in many capacities, including a stint as the 23rd superintendent of the U.S. Naval Academy and as the commander of Allied Naval Forces along the Pacific Coast during the war. General Pershing appointed Major General Mason M. Patrick to command the Air Service in France during World War I, and Captain St. Claire Street was the commander of the famous Alaskan flight. Captain Guy de Lavergne was the air attaché of the French Embassy as part of the Diplomatic Service to the United States, stationed in the Capital City. Fred C. Hicks Jr. was currently a U.S. Congressman, who had represented his New York district through the war.

The audience included not only many of aviation's leading men, but some of America's most distinguished leaders who had taken a keen interest in the future of aviation. They realized the profound potential and opportunity for aviation as an avenue for tremendous investment. A few of the notables in the 100 plus crowd were Edwin and Harry Guggenheim, F. Trubee Davison, Caleb S. Bragg, Otto Praeger, Eddie Stinson, Pierre S. du Pont, Vincent Astor, William A. Rockefeller, Fiorello H. La Guardia and Nelson Doubleday.

At the start of the meeting, the toastmaster lightheartedly noted that due to prohibition, the gathering would not be able to officially toast as in the good old days. Kittering then read a few letters and telegrams from noted individuals who were unable to attend but had sent forth their good wishes. One from President Harding read: "Greatly regret my inability to accept your invitation and be with the Aero Club at its Banquet tonight. I shall hope that the occasion may bring further encouragement to American interest and effort in the growing field of aeronautics."[7]

Statements from Orville Wright and other exceptional Americans were also read. The Aero Club felt that with airplane races surfacing all over the world the United States should compete in the major events to demonstrate America's great technology. Rear Admiral Fullam stated that because wars would not cease, but rather only be postponed, the nation which controlled the air would dominate land and sea operations. Later Captain Rickenbacker mentioned in his speech that "the presence here tonight of the Chiefs of the Army, Navy and Marine Corps flying services, and of leading engineers and executives in the automotive world is highly significant of the recognition being accorded the science of aeronautics."[8]

Challenges existed in the air for speed, distance and dependability, and those who broke records often received awards. Grover Cleveland Loening received two notable trophies: the Collier Trophy and the Wright Trophy. He received the latter for the design and performance of his dependable seaworthy plane, which could seat four, travel at 135 mph and fly up to 17,500 feet.

Captain Hamilton was quickly becoming recognized by the top echelon of aviators for his future potential contributions. Although there does not appear to be a record of any speech he might have made, he was now primed for speaking at future aeronautical gatherings. Because Hamilton could not resist a challenge, he had to be thinking in the back of his mind about what current record he planned to break. His life was on track again, and he was focused on his bright future.

On the first day of February, Hamilton officially put in a written request to be assigned for aviation duty in the Dominican Republic.[9] The current commander of the First Marine Air Squadron in Santo Domingo was none other than Major Alfred Cunningham. Major Geiger, the aviation Third Brigade commander, endorsed Hamilton's request the following day and sent it on to Commandant Lejeune. Somewhere along the paper trail the process was slowed down, and for the time being Hamilton remained stationed at Quantico.

Unquestionably, he had faced death numerous times throughout his service in the war. Side conversations at the Aero Club and other aviation gatherings always touched upon men they knew who had either come close to death or had perished chasing their ambitions. All aviators tried to learn from the mishaps of others to attain additional knowledge and experience.

On March 23, 1922, Hamilton was flying in a Vought VE-7 "Bluebird," Number A-5958 biplane, along with his mechanic. Because of its speed the limited-production trainer plane was distinguished as being among the first U.S. Navy fighter planes. The men, on a return flight to the Quantico aviation field at Reid, made an initial landing that was rather hard, and the plane was soon airborne again. Instantly the engine failed. Hamilton tried to turn and make a landing at the second runway, but with insufficient altitude the plane dropped the final 50 feet and crashed into the Chappawamsic swamp. The location was near a new bridge connecting the roadway between the aviation field and the Quantico barracks. Although most of the plane, including the wings, was damaged beyond repair, the two men lived to fly again, escaping this time with only bruises.[10]

A swamp was an aviator's best friend as it generally offered a soft landing. The cushion of such terrain saved many lives during early aviation and throughout World War I. The numerous airfields located next to marshy water were a blessing to many.

An investigation bureau determined that the likely cause of the engine failure was carburetor screws becoming loose. A second board, however, disagreed with the findings, but could not identify the critical factors that created the accident.[11]

Aviation was certainly capturing the hearts and minds of the most courageous and adventurous youths in America. During the following month of April 1922, a 20-year-old named Charles A. Lindbergh took to the air for the very first time as a passenger in a 220 HP Lincoln Standard Tourabout.[12] The daring young man, who was initially awestruck by aviation, was now instantly hooked and could not wait for his day to fly solo.

In May, Major Geiger made his own headlines by breaking a world record for combined speed and distance. Flying in a DH-4 he flew from Quantico to the training facility in Pensacola, Florida, averaging about 110 miles an hour. His two stops were included in the calculations covering the 1,000 mile distance.

On Memorial Day 1922 an official ceremony was held to reveal to the public the recently completed Lincoln Memorial. President Taft, while in office began the project and now, as the chairman of the Memorial Commission and chief justice of the Supreme Court, he turned the historic structure over to the United States government for dedication. President Harding accepted on behalf of the government. In attendance were several soldiers from both the "Blue" and the "Gray," extended members of the Lincoln family, sculptor Daniel French and many government officials. Hidden amplified speakers carried the many speeches to the crowd, which extended back for about a quarter of a mile. The massive marble structure with Doric columns, located on the western end of the Washington Mall by the Potomac River, gave the Capital City its third dominant structure. To the east was the impressive dome of the Capitol Building and situated in the middle, with proportionate distances between the Capitol and the Lincoln Memorial, was the tall granite and marble Washington Monument.

With the start of summer, it would be natural for Hamilton to long to get back to Conesus Lake once again, even if for a long weekend. In early summer, though Mary might not have realized the changes, she was now pregnant with her second child, a future son, who would be a nephew to George.

The annual mock battle at Gettysburg, Pennsylvania, was going to be held during the summer, and Hamilton planned to be in attendance at Camp Harding. He first laid eyes on this location back on July 18, 1914, as a young 22-year-old Marine, when he and other members of the Corps attended training camp for several weeks.

One of the Marine Corps' most decorated men, Brig. General Smedley D. Butler, the commandant of Quantico, was once again designated to preside over the camp. President Harding and his wife planned to arrive on July 2 to view the exercises on the 59th anniversary of Pickett's charge. They looked forward to camping with the Marines and spending time with other notable guests, including the widow of Confederate General James Longstreet.

About 5,000 Marines had been camping in Maryland, and on Sunday morning, June 25, they broke camp and hiked 18 miles towards Gettysburg, Pennsylvania. Crowds of folks stopped what they were doing to cheer the Marines along their route, and when evening came they halted and camped near Thurmont, Maryland. The following day, June 26, they broke camp for the final leg of their march, which would bring them to Camp Harding in the afternoon. As the troops traversed woods and fields with full gear, a number of the leathernecks instantly recalled the lush wheat fields of days past. This would be the largest group of military troops assembled at Gettysburg since the Civil War.

Thirty planes were scheduled to assist the ground troops in the mock battle. Hamilton, as a Marine Corps squadron commander, was chosen to provide air support in the battle. He looked forward to spending free time reuniting with some of his "Boys" and other veterans of the war. It would be a festive reunion filled with late night conversations, swapping stories and good cheer.

On Monday June 26, 1922, Hamilton warmed up his DH-4B biplane number 6157 at the Quantico Marine Base in preparation for his flight to Gettysburg. Seated behind him was his observer and mechanic, Gunnery Sergeant George R. Martin.

To a common person at ground level it appeared to be a fairly nice day for a flight to Gettysburg. The previous day the high temperature had been close to 93 degrees, but today a front was moving in and the unsettled forecast called for fair and cooler weather. The published "Flying Weather Forecast" from Washington to Long Island called for partly cloudy skies and fresh northwest winds up to 5,000 feet, while the forecast from Washington to Dayton, Ohio, mentioned generally clear skies with moderate to fresh north and northeast winds up to 5,000 feet.[13] Before long Captain Hamilton was airborne cruising with his squadron at the normal speed of 90 miles per hour.

Shortly after 1300 Hamilton, commanding the Second Squadron, was leading five biplanes in battle formation engaged in mock scouting ahead of the ground troops over the battlefield at an altitude of 1,000 feet. He circled the field and signaled to his other planes that he was preparing to land. As he was making a banked left turn and descending through scattered clouds his plane began to shake, apparently due to turbulent air. The biplane then began

A DH-4B biplane similar to the one Hamilton flew (courtesy National Archives).

a tailspin from which he could not recover. The plane crashed nose down on the battlefield, within yards of a vendor's tent and just a little north of where Pickett made his famous charge. The time was noted in reports as 1:10 P.M.

The noise from the plane's descent caught the attention of several thousand Marines preparing camp nearby. The first person to arrive on the scene was USMC Lieutenant Howard Enyart, a friend of Captain Hamilton's. The lieutenant soon realized it was Hamilton's biplane; however, the captain's body was injured beyond initial recognition. Hamilton's companion, Gunnery Sergeant George R. Martin, died shortly after reaching the local hospital. Captain Hamilton's death was naturally front-page news in the *Washington Post*.[14]

An investigation committee was immediately formed, headed by Brig. General Butler. Most aviation accidents were attributed to faulty equipment or weather conditions rather than pilot error, and Captain Hamilton's plane crash appeared to be no different. The findings from the inquiry board were as inconclusive and sketchy as the initial eyewitness reports. The board's review could not fully determine the cause of the accident, which was likely a combination of factors. It appears that the fresh northeast winds had picked up, as one official report mentions that wind played a significant role in the crash. What was certain, through another official written review, was that the "board found [Hamilton's] death in line of duty and not result of own misconduct" and that the board could not "attach blame or culpability to any person in the Naval Service."[15]

The fierce competitor's days of striving to be the best of the best were over. The undeniable fact was that Hamilton had taken his last breath.

Back in 1918, upon losing his son Quentin to an airplane crash, Theodore Roosevelt philosophically stated:

> In America today all our people are summoned to service and sacrifice. Pride is the portion only of those who know bitter sorrow or the foreboding of bitter sorrow. But all of us who give service, and stand ready for sacrifice, are the torchbearers. We run with the torches until we fall, content if we can pass them on to the hands of other runners. The torches whose flame is brightest are borne by the gallant men at the front, and by the gallant women whose husbands and lovers, whose sons and brothers are at the front. These men are high of soul, as they face their fate on the shell-shattered earth, or in the skies above or in the waters beneath; and no less high of soul are the women with torn hearts and shining eyes; the girls whose boy lovers have been struck down in their golden morning, and the mothers and wives to whom word has been brought that henceforth they must walk in the shadow.
>
> These are the torch-bearers; these are they who have dared the Great Adventure.[16]

20. Funeral

On Tuesday, June 27, Captain Hamilton's body was escorted back to the Capital City by officers from his squadron. The skies above Gettysburg were still a little turbulent, and most of the roughly one dozen Marine Corps aviation planes in the area remained on the ground.

The Hamilton family hastily put together a farewell tribute service at locations that would have pleased the mighty warrior. The Marine Corps also offered their full assistance. A formal military funeral, open to the public, was set for Thursday, June 29, starting with a 9:30 A.M. service at Central High School. Final rites would be administered at 11:00 A.M. in Arlington National Cemetery. A section of the Marine Corps Band, along with a company of Marines, would be present at both Central High and the grave site.

On Thursday morning throngs of people, wishing to pay their final respects to Captain Hamilton, entered the doors of Central High. The overflow crowd consisted of family, relatives, school alumni, comrades from the Marine Corps, and a wide assortment of family friends and professional business associates. There were many dignitaries present, including Assistant Secretary of the Navy Theodore D. Roosevelt Jr. The Congregational Church service conducted by U.S. Navy Chief of Chaplains Captain Evan Walter Scott began promptly as scheduled.

In his short life span Hamilton had lived each day of life to its fullest and touched many lives. Since graduating from high school in 1912, he had achieved many accomplishments, but needless to say this was not the tenth high school reunion anyone was looking for.

The commanders who inspired and guided him in the Great War had a final role to play. Serving as honorary pallbearers were the Commandant of the Marine Corp Maj. General Lejeune, Maj. General Neville, Brig. General Feland, Lt. Colonel Turrill and Lt. Colonel Turner.[1]

HONORARY PALLBEARERS

Major General John A. Lejeune   During World War I he was the highest ranking member of the Marine Corps serving in the AEF as the Second Division Force Commander. He was currently the USMC's 13th commandant.

Major General Wendell C. Neville   He later served as the 14th commandant of

Marine Corps. At Belleau Wood he was the commanding officer over the Fifth Regiment and later commanded the Fourth Brigade.

Brigadier General Logan Feland   He was the officer who sincerely thought so much of Hamilton. At Belleau Wood he was Second in command of the Fifth Regiment. When Hamilton commanded 1/5, Feland was his commanding officer over the Fifth Regiment. He later became a major general.

Lieutenant Colonel Julius S. Turrill   He commanded 1/5 when Hamilton first joined the 49th Company in the U.S. and served as Hamilton's commander at Belleau Wood.

Lieutenant Colonel Thomas C. Turner   He presided as the officer in charge/senior aviator attached to Headquarters U.S. Marine Corps at the Quantico base where Hamilton departed from on his last flight.[2]

It has been said you can tell a lot about a person by the friends that he keeps. Taking a glimpse at the active pallbearers speaks volumes as to the men who were close to Hamilton. Those carrying the flag-draped coffin, wearing the requested full khaki uniform with fair leather belts, were Major Puryear, Major Shearer, U.S. Navy Surgeon Boone, Major Geiger, Captain Wright and Captain Whitehead.[3]

Hamilton was a man of convictions and always stood up for what he deemed to be right, and he surrounded himself with men who had similar traits. It should be noted that back when General Pershing released USMC Brig. General Doyen of his command of the Fourth Brigade, replacing him with U.S. Army Lt. Colonel Harbord, a couple of the men who would be Hamilton's active pallbearers stepped forward and protested the decision. As one historian wrote: "Junior officers were admonished to keep quiet, and several brigade staff members were placed under arrest for continuing to question the relief after being told to shut up. Holland Smith listed staff majors Bennett Puryear, Maurice E. Shearer, and Henry N. Manney Jr. as members of the Marine cabal opposed to Doyen's ouster."[4]

ACTIVE PALLBEARERS

Major Bennet Puryear Jr.   Puryear served in World War I as quartermaster under Pershing. At the time of Hamilton's death, Puryear was assigned to Marine Headquarters in Washington, D.C. In April 1919 seven majors were officially recommended for promotion to lieutenant colonel, two of whom were Hamilton and Puryear. He rose to the rank of major general and retired in 1943.

Major Maurice E. Shearer   At Belleau Wood, he took command of 3/5 when Major Berry was wounded. On June 26 he declared "Belleau Woods now U.S. Marine Corps entirely." He fought in the Spanish-American War and joined the Marine Corps in 1905. He retired as a brigadier general.

Surgeon Joel T. Boone   In France he served as a medical officer under Division Surgeon Derby. He received the Medal of Honor for deeds performed at Soissons. As a personal physician to President Hoover and others, he later became chief medical director of the Veterans Administration and a vice admiral of United States Navy.

Major Roy S. Geiger   After joining the Marines as a private he rose to become a major general in the Marine Corps and was posthumously promoted to four star general. Like Hamilton, he was one of the few who served on the sea, on land and in the air.

Captain Lee W. Wright   He was assistant paymaster with the Marine Corps Headquarters in Washington, D.C. As a member of "The Society of the Sons of the Revolution," in 1920 he served as vice-chairman of the Triennial Convention, General Society. He does not appear to have been a close relative to Hamilton, as other Wrights were.

Captain Frank Whitehead   Whitehead was one of the most liked captains of the Fourth Brigade. At Blanc Mont he was wounded in "The Box," but recovered to lead his company across the Meuse River. In his later years he was the commandant of the Army Industrial College and the first commander of the college outside the Army.

Following the Central High service, the captain's flag-draped coffin was placed on the back of the flatbed funeral vehicle. Such a large crowd had never gathered outside the high school and been so silent. The coffin was then slowly transported with a full military procession to Arlington National Cemetery. At the Fort Myer Gate entrance the casket was carefully transferred to a caisson. The final path forward then led to grave lot number 4585 in the southern section.

The Air Service wished to fly several open cockpit biplanes over Hamilton's grave as a final tribute. When Margaret, who idolized her older brother, heard of the plan she immediately contacted officials and pleaded that the flyover be canceled. She stated, through constant tears, "They will meet their death soon enough, just as my brother did. Please don't let them take unnecessary chances. George is gone. He went without fear, but the others must not take the chances when there is no need for it."[5]

As distraught as Margaret was, her plea was real. Recollections of a famous mishap most certainly were in her mind. The date was September 17, 1908, when Margaret was just a couple of months shy of becoming a teenager and a middle school student in the Capital City. The U.S. Signal Corps had challenged developers to build a plane that could carry two people at 40 miles per hour for a minimum one hour flight. Orville Wright took his plane to Fort Myer, Virginia, which was in close proximity to Arlington Cemetery. Among the very large crowd were President Roosevelt and members of his Cabinet, including U.S. Secretary of War Taft. Orville's observation passenger was U.S. Army 1st Lieutenant Thomas E. Selfridge. The plane rose and shortly thereafter the wooden propeller split causing the plane to crash near the cemetery's western wall. Orville's injuries were extensive but not life threatening,

The grave of George Wallis Hamilton at Arlington National Cemetery (courtesy Michael Robert Patterson, Arlington National Cemetery Website).

while Selfridge died. As the first causality of modern aviation, he was buried in Arlington National Cemetery with full military honors and the western cemetery gate was then named Selfridge Gate.[6]

Aviation officials adhered to Margaret's wishes, and the flyover was canceled. At 11:00 A.M. the graveside service began. For the final tribute the U.S. Navy chaplain said a few prayers. A final rifle volley was followed by a moment of silence and then came the bugler sounding taps. The flag covering the casket was carefully folded and presented to Charles Hamilton. Captain Hamilton's body was then laid to rest.

21. Life Goes On

When Hamilton passed away life continued on for the others around him. Listed below are a few of the notable people.

Charles A. Hamilton

Hamilton's father became the dean of Washington newspaper correspondents, treasurer of the National Press Club, president of the Washington Press Club and president of the "Old-Timers," an organization composed of senators, representatives and Washington correspondents, who enjoyed fellowship relating to past times and history. When he died on August 23, 1942, World War II was in full force, and the First Battalion, Fifth Regiment, that his son once commanded was involved with Guadalcanal.[1] Like his son, his death was also front-page news for the *Washington Post*.

His service as a member of the Congressional Press Galleries for 60 years (1883–1942) was longer than anyone prior, and he knew and interviewed each U.S. President from Chester A. Arthur to Franklin D. Roosevelt. In 1922, at 66 years old, he was actively enjoying the peak of his career when his son George passed away.

In 1942 during a press conference with President Franklin D. Roosevelt, Charles said, "When T.R. [Theodore Roosevelt] was in the White House he had a big stick. It's time you had one too." And he awarded the President a black cane.[2]

One peer summed up his lengthy public career by saying, "I think, perhaps, Charlie Hamilton has helped make more good newspapermen than any school of journalism ever did."[3]

Mary Hamilton Barnard

Of all the children born to Charles and Ida, only Mary, George's older sister, whom he called "Flax," took wedding vows. She therefore was the only sibling to have children, one daughter and one son.

Charles Burwell Hamilton

There's no question that Burley would have been George's closest friend. He was working in Philadelphia, not far from Gettysburg, when he heard the news of the death of his brother. Burley later lived most of his life near New York City employed as a professional executive with the Canada Dry Corporation. He also became an expert in crystals, and through his association with the Signal Corps, he made several trips to Brazil to purchase crystals for communication equipment.

Margaret Dorothy Hamilton

Margaret, the younger sister, who had trouble standing when notified of her brother's death, never married. For a period of time, she was employed by the U.S. Navy Department. In her earlier years, when her brothers were at war, she looked after her dying mother, and in later years she assisted her dying father. She outlived her brother George by about 49 years.

Margaret H. Barnard

Hamilton's only niece was two years old when he passed away. She passed away in 1991.

Roger Conant Barnard Jr.

Mary E. Barnard was newly pregnant with Roger when George died. As a result Roger C. Barnard Jr. never got the chance to meet his honored uncle. Through his mother he has the "Hamilton" blood in him. He is very proud of his uncle, but he remains humble and does not boast, which was one very notable trait of his Uncle George. He was 19 years old when his grandfather, Charles A. Hamilton, passed away. Roger C. Barnard Jr., who actively served with the Air Force Flying Tigers, is yet another great World War II veteran with strong ties to World War I.

James Lloyd Wright

Hamilton's first cousin and older brother of Carlton and George Wright followed in the path that Charles Hamilton had blazed. Using connections he became a journalist and correspondent for the *Buffalo Evening News*. Based in Washington, D.C., he blazed his own trail in the Capital City for a 40 year span that overlapped the career of his uncle Charles A. Hamilton. During 1924–1925 he served as chairman of the Standing Committee of Correspondents, a group that governs the Congressional Press Galleries. He was with President Calvin Coolidge in the Black Hills of South Dakota in 1927 when the President declared, "I do not choose to run." In 1934 he presided as president of the Gridiron Club.[4]

Carlton Herbert Wright

Hamilton's first cousin, who was the same age, graduated from the U.S. Naval Academy in 1912 and experienced some amazing firsthand history of his own. On Saturday, August 9, 1941, he was commanding the USS *Augusta*, the flagship of the Atlantic Fleet, recently donned with camouflage, off the coast of Newfoundland. On board the *Augusta* was President Franklin D. Roosevelt. The stage was set on the rolling seas for the president to officially meet Winston Churchill for the first time. Churchill's ship, the *Prince of Wales*, pulled alongside the *Augusta*, and Churchill, wearing his best attire, stepped aboard the *Augusta*. Following formal ceremonies they agreed to the "Atlantic Charter."[5] Carlton H. Wright saw extensive action in World War II and went on to become known as Vice Admiral Wright.

George Charles Wright

Hamilton's first cousin graduated from Central High in 1921, the U.S. Naval Academy in 1925, and then received his master's degree in mechanical engineering from Columbia University. During the Korean War he commanded the USS *Missouri*, known as the "Mighty Mo," the U.S. Navy's most notorious battleship, which every naval officer dreamed of commanding. George C. Wright was, at one point in time, also the director of the Navy's Atomic Energy Division. He too became known as Vice Admiral Wright.

George K. Shuler

Shuler was Hamilton's good friend with whom he shared many ties. After Hamilton died the Teapot Dome scandal was taken to another level. Albert B. Fall, the secretary of the interior, had leased oil fields in Wyoming to special-interest individuals without competitive bidding. When yet another individual began unauthorized drilling, Fall persuaded President Harding to have

USMC Commandant Lejeune handpick one Marine to lead an assault team to settle the issue. The chosen Marine was none other than Captain Shuler; upon Shuler accepting the mission, Lejeune asked him how many Marines he would need to handle the situation. Shuler replied, "If we are going out there and fight the whole state of Wyoming, we would probably have to take quite a few."⁶ Hamilton would have been proud of his friend.

John W. Thomason Jr.

Everyone missed Hamilton, but aside from Shuler and Feland, if there was one Marine, who would forever miss his presence, it would be the aristocratic Texas gentleman John W. Thomason Jr., who was so fond of his "skipper." Like many Marines he had many talents, and by free will he too chose the Corps for his career. He later became Lt. Colonel Thomason, but it was his side career as a famed writer, illustrator, and artist — producing eleven illustrated books, eight full-length books, of which five were about Marines, and more than five dozen articles for magazines, such as *Scribner's* and the *Saturday Evening Post*— that made him one of the best known Marines of the "Old Breed" and earned him the label "Kipling of the Corps."

Mary Hamilton Barnard took control of the BUR-GEO-MAR Farm at Conesus Lake, and her family used it in fashion similar to her own childhood days. The lake home was still primarily a summer retreat, and as a "family compound" it was open to the extended Hamilton family. Her children, Margaret and Roger, got to know Uncle George, not only through their mother, but from their grandfather Charles, Uncle Burley and Aunt Margaret. George Hamilton's uncle, George Cyrus Wright, the father of James, Carlton and George, often accompanied Charles Hamilton on extended vacations to Conesus Lake in the decades to follow, as the connection between the two brothers-in-law became even closer.

Hamilton was the model for the famous painting of 1/5 crossing the Meuse River, and in a way he appeared to be the model candidate for a person who was to receive amends on a later date. After much thought Charles Hamilton, a man full of his own drive and passionate willpower, was determined to see that his son's day would come in his lifetime. He drafted a letter to the Marine Corps commandant conveying his thoughts. The letter, printed on "*The Troy Times*" stationary, is as follows:

SUBJECT: RECOMMENDATION FOR MEDAL OF HONOR
To: Major General John A. Lejeune, Commandant U.S. Marine Corps:
General: In response to your verbal request for a copy of the communication from Colonel Neville to the commanding General of the 4th Brigade [U.S.

Army Brig. Gen. James Harbord], Marine Corps, American E. F., recommending the award of a congressional [sic] Medal of Honor to my son, George Wallis Hamilton, late Captain of the 49th Co. 5th Regt. U.S. Marines, A. E. F., I have the honor to transmit herewith a copy of that document dated June 10th, 1918, for your consideration.

I also take occasion to call to your attention to a communication from my son addressed to you, as Commandant of the Marine Corps, dated November 19, 1919, wherein Captain Hamilton sets forth his reasons for objecting to the wording of the citation in which he was awarded the Distinguished Service Cross, which communication appears to have escaped your attention.

Further, General, your attention is respectfully invited to the Military History of Captain Hamilton with particular reference to the facts therein set forth showing that his services in the World War were recognized as of such conspicuous character as to entitle him to "Citations" for gallantry and "extraordinary heroism" at "Hill 142" "St. Mihiel" "Blanc Mont Ridge" and particularly for the manner in which he carried out the order to cross the Meuse on the night of November 10-11 AFTER OTHER ATTEMPTS HAD FAILED.

There is attached hereto a clipping from the Rochester Post Express of June 27 last, written by Lieutenant Brady U. S. M. C., who tells of his knowledge of the exploit of Captain Hamilton on Hill 142, which led to the recommendation of General (then Colonel) Neville, that the Medal of Honor be awarded to Captain Hamilton.

I feel certain, General that if you will look carefully into the record of my son and compare that record with that of others to whom the Congressional Medal has been awarded, you will feel justified in suggesting to the Board that General Neville's recommendation be carried out and that the Medal of Honor should be awarded, posthumously, to George Wallis Hamilton, either as a Captain of the 49th Company, or as a Major of the 1st Battalion 5th Regiment, U.S. Marines.

I have the honor to be, General,
Most sincerely yours,
(signed) Chas. A. Hamilton[7]

Lejeune had not been in France during Belleau Wood, but he did receive Neville's paperwork recommending Hamilton for the Medal of Honor. In conjunction with the Medal of Honor request, Lejeune issued the General Orders, No. 40, personal citation on July 5, 1918.

This time the official process for recommending that the Medal of Honor be issued posthumously started with the Marine Corps sending paperwork to the adjutant general of the U.S. Army. Protocol still recognized the American Expeditionary Force's bureaucratic structure for postwar awards and citations. On March 12, 1923, Neville sent his paperwork forward, along with affidavits from eyewitnesses: Medal of Honor recipient Sergeant Ernest A. Janson (formerly Charles Hoffman), Arthur Lyng and Medal of Honor recipient, current Captain Louis Cukela.

It was difficult to identify witnesses at Belleau Wood due to the many casualties. Sergeant Stahl later officially replied stating:

> Am very sorry that I can't tell you anything about Captain Hamilton, as I was wounded and sent to the rear but will say that Captain Hamilton was about as game as anyone I ever saw and by his personal courage kept what was left of the 49th., Company from scattering.
> He was my ideal of what a Marine Officer should be.[8]

However, Lyng, who was then a gunnery sergeant and one of the few who observed Hamilton's actions, stated under sworn testimony:

> During a respite in the attack and while we were re-organizing our lines, I observed from the right flank where my platoon was, Captain George W. Hamilton and Gunnery Sergeant Charles Hoffman suddenly jump from cover and attack a group of Germans who were attempting to set up machine guns. Alone and unaided these two made quick work of about twelve Germans and when we advanced we found five light machine guns, which the Germans were going to use.
> Beyond a doubt, Captain Hamilton and Gunnery Sergeant Hoffman saved the 49th Company from complete annihilation by their extraordinary heroism and alertness in this particular deed.[9]

A week later Lejeune issued his own paperwork noted below:

1st Endorsement
Headquarters U.S. Marine Corps, Washington, 19 March 1923

From: The Major General Commandant
To: The Adjutant General of the Army, War Department, Washington, D.C.
Subject: Recommendation for the posthumous award of a Medal of Honor to Captain George W. Hamilton, U.S. Marine Corps, for extraordinary heroism beyond the call of duty in battle.
Enclosures: (3)

1. Forwarded. It is obvious from the above recommendation that Captain Hamilton showed extraordinary heroism in attacking with the bayonet twelve of the enemy who were fully armed. Furthermore, it appears to me that Captain Hamilton would have fully performed his duty as company commander if he had attacked the enemy with such men as he had immediately available, rather than almost alone. Therefore in my opinion, he exceeded the ordinary requirements of the duties in his office and performed an act *beyond the call of duty* in attacking without thought of assistance twelve of the enemy. His deed, to my mind, satisfies the requirements for the award of a Medal of Honor, in that it was one of extraordinary heroism at the risk of his life on the field of battle and beyond the call of duty.

2. Attention is invited to the fact that a Medal of Honor was awarded to Sergeant Ernest A. Janson, U.S. Marine Corps, (then Gunnery Sergeant Charles Hoffman), for his part in the above described attack with Captain Hamilton on

the enemy. It appears just that captain Hamilton, as the Commanding Officer of Janson, and as the instigator of the attack, should have an award for his valor equal to that awarded his subordinate.

3. I strongly recommend that the award recommended above be made in recognition of the extraordinary heroism beyond the call of duty of the late Captain George W. Hamilton.

JOHN A. LEJEUNE.[10]

The recommendations from Neville and Lejeune were officially turned down by the U.S. Army War Department Adjutant General Robert C. Davis in a letter dated April 28, 1923.[11] Instead, an Oak Leaf Cluster was issued posthumously to Hamilton.

Years later, Charles Hamilton tried another approach for lesser recognition to honor his deceased son. The old saying "it would take an Act of Congress" is tried and true, and through his efforts the following was proclaimed: "The records of the Marine Corps have been amended in accordance with section one of an Act of Congress approved 21 June 1930, to show that your late son, Captain George W. Hamilton, who died on June 26, 1922, was advanced to the rank of Major in the Marine Corps on that date."[12]

Hamilton was so active and driven that he did not take time to notice how many friends he truly had. He was an honest straight shooter in more ways than one. He touched so many lives, and those who knew him liked what they saw. True friendship is mutual, and Hamilton thought just as much of his friends and comrades as they thought of him.

On the tenth anniversary of Hamilton's death, his friends took time to honor him again. On June 21, 1932, George K. Shuler sent a letter to USMC Major General Ben H. Fuller notifying him that a service in memory of Major George W. Hamilton would be held at his graveside in Arlington National Cemetery at 3 P.M. on Sunday, June 26. Shuler enclosed a notice within the letter to be circulated at Marine Corps Headquarters.[13]

Still years later many World War I Marine veterans continued to enjoy thoughts of Hamilton. They would occasionally reunite as evidenced by one special gathering when John W. Thomason Jr. and other "Devil Dogs" met in New York City. The 1934 formal reunion, 16 years after 1918 and 12 years after Hamilton's death, was documented through a personal letter to Hamilton's father.

Hotel Astor, NY, NY
June 9th 1934

Mr. Charles A. Hamilton
National Press Club
Washington, D.C.
Dear Mr. Hamilton,

Never have two or more men of the Old Forty Ninth Company gathered together without thinking and talking of your splendid son, George W. Hamilton.

As a fine young First Lieutenant, he organized our Company in the United States, whipped it together in the training areas, taught us to hike and drill and fight, led us into action and throughout the War as Captain and Major; and yet remained to us, as always will be, just plain "Skipper George." A true Shipmate, a splendid Soldier, an inspired Leader, a real Marine, he bore a charmed life through out the War, and seemed especially destined to amalgamate and command one of the finest companies of fighting men ever assembled in any Army. He nobly commanded a Combat Company and a front Line Battalion in the severest battles in which American troops participated during the World War. He will go down in history as one of the greatest Company Commanders in the American Expeditionary Forces.

We can not too strongly express our love and admiration for the son whom you gave to us and to the Service of his Country; and we deeply mourn with you his passing in a simple peace time maneuver. However, like a true Marine, he died in action, leading his Squadron in the field. May God preserve his soul, and keep his memory ever glorious through out the Ages. His spirit will ever be an inspiration to us, so long as one single Old Forty Niner remains upon this earth, and until such time as we all have reported "present" to dear old "Skipper George" in that Realm Beyond the Skies.

We sincerely trust that the passing years have been kind to you, and that you are carrying on in this life as nobly as your son did upon the fields of France. We regret that you were unable to be with us today, when so many of us have gathered here in reunion. We sincerely hope that you may be able to attend some future reunion of the Old Company and meet those Veterans whom your son called his "Boys."

With sincerest wishes for your continued health and happiness from each and every man of the Old Forty Ninth Company, First battalion, Fifth Regiment, U.S. Marines, Second Division, American Expeditionary Forces.

(signed)[14]

The letter was personally signed by close to 50 of Hamilton's "Boys"

USMC Major John W. Thomason Jr. in 1934, the year of the New York City reunion (courtesy National Archives).

from his old 49th Company of 1/5 who were so loyal to him. Among the noted signatories were Murl Corbett, captain USMC, on the top left column; John W. Thomason Jr. on the top right column; Frank Garvin, the 49th Company historian; and John Culnan, a sergeant who survived the attack of June 6.

It is common for a parent who has lost a son or daughter to think of them often, and there is no question that even though Charles Hamilton remained very active, he lived the remaining 20 plus years of his life with his deceased son constantly on his mind. This is exemplified by another personal letter he received from President Roosevelt in 1941, before America declared war again and roughly eighteen and a half years after his son's death:

THE WHITE HOUSE
WASHINGTON

February 6, 1941
Dear Charlie:

Thank you very much for the copy of that historic painting "The Last Night of the War." As a father you have every reason to be proud of the memory of such a son.

I am delighted to have the photograph. I shall frame it and place it with a German machine gun which I have which was captured on the last day of the war.

Very sincerely yours,
(Sgd.) Franklin D. Roosevelt

Charles A. Hamilton, Esq.,
National Press Club
Washington, D.C.[15]

After Charles Hamilton passed away, Margaret found herself as the guardian of some of her brother's possessions, including his World War I medals. The world was in turmoil with World War II in full motion, and patriotism across every corner of the nation was at an all-time high. Margaret had lived in the nation's capital through the First World War, viewing the headlines each day with concern for her two brothers. The current atmosphere in the Capital City would certainly bring back many memories of her big brother, the national hero, who if alive would once again be giving his all. Many of Hamilton's peers were now earning their stars as active generals with great responsibility. Evidentially Margaret made an assessment and thought the time was right to loan some of his medals to the Marine Corps Museum, to not only honor her beloved brother, but to share a piece of his life with the rest of America. Twenty-five years had elapsed since Americans took to the front lines and proceeded forward in World War I, but those who knew history had not forgotten Hamilton, as evidenced by the response letter from the U.S. Marine Corps:

HEADQUARTERS U.S. MARINE CORPS
WASHINGTON

28 July 1943

Miss Margaret D. Hamilton
Apt. B 128
3800 39th Street
Washington, DC

Dear Miss Hamilton,

This is to acknowledge the receipt of certain banners, medals, and decorations left by your brother, the late Major George W. Hamilton, which you have loaned the Marine Corps Museum at Quantico, Virginia, subject to your control or, in your absence, to the control of Mr. Charles B. Hamilton and Mrs. Mary H. Barnard, brother and sister of the late Major Hamilton, and Mr. Roger C. Barnard, his nephew. The following is a list of the articles received:

- one silk embroidered banner of the 67th Company, 1st Battalion, 5th Regiment, U.S. Marines
- one silk embroidered banner of the 17th Company, 1st Battalion, 5th Regiment, U.S. Marines
- one silk embroidered banner of the 49th Company, 1st Battalion, 5th Regiment, U.S. Marines
- one Victory Medal with four stars and five clasps
- one Fourragere with two palms 1914–18
- one Distinguished Service Cross with oak leaf cluster
- one Navy Cross
- one Campaign Medal — First Haitian Campaign
- one conspicuous Service Medal with seven miniatures presented by the state of New York, No. 1477

The above listed objects are received for the purpose of displaying them in the Marine Corps Museum and preserving them as mementos of the late George W. Hamilton, USMC, who, in the opinion of the undersigned, was the most outstanding Marine Corps hero in World War I.

Sincerely yours,
C. H. METCALF
Colonel, U.S. Marine Corps[16]

Copy for Mr. Roger C.
Barnard

Epilogue

Words cannot express the true honor and privilege I felt at all times when trying to put the pieces of George W. Hamilton's life together. I have always greatly respected the heritage of the Marine Corps, and as one who is on the outside looking in, I wanted to be certain that I did my very best in unraveling the past of this great American.

In the fall of 2009, following the Wake Forest/Stanford football game, my in-laws had dinner with a small group, which included Colonel John C. Scharfen USMC (Ret.) and his wife. I did not know Colonel Scharfen, but realizing he had written a few books, I decided to send him a short note mentioning my involvement in the ongoing project of George W. Hamilton's biography. He replied, "I assume that you are enjoying all the satisfaction of doing something so creative yet suffer the pangs of 'Am I getting this right?'"[1] He was so correct, as wherever the trail of facts and information led me, I was always consumed with "Am I getting this right?" I believe that I have it right.

My quest for information was fueled by the fact that information regarding Hamilton's personal life was truly lacking, and I was determined to get to the bottom of the story. My contention was that for such a remarkable man to get lost in history, two elements must have been in play. First, he must have been raised in a city where notable people are very common, but not necessarily heroes. One can tend to get lost in such an atmosphere over time. Second, he must have come from a rather prominent family with few living relatives. If he had been raised in a small or mid-sized town by a common large family, the entire community would have given recognition to the man for decades and even centuries.

Although his legal residence was Conesus Lake, known as Groveland, New York, this location always served as his quiet escape to enjoy life without distractions. The casual retreats to BUR-GEO-MAR Farm worked to perfection as the Conesus Lake residents left the Hamilton family alone. His hometown was Washington, D.C., and yes he occasionally made the headlines, but so too did many other famous residents and folks who were just passing through the metropolis. Such was the background setting for a youthful man to fade away.

The Great War was intended to be the war to end all wars. American heroes were, in fact, on the horizon, and when called upon they stepped forward with honorable courage and stood out among the over 4,800,000 military personnel in the U.S. Army, U.S. National Guard, U.S. Navy and U.S. Marine Corps.

When the war ended America was undeniably the greatest nation on earth, and the Marine Corps was firmly set in its glory. While the United States looked to get back to normalcy the whole story of the war was never fully told. The activities and events regarding the Marines at Belleau Wood have been thoroughly recorded, but you now understand that World War I was much more than the initial battle.

All three battles, Belleau Wood, Blanc Mont and the crossing of the Meuse River, were unique in scope, and each played a significant role in ending the war. The terrain varied for all three engagements, from woods and wheat, to barren turf with clay craters, to a gushing river. In each instance, the sole common objective was to dislodge the entrenched enemy from an elevated piece of terrain containing a well-trained, determined force armed with an assortment of artillery and many hot machine guns.

The battle at Belleau Wood was instrumental in saving Paris, and it turned the tide from Allied Forces being on defense to attacking the Central Powers offensively. Belleau Wood was our nation's first major battle in the war, and Captain Hamilton was one of two company commanders who jumped off first with the wave of Americans at 0350. He served as a calm leader issuing orders and offering guidance to those in need. At the same time the captain was also a very active participating warrior in the middle of the action, displaying acts of bravery by jeopardizing his life to save the lives of his men. His honorable performance and accomplishments further inspired many men back home in the United States to rally for the American cause and enlist in the Marine Corps.

Many replacements were needed to fill the ranks for the battles of Soissons and Saint Mihiel. Through extra training exercises Hamilton perfected his new recruits to be fully prepared for future engagements, and in the process his leadership style bonded his "Boys" together as one solidified unit.

Blanc Mont was fought under the most horrific conditions. Major Hamilton was beside his men the entire way, and when they were surrounded on all four sides in "The Box," he again remained calm and led his men to safety. When all objectives were completed, the enemy was forced into a hastened retreat 18 miles off their stronghold.

Finally, if there ever was a life-threatening mission, crossing the Meuse River single file on flimsy, narrow wooden planks late on the evening of November 10, would be it. Major Hamilton was in command of the entire southern crossing, which ended up being the only crossing on the eve of the Armistice. During the final 24 hours of the war, his leadership responsibility was over two U.S. Marine battalions, one U.S. Army battalion and a detachment of Second Engineers. He faithfully followed the orders that he was given and charged ahead with his men completing the final objectives.

Eight U.S. Marines who fought in World War I received the Medal of Honor, half of them posthumously, with the final posthumous award being issued in 1939. Two of the eight were aviators, who were not under the control of General Pershing and the U.S. Army, and therefore did not need his staff approval prior to Congressional authorization. Of the six U.S. Marines on the ground, the highest ranking was a gunnery sergeant. No U.S. Marine commissioned officer in the Fourth Brigade received the award. Listed below are the eight who did receive the award:

USMC Aviation Forces
2nd Lieutenant Ralph Talbot
Gunnery Sergeant Robert Guy Robinson

USMC Fourth Brigade
Gunnery Sergeant Ernest A. Janson (who served under the name Charles F. Hoffman)
Gunnery Sergeant Fred W. Stockham
Sergeant Louis Cukela
Sergeant Matej Kocak
Corporal John Henry Pruitt
Private John Joseph Kelly

Hamilton was nominated twice for the Medal of Honor for his active role as a captain at Belleau Wood, and he was worthy of the same award for action as a major at Blanc Mont and during the Meuse River crossing.

One other great leader and military warrior comes to my mind, a man who also led from the front and was admired by officers above and men below him in rank. Through his examples, many believed he deserved the Medal of Honor, and he also felt justified to receive the honor. It is said the politics might very well have played a role as to why he did not initially receive the award. Although it was more than 100 years later, destiny finally prevailed. The citation to the man is a follows:

> The President of the United States of America, authorized by Act of Congress, March 3, 1863, has awarded in the name of The Congress the Medal of Honor to: LIEUTENANT COLONEL THEODORE ROOSEVELT UNITED STATES ARMY
> for conspicuous gallantry and intrepidity at the risk of his life above and beyond the call of duty.

Lieutenant Colonel Theodore Roosevelt distinguished himself by acts of bravery on 1 July 1898, near Santiago de Cuba, Republic of Cuba, while leading a daring charge up San Juan Hill. Lieutenant Colonel Roosevelt, in total disregard for his personal safety, and accompanied by only four or five men, led a desperate and gallant charge up San Juan Hill, encouraging his troops to continue the assault through withering enemy fire over open countryside. Facing the enemy's heavy fire, he displayed extraordinary bravery throughout the charge, and was the first to reach the enemy trenches, where he quickly killed one of the enemy with his pistol, allowing his men to continue the assault. His leadership and valor turned the tide in the Battle for San Juan Hill. Lieutenant Colonel Roosevelt's extraordinary heroism and devotion to duty are in keeping with the highest traditions of military service and reflect great credit upon himself, his unit, and the United States Army.[2]

On January 16, 2001, President William Jefferson Clinton honored Theodore Roosevelt posthumously with the Medal of Honor. Mr. Roosevelt became the first President to be honored with the Medal of Honor, and he rests in history as the only President to receive both the Medal of Honor, as well as the Nobel Prize for Peace.

I know, deep inside, Hamilton was confident he had proven his merit and displayed the credentials to be honored with such an award. What more could he possibly have done? How much more could he have given of himself?

Hamilton led the first wave of Marines to signal the start of America's very first major battle on the Western Front, and he was later the last American officer to shut down the war on the Western Front. How he survived it all is a miracle. In his active role, he followed all the orders he was given, correspondingly issued his own orders, displayed personal courage and leadership, fought in hand to hand combat and was successful each and every time. Throughout the war his individual contribution was second to none. He was revered by high-ranking officers above him, his peers and the many men he commanded. This mutual respect throughout all the ranks was quite rare and should be acknowledged among his lasting accomplishments. His true enjoyment came through leading from the front while fighting alongside his men, and he had a natural talent to feel most comfortable under these intense conditions. Above all, George W. Hamilton's greatest accomplishments should be remembered in history, as Secretary of the Navy Joseph Daniels proclaimed: "More than faithful in every emergency, accepting hardships with admirable morale, proud of the honor of taking their place as shock troops for the American legions, they have fulfilled every glorious tradition of their corps, and they have given to the world a list of heroes whose names will go down to all history."[3]

Hamilton never married, sadly missing that piece of life's adventure.

Many other men found the right person to marry immediately after the war and settled down. We know he dated a woman in Toronto, and he enjoyed receiving a memorable kiss in front of his men from a beautiful French woman. His sister Mary got married at 35 years of age. Hamilton was extremely ambitious and focused on making a career in the Marine Corps. From what we know of the energetic man, it appears he was simply not yet ready to settle down and had not met his soul mate.

The Great War turned out to be an adventure like no other. Yes, there were terrible moments when the path forward was more tragic than one wished it to be. Times that a man tried constantly to forget, but such is war. Many Americans at home in the United States played a supporting part in the war, while others were shipped overseas and saw a small piece of the action. Hamilton was fully engaged in the adventure and played the most active role.

When the war was over Hamilton could look back at his personal accomplishments and know that he had set the bar high as a role model for other warriors to follow if ever there was to be another such war. Though World War II was much larger in scale, it does not in any way diminish the courage and deeds that Hamilton and his men displayed in World War I.

His reputation stood the test of time, as evidenced by the written statements of others in the years following the war and after his death. Some can certainly envision the profound thought of someday seeing Hamilton in his full dress whites, in the "Realm Beyond the Skies," as "The Marines' Hymn" concludes:

> If the Army and the Navy ever look on Heaven's scenes,
> They will find the streets are guarded by United States Marines

USMC Lieutenant General Victor H. Krulak, who passed away in 2008, knew as well any man what the Marine Corps is all about. In his book *First to Fight: An Inside View of the U.S. Marine Corps*, he wrote, "The Marines are an assemblage of warriors, nothing more."[4] As a commissioned officer, Hamilton could be described in many ways, but first and foremost, he was that noted warrior.

In World War I he gave his all and served our country well beyond expectations. If it were possible to view the Great War through one set of eyes, that person without a doubt, would be George Wallis Hamilton. He was a true American patriot who chose to become a U.S. Marine. He kept his head high with eyes forward, and as a leader and warrior, he continuously set examples in each of the great battles. Always victorious from start to finish, he was, hands down, the greatest American hero of World War I.

Appendix A

Allied Nation	War Declared by Central Powers	War Declared Against Central Powers
Serbia	July 28, 1914	August 9, 1914
Russia	August 1, 1914	November 3, 1914
France	August 3, 1914	August 3, 1914
Belgium	August 4, 1914	April 7, 1917
Great Britain	November 23, 1914	August 4, 1914
Montenegro	August 9, 1914	August 6, 1914
Japan	August 27, 1914	August 23, 1914
Portugal	March 9, 1916	November 23, 1914
Italy	-	May 23, 1915
San Marino	-	June 6, 1915
Romania	August 29, 1916	August 27, 1916
Greece	-	November 23, 1916
United States	-	April 6, 1917
Panama	-	April 7, 1917
Cuba	-	April 7, 1917
Siam	-	July 22, 1917
Liberia	-	August 4, 1917
China	-	August 14, 1917
Brazil	-	October 26, 1917
Guatemala	-	April 21, 1918
Nicaragua	-	May 6, 1918
Haiti	-	July 12, 1918
Honduras	-	July 19, 1918[1]

Russia stopped fighting in the fall of 1917 after suffering a loss of roughly 1,700,000 men. They signed a treaty on March 3, 1918, ending their Allied involvement in the Great War, before America entered into major fighting. Romania followed, signing their treaty on March 6, 1918.

The American Expeditionary Forces could generally be categorized into three groups.[2]

Classification	Make Up of Troops	Division Number
Regular Army	professional soldiers and selected volunteers	1–25
National Guard	volunteers	26–75
National Army	drafted men	76–93

At full strength each of the AEF divisions consisted of roughly 979 officers and 27,080 men for a total of 28,000. The breakdown within a division was basically as follows:

2 infantry brigades (246 officers and 8,169 men each)
4 regiments (2 regiments to 1 brigade, 112 officers and 3,720 men in each regiment)
12 battalions (3 battalions to 1 regiment, 26 officers and 1,000 men in each battalion)
48 companies (4 companies to 1 battalion, 6 officers and 250 men in each company)
1 field artillery brigade

Support units included engineers, military police, field signal battalion, extra machine gun battalion, an engineer train, ammunition train, supply train, sanitary train, and a headquarters train. Medical personnel were also filtered into each fighting force.[3]

SECOND DIVISION

Nickname: Indian Head Division
Also known as: "Race Horse Division" and "Second to None"

Fourth Infantry Brigade (Marine)

FIFTH REGIMENT

First Battalion	Second Battalion	Third Battalion
17th (A) Company	18th (E) Company	16th (I) Company
49th (B) Company	43rd (F) Company	20th (K) Company
66th (C) Company	51st (G) Company	45th (L) Company
67th (D) Company	55th (H) Company	47th (M) Company

Eighth Machine Gun Company, Supply Company, Medical Unit, Headquarters Company

SIXTH REGIMENT

First Battalion	Second Battalion	Third Battalion
74th (A) Company	78th (E) Company	82nd (I) Company
75th (B) Company	79th (F) Company	83rd (K) Company
76th (C) Company	80th (G) Company	84th (L) Company
95th (D) Company	96th (H) Company	97th (M) Company

73rd Machine Gun Company, Supply Company, Medical Unit, Headquarters Company

Sixth Machine Gun Battalion
15th (A) Company
23rd (B) Company
77th (C) Company
81st (D) Company

Third Infantry Brigade

Ninth Infantry Regiment
23rd Infantry Regiment
Fifth Machine Gun Battalion

Second Field Artillery Brigade

12th Field Artillery
15th Field Artillery
17th Field Artillery
Second Trench Mortar Battery

Assisting Units

Second Engineers
Fourth Machine Gun Battalion
First Field Signal Battalion
Second Headquarters Train and Military Police
Second Ammunition Train
Second Engineer Train
Second Supply Train
Second Sanitary Train[4]

Appendix B

In the final analysis, fighting a war is not about promotions, medals or awards, as they alone are not capable of telling the full story. Hamilton was the man at his sister's wedding who was proud to display the awards bestowed upon him, but as noted by a firsthand witness, the humble warrior did not care to elaborate upon his deeds. His dedication and faithful service as a Marine went well beyond his military decorations, but still a list of his medals should be mentioned.

Upon inspection it is obvious that the only specific awards he received from the United States government were for action at Belleau Wood in the Château-Thierry sector in June 1918. He was also recognized with numerous citations for extreme individual bravery. The French government issued their Croix de Guerre award twice to Hamilton, first for action at Belleau Wood and later for service at Blanc Mont.

Awards Received

Distinguished Service Award (Army) No. 661
Location: Belleau Wood
Citation:
> "For extraordinary heroism in action near the Bois de Belleau, Chateau-Thierry, France, June 6, 1918. He displayed the highest type of courage and leadership when on the first day of the Chateau-Thierry Battle his command was under decimating fire of machine guns from the front and both flanks. All of his officers but one, and most of his non–commissioned officers having been killed or wounded, he passed up and down his front line and, by his personal bravery, inspired his men to valiant and successful combat under especially difficult conditions."[1]

General Orders No. 15 page 21
Date: January 21, 1919

Navy Cross
Location: Belleau Wood
Citation:

"For extraordinary heroism in action near the Bois de Belleau, Chateau-Thierry, France, June 6, 1918. He displayed the highest type of courage and leadership when on the first day of the Chateau-Thierry Battle his command was under decimating fire of machine guns from the front and both flanks. All of his officers but one, and most of his non–commissioned officers having been killed or wounded, he passed up and down his front line and, by his personal bravery, inspired his men to valiant and successful combat under especially difficult conditions."[2]
Date: November 11, 1920

Oak Leaf Cluster (posthumous)
Location: Belleau Wood
Citation:
"George W. Hamilton, captain, 49th Company, 5th regiment, United States Marine Corps, 2d Division. For extraordinary heroism in action at Hill 142 west of Belleau Wood and northwest of Chateau-Thierry June 6, 1918. While in command of Company B (49th Company), 5th Regiment, U.S. Marine Corps, during the attack upon Hill 142 at 3:45 A.M., June 6, 1918, he led his company to its objective. While his company was engaged in digging in, twelve enemy machine gunners stealthily approached and proceeded to set up their guns for purpose of firing upon Captain Hamilton's company. He discovered the enemy before the guns were in position and in attacking them with a bayonet, dispatched several and driving the remaining men to flight capturing their machine guns. The undaunted bravery and soldierly conduct displayed by Captain Hamilton served to inspire the men in his regiment with increased determination and incited them to heroic endeavors."[3]
Date: May 16, 1923

CROIX de GUERRE with Palm
Location: Belleau Wood
Citation:
"During the attack of the enemy of the Cote 142, displayed exceptionally bright qualities of training, led his company 1 kilometer ahead, close to an enemy entrenched behind machine gun positions, crossing several points swept by heavy fire. In spite of the very severe casualties suffered by his unit and of nearly all his officers, he carried his men ahead with his splendid impulse by his grit and superb example."[4]
Order No. 10.965 "D" Extract
Date: October 28, 1918

CROIX de GUERRE with Palm
Location: Blanc Mont
Citation:
"Major George W. Hamilton commanding the 1st Battalion, 5th Marine Regiment
   He displayed great courage and hugh [sic] maneuvering ability while leading his battalion during the combats of 3, 4, 5, and 6 October 1918, in the battle of BLANC MONT."[5]
Order No. 11.697 "D"
Date: November 16, 1918

Recommended Awards Later Disapproved

Medal of Honor
On June 10, 1918, Neville officially processed paperwork for Hamilton to receive the Medal of Honor for action at Belleau Wood. A second attempt to have the nation's highest award issued to Hamilton (posthumous) was issued by Neville on March 12, 1923, and Lejeune on March 19, 1923.

Distinguished Service Cross
Location: Blanc Mont
Citation:
"During 4th October, southeast of St. Etienne, in the Battle of Blanc Mont Ridge, while his battalion was in the reserve position advanced to the position of the support Battalion and there finding that certain elements had become disorganized by the shock of the battle, displayed the highest type of leadership by immediately taking charge of the situation and reorganizing the position. In carrying out this self-assumed task he displayed extraordinary heroism by fearlessly exposing himself to heavy shelling and direct and indirect machine-gun fire, while personally placing in line the elements which had become disorganized."[6]
Date: November 13, 1918
Recommended by: Colonel Logan Feland
Witness: Captain J. A. Nelms.

Distinguished Service Cross
Location: Meuse River
Citation:
"On the night of November 10–11, 1918, near Pouilly, France, Major Hamilton was assigned the difficult task of crossing the MEUSE RIVER, and placed on command of the 1st and second [sic] Battalions, 5th Regiment Marines, the 2nd Battalion, 356th Infantry, and Bridge building detail from the 2nd Regiment Engineers. Immediately the operations started, the enemy laid down a terrific counter-barrage which destroyed one bridge and made the crossing of the river most difficult. With an absolute disregard of his own personal safety, Major Hamilton undertook the crossing over one narrow foot bridge, pushed the attack against strongly organized positions on the right bank, and established a strong bridge head. On the morning of November 11, 1918 he pushed his forces forward to a depth of three kilometers over extremely difficult ground and when the Armistice commenced at 11 o'clock, A.M. had organized an impregnable position on the commanding hills to the East."[7]
Date: December 11, 1918
Recommended by: Colonel Logan Feland
Witnesses: Captain Charley Dunbeck, MC. and Captain LeRoy P. Hunt, MC.

Belgian Decoration
Location: General, entire time period in France
Citation:
"MAJOR GEORGE W. HAMILTON, FIFTH REGIMENT, U.S. MARINES, An officer of exceptional courage, zeal and devotion to duty. At Hill 142 on June 6, 1918 he led his company in a dashing attack which swept the enemy before it in

confusion. On this occasion he distinguished himself by his disregard of personal safety and by the example he set for his men. At Soissons on July 18, 1918, as second in command of a battalion he was distinguished for his zeal, enthusiasm, courage and good judgment. East of St. Mihiel, Sept. 12–15, 1918 in command of a battalion he exhibited the same high qualities of leadership.

"In front of Blanc Mont, east of Reims, on October 4th, 1918 while commanding a battalion and when both flanks of the regiment were exposed and the troops under a terrific bombardment and machine gun fire, his coolness, personal bravery and good judgement inspired confidence in all around him and in my judgement, more than any other factor, enabled the regiment to hold its gains against the repeated and desperate counter attacks of the enemy.

"In the attack of November 1st, 1918, his battalion in the front line, under the inspiration of his leadership assaulted and carried in a brilliant manner the last portion of the Hindenburg line held by the enemy.

"On the night of November 10–11, 1918 Major Hamilton commanded a mixed force, consisting of the 1st and 2d battalions, 5th Marines and a battalion of the 355th Infantry, U.S.A. This command, under his brilliant leadership and against the most desperate resistance of the enemy, forced its way over narrow foot bridges across the MEUSE, advanced unflinchingly and seized a commanding position on the eastern bank."[8]

Date: November 13, 1918
Recommended by: Colonel Logan Feland

Navy Distinguished Service Medal
Location: General, entire time period in France

"1. The award of the Navy distinguished service medal [*sic*] to Major George W. Hamilton, U.S.M.C., is earnestly recommended.

2. This officer, then a captain, sailed overseas in June 1917, with the Fifth Regiment of Marines, and served with the first battalion of that regiment as a company commander until August, 1918, when he was assigned to the command of that battalion, and continued in that capacity until February 1919.

3. As company commander he participated in the occupation of the Toulon-Tryon sector; the engagements in the Chateau-Thierry sector, the battle southwest of Soissons, and the occupation of the Marbache sector. As battalion commander participated in the battles of St. Mihiel, Blanc Mont Ridge and Meuse-Argonne; the march to the Rhine and the occupation of the Coblenz Bridge Head.

4. Major Hamilton's service as a battalion commander was of the highest order he showed himself to be an officer of exceptional ability, great energy, and the possessor of remarkable qualities of leadership.

5. His service was conspicuous, highly meritorious, and in duty of great responsibility."[9]

Date: December 9, 1919
Recommended by: Maj. General John A. Lejeune

Distinguished Service Medal (posthumous)
Location: Meuse River
Citation:

"1. As former commander of the Second Division A.E.F., I recommend the posthumous award of a Distinguished Service Medal to Major George W. Hamilton. His highly honorable and distinguished career was terminated in an airplane accident in June, 1922.

2. From June, 1917 to August, 1918 Major Hamilton served in the Toulon Sector, near Verdun; in the Aisne Defensive; in the desperate fighting in the Chateau Thierry Sector, where he was awarded the Distinguished Service *Cross* for extraordinary heroism; and in the Aisne-Marne Offensive (Soissons). As major in the Fifth Regiment, Second Division, A.E.F., he served as Second in Command and battalion commander in the battle of St. Mihiel; then as battalion commander in the Fifth Regiment he rendered distinguished service in the battles of Blanc Mont Ridge (Champagne) and of the Meuse-Argonne.

3. Major Hamilton's record was so distinguished by the highest type of courage, by excellent judgment and initiative, and by such exceptional qualities of leadership that in the battle of the Meuse-Argonne he was chosen for a position of great responsibility and placed in immediate command of two battalions of the Fifth Regiment and a battalion of the Eighty-Ninth Division, A.E.F. for the crossing of the Meuse River near Beaumont, France, on the night of November 10–11, 1918. Higher command attached great importance to the depressing effect on enemy morale of crossing the Meuse and pushing the attack to the last moment before the Armistice. It is obvious that the enemy would have been correspondingly encouraged if they had succeeded in preventing the crossing. The importance of the command held by Major Hamilton in this crossing operation is apparent. Major Hamilton with these troops, in spite of very severe losses and in the face of heavy artillery and machine gun fire, crossed the Meuse on two hastily constructed footbridges and drove back the enemy. Towards morning a fourth battalion (from the Ninth Infantry) was added to Major Hamilton's force, and he occupied the heights east of the Meuse and continued pursuing the enemy the Armistice Hour, 11:00 A.M., November 11, 1918.

4. It is recommended that the posthumous award of a Distinguished Service Medal be made to George W. Hamilton, U.S. Marine Corps, in that he rendered exceptionally distinguished service in a position of great responsibility on the night of November 10–11, 1918 while in command of three battalions of the Second Division and the Eighty-Ninth Division A.E.F., in forcing a crossing of the Meuse River in spite of severe losses and in the face of very heavy shell and machine gunfire, defeating the enemy and harassing him until the Armistice Hour, 11:00 A.M.,11 November1918,and thereby successfully assisting in confirming in the enemy's mind the hopelessness of further resistance to the Allies.

5. I would be glad to amplify the above by personal testimony."[10]
Date: December 29, 1922
Recommended by: Maj. General John A. Lejeune

Individual Citations Received

Location: Belleau Wood
Citation:

"During an attack on the enemy, showed exceptionally brilliant leadership. He advanced his company a kilometer to his final objective against an enemy in trenches and equipped with machine guns. He and his company passed through several zones of machine gun fire. When it is known that this company lost approximately ninety per cent, of company in casualties, Captain HAMILTON'S rare quality of leadership is apparent. During the latter stages of the attack, after the men had lost their leaders, he ran up and down his line under severe fire, leading his men forward and urging them on, by cheering and similar efforts. He did this at great personal exposure. Captain HAMILTON displayed a quality of extraordinary heroism."[11]

Order No. 40, p. 19
Award Date: July 5, 1918
Issued By: Major General Omar Bundy, Second Division

Location Blanc Mont
Citation:
"For gallantry in action southeast of ST. ETIENNE in the battle of BLANC MONT RIDGE, October 4, 1918, and for brilliant leadership."[12]

Order No. 2, p. 46
Date: Not recorded
Issued By: U.S. Army General John J. Pershing, AEF

Location: Blanc Mont
Citation:
"The above-named is cited for gallantry in action against the enemy in BLANC MONT"[13]

Order No. 64, p. 33
Date: June 25, 1919
Issued By: Major General John A. Lejeune, Second Division

Location: Meuse River
Citation:
"Was assigned the difficult task of crossing the MEUSE RIVER near POUILLY, France, on the night of November 10–11th 1918. He was placed in command of the First and Second Battalions, Fifth Marines, the Second Battalion 356th Infantry, and a bridge detail from the 2nd. Regiment of Engineers. When the movement started the enemy laid down a terrific counter-barrage which destroyed one bridge and made the crossing of the river most difficult. With absolute disregard of his own personal safety, Major Hamilton undertook the crossing over one narrow foot bridge, and pushed the attack against strongly organized position on the right bank and established a strong bridge head. On the morning of November 11th 1918, he pushed his forces forward to a depth of three kilometers over extremely rough ground, and when Armistice became effective at 11:00 A.M. he had organized an impregnable position on the commanding hills to the east."[14]

Order No. 88, p. 69
Date: December 31, 1918
Issued By: Maj. General John A. Lejeune

Notes

Preface

1. The corporal through his promotion was then known as Sergeant York.
2. U.S. War Department, Report of the Adjutant General, *War Department Annual Reports 1919*, vol. 1 (Washington, D.C.: Government Printing Office, 1920), 4.
3. C. H. Metcalf to Margaret D. Hamilton, 28 July 1943, Roger C. Barnard Jr. Papers, private collection.
4. George B. Clark, *Devil Dogs: Fighting Marines of World War I* (Novato, CA: Presidio Press, 1999), 438.
5. The Marines' Hymn is now public domain. The wording "In air" was added on November 21, 1942.
6. "Capt. Hamilton of U.S. Marines Killed on Duty," *Rochester* (New York) *Post Express*, 27 June 1922.
7. Alan C. Bevilacqua, "TOP-10 BADASS* MARINES," *Leatherneck,* April 2009, 12.
8. No time period in history is perfect. The rights of minorities and women were lacking.
9. Will Durant and Ariel Durant, *The Lessons of History* (New York: Simon and Schuster, 1968), 81.
10. Jon Meacham, *Franklin and Winston: An Intimate Portrait of an Epic Friendship* (New York: Random House, 2003), 36.
11. Frederick Palmer, *America in France* (New York: Dodd, Mead, 1919), 3.

Chapter 1

1. *The Sunday Star* (Washington, D.C.), 3/22 March 1936, 3(M).
2. "A Polar Bear and a Pirate," *Washington Post*, 4 June 1926, sec. Letters to Editor.
3. *Biographical sketch of Charles A. Hamilton*, Office of the Town Historian, Town of Aurora and Village of East Aurora, New York, November 1938.
4. "Charles A. Hamilton Celebrates 57th Year in Journalism," *The Evening Star* (Washington, D.C.), 16 January 1939.
5. *The Nation*, 6 March 1890, 191.
6. Charles Hamilton ran errands for Mr. Cleveland's law office around 1869 when Frances Folsom was five years old and Mr. Cleveland was 32. In 1875 when Cleveland's law partner Oscar Folsom passed away, Cleveland served as guardian to his 11-year-old daughter Frances. Mr. Cleveland fell secretly in love with Miss Folsom when she was in her late teens.
7. Theodore Roosevelt, *The Rough Riders* (New York: Charles Scribner's Sons, 1899), 22.
8. "Welcome to New Year," *Washington Post*, 1 January 1900.
9. Years later Roger C. Barnard Jr. used the shed to play childhood war games. He envisioned his uncles George and Burley as youths creating an imaginary charge up San Juan Hill and sinking Spanish fleets in Conesus Lake.
10. *Complaints of Cities, Towns, Associations, Individuals, Etc.*, Nineteenth Annual Report of the Board of Railroad Commissioners of the State of New York. For 1901, vol. 1 (Albany: J.B. Lion Company, State Printers, 1902), 7.
11. John W. Tyler, *The Life of William McKinley* (Philadelphia: P. W. Ziegler, 1901), 196.

12. The Hamiltons at some point moved from 1205 Kenyon Street to 1032 Lamont Street. Both residences in the northwest section were the same distance from the U.S. Capitol.

13. Burnham was the lead architect along with McKim and Olmsted Sr. who designed New York's Central Park.

14. The guest list was not published and there is no common agreement as to the few attendees. Some descendants of Samuel Adams firmly believe that North Carolina Superior Court Judge Spencer Bell Adams was in attendance. Although unsuccessful as the Republican candidate for governor in 1900, he was the most prominent Republican in the bordering state and a personal friend of Roosevelt's.

15. "White House Christmas," *New York Times*, 20 December 1903, sec. part II. The Roosevelt children were always causing commotion in the house. Once Quentin brought a few snakes into the study to show his father, and later he brought his Algonquin pony upstairs in the White House to visit an older brother who was ill.

16. A. Scott. Berg, *Lindbergh* (New York: G. P. Putnam's Sons, 1998), 61.

17. "Washington Station Opens," *New York Times*, 28 October 1907.

Chapter 2

1. "George C. Wright Dies at 84; Revenue Deputy 20 Years," *Washington Post*, 7 March 1943. Mary Jane Hamilton and George C. Wright took wedding vows in Buffalo in 1884, one year after Charles and Ida were married. Mr. Wright was affiliated with the Internal Revenue Service, as was George Hamilton's grandfather.

2. Taft's father co-founded the Skull and Bones secret society at Yale.

3. "High School Notes," *Washington Post*, 12 December 1909, sec. Sporting.

4. "To Enter High School," *Washington Post*, 29 January 1910.

5. Daniel C. French of Concord, Massachusetts, was a personal friend of residents Ralph Waldo Emerson and Louisa May Alcott. At age 24 he created his first well known sculpture, the bronze statue of "The Minute Man" located at Concord's Old North Bridge. The National Monument was unveiled and dedicated for the centennial event April 19, 1875.

6. National Archives, Personnel file of George W. Hamilton, letter of recommendation from Clarence D. Clark, Chairman United States Senate Committee on the Geological Survey to U.S.M.C. Board of Examiners, 29 July 1913.

7. "High School Teams Ready for Schedules of the Week," *Washington Post*, 30 March 1913, sec. Sporting.

8. "Rain Balks Athletes," *Washington Post*, 24 April 1911.

9. "Seek Local Athletes," *Washington Post*, 8 February 1911.

10. *Ibid*.

11. "Central's Athletes Take Honors in M.A.C. Games," *Washington Post*, 12 May 1912, sec. Sporting.

12. "Diplomas Given to 141," *Washington Post*, 19 June 1912.

13. "Taft to Give Diplomas," *Washington Post*, 29 May 1912.

14. "New Athletic Club Launched," *Washington Post*, 19 August 1912.

15. The pentathlon involved five activities: the discus, broad jump, javelin and a couple of running events. The decathlon involved ten varied track events that also included the pole vault and hurdles. Off to College! "Local Schools Lose Athletes," *Washington Post*, 9 June 1912, sec. Sporting.

Chapter 3

1. "Local Schools Lose Athletes," *Washington Post*, 9 June 1912, sec. Sporting.

2. "Central Coach has Notable Record in a Athletic World," *Washington Post*, 29 September 1912, sec. Sporting.

3. James Albert Woodburn, *Political Parties and Party Problems in the United States* (New York: G. P. Putnam's Sons, 1914), 194.

4. *Ibid.* His biggest contributor was Frank A. Munsey, who had amassed great wealth through owning newspapers. He donated $70,000, which was about 23 percent of the total campaign funds. Two top ten donors, who donated $500 each, were Thomas Edison and Charles Scribner.
5. "G.U. Football Starts Today," *Washington Post*, 16 September 1912.
6. "Big Elevens Get Jolt in Games of Saturday," *Washington Post*, 28 October 1912.
7. The most noted football player at G.U. was Al Bloizs an All-American in the class of 1942. His jersey number 32 was retired from the New York Giants. While at the Army's Fort Benning facility he supposedly threw a hand grenade a record distance of more than 94 yards. He died during World War II.
8. Lars Anderson, *Carlisle vs. Army: Jim Thorpe, Dwight Eisenhower, Pop Warner and the Forgotten Story of Footballs Greatest Battle* (New York: Random House, 2007), 271.
9. *Ibid.*, 5.
10. "Georgetown Loses Dailey, Its Director of Athletics," *Washington Post*, 24 January 1913.
11. "Quits Football," *Washington Post*, 18 September 1913.

Chapter 4

1. "High School Teams Ready for Schedules of the Week," *Washington Post*, 30 March 1913, sec. Sporting.
2. Application, 14 April 1913, National Archives.
3. Emory M. Wilson to Josephus Daniels, 7 April 1913, National Archives.
4. "Attack on Navy Rule," *Washington Post*, 31 March 1913.
5. "Settle Marine Row," *Washington Post*, 11 November 1913.
6. Personal Description of Officers, 3 December 1913, National Archives.
7. *My Rifle*, suggested by William H. Rupertus, Division of Public Relations, United States Marine Corps, Navy Department, Arlington Annex, Washington, D.C.
8. In 1777 the Springfield Armory started supplying American troops in the Revolutionary War with gun cartridges.
9. *Dear Folks at Home: The Glorious Story of the United States Marines in France as Told by Their Letters from the Battlefield*, comp. Kemper F. Cowing, ed. Courtney R. Cooper (Boston: Houghton Mifflin, 1919), 55–56. Letter dated 25 June 1918 from GWH to a friend in Washington, D.C.
10. "Central High's Class," *Washington Post*, 17 June 1914.
11. Peter Collier and David Horowitz, *The Fords: An American Epic* (New York: Summit Books, 1987), 63. Danish born Charles E. Sorensen came to America at an early age, and as Ford's Highland Park plant superintendent, he is credited with implementing the assembly line.
12. G. Waldo Browne and Rosecrans W. Pillsbury, comps., *The American Army in the World War: A Divisional Record of the American Expeditionary Forces in Europe* (Manchester, NH: Overseas Book Company, 1921), 54.
13. Ronald J. Brown, "George Wallis Hamilton: The Forgotten Hero of World War I," *Leatherneck*, November 2003, 46.
14. "German Embassy Issues Warning," *New York Times*, 1 May 1915.
15. In 1916 civilians could enter the National Match through a state represented team.
16. "Three Rifle Honors Go to New Yorkers," *New York Times*, 11 September 1915.
17. "Dryen Cup to Marines," *Washington Post*, 16 September 1915.

Chapter 5

1. After World War II the *Arkansas* was sent to Bikini Atoll in the Pacific Ocean. On July 1, 1946, it survived the 500-foot altitude nuclear test bomb Able, but it was sunk a few weeks later on July 25 with nuclear explosion Baker.
2. "Army and Navy News," *Washington Post*, 22 December 1915.
3. "Heavy Guard Put Over Navy Yard," *New York Times*, 22 April 1916.
4. "Show Marines Under Fire," *New York Times*, 24 April 1916.

5. Commandant Barnett to Charles W. Stewart, 16 May 1916, National Archives.
6. "Miss Mary Ligon a Bride," *Washington Post*, 18 May 1916.
7. "Sailors Cheer Mayo, New Chief of Fleet," *New York Times*, 20 June 1916.
8. "Reports on Navy Gunnery," *New York Times*, 8 July 1916.
9. "Fleet Starts War Games," *New York Times*, 11 July 1916.
10. Leonard Wood, et al., *The Story of the Great War: History of the European War from Official Sources*, ed. Francis J. Reynolds, Allen L. Churchill and Francis Trevelyan Miller (New York: Collier and Son, 1916), 184–185.
11. "The Mighty Arizona Now a Part of Navy," *New York Times*, 18 October 1916, sec. I. The ship was launched on June 19, 1915, but with new extra equipment installed it was now commissioned. Its days on the seas ended on December 7, 1941, at Pearl Harbor.
12. "Battleship Elevens Play," *New York Times*, 22 October 1916, sec. 8.
13. "Hamilton Wins for Tars," *New York Times*, 4 November 1916.
14. "50,000 Cheer Cadets," *Washington Post*, 26 November 1916.
15. "Sailors Overcome in Fire," *New York Times*, 6 January 1917.
16. "Military, Official and Civic Representatives in Funeral," *Washington Post*, 21 January 1917.
17. Browne and Pillsbury, *American Army*, 22.
18. *Annual Report of the Secretary of the Navy for the Fiscal Year 1918* (Washington, D.C.: GPO, 1918), 45. Prophetic comments made in 1918.
19. National Archives. Personnel file of George W. Hamilton.
20. *Congressional Record*, 65th Cong., 1st sess., 1917, vol. 55, 412–413.
21. Wood et al., *Story of the Great War*, 333–334.
22. "Army and Navy Changes of the Day," *Washington Post*, 16 May 1915.
23. Edwin N. McClellan, *The United States Marine Corps in the World War* (Washington, D.C.: GPO, 1920): 18.
24. Hamilton to Gen. John A. Lejeune, telegram, 14 May 1917, National Archives.
25. Naval Dispatch to Hamilton, 21 May 1917, National Archives.

Chapter 6

1. U.S. War Department, Report of the Adjutant General, *1919*, vol. 1, 3–4.
2. McClellan, *United States Marine Corps*, 9.
3. *The American Army in the European Conflict*, trans. Colonel De Chambrun and Captain De Marenches (New York: Macmillan, 1919), 84.
4. Frederick Palmer, *John J. Pershing: General of the Armies* (Westport, CT: Greenwood Press, 1948), 67.
5. Historically the Fifth Regiment originated in early 1914 but was disbanded later that same year.
6. Bennie Scarton, "Down Home in Quantico," *Cooperative Living*, February 2007, 38. The Marine Corps purchased the property in 1918.
7. The term may have originated from the early days when Marines wore a leather neck collar, or it could have derived from their salty tanned necks from days at sea.
8. McClellan, *United States Marine Corps*, 15.
9. "Texas Giant in Washington," *Washington Post*, 13 August 1919. Texas cowpuncher R.E. Madsen, at 7'7" said to be the tallest person in the world, was denied for being a big target.
10. Willis J. Abbot, *Soldiers of the Sea: The Story of the United States Marine Corps* (New York: Dodd, Mead, 1918), 291. Married men could serve if they attained permission from their spouse.
11. "Marines Chief Reports," *New York Times*, 15 December 1918.
12. McClellan, *United States Marine Corps*, 34.
13. Browne and Pillsbury, *American Army*, 38. English divisions comprised roughly 15,000 men, while French and German divisions usually contained 12,000 men.
14. McClellan, *United States Marine Corps*, 10.
15. Edward V. Rickenbacker, *Fighting the Flying Circus* (New York: Frederick A. Stokes, 1919), 168–169.

16. U.S. War Department, Report of the Adjutant General, *1919*, vol. I, 886.
17. *American Army in the European Conflict*, 54.
18. Heywood Broun, *Our Army at the Front* (New York: Charles Scribner's Sons, 1918), 103.
19. Bruce N. Canfield, *U.S. Infantry Weapons of the First World War* (Lincoln, RI: Andrew Mowbray, 2000), 107.
20. Palmer, *John J. Pershing*, 322. This was before common penicillin.
21. Many Armenians were a part of the civilian deaths.

Chapter 7

1. Leroy P. Hunt, *History of the Fifth Regiment Marines: 5/1917–12/31/1918*, Reprint no. 3 (Pike, NH: Brass Hat), 5.
2. In the fall of 1918, Torrey as a major was aboard a transport ship headed to France when he acquired either pneumonia or the Spanish Flu and died.
3. "Chats with Visitors in Washington," *Washington Post*, 26 October 1920.
4. Frank Hunt Garvin, *A History of the 49th Company*, Stories from the Veterans History Project, Library of Congress, 1.
5. William A. Carter and Pascal J. Plant, *The Tale of a Devil Dog* (Washington, D.C.: Canteen Press, 1920), 26.
6. National Archives. Personnel file of George W. Hamilton.
7. Hunt, *History of the Fifth Regiment Marines*, 5.
8. Rickenbacker, *Fighting*, vi.
9. "Cheering Crowds Greet Pershing Arriving in Paris," *New York Times*, 14 June 1917.
10. Hamilton to USMC Major General Commandant, report, 5 April 1915, National Archives. Debt of $10.25 to Burke-Hume Piano.
11. Elias S. Longstreet, "Gunner Nice of the Devil Dogs," *Asbury Park* (New Jersey) *Sunday Press*, 10 September 1933.
12. "Feland of the Marines a General," *The Technology Review* 21 (January 1919): 178.
13. Josephus Daniels, *The Navy and the Nation: War-Time Addresses* (New York: George H. Doran, 1919), 290. Credit for the quote went to Pershing, but there is belief that it was stated by one of his senior staff officers.
14. Broun, *Our Army*, 35.
15. Palmer, *America in France*, 28.
16. Broun, *Our Army*, 71.
17. Palmer, *America in France*, 43.
18. Broun, *Our Army*, 75.
19. Ronald J. Brown, *A Few Good Men: The Story of the Fighting Fifth Marines* (Novato, CA: Presidio Press, 2001), 19.
20. Garvin, *History of the 49th Company*, 3.
21. Carter and Plant, *Tale of a Devil Dog*, 33.
22. Hamilton to Mary E. Hamilton, 1 October 1917, Roger C. Barnard Jr. Papers. The cafes in France generally remained open until 7:30 P.M. serving wine or beer to service men in uniforms, but no hard liquor.
23. Longstreet, "Gunner Nice," *Asbury Park* (New Jersey) *Sunday Press*.
24. U.S. Congress, House Committee Naval Investigation, *Hearings Before the Subcommittee of the Committee on Naval Affairs United States Senate*, 66th Cong., 2nd sess., vol. 2, 1921, 2622.
25. Rickenbacker, *Fighting*, 1–2. Each plane in the 94th Squadron, nicknamed the "Hat-in-the-Ring Squadron," was adorned with the Uncle Sam stovepipe hat and Stars and Stripes hatband.
26. *American Army in the European Conflict*, 130.
27. Garvin, *A History of the 49th Company*, 4.
28. "Two Long-Separated Washington Brothers Meet in German Trench," *Washington Post*, 2 June 1918. Toul had a population of 20,000 and served as the current location for the 2nd Division Headquarters and the home base for the 94th Squadron.
29. "Pershing Tells How We Fought," *New York Times*, 14 December 1919, sec. I.

30. "Mrs. C. A. Hamilton Dead," *Washington Post*, 25 April 1918. The original thought was cancer might have been the cause, but 1918 was the devastating year for the Spanish Flu. Her sister-in-law, Jane Wright, also died in 1918.

31. "George C. Wright Dies at 84; Revenue Deputy 20 Years," *Washington Post*, 7 March 1943.

32. Hamilton letter quoted in "Timely Topics Discussed by Capital Visitors," *Washington Post*, 21 June 1918.

33. Omar Bundy, "The Second Division at Château-Thierry," *Everybody's Magazine*, March 1919, 12.

34. *Ibid.*

35. Carter and Plant, *Tale of a Devil Dog*, 43.

36. Daniels, *Navy and the Nation*, 279.

37. The quote was attributed to Captain Williams, who died several days later on June 12, 1918, during Belleau Wood action. Colonel Manus McCloskey commanding the Second Division, 12th Field Artillery, claimed the quote was actually his own words.

38. James G. Harbord, *The American Army in France: 1917–1919* (Boston: Little, Brown, 1936), 289.

39. Albertus W. Catlin, *With the Help of God and a Few Good Marines* (New York: Doubleday, 1919), 105.

Chapter 8

1. Alan Axelrod, *Miracle at Belleau Wood: The Birth of the Modern U.S. Marine Corps* (Guilford, CT: Lyons Press, 2007), viii.

2. Hunt, *History of the Fifth Regiment Marines*, 11.

3. Alexander Merrow, Gregory Starace, and Agostino von Hassell, "Belleau Wood: From the German Perspective," *Marine Corps Gazette*, November 2008, 44.

4. *Dear Folks at Home*, 55.

5. Axelrod, *Miracle at Belleau Wood*, 114.

6. *Dear Folks at Home*, 55.

7. *Ibid.*

8. *The History and Achievements of the Fort Sheridan Officers' Training Camps* (Myron E. Adams and Fred Girton for Fort Sheridan Association, 1920), 134.

9. David C. Homsher, "Securing the Flanks at Belleau Wood," *Military History* 14, no. 2 (June 1997): 3.

10. Elton E. Mackin, *Suddenly We Didn't Want to Die* (Novato, CA: Presidio Press, 1993), 143.

11. Charles C. Krulack, "Through the Wheat to the Beaches Beyond: The Lasting Impact of the Battle for Belleau Wood," *Marine Corps Gazette*, July 1998.

12. The German name also appears as Teufelhunden and Teufelshunde.

13. *Dear Folks at Home*, 55–56.

14. Roger C. Barnard Jr., letters to author and copies of official documents, various dates.

15. "Capt. Hamilton of U.S. Marines Killed on Duty," *Rochester* (New York) *Post Express*, 27 June 1922. The messenger, later employed by the newspaper, appears to have been Chaplain John J. Brady. He was from New York and received the NC, DSC and several citations. Father Brady's mission under these conditions would be reason for such awards.

16. *Ibid.*

17. Garvin, *History of the 49th Company*, 5. Charles Hoffman later changed his name to Ernest August Janson. Gunnery Sergeant Robert G. Stockham of the 96th Company in 2/6, received the Medal of Honor for action at Belleau Wood years later.

18. Longstreet, "Gunner Nice," *Asbury Park* (New Jersey) *Sunday Press*.

19. Arthur Russell Collection, Oshkosh Public Museum, Record Group 59 history.

20. Longstreet, "Gunner Nice," *Asbury Park* (New Jersey) *Sunday Press*.

21. Robert B. Asprey, *At Belleau Wood* (Denton: University of North Texas Press, 1996), 153.

22. According to some sources he said a variation of the quote attributed to him. One of his Medal of Honor awards was for action in China in 1900 and the other for service in Haiti in 1915.

23. Clark, *Devil Dogs*, 128.
24. Donald R. Morris, "Thomason U.S.M.C.," *American Heritage*, November 1993, 1–2. He met Lawrence Stallings of 3/5 (later Lt. Colonel) as classmates at the Quantico Marine officer training school. After the war they renewed their acquaintance and Stallings introduced him to his contacts at *Scribner's Magazine*. Stallings was involved with his own works including the theatrical "What Price Glory." Following the war Stallings married Helen Poteat, whose father was president of Wake Forest College.
25. Homsher, "Securing the Flanks," 2.
26. "Flock to the Marines," *New York Times*, 9 June 1918, sec. I
27. John S. D. Eisenhower with Joanne Thompson Eisenhower, *Yanks: The Epic Story of the American Army in World War I* (New York: Free Press, 2001), 138.
28. Catlin, *With the Help*, 268.
29. Abbot, *Soldiers of the Sea*, 306.
30. George W. Hamilton letter to Mary E. Hamilton, 21 June 1918.
31. Mackin mentioned in his book that a few men enjoyed killing and made a sort of game of it. Hamilton was not one of them.
32. Asprey, *Belleau Wood*, 322.
33. Clark, *Devil Dogs*, 128–129.
34. Catlin, *With the Help*, 180–181.
35. Due to weak flank support one might contest that the French were elbows away.
36. John W. Thomason Jr., "Into Belleau Wood," *Scribner's Magazine* 79, no. 23 (1926): 311.
37. Richard J. Beamish and Francis A. March, *America's Part in the World War* (Philadelphia and Chicago: John C. Winston, 1919), 294.
38. Thomason, "Into Belleau Wood," 313.
39. Harbord, *American Army*, 300.
40. General W. C. Neville to Hamilton, Official Business, 10 June 1918, Roger C. Barnard Jr. Papers.
41. Palmer, *America in France*, 256.

Chapter 9

1. Major General Omar Bundy to Hamilton, 5 July 1918, National Archives.
2. Brigadier General Preston Brown Chief of Staff, by Command of Major General Lejeune to Hamilton, 5 July 1918, Roger C. Barnard Jr. Papers.
3. "14th an A.E.F. Holiday," *Stars and Stripes* (France), 12 July 1918.
4. Gilson Willets, *Inside the History of the White House* (New York: Louis Klopsch, 1908), 235.
5. Rickenbacker, *Fighting*, 196.
6. Rickenbacker, *Fighting*, 196. No American witnessed his death.
7. "*Quentin Roosevelt Had Soldier Burial*," *New York Times*, 22 July 1918.
8. Theodore Roosevelt, *The Great Adventure* (New York: Charles Scribner's Sons, 1919), 1.
9. Richard Derby, "*Wade in, Sanitary!*": *The Story of a Surgeon in France* (New York: G. P. Putnam's Sons, 1919), 86. Ethel, one year older than George, made her debut in society during a White House Christmas Ball at age 17 in 1908. Derby, like his father-in-law, was educated at Harvard.
10. Clark, *Devil Dogs*, 223.
11. Browne and Pillsbury, *American Army*, 73.
12. John W. Thomason Jr., *Fix Bayonets!: With the U.S. Marine Corps in France, 1917–1918* (London: Greenhill Books, 1989), 76.
13. Floyd Gibbons, *And They Thought We Wouldn't Fight* (New York: George H. Doran, 1918), 363.
14. Thomason, *Fix Bayonets*, 88.
15. Catlin, *With the Help*, 187.

16. *Official History of the SECOND ENGINEERS in the World War: 1916–1919*, comp. Regimental Headquarters Second Engineers (Gift, 1920), 33.

17. Often the absence of Allied planes meant they were in some other remote location over enemy territory attacking and performing surveillance.

18. Longstreet, "Gunner Nice," *Asbury Park* (New Jersey) *Sunday Press.*

19. *The Americans in the Great War*, vols. 1 and 2 (France: Michelin and Cie, 1920): 1:26.

20. *Official History of the SECOND ENGINEERS*, 37.

21. McClellan, *United States Marine Corps*, 46.

22. Harbord, *American Army*, 337.

23. *Ibid.*, 265. Lejeune took command of the Fourth Brigade and three days later became commander of the Second Division.

24. McClellan, *United States Marine Corps*, 39. Doyen was the first Marine to command an Army division and Lejeune was the second.

25. Karl Schuon, *U.S. Marine Corps Biographical Dictionary: The Corps' Fighting Men What They Did Where They Served* (New York: Franklin Watts, 1963), 107. Holcomb rose to become the 17th commandant of the Marine Corps.

Chapter 10

1. "Traveling in the Northwest," *Washington Post*, 1 September 1918, sec. Editorial and Society.

2. Most of the songs were not carried back home across the Atlantic Ocean. The song "Parley-Vous" was also known as "Hinky Dinky Parley-Vous."

3. W. E. Christian, *Rhymes of the Rookies: Sunny Side of Soldier Service* (New York: Dodd, Mead, 1917), 23–24.

4. Mackin, *Suddenly*, 143.

5. Arthur E. Hartzell, *Meuse-Argonne Battle: Sept. 26–Nov. 11, 1918*, reprinted by Visitors Bureau G-1 American Forces in France, Central Printing Plant Q.M.C (1919), 23.

6. John J. Pershing, *Final Report of Gen. John J. Pershing* (Washington, D.C.: GPO, 1919), 38.

7. The event was a "Shock and Awe" of unprecedented proportion.

8. Broun, *Our Army*, 271.

9. Mackin, *Suddenly*, 156.

10. Hunt, *History of the Fifth Regiment Marines*, 4.

11. The sergeants were three of only 19 men in American history to be honored with the Double Medal of Honor since it was issued from both the U.S. Army and U.S. Navy. The designated award was later phased out.

12. Derby, *"Wade in, Sanitary!"* 112.

13. Leonard P. Ayres, *The War with Germany: A Statistical Summary* (Washington, D.C.: GPO, 1919), 118.

14. Palmer, *America in France*, 428.

15. Clarence L. Richmond, personal World War I diary, "Somewhere in France," episode 13.

16. Rickenbacker, *Fighting*, 232.

17. Browne and Pillsbury, *American Army*, 89.

18. Charles Woolley and Bill Crawford, *Echoes of Eagles* (New York: Dutton, 2003).

19. *Americans in the Great War*, 2.

20. "Soldiers Letter," *Winchester* (Massachusetts) *Star*, 17 January 1919.

21. Mackin, *Suddenly*, 169.

22. *Ibid.*, 171.

23. Ben H. Chastaine, *The Story of the 36th: The Experiences of the 36th Division in the World War* (Oklahoma City: Harlow Publishing, 1920), 17.

24. Gibbons, *And They Thought*, 358–359.

25. McClellan, *United States Marine Corps*, 49.

26. Derby, *"Wade in, Sanitary!"* 123–124.

Chapter 11

1. Brown, "George Wallis Hamilton" *Leatherneck*. November 2003, 49.
2. *Ibid.*
3. J. H. Craige, "Breaking the Hindenburg Line at Blanc Mont Ridge," *Daughters of the American Revolution Magazine*, December 1919, 699. Before the war Craige was a newspaper editor. During World War I he served with the 11th Marines as regimental adjutant, intelligence officer and war correspondent. After the war he was an aide to Lejeune and a professor of journalism at Quantico.
4. Louis E. Orcutt, *Supplementary Volume in the Great War History: From the Armistice November 11, 1918 to the Ratification of the Peace Treaty* (New York: Christian Herald, 1920), 202.
5. *History of the Seventy Seventh Division: August 25th. 1917, November 11th. 1918*, ed. J.O. Adler (New York: 77th Division Association, 1919), 199.
6. *Ibid.*, 206.
7. Derby, "*Wade in, Sanitary!*" 131–132.
8. Rickenbacker, *Fighting*, 4.
9. Carter and Plant, *Tale of a Devil Dog*, 70.
10. Broun, *Our Army*, 279.
11. Derby, "*Wade in, Sanitary!*" 146.
12. Robert Messersmith died in 1929 at Quantico. His brother George, who was two years older, had a distinguished career in the U.S. Foreign Service and was featured on the front cover of *Time* magazine, December 2, 1946, as a prominent diplomat.
13. Carter and Plant, *Tale of a Devil Dog*, 71.
14. Thomason, *Fix Bayonets*, 168. Corporal Pruitt died later in the day, one day before his 22nd birthday.
15. *Ibid.*, 171.
16. Longstreet, "Gunner Nice," *Asbury Park* (New Jersey) *Sunday Press.*
17. *Blanc Mont: (Meuse-Argonne-Champagne)*, prepared in the Historical Branch War Plans Division General Staff. (Washington, D.C.: GPO, 1922), 14
18. Derby, "*Wade in, Sanitary!*" 134.
19. *Ibid.*, 24.
20. Clark, *Devil Dogs*, 314–315. First Lieutenant. Nelms was commander of the 8th Machine Gun Company. I purposefully omitted the names from the original text.
21. Roosevelt, *Rough Riders*, 142–143.
22. Clark, *Devil Dogs*, 323.
23. "Soldiers Letter," *Winchester* (Massachusetts) *Star*, 17 January 1919.
24. Today the annual Hulbert Trophy for Outstanding Leadership Award is given in his honor.
25. Allan C. Bevilacqua, "From Exile to Hero," *Leatherneck*, January 1999, 28.
26. *Ibid.* 2
27. Longstreet, "Gunner Nice," *Asbury Park* (New Jersey) *Sunday Press.*
28. Allan C. Bevilacqua, "The Battle of Blanc Mont Ridge," *Leatherneck*, November 2000, 5.
29. Clark, *Devil Dogs*, 316.
30. *Ibid.*, 316–317.
31. *Ibid.*, 324. Mackin gave the total that walked out as 134 and reserve officer Eugene West mentioned 243 out of 1,057. Muster rolls were not an exact science, and Hunt's figure of 168 appears to be the more accurate.
32. *Official History of the SECOND ENGINEERS*, 53–54.
33. *Blanc Mont: (Meuse-Argonne-Champagne)*, 16.
34. Derby, "*Wade in, Sanitary!*" 146–148.
35. Clark, *Devil Dogs*, 318. No specific time given.
36. *Ibid.*, 324.
37. *Blanc Mont: (Meuse-Argonne-Champagne)*, 16. F.O. 38 was issued at 0400 on 10/5 to continue a general advance, but morning orders stated no formal attack.
38. *Ibid.*, 30. *Blanc Mount* provided the total of enlisted men at 4,771, but the actual total based on the numbers is 4,764.

39. Bevilacqua, "Battle of Blanc Mont Ridge," 6.
40. Clark, *Devil Dogs*, 423.
41. Morris, "Thomason U.S.M.C.," 3.
42. Stephanie Cassidy, Art Students League of New York, archivist. The school had about 20 teachers. Thomason registered for the 1914-15 season and studied under Frank Vincent DuMond and George Bridgman. He also registered for the 1929-30 season and studied a few months under Bridgman. While Thomason was in New York he was taken by the large naval ships at the New York Yard, which prompted him to join the Marine Corps.
43. Hunt, *History of the Fifth Regiment Marines*, 17–18.
44. Catlin, *With the Help*, 231–232.
45. McClellan, *United States Marine Corps*, 295.
46. Captain Dirksen was honorably discharged from the Marine Corps on August 6, 1919.
47. Today the Fifth Regiment, stationed at Camp Pendleton, California, and the Sixth Regiment at Camp Lejeune, North Carolina, are honored to still wear the French Fourragere.
48. James Brown Scott, *Official Statements of War Aims and Peace Proposals: December 1916 to November 1918* (Washington, D.C.: Carnegie Endowment for International Peace, 1921), 415.
49. Clark, *Devil Dogs*, 344.
50. Frederick Palmer, *Our Greatest Battle: The Meuse-Argonne* (New York: Dodd, Mead, 1919), 269.
51. Ferdinand Foch, *The Memoirs of Marshal Foch*, trans. Bentley T. Mott (Garden City, NY: Doubleday, Doran, 1931): 434–436.
52. Frederick Palmer, *Our Greatest Battle: The Meuse-Argonne* (New York: Dodd, Mead, 1919), 269.
53. Mackin, *Suddenly*, 225.
54. *Ibid.*, 227.
55. Richmond, "Somewhere in France," episode 17.
56. Charles P. Summerall, "Leadership," ed. Robert C. Richardson Jr., *The Cavalry Journal* 30, no. 122 (January 1921): 3.
57. Louis E. Orcutt, *Supplementary Volume in the Great War History*, 206.

Chapter 12

1. Derby, *"Wade in, Sanitary!"* 165.
2. Louis E. Orcutt, *Supplementary Volume in the Great War History*, 206.
3. Derby, *"Wade in, Sanitary!"* 166–167.
4. *Ibid.*, 167.
5. Hartzell, *Meuse-Argonne Battle*, 34.
6. Brehon B. Somervell, who was born in Arkansas, later entered West Point and made a career in the U.S. Army rising to a four-star general during World War II. With his engineering background he was instrumental in building the Pentagon.
7. Thomason later rejoined the 49th Company during the "Occupation of Germany."
8. *Official History of the SECOND ENGINEERS*, 76, 238.
9. U.S. Congress, House Select Committee on Expenditures in the War Department. *Hearings Before Subcommittee No. 3 (Foreign Expenditures)*, 66th Cong., 2nd sess., 1920, vol. 3, Serial 4-Parts 51–74, 3768.
10. *Official History of the SECOND ENGINEERS*, 239.
11. Richmond, "Somewhere in France," episode 20.
12. Mackin, *Suddenly*, 252.
13. *Ibid.*, 254–255.
14. In the 1930s Louis Cukela as a captain was in officer training. A case study scenario was presented to a group. The proper solution was to pull back, however Cukela defended his opposing view, stating he attacked at all times and showed his Medal of Honor as proof.
15. Clark, *Devil Dogs*, 374–375.
16. U.S. Congress, House Select Committee on Expenditures in the War Department, *Hearings Before Subcommittee No. 3 (Foreign Expenditures)*, 66th Cong., 2nd sess., 1920, vol. 2, Serial 4-Parts 26–50, 2363.

17. Henry K. Kindig, personal diary, 83rd Company, 3/6.
18. Richmond, "Somewhere in France," episode 21.
19. Foch, *Memoirs*, 486.
20. U.S. Congress, House Select Committee on Expenditures in the War Department, 1920, vol. 2, Serial 4-Parts 26–50, 1965.
21. *Ibid*.
22. James C. Russell and William E. Moore, *The United States Navy in the World War* (Washington, D.C.: Pictorial Bureau, 1921): 299.
23. Garvin, *"A History of the 49th Company,"* 15.
24. Clark, *Devil Dogs*, 375.
25. Alan C. Bevilacqua, "Major Louis Cukela," *Leatherneck* (October 2006).
26. Brown, *Few Good Men*, 83.
27. Robert Wallace Blake, *From Belleau Wood to Bougainville: The Oral History of Major General Robert Blake USMC and the Travel Journal of Rosselet Wallace Blake* (Bloomington, IN: AuthorHouse, 2004): 23–24. Oral history transcript of tape-recorded interview between Major General Robert Blake and Marine Corp historian Benis Frank, March 28, 1968.
28. U.S. War Department. Report of the Adjutant General, *1919*, vol. 1, 598–599.
29. The Great War had a "Christmas Truce" on December 25, 1914. Both British and German troops spontaneously emerged from trenches to celebrate. The British noted then how harmonious the Germans were.
30. Richmond, "Somewhere in France," episode 21.
31. Foch, *Memoirs*, 488.
32. Russell and Moore, *United States Navy*, 299.
33. Carter and Plant, *Tale of a Devil Dog*, 75.
34. Russell and Moore, *United States Navy*, 298.
35. Brown, *Few Good Men*, 75.

Chapter 13

1. McClellan, *United States Marine Corps*, 81.
2. Leonard P. Ayres, *The Official Record of the United States' Part in the Great War* (Washington, D.C.: War Department), 126–128. Total prisoner figures in John. J. Pershing's *Final Report* vary slightly.
3. Pershing, *Final Report*, 86.
4. "Marines' Chief Reports," *New York Times*, 15 December 1918.
5. Bartlett, *Lejeune*, 114. The division also captured 1,350 machine guns and many pieces of artillery.
6. Clark, *Devil Dogs*, 129. For the period March 15 to November 15.
7. Derby, *"Wade in, Sanitary!"* 44–45.
8. *Ibid*.
9. Frank Tousic, "In the Thick of the Fight," *The Hospital Corps Quarterly and Supplement to the Untied States Naval Medical Bulletin*, no.12 (January 1920): 39.
10. Derby, *"Wade in, Sanitary!"* 26.
11. Robert L. Denig, "Address by Major Robert L. Denig, U.S.M.C.," *Annual Proceedings Pennsylvania Society of Sons of the Revolution 1918–1919* (1919): 79–80.

Chapter 14

1. "First 'Devil Dogs' Come Home Today," *New York Times*, 3 August 1919.
2. "Clash Over Deaths on Armistice Day," New York Times, 2 March 1921.
3. Joseph E. Persico, *Eleventh Month Eleventh Day Eleventh Hour: Armistice Day, 1918, World War I and Its Violent Climax* (New York: Random House, 2004), 378. The total one day estimate of casualties of those countries fighting on November 11, 1918, was 10,944 versus approximately 10,000 on D-Day.

4. Jack Ausland, "The Last Kilometer," *Saturday Evening Post*, 13 November 1937, 85. It appears that Jack Ausland was officially known as Corporal John E. Aasland, who as a member of the 55th Company was awarded a Silver Star for action on November 1, 1918. The article was illustrated by the highly reputable John W. Thomason Jr. He also wrote under the name John E. Ausland.
5. *Ibid.*
6. *Ibid.*, 86.
7. Byron D. Stokes, "Shell Gets 'Burley' as George Keeps Going," *The Sigma Chi Quarterly* 38 (1918–1919): 171.
8. Robert Lawler to USMC Medical Department, 16, November 1918, National Archives. It should be noted that the U.S. Army in France still controlled all protocol.
9. For this reason, different diaries and reports contain a variety of village listings.
10. Derby, "*Wade in, Sanitary!*" 184.
11. *Stars and Stripes* (France). vol. 1, no. 42.
12. "Soldiers Letter," *Winchester* (Massachusetts) *Star*, 17 January 1919.
13. Thomason, *Fix Bayonets*, 227.
14. Hamilton's 66th Company under Capt. Blake billeted at Wolfenucker and the 17th under Capt. Hunt billeted at Kurtscheid.

Chapter 15

1. "Washington Sorrow Keen," *New York Times*, 7 January 1919.
2. Derby, "*Wade in, Sanitary!*" 199.
3. *Ibid.*, 200.
4. "Nation to Mourn at the Bier of Roosevelt Today," *New York Times*, 8 January 1919.
5. Commander Feland to Commander General Lejeune, Official Documents, 12 January 1919, Roger C Barnard Jr. Papers.
6. Commander Feland to Chief of Staff 2d Division, Official Documents, 25 January 1919, Roger C Barnard Jr. Papers.
7. General Lejeune to Hamilton, 14 March 1919, U.S.M.C. History Division Reference Branch, George W. Hamilton File.
8. Allan C. Bevilacqua, "The Strange Case of Edmund Chamberlain," *Leatherneck* (May 2009).
9. "Chamberlain Tells of his Air Exploit," *New York Times*, 16 September 1918.
10. *Ibid.*
11. *Ibid.*
12. Bevilacqua, "Strange Case."
13. Abbot, *Soldiers of the Sea*, 313.
14. Bevilacqua, "Strange Case."
15. Rickenbacker, *Fighting*, 187–188.
16. A pilot with five confirmed down planes became an "Ace."
17. "Flyers Return from War," *New York Times*, 1 June 1919, sec. I.
18. *Ibid.*.
19. "Maj. Hamilton Returns," *Washington Post*, 2 June 1919.
20. "Society," *Washington Post*, 2 June 1919. According to Roger C. Barnard Jr., the BUR-GEO-MAR sign was still hanging in 2002.

Chapter 16

1. *History of the Third Battalion: Sixth Regiment, U.S. Marines* (Hillsdale, MI: Akers, Mac Ritchie and Hurlbut, 1919), 123.
2. Susan Conant Barnard to daughter Eleanor, 11 July 1919, Roger C. Barnard Jr. Papers. Roger C. Barnard Sr., Harvard '02 came from a family with a long line of Harvard graduates.
3. Susan Conant Barnard to daughter Eleanor, 11 July 1919, Roger C. Barnard Jr. Papers.

4. USMC Major General Commandant to Hamilton, official memo, 15 July 1919, National Archives.
5. McClellan, *United States Marine Corps*, 78.
6. FDR and his wife Eleanor also maintained a town home at 49 East 65th Street in NYC.
7. "Devil Dog Division Captures Fifth Av.," *New York Times*, 9 August 1919.
8. "The Second Division to Be Paraded Here," *New York Times*, 4 August 1919. There was no mention of the dog "Parade Rest." Many thought "Jimmy" was an anteater, but he was a coatimundi, who preferred hard tack over ants and at times wore a specially constructed gas mask. During the Spanish-American War, Colonel Roosevelt's Rough Riders had three mascots: a young mountain lion named Josephine, who was usually tied up, a war eagle and a dog named Cuba.
9. *History of the Third Battalion: Sixth Regiment, U.S. Marines*, 129.
10. "Band Concert Today," *Washington Post*, 11 August 1919.
11. "The United States Marines," *Washington Post*, 12 August 1919.
12. Garvin, "A History of the 49th Company," 16. James Edward "Ted" Meredith was one year older than Hamilton and also graduated from high school (Mercersberg Academy in Pennsylvania) in 1912 . He won two gold medals at the 1912 Summer Olympics. In the 880 meters he set a world record and also won in the 400 meter relay. The middle distance runner later set a world record for the half mile. During World War I he saw limited action as a U.S. Army Air Corps pilot and shunned the limelight.
13. Bartlett, *Lejeune*, 116.
14. "Ready for Marines," *Washington Post*, 12 August 1919.
15. *Congressional Record*, 65th Cong., 1st sess., 1919, vol. 58, pt. 4, 3783–3784.
16. "Lodge Outlines Five Reservations To League Plan," *New York Times*, 13 August 1919.
17. "Cheers in Senate as Lodge Says League Invites More Wars," *Washington Post*, 13 August 1919.
18. "Society," *Washington Post*, 13 August 1919.
19. McClellan, *United States Marine Corps*, 82.
20. *Ibid.*, 81. The Marine Fifth Brigade that did not see action in France released 6,671.
21. Ove Mortensen, U.S.M.C., personal discharge papers, 13 August 1919. Additional discharge comments on a scale of 5: Military Efficiency: 4.5 (no easy grading, as a sharpshooter there was still expert classification as Hamilton) Obedience: 5, Sobriety: 5. He would outlive his major by roughly 58 years.
22. It also appears that 1st Lt. Charles H. Woolley the commander of the 49th Aero Squadron, who was earlier affiliated with the 95th Aero Squadron, came home to Winchester in March 1919. Julia E. Hamblet was born in town 1916. In the 1950s Colonel Hamblet was director of Women Marines. In 1960 Winchester native Joe Bellino won the Heisman Trophy while at the U.S. Naval Academy. Native Mark P. Fitzgerald became a U.S. Navy Four-Star Admiral.
23. The 92nd Division was comprised of all black men except for the officers.
24. Lt. Colonel Harllee, Fitness Report of Hamilton, 30 September 1919, National Archives.
25. "Wilson Stronger, His Weight Normal," *New York Times*, 20 August 1920. By the summer of 1920 the President could get out of bed and raise his left hand to his head.
26. U.S. Congress, House Committee on Naval Affairs, *Hearings to Increase the Efficiency of the Personnel of the Navy and Coast Guard Through the Temporary Provision of Bonuses or Increased Compensation*, Bill H. R. 11927, 66th Cong., 2nd sess., 1920, 350.
27. U.S. Congress, House Select Committee on Expenditures in the War Department, 66th Cong., 2nd sess., 1920, vol. 3, Serial 4-Parts 51–74, 3767–3768.
28. *Ibid.*, 3768.
29. Brown, *Few Good Men*, 75.
30. *Ibid.*
31. Hamilton to Commandant Barnett, 19 November 1919, National Archives.

Chapter 17

1. Thomason, *Fix Bayonets*, 171.
2. Rickenbacker, *Fighting*, 355.
3. *Ibid.*, 358. The book was published in 1919 prior to the hearings.

4. Foch, *Memoirs*, 476.
5. In 1916, when Lt. Hamilton was stationed aboard the *Arkansas* in Newport, Rear Admiral Austin M. Knight served as president of the Newport Naval War College.
6. U.S. Congress, House Committee on Awarding of Medals in the Naval Service, *Hearings Before a Subcommittee on Naval Affairs United States Senate, S. RES. 285*, 66th Cong., 2nd sess., 1920, 393.
7. *Ibid.*, 394.
8. *Ibid.*, 435.
9. Brig. General Feland to Hamilton, 19, February 1920, Roger C. Barnard Jr. Papers. Evidently Feland in the islands had not heard that Hamilton was a captain.
10. Commandant Barnet to Secretary Daniels, 8 March 1920, National Archives.
11. "Bulletin," *The Norwegian American Chamber of Commerce* 3, no. 1 (January 1919): 5. The address was also known as "Newspaper Row" due to its proximity to City Hall.
12. *The New International Year Book: Compendium of the World's Progress for the Year 1921*, ed. Frank More Colby (New York: Dodd, Mead, 1922), 4.
13. Ladislas D'Orcy, ed., "Alaskan Flying Expedition Completes Flight," *Aircraft Journal* 7, no. 17 (25 October 1920): 5–6.
14. "Text of the Proclamation Signed by Colby Certifying Ratification of 19th Amendment," *New York Times*, 27 August 1920.
15. Hamilton to M.G.C., telegram, 1 October 1920, National Archives.
16. "Chats with Visitors in Washington," *Washington Post*, 26 October 1920.
17. Armistice Day was renamed Veterans Day on June 1, 1954 by President Dwight D. Eisenhower. The national holiday continues to be observed on November 11, the last day of the Great War, no matter what day of the week it falls on. On this day, veterans often pass out poppies as a remembrance of the fields of France. The day is set aside for two distinct purposes: to both honor all veterans who have and are currently serving our fine country, and through its origin, to honor a new era of world peace.

Chapter 18

1. Bevilacqua, "Strange Case."
2. "Flier Fights Fire in Plane Over City," *New York Times*, 5 February 1921.
3. USMC Commandant Lejeune to Hamilton, 22 March 1921, National Archives.
4. Captain Dearing to Commandant Lejeune, memo, 15 April 1921, National Archives.
5. "Big Curtiss-Eagle Falls," *New York Times*, 30 May 1921.
6. "Rickenbacker Ends Continental Flight," *New York Times*, 29 May 1921.
7. "Express Plane Carries 23 to Atlantic City," *New York Times*, 30 May 1921.
8. "Central '21, Seagoing Class, Produced 13 Navy Officers," *Washington Post*, 1 October 1950. All 13 became officers.
9. "Countryside Joins President in Camp," *New York Times*, 25 July 1921.
10. "President Watches Battle of Marines," *New York Times*, 2 October 1921.
11. Phillip Bigler, *In Honored Glory: Arlington National Cemetery The Final Post* (Arlington: Vandamere Press, 1994), 63.
12. "President Harding's Address at the Burial of an Unknown American Soldier," *New York Times*, 12 November 1921.
13. "Amplifiers Tested for Armistice Day," *New York Times*, 10 November 1921.
14. Aviation Training Journal, Completing School Report, 22 December 1921, National Archives.

Chapter 19

1. *Aircraft Year Book* (New York: Aeronautical Chamber of Commerce of America, 1922), 174.
2. U.S. Congress, House Committee Naval Investigation, *Hearings Before the Subcommittee of the Committee on Naval Affairs United States Senate*, 66th Cong., 2nd sess., vol. 2, 1921, 2680.

3. Marc Wortman, *The Millionaires' Unit: The Aristocratic Flyboys Who Fought the Great War and Invented American Air Power* (New York: Public Affairs, 2006), 212.

4. U.S. Congress, House Committee in Charge of Army Appropriation Bill, 1922, *Hearing Before Subcommittee of House Committee on Appropriations*, 66th Cong., 3rd sess., 1921, 229–230.

5. *The New International Year Book: Compendium of the World's Progress for the Year 1921*, ed. Frank More Colby (New York: Dodd, Mead, 1922), 10.

6. Douglas G. Wardrop, ed., "Aero Club Banquet Inaugurates Era of Aeronautic Co-operation and Co-ordination," *Aerial Age Weekly* 14, no. 20 (23 January 1922), 464.

7. Ibid., 465.

8. Ibid., 469.

9. Hamilton to USMC Commandant Lejeune, memo, 1 February 1922, National Archives.

10. "Airplane Crashes into Swamp," *Washington Post*, 27 March 1922. On October 17, 1922, a VE-7 took off from the USS *Langley*, marking the first successful takeoff from an aircraft carrier.

11. Report 1240-25/202, 3 November 1922, National Archives.

12. A. Scott Berg, *Lindbergh*, 63–64. Lindbergh shared the cockpit seat with sixteen-year-old Harlan "Bud" Gurney, with Otto Timm as the pilot. In 1927 he flew solo for 33½ hours nonstop from America to Paris.

13. "Weather Conditions," *Washington Post*, 26 June 1922.

14. "5,000 See Hero Die," *Washington Post*, 27 June 1922. George R. Martin was from Buffalo. Reports varied as to the altitude from which the tail spin began from 1,000 feet to 400 feet.

15. National Archives. Personnel file of George W. Hamilton. Military records state plane #6157, but non military photograph of plane displays #6679.

16. Roosevelt, *Great Adventure*, 7–8.

Chapter 20

1. "Highest Honors Paid Capt. G. W. Hamilton," *Washington Post*, 30 June 1922.

2. In 1936 the title was changed from Officer in Charge, Aviation, to Director of Aviation.

3. "Highest Honors Paid Capt. G. W. Hamilton," *Washington Post*, 30 June 1922.

4. Brown, *Few Good Men*, 24, 25.

5. "Honor Girl's Plea for Rites to Hero," *Washington Post*, 28 June 1922. The very first "flyover" may have been performed during the Great War by British aviators to honor the death of the German "Red Baron."

6. Bigler, *In Honored Glory*, 49–50.

Chapter 21

1. Colonel Leroy P. Hunt commanded the Fifth Regiment at Guadalcanal. As the senior 1/5 captain under Major Hamilton, he survived "The Box" and the Meuse River crossing.

2. "Charles A. Hamilton Newspaper Man," *New York Times*, 25 August 1942.

3. "Washingtonians of the Week," *Washington Post*, 16 March 1941.

4. "James Lloyd Wright," *New York Times*, 8 December 1952.

5. Meacham, *Franklin and Winston*. The two were briefly introduced many years prior.

6. Layton McCartney, *The Teapot Dome Scandal: How Big Oil Bought the Harding White House and Tried to Steal the Country* (New York: Random House, 2008), 133. The answer was four Marines would be sufficient. Fall was later convicted of accepting bribes, becoming the first Cabinet member to go to prison.

7. Charles Hamilton to USMC Commandant Lejeune, not dated, National Archives.

8. Sergeant Stahl to Brig. General Rufus H. Lane, 15 March 1923, National Archives.

9. Arthur Lyng to Div. Opns. & Trg., 8 February 1923, National Archives.

10. USMC Commandant Lejeune to Adjutant General of the Army, 19 March 1923, National Archives.

11. Robert C. Davis to USMC Commandant Lejeune, 28 April 1923, National Archives.

12. President Hoover, Greeting, 21 June 1930, National Archives.

13. Shuler to USMC Major General Ben Fuller, 21 June 1932, National Archives. Shuler used stationary from Plain Talk Magazine, Inc., Washington, D.C., where he was the business manager.

14. Hamilton's "Boys" to Charles Hamilton, 9 June 1934, Roger C. Barnard Jr. Papers. John Culnan, who also signed the letter, published a Marine ballad book in 1927 titled *Semper fidelis (ever faithful)*.

15. President Roosevelt to Charles Hamilton, 6 February 1941, Roger C. Barnard Jr. Papers.

16. C. H. Metcalf to Margaret D. Hamilton, 28 July 1943, Roger C. Barnard Jr. Papers. It should be noted that Hamilton was appropriately referred to as a major in the letter. The Haitian Campaign Badge No. 137 and ribbon bar were posthumously issued on June 2, 1923, as recognition for Hamilton's brief service in Haiti during December 1919, while attached to the USS *Delaware*.

Epilogue

1. John C. Scharfen, letter to author, 22 November 2009.

2. *Theodore Roosevelt Association Journal* 24, no. 2 (2001): 9. My intent in mentioning the Medal of Honor facts is for historical reference only and should not be construed as an attempt to promote a third request for issuing the Medal of Honor to GWH.

3. Daniels, *Navy and the Nation*, 289.

4. Victor H. Krulak, *First to Fight: An Inside View of the U.S. Marine Corps* (Annapolis: Naval Institute Press, 1984), 252.

Appendix A

1. Ayres, *Official Record*, 54.
2. Ayres, *War with Germany*, 26–27.
3. *American Army in the European Conflict*, trans. Chambrun and Marenches, 21, 29, 49, 50.
4. McClellan, *United States Marine Corps*, 29, 38.

Appendix B

1. Military Record, Hamilton, National Archives.

2. *Ibid.* Since President Harding was in Texas on the second anniversary of Armistice Day, the award was mailed to Hamilton along with an additional letter from Lejeune, dated November 11, 1920.

3. *Ibid.*

4. Military Record, Hamilton, Translation not identified, National Archives.

5. Military Record, Hamilton, trans. USMC Colonel John W. Barker, National Archives.

6. Military Record, Hamilton, Roger C. Barnard Jr., Papers.

7. Regimental Commander Feland to Commander in Chief, G.H.Q., 11 December 1918, National Archives.

8. Commanding Officer Feland to Commanding General Neville, 13 November 1918, National Archives.

9. Major General John A. Lejeune to the Secretary of the Navy, 9 December 1919, National Archives.

10. Major General John A. Lejeune to the Adjutant General of the Army, 29 December 1922, National Archives.

11. Military Record, Hamilton, National Archives.

12. *Ibid.*

13. *Ibid.*

14. *Ibid.*

Bibliography

Books

Abbot, Willis J. *Soldiers of the Sea: The Story of the United States Marine Corps*. New York: Dodd, Mead, 1918.
The American Army in the European Conflict. Translated by Colonel De Chambrun and Captain De Marenches. New York: Macmillan, 1919.
The Americans in the Great War. Volumes 1 and 2. France: Michelin and Cie, 1920.
Anderson, Lars. *Carlisle vs. Army: Jim Thorpe, Dwight Eisenhower, Pop Warner and the Forgotten Story of Footballs Greatest Battle*. New York: Random House, 2007.
Asprey, Robert B. *At Belleau Wood*. Denton: University of North Texas Press, 1996.
Axelrod, Alan. *Miracle at Belleau Wood: The Birth of the Modern U.S. Marine Corps*. Guilford, CT: Lyons Press, 2007.
Bartlett, Merrill L. *Lejeune: A Marine's Life 1867–1942*. Columbia: University of South Carolina Press, 1991.
Beamish, Richard J., and Francis A. March. *America's Part in the World War*. Philadelphia and Chicago: John C. Winston, 1919.
Berg, A. Scott. *Lindbergh*. New York: G.P. Putnam's Sons, 1998.
Bigler, Phillip. *In Honored Glory: Arlington National Cemetery: The Final Post*. Arlington: Vandamere Press, 1994.
Blake, Robert Wallace. *Bayonets and Bougainvilleas: A Memoir of Major General Robert Blake, USMC, 1894–1983*. Robert Wallace Blake, 2001.
———. *From Belleau Wood to Bougainville: The Oral History of Major General Robert Blake USMC and the Travel Journal of Rosselet Wallace Blake*. Bloomington, IN: AuthorHouse, 2004.
Broun, Heywood. *Our Army at the Front*. New York: Charles Scribner's Sons, 1918.
Brown, Ronald J. *A Few Good Men: The Story of the Fighting Fifth Marines*. Novato, CA: Presidio Press, 2001.
Browne, G. Waldo, and Rosecrans W. Pillsbury, comps. *The American Army in the World War: A Divisional Record of the American Expeditionary Forces in Europe*. Manchester, NH: Overseas Book Company, 1921.
Boyd, Thomas. *Through the Wheat*. New York: Charles Scribner's Sons, 1923. Fiction.
Canfield, Bruce N. *U.S. Infantry Weapons of the First World War*. Lincoln, RI: Andrew Mowbray, 2000.
Carter, William A., and Pascal J. Plant. *The Tale of a Devil Dog*. Washington, DC: Canteen Press, 1920.
Catlin, Albertus W. *With the Help of God and a Few Good Marines*. New York: Doubleday, 1919.
Chastaine, Ben H. *The Story of the 36th: The Experiences of the 36th Division in the World War*. Oklahoma City: Harlow, 1920.
Christian, W. E. *Rhymes of the Rookies: Sunny Side of Soldier Service*. New York: Dodd, Mead, 1917.
Clark, George B. *Devil Dogs: Fighting Marines of World War I*. Novato, CA: Presidio Press, 1999.
———. *His Road to Glory: The Life and Times of "Hiking Hiram" Bearss Hoosier Marine*. Pike, NH: Brass Hat, 2000.
Collier, Peter, and David Horowitz. *The Fords: An American Epic*. New York: Summit Books, 1987.
Daniels, Josephus. *The Navy and the Nation: War-Time Addresses*. New York: George H. Doran, 1919.

Dear Folks at Home: The Glorious Story of the United States Marines in France as Told by Their Letters from the Battlefield. Compiled by Kemper F. Cowing, Edited by Courtney R. Cooper. Boston and New York: Houghton Mifflin, 1919.

Derby, Richard. *"Wade in, Sanitary!": The Story of a Surgeon in France.* New York and London: G. P. Putnam's Sons, 1919.

Durant, Will, and Ariel Durant. *The Lessons of History.* New York: Simon and Schuster, 1968.

Eisenhower, John S. D., with Joanne Thompson Eisenhower. *Yanks: The Epic Story of the American Army in World War I.* New York: Free Press, 2001

Foch, Ferdinand. *The Memoirs of Marshal Foch.* Translated by Bentley T. Mott. Garden City, NY: Doubleday, Doran, 1931.

Gibbons, Floyd. *And They Thought We Wouldn't Fight.* New York: George H. Doran, 1918.

Gross, Charles J. *American Military Aviation: The Indispensable Arm.* College Station: Texas A&M University Press, 2002.

Harbord, James G. *The American Army in France: 1917–1919.* Boston: Little, Brown, 1936.

Krulak, Victor H. *First to Fight: An Inside View of the U.S. Marine Corps.* Annapolis, MD: Naval Institute Press, 1984.

Mackin, Elton E. *Suddenly We Didn't Want to Die.* Novato, CA: Presidio Press, 1993.

McCartney, Layton. *The Teapot Dome Scandal: How Big Oil Bought the Harding White House and Tried to Steal the Country.* New York: Random House, 2008.

McClellan, Edwin N. *The United States Marine Corps in the World War.* Washington, DC: GPO, 1920.

Meacham, Jon. *Franklin and Winston: An Intimate Portrait of an Epic Friendship.* New York: Random House, 2003.

Metcalf, Clyde H. *A History of the United States Marine Corps.* New York: G. P. Putnam's Sons, 1939.

The New International Year Book: Compendium of the World's Progress for the Year 1921. Edited By Frank More Colby. New York: Dodd, Mead, 1922.

Orcutt, Louis E. *Supplementary Volume in the Great War History: From the Armistice November 11, 1918, to the Ratification of the Peace Treaty.* New York: Christian Herald, 1920.

Palmer, Frederick. *America in France.* New York: Dodd, Mead, 1919.

———. *John J. Pershing: General of the Armies.* Westport: Greenwood Press, 1948.

———. *Our Greatest Battle: The Meuse-Argonne.* New York: Dodd, Mead, 1919.

Persico, Joseph E. *Eleventh Month Eleventh Day Eleventh Hour: Armistice Day, 1918, World War I and Its Violent Climax.* New York: Random House, 2004.

Rickenbacker, Edward V. *Fighting the Flying Circus.* New York: Frederick A. Stokes, 1919.

Roosevelt, Theodore. *The Great Adventure.* New York: Charles Scribner's Sons, 1919.

———. *The Rough Riders.* New York: Charles Scribner's Sons, 1899.

Russell, James C., and William E. Moore. *The United States Navy in the World War.* Washington, DC: Pictorial Bureau, 1921.

Schuon, Karl. *U.S. Marine Corps Biographical Dictionary: The Corps' Fighting Men What They Did Where They Served.* New York: Franklin Watts, 1963.

Scott, James Brown. *Official Statements of War Aims and Peace Proposals: December 1916 to November 1918.* Washington, DC: Carnegie Endowment for International Peace, 1921.

Thomason, John W., Jr. *Fix Bayonets!: With the U.S. Marine Corps in France, 1917–1918.* London: Greenhill Books, 1989.

Tyler, John W. *The Life of William McKinley.* Philadelphia and Chicago: P. W. Ziegler, 1901.

Washington Post. Various dates.

Willets, Gilson. *Inside the History of the White House.* New York: Louis Klopsch, 1908.

Wood, Leonard, Austin M. Knight, Frederick Palmer, Frank H. Simonds, and Arthur Ruhl. *The Story of the Great War: History of the European War from Official Sources.* Edited by Francis J. Reynolds, Allen L. Churchill, and Francis Trevelyan Miller. New York: Collier and Son, 1916. (Visible notice of stated 1916 copyright.)

Woodburn, James Albert. *Political Parties and Party Problems in the United States.* New York: G. P. Putnam's Sons, 1914.

Woolley, Charles, and Bill Crawford. *Echoes of Eagles.* New York: Dutton, 2003.

Wortman, Marc. *The Millionaires' Unit: The Aristocratic Flyboys Who Fought the Great War and Invented American Air Power.* New York: Public Affairs, 2006.

Magazine and Newspaper Articles

Alexander, Joseph H. "The U.S. Marines in World War I." *Leatherneck*, November 2008.
Ausland, Jack. "The Last Kilometer." *Saturday Evening Post*, 13 November 1937.
Bartlett, Merrill L. "'Whispering Buck' Neville: Marine." *Marine Corps Gazette*, December 1995.
Bettez, David J. "Quiet Hero: Maj. Gen Logan Feland." *Marine Corps Gazette*, November 2008.
Bevilacqua, Allan C. "The Battle of Blanc Mont Ridge." *Leatherneck*, November 2000.
_____. "From Exile to Hero." *Leatherneck*, January 1999.
_____. "Major Louis Cukela." *Leatherneck*, October 2006.
_____. "Soissons, France 1918." *Leatherneck*, November 2001.
_____. "The Strange Case of Edmund Chamberlain." *Leatherneck*, May 2009.
_____. "TOP-10 BADASS* MARINES." *Leatherneck*, April 2009.
Brown, Ronald J. "George Wallis Hamilton: The Forgotten Hero of World War I." *Leatherneck*, November 2003.
"Bulletin." *The Norwegian American Chamber of Commerce* 3 (January 1919).
Bundy, Omar. "The Second Division at Château-Thierry." *Everybody's Magazine*, March 1919.
Craige, J.H. "Breaking the Hindenburg Line at Blanc Mont Ridge." *Daughters of the American Revolution Magazine*, December 1919.
Daugherty, Leo J. III. "General Thomas Holcomb, USMC 1879–1965." *Marine Corps Gazette*, August 1997.
Denig, Robert L. "Address by Major Robert L. Denig, U.S.M.C." *Annual Proceedings Pennsylvania Society of Sons of the Revolution 1918–1919* (1919).
D'Orcy, Ladislas, ed. "Alaskan Flying Expedition Completes Flight." *Aircraft Journal* 7 (25 October 1920).
"Feland of the Marines a General." *The Technology Review* 21 (January 1919).
Homsher, David C. "Securing the Flanks at Belleau Wood." *Military History* 14 (June 1997).
Krulak, General Charles C. "Through the Wheat to the Beaches Beyond: The Lasting Impact of the Battle for Belleau Wood." *Marine Corps Gazette*, July 1998.
Lee, Robert E., ed. "Planting Trees as Memorials." *The Modern City* 4 (December 1919).
Longstreet, Elias S., "Gunner Nice of the Devil Dogs," *Asbury Park* (New Jersey) *Sunday Press*. 10 September 1933.
Merrow, Alexander, Gregory Starace, and Agostino von Hassell. "Belleau Wood: From the German Perspective." *Marine Corps Gazette*, November 2008.
Morris, Donald R. "Thomason U.S.M.C." American Heritage 44 (November 1993).
The Nation, 6 March 1890, 191.
New York Times. Various dates.
Norris, Edwin M., ed. "'11." *Princeton Alumni Weekly*, 5 February 1919.
Roosevelt, Archibald. "Lest We Forget." *Everybody's Magazine*, May 1919.
Rochester (New York) Post Express. 27 June 1922.
Scarton, Bennie. "Down Home in Quantico" *Cooperative Living*, February 2007.
"Soldiers Letter," *Winchester* (Massachusetts) *Star*. 17 January 1919.
Stars and Stripes (France). Various dates.
Stokes, Bryon D. "Shell Gets "Burley" as George Keeps Going." *The Sigma Chi Quarterly* 38 (1918–1919).
The Sunday (Washington, D.C.) *Star*. 22 March 1936 and 16 January 1939.
Summerall, Charles P. "Leadership." Edited by Robert C. Richardson, Jr. *The Cavalry Journal* 30 (January 1921).
Thomason, John W., Jr. "Into Belleau Wood." *Scribner's Magazine* 79, no. 23 (1926).
Tinker, Clifford Albion. "Josephus Daniels and the Medal Muddle." *U.S. Air Service*, February 1920.
Tousic, Frank. "In the Thick of the Fight." *The Hospital Corps Quarterly & Supplement to the Untied States Naval Medical Bulletin* (January 1920).
"TR Awarded Medal of Honor." *Theodore Roosevelt Association Journal* 24, no. 2 (2001).
Ward, Geoffrey C. "Ollie and Old Gimlet Eye." *American Heritage* 38 (November 1987).
Wardrop, Douglas G., ed. "Aero Club Banquet Inaugurates Era of Aeronautic Co-operation and Co-ordination." *Aerial Age Weekly*, 23 January 1922.

Government Documents and Historical Papers

Aircraft Year Book. New York: Aeronautical Chamber of Commerce of America, 1922.
Annual Report of the Secretary of the Navy for the Fiscal Year 1918. Washington, DC: GPO, 1918.
Annual Reports of the Navy Department for the Fiscal Year 1915. Washington, DC: GPO, 1916.
Annual Reports of the Navy Department for the Fiscal Year 1920. Washington, DC: GPO, 1921.
Ayres, Leonard P. *The Official Record of the United States' Part in the Great War.* Washington, DC: War Department.
———. *The War with Germany: A Statistical Summary.* Washington, DC: GPO, 1919.
Biographical Sketch of Charles A. Hamilton. Office of the Town Historian, Town of Aurora and Village of East Aurora, New York. November 1938.
Blanc Mont: (Meuse-Argonne-Champagne). Prepared in the Historical Branch War Plans Division General Staff. Washington, DC: GPO, 1922.
Complaints of Cities, Towns, Associations, Individuals, Etc. Nineteenth Annual Report of the Board of Railroad Commissioners of the State of New York, 1901. Volume 1. Albany: J.B. Lion Company, State Printers, 1902.
Congressional Medal of Honor the Distinguished Service Cross and the Distinguished Service Medal Issued by the War Department. Complied in the Office of the Adjutant General of the Army. Washington, DC: GPO, 1920.
Congressional Record. 65th Cong., 1st sess., 1917. Volume 55. Washington, DC: GPO, 1917.
Congressional Record. 65th Cong., 1st sess., 1919. Volume 58, part. 4. Washington, DC: GPO, 1919.
English, George H., Jr. *History of the 89th Division, U.S.A.* Denver: War Society of the 89th Division, 1920.
Garvin, Frank Hunt. *A History of the 49th Company.* Stories from the Veterans History Project, Library of Congress. http://lcweb2.loc.gov/diglib/vhp-stories/loc.natlib.afc2001001.01339/pageturner?ID=pm0007001&page=1.
Hartzell, Arthur E. *Meuse-Argonne Battle: Sept. 26 — Nov. 11, 1918.* Reprinted by Visitors Bureau G-1 American Forces in France. Central Printing Plant Q.M.C, 1919.
The History and Achievements of the Fort Sheridan Officers' Training Camps. Myron E. Adams and Fred Girton for Fort Sheridan Association, 1920.
History of the Seventy Seventh Division: August 25th. 1917, November 11th. 1918. Edited by J.O. Adler. New York: 77th Division Association, 1919.
History of the Third Battalion: Sixth Regiment, U.S. Marines. Hillsdale, MI: Akers, Mac Ritchie and Hurlbut, 1919.
Hunt, Leroy P. *History of the Fifth Regiment Marines: 5/1917–12/31/1918.* Reprint no. 3. Pike, NH: Brass Hat.
My Rifle. Suggested by William H. Rupertus. Division of Public Relations United States Marine Corps Navy Department Arlington Annex. Washington, D.C.
Official History of the SECOND ENGINEERS in the World War: 1916–1919. Compiled by the Regimental Headquarters Second Engineers. Gift, 1920.
Pershing, John J. *Final Report of Gen. John J. Pershing.* Washington, DC: GPO, 1919.
Register of the Commissioned and Warrant Officers of the United States Navy and Marine Corps: January 1, 1920. Washington, DC: GPO, 1920.
U.S. Congress. House Committee in Charge of Army Appropriation Bill, 1922. *Hearing Before Subcommittee of House Committee on Appropriations.* 66th Cong., 3rd sess., 1921.
U.S. Congress. House Committee Naval Investigation. *Hearings Before the Subcommittee of the Committee on Naval Affairs United States Senate.* 66th Cong., 2nd sess., vol. 2, 1921.
U.S. Congress. House Committee on Awarding of Medals in the Naval Service. *Hearings Before a Subcommittee on Naval Affairs United States Senate.* S. RES. 285. 66th Cong., 2nd sess., 1920.
U.S. Congress. House Committee on Naval Affairs. *Hearings on Estimates Submitted by the Secretary of the Navy 1919: Part 2.* 66th Cong., 2nd sess., 1919.
U.S. Congress. House Committee on Naval Affairs. *Hearings to Increase the Efficiency of the Personnel of the Navy and Coast Guard through the Temporary Provision of Bonuses or Increased Compensation. Bill H. R. 11927.* 66th Cong., 2nd sess., 1920.
U.S. Congress. House Committee on United Air Service. *Hearing Before a Subcommittee of the Committee on Military Affairs.* 66th Cong., 2nd sess., 1921.
U.S. Congress. House Select Committee on Expenditures in the War Department. *Hearings Before*

Subcommittee No. 3(Foreign Expenditures). 66th Cong., 2nd sess., 1920. Vol.2, Serial 4-Parts 26–50. Vol. 3, Serial 4-Parts 51–74.
U.S.M.C. History Division Reference Branch. *George W. Hamilton file.*
U.S. War Department. Report of the Adjutant General. *War Department Annual Reports 1919.* Vol. I. Washington, DC: GPO, 1920.

Personal Papers

Barnard, Roger C., Jr. Papers. Private collection.
Cassidy, Stephanie. (Archivist) Art Students League of New York, information April 2008.
Department of the Navy, Naval History and Heritage Command.
Kindig, Henry K. Personal diary http://www.worldwaronediary.com/.
Metcalf, C. H. Letter to Miss Margaret D. Hamilton, 28 July 1943.
Mortensen, Ove. U.S.M.C. personal discharge papers, 13 August 1919.
National Archives. Personnel file of George W. Hamilton.
Richmond, Clarence L. Personal diary "Somewhere in France," http://my.en.com/~robinr/wardiary/diary.htm.
Russell, Arthur. Collection, Oshkosh Public Museum, Record Group 59 history.
Scharfen, John C. Letter to author, 22 November 2009.

Index

Page numbers in ***bold italics*** indicate illustrations.

Academy at East Aurora 10
Adkins, J.W. 228
Adrian, Minnesota 136
Aero Club of America 230, 232–234
Air Corps 50; *see also* Air Service
Air Service 226, 232–233, 24; *see also* Air Corps
Aisne 168, 175; defensive 70; offensive 96; river 118
Allied Forces 33, 64, 67, 69, 71, 78, 85, 94, 96, 102, 106, 108–109, 113, 115, 118, 144, 167, 172, 180, 216–217, 254; Allied air force 114, 117, 132; Allied army 58, 66, 122–123, 142, 145, 167, 174; Allied artillery 151; Allied countries 180, 230; Allied Nations 66, 174, 185; Allied Naval Forces 233; Allied Powers 33; Allied soldiers 54, 172; Allied troops 48, 164
Alpine Chasseurs 58–60, 77
American Automobile Association 226
American Expeditionary Forces 2–3, 45–47, 49–51, 54–56, 62–63, 65, 70, 81, 85, 90–91, 96, 98, 104, 106, 111, 115–117, 120, 122, 146, 151, 153, 164, 165–166, 168, 170–171, 174, 178, 185–186, 191, 215, 218, 220, 239, 247, 250; American Army 56–57, 145, 174
American Flying Club 230
American Indians *see* Native Americans
American Revolution 5
American Telephone & Telegraph 49
Annamites 97
Annapolis, Maryland 39, 226–227, 231
Ansauville-Royaumeix, France 116
Anselm, William B. 160
Argentina 60
Argonne *see* Meuse Argonne
Arizona 42
USS *Arizona* 41–42
USS *Arkansas* 37–43, 191
Arlington National Cemetery 4, 42, 229, 239, 241, ***242***, 249

Arlon, Belgium 180
Armistice 3, 120, 156, 163–164, 167, 174–176, 180, 192, 196, 209, 215–217, 255
Armistice Day 51, 208, 223, 228, 230, 232
Army Industrial College 241
Art Students League 141
Arthur, Chester A. 11, 243
Ashley, Thomas W. 211
Astor, Vincent 233
Atlantic Charter 245
Atlantic City, New Jersey 226
Atlantic Fleet 37–43
Atomic Energy Division 245
USS *Augusta* 245
Aurora Times 11
Ausland, Jack (John E. Aasland) 175–176
Austria 33

Bacon, Henry 20
Baker, Newton D. 45–46, 65, 114, 146, 204
Baltimore Polytechnic Institute 22
Barnard, Margaret H. (niece) 220, 244, 246
Barnard, Mary H. (sister) 220, 235, 243, 246, 252; *see also* Hamilton, Mary E.
Barnard, Roger C. (brother-in-law) 195
Barnard, Roger C., Jr. (nephew) 7, 244, 246, 252
Barnett, George 39, 46, 93, 111, 170, 190–191, ***192***, 193–194, 200, 206, 210, 217–218, 220–221
Bastille Day 94–95
Bayonville, France 150, 175
Bearss, Hiram 62–63; "Hiking Hiram" 63, 99
Beauchamp, Felix 136
Beaumont, France 153–157, 166, 174
Beauvais, France 66
Belgium 33, 178–180, 187; military forces 96, 122; Ypres 121
Belleau Wood xii, 3–5, 72, 74–75, ***77***, 84–85, 88–92 ***93***, 94–96, 100–101, 109, 111,

291

113, 115, 120, 123, 128, 131, 135, 143–144, 153–154, 172, 193, 210, 214, 240, 247–248, 254–255; Belleau 70, 74; Bois de Belleau 72, 74, 89–90, 219
Benjamin, Ray N. 138
Benson, William S. 204
Berkley, California 144
Berry, Benjamin S. 75, 87–88, 240
Biddle, William P. 28
Bissell, W.S. 12
Black Hills, South Dakota 245
Black Point Military Reservation 35
Blackstone, Paul J. 22
Blake, Robert 84, 144, 160, 165, *177*, 206
Blanc Mont 4, 64, 120, *123*, 124, *125*, 127, *129*, 130–131, 138–140, *141*, 142–144, 147, 150, 154, 160, 172, 186, 208, 215, 241, 254–255; Blanc Mont Ridge 118, 120–121, 124, 126, 129, 132, 135, 142–143, 172, 174, 247
Bliss, Tasker H. 67
Bois de Retz 99
Bois de Veuilly, France 71–72
Bois de Vipre, France 130
Bois des Flaviers, France 162
Boone, Daniel 118
Boone, Joel T. 118, 127, 151, 240
Boston, Massachusetts 86, 206, 215; Boston Common 16; Red Sox 215
Boulogne, France 54
Bouresches, France 75, 90–91
Bourmont, France 60, 64
Bowers, Lawrence 160
"The Box" 3, 138, 140–141, 143, 154, 162, 241, 254
Brady, John J. 81, 247
Bragg, Caleb S. 233
Brazil 244
Brest, France 59, 196
Breuvannes, France 60, 194
Briey iron fields 108
British Expeditionary Forces 109; Northern Bombing Group, reference to 34, 39, 85, 96, 114, 121, 122, 123, 145, 172; Royal Air Force 218; squadron 188
Brittany, France 88
Brown, Preston 93, *109*
Budde, George W. 160, 162
Buffalo, New York 9–10, 12–13, 15–16, 83, 85
Buffalo Commercial Advertiser 11
Buffalo Evening News 244
Bulgaria 118; Bulgars 123
Bullard, Robert L. 98
Bundy, Omar 62, 69–70, 72, 85, 89, 93, 96, *105*, 146
Bur-Geo-Mar Farm 194, 196, 246, 253; *see also* Conesus Lake

Burtt, Wilson B. 164
Bussiares, France 212
Butler, Smedley D. 236, 238

California 226
Cambrai, France 122, 142
Camp Bois de l'Eveque 104
Camp Douzaine 65
Camp Harding 228, 235–236
Camp Perry 228
Campbell, Douglas W. 64
Canada 107
Canada Dry Corp. 244
Cannon House office building 17
Canton, Ohio 16
Cape May, New Jersey 12, 14
Capital City 12, 15–16, 22, 26, 32, 63, 68, 107, 198, 200, 222, 226, 233, 235, 239, 241, 245, 251; *see also* District of Columbia; Washington, D.C.
Carlisle, Pennsylvania 24
Carlisle Indian Industrial School 24–25
Carnegie, Andrew 19, 198
Casey, John 83
Catlin, Albertus W. 68, 71–72, 87–88, 204
censorship issues 85–86, 180–181
Central High 18–23, 27–28, 32, 34, 68, 75, 154, 226–227, 239, 241, 245; reference to 200
Central Powers 33, 69, 118, 140, 143, 147, 203, 230
Chamberlain, Edmund G. 187–191, 224, 231
Champagne (sector) 4, 64, 118, 120, 124, 127, *141*, 168, 174, 219
Chandler Theater 39
Chappawamsic Swamp 234
Château-Thierry 4, 69–70, 72, 89–90, 92, 96, 124, 145, 172, 174, 181, 186, 193, 203, 211
Chauchat 50
Chaudin, France 103
Chautmont-en-Vexin, France 69
Chicago, Illinois 226
Chicago Tribune 84
China 37, 97
Christian IX, King of Denmark 14
Christmas, Walter E. 14
Churchill, Winston 6, 245
Civil Service Act 11
Civil War 1, 5, 33, 77, 85, 228, 236
Cleveland, Grover 10, 12–13
Clemenceau, Georges 67, 145–146
Clinton, William J. 256
Cochran, Kenyon H. 144, 150, 154
Coffman, De Whitt 39
Colby, Bainbridge: as Secretary of State 221
Collier Trophy 234

Columbia University 41, 245
Columbus, Ohio 136
Cone, H.J. 188
Conesus Lake 14–16, 20, 28, 32, 34, 61, 66–67, 75, 107, 194–195, 221, 235, 246, 253; *see also* Groveland, New York
Congressional Press Corps 5; gallery 11, 217, 228, 243, 245
Conner, Robert E. 52, 130, 135
Conway, Peter 83
Coolidge, Calvin 229, 245
Corbett, Murl 82, 87, 101, 135, 218, 251
Cornell, Percy D. 126, 142
Cornell University 21
USS *Corsair* 187
Costello, Harry 24
Courtesols, France 118
Cox, James M. 223
Crabbe, William 100
Craige, John H. 120
Crawley, T.B. 228
Croix de Guerre (for 4th Brigade) 89–90, 103, 143
Cronin, Raymond P. 83, 213
Crouttes, France 94
Crowell, Benedict 232; as Toastmaster 233
Crowther, Orlando C. 75–76, 78, 81, 211, 213
Cuba 13, 37, 42, 256; *see also* Guantanamo
Cukela, Louis 111, 135, 160, 165, *177*, 214, 247, 255
Culnan, John H. 83, 251
Cunningham, Alfred A. 188, 226, 234
Curtis-Eagle 226

D-Day 175
Dailey, Vincent 26
Dale, Thomas 212
Daly, Daniel 84
Danforth, Henry G. 27
Daniels, Josephus 28, 30, 39, 43, 184, 194, 204, 220, 256
Danish West Indies 14
Davis, Claude E. 212
Davis, Robert C. 249
Davison, F. Trubee 233
Dayton, Ohio 236
Dayton Daily News 223
Dean, James 3
Dearing, A.C. 225
DeCarre, Alphonse 186, 191–192
Degoutte, Jean 90
De Havilland (DH-4, DH-4B) 64, 188, 221, 228, 231–232, 235–236, *237*
USS *DeKalb* 54–55, 63, 188
de Lavergne, Paul 226, 233
USS *Delaware* 214

Democratic Party 23, 222–223
Denig, Robert L. 172
Denmark 111; *see also* Jutland
Derby, Richard 95–96, 118, 131, 133, 139, 151, 153, 171, 180, 184, 240
Detroit, Michigan 18
Devil Dog (as definition) 79
Dewey, George 42
DeWitt, John 41
Dickinson, D. Jr. 127
Dickman, Joseph 110, 178
Dirksen, Raymond F. 106, 126, 134, 142
District of Columbia 14–16, 20, 30, 232; *see also* Capital City; Washington, D.C.
Dogan (French general) 96
Doubelday, Nelson 233
Dowd, Michael 27–28, 52
Dowd Military Academy 27
Doyen, Charles A. 46, 53, 55–56, 60, 62, 68, 93, 143, 240
Drum, Andrew B. 52
Dudley, Robert W. 160
Dumas (French general) 54
Dunbeck, Charles 156, 159, 161–162, 165–166, 175
Dunlap, Robert H. 204
Dunn, Jim 24
du Pont, Pierre S. 233
Dye, Leon L. 207

East Aurora, New York 10, 11, 34
East Coast Expeditionary Force 231; *see also* 2nd Squadron
Edison, Thomas 11, 13, 227
18th Amendment 217
18th Company (USMC) 156, 176
8th Machine Gun Company (USMC) 76, 102, 126, 128, 136, 161
80th Division 149
81st Machine Gun Company 126
82nd Division 110, 122
89th Division 110, 115, 146, 149, 151, 153, 157–158, 162, 165, 171
Eisenhower, Dwight D. 25
Ellis Island 6
Ely, Hanson 113, 126, 140
Enyart, Howard 237
Epiez aerodrome 64
Erzberger, Matthias 163
Essen Hook (Essen Trench) 124, 127–128, 130
Evans, Francis 189
Evans, Frank E. 204
Exermont, France 144

Fall, Albert 228, 245
Fay, William G. 204

294 Index

Feland, Logan 53–54, 56, 60, 62, 96, 100, 126, 130, 132, 139, 141, 150, 165, 175, 177, *181*, 183, 185–186, 191, 194, 204, *218*, 219–221, 239–240, 246
Ferch, Aaron 150
Ferdinand, Franz 33
15th Company (USMC) 52
15th Machine Gun Company 126
5th Army Corps (Fifth Corps, V Corps) 146–147, 149, 151, 164, 166, 168, 178
5th Division 110, 149
"5th Marines at Champagne" *141*
5th Regiment (USMC) xii; 46–47, 53–56, *57*, 58, 60–65, 68, 71–73, 84, 90, 96, 100–103, 115, 120, 126, 128, 130–132, 135, 140, *141*, 149–150, 161, 163, 165, 168, 179–180, 183, 185–186, 196, 200–201, 206, 210, 219–220, 240, 247, 250
51st Company (USMC) 72, 156, 176
55th Company (USMC) 129, 156, 175–176
Fillmore, Milliard 10
Finnegan, Gerald R. 83, 213
Firestone, Harvey 227
First Army 123, 164, 166, 175
1st Army Corps (First Corps, I Corps) 110, 149
1st Aviation Force (USMC) 187; Squadron Santo Domingo 234; *see also* East Coast Expeditionary Force
1st Battalion 5th Regiment (USMC) 3, 47, 52–55, 57–58, *59*, 60, 62–66, 71, 75–76, 84, 87, 92, 94, 97, 102, 106–107, 111, 116, 126, 128, 131–133, *137*, 138, 150, 156–160, *161*, 162, 165, 168, 175–176, *177*, 179, 181, 183, 185, 187, 191, 196, 200, 204, 240, 243, 246–247, 250–252; First Battalion 211; motto 116; reference to Hamilton's battalion 134, 136, 139, 144, 146
1st Battalion 6th Regiment (USMC) 87, 126, 157
1st Division 55–56, 60, 62, 65, 96, 98–99, 110, 146, 153, 170–171, 178, 184, 195; Big Red One 146, 153, 172; "Pershing's Own" 172
First Field Hospital 172
First Moroccan Division 96, 98, 101, 103, 104; Moroccan 172
1st Regiment 208
First World War *see* World War I
Fisk, USMC Capt. 144
Flying Circus 71
Foch, Ferdinand 66–67, 90, 92, 96, 109, 117, 121, 145–146, 155, 163–164, 166–167, 229; as Commander in Chief 123
Fokker 71
Foley, William 23
Folsom, Frances 12

Force School 94, 209
Ford, Henry 227
Ford Model T 18, 32
Forest of Beival 175
Fortune 9–10
Fosse, France 175
4th Army Corps (Fourth Corps, IV Corps) 110
4th Brigade (USMC) 46–47, 62–64, *65*, 72, 75, 79–81, 84–85, *86*, 87–92, 94, 96–98, 103, 106, 111, 117, 120, *121*, 122, 126–128, 130, 140, 143, 148, 154, 163–164, 168, 170, 179–180, 191, 196, 198–200, *201*, *202*, 204, 240–241, 246, 255; Marine Brigade 5, 46, 62, 64, 68, 84, 92, 104, 120, 126, 127, 135, 143, 146, 153, 155–157, 167, 170, 183, 198; reference to brigade 144, 152
4th Division 178
4th Machine Gun Battalion 97, 101
42nd Division (Rainbow) 110, 115, 171, 178
43rd Company (USMC) 147, 156, 177
49th Company (USMC) 47, 52, 54–56, 58, 60, 64, 66, 70, 73, 75–76, 78–79, 81, 83, 85, 91–92, 94, 96, 100–101, 108, 111, 126, 128, 130, 134–135, 137–138, 140, 144, 154, 156, 160, 182, 193, 200, 211–213, 240, 247–248, 250–252; slogan 53
Fox, Daniel R. 136
Frazier, Walter D. 73, 213
French, Daniel C. 20, 235
French Army 58, 145
French Foreign Legion 58, 96
French Fourragere 143, *218*
French military forces (specific): First Brigade 96; Second Brigade 96; 2nd Battalion tanks 126; 4th Army 117–119, 123, 174; VI Army 90; XXI Corps 126; 21st Division 126–128, 130–131; 22nd Division 130–131; 170th Division 126; 252nd Aviation Squadron 132; *see also* Alpine Chasseurs; First Moroccan Division; French Army; French Foreign Legion; Senegalese
Freya Stellung 152, 219
Frost, David H. 160
Frye, William P. 11
Fullam, William F. 232–233
Fuller, Alvan T. 209, 215
Fuller, Ben H. 53, 249
Furguson, William J. 162

Galliford, Walter T. 61, 134
Gallipoli 117
Garfield, James A. 11, 229
Garvey, James B. 81, 213
Garvin, Frank H. 200, 251
gases (description) 49
Gates, Isabel Likens xii, 200

Geier 43
Geiger, Roy S. 187, 231, 234–235, 240–241
General Electric 13
Genesco, New York 195
Geological Survey Field Corps 21, 75
George, D. Lloyd 67
USS *George Washington* 196, 198
George Washington University 18, 27
Georgetown University 21, 23–26, 190
German Chancellor 216
German Mauser Company 31
German military forces (specific) 28th Division 74; 200th Division 126; 213th Division 126; 362nd Division 74; U-53 (submarine) 41; *see also* Prussians
Geronimo 15
Gettysburg, Pennsylvania 32, 235–236, 239, 244; Gettysburg Battlefield 228
Gibbons, Floyd 82, 84–86, 91, 100
Gideon, William C. 160
Gondrecourt Training Area *57, 59*
Goree, Thomas 85
Gouraud, Henri 117–118, 141–142
Govillers, France 106
Great Adventure 95, 238
Great Britain *see* England
Great War *see* World War I
Greene, Edward A. 64–65
Gresuell, Arthur B.W. 214
Gridiron Club 245
Grimm, Charles ***222***
Groveland, New York 14, 27; *see also* Conesus Lake
Guadalcanal 243
Guantanamo, Cuba 14, 38
Guggenheim, Edwin 233
Guggenheim, Harry 233
Guiteau, Charles J. 11

Haig, Douglas 67, 109
Haines, Henry C. 204
Haiti 35, 37–39, 42, 198, 214; Port Au Prince 231
Hale, Frederick 217
Hamilton, Alexander 203
Hamilton, Charles A. (father) 5, 9–16, 19, 21, 32, 63, 67, 68, 107, 222–223, 242–246, 249, 251; letter from FDR 251; letter to Lejeune 246–247
Hamilton, Charles B. "Burley" (brother) 12–14, 18, 19, 153, 178, 196, 244, 246, 252
Hamilton, Edwin P. (brother) 12
Hamilton, George, W. 7, 20, 23, 26, ***31***, 32–33, ***40***, 45, 51, 67, 89, 95, 103, 106, 111, 117, 120, 141, 153, 160, ***161***, 165, 169, 182, 191, ***196***, 203–204, 224, 228, 232–233, 239–241, 243, 253; Aero Club banquet 232; airplane crash 234, 237; ancestry 9; appreciation of nature 15, 61, 68–69; with USS *Arkansas* 37–43; Armistice notification 166; arrival in France 55; as athlete 19–26, 28, 41, 200; awards 3–4, 90–91, 93, 143, 169, 201, 210, 246–249, 252, 255; birth of 12; Capt. Chamberlain trial 186, 187, 190; certified as Marine aviator 230; character of 2–5, 9, 20, 22, 27–28, 88, 91, 110, 118, 120, 133, 156, 186, 190, 195, 200, 207, 210, 219, 220, 240, 247, 249–252, 254–257 childhood of 14–18; commands 1/5 3, 47, 62–64, 116–119, 123, 126–139, 143–144, 146–148–152, 154–155, 177–181, 183; commands 1/5 and 2/5 47, 156–159, 162–163, 165–166, 175–176, 200, 216, 255; commands 49th Company 47, 52–60, 64–66, 68–85, 87–88, 91–92, 94, 96, 98–102, 104, 107–108, 110, 112, 114; death of 237–238; with USS *DeKalb* 54–55; with USS *Delaware* 214–215; departs Marine Corps 220; Dowd Military Academy 27–28; East Coast Expeditionary Force 232; employed Geological Survey Field Corps 21; employed Hoff, Kleve Corp., 220–221; employed National Savings and Trust Co. 26–27; employed U.S. Forest Service 21; enters Marine Officer's School 30; friendship with Burley 66, 244; friendship with Feland 56, 219–220, 240, 246; friendship with Shuler 52, 222–223, 245–246, 216; friendship with Thomason 246; Gettysburg 32, 235–236; home from France 193; letters 61, 66, 68, 76–77, 79–80, 88, 210–214; lt. col. recommendation 178, 185–186; with USS *Louisville* 191; made 1st lt. 43; made assistant to 1/5 94; made captain 61, 196, 225; made major 108, 249; medical leave 183; meeting with Barnett 193; messages 44, 83–84, 132–133, 139, 162, 221–222; with USS *New Hampshire* 43–44; Norfolk Barracks 30, 32, 34, 43; notable quote 4, 81; oath of office 30, 158, 225; Pensacola station 227, 230; Philadelphia Barracks 35, 208, 210, 214–215; physical appearance 3, 27, 30, 108; poem dedication xii 200; Quantico Barracks 44, 52, 215, 226, 230- 231, 234, 236; request for Caribbean duty 39, 234; rifle and war 32, 50, 75; rifle competition 31–32, 35–36, 193–196, 198, 206–207; rifle practice 31–32, 59; romance 108, 196; Student Naval Aviator program 227, 230; Victory Parade 200; Washington, D.C., barracks 44, 49, 207–208, 225, 227
Hamilton, Ida P. (mother) 11–14, 32, 63, 67, 107, 195, 243; *see also* Persons, Ida M.

Hamilton, Margaret D. (sister) 13, 20, 32, 34, 63, 67, 107, 222, 241–242, 244, 246, 252
Hamilton, Mary E. (sister) 12–13, 32, 61, 63, 67, 88, 107, 195, 257; *see also* Barnard, Mary H.
Hamilton, Mary J. (aunt) 19; *see also* Wright, Mary H.
USS *Hancock* 55
Hanna, Maj. Mark 157, 162
Hansen, Hans Peter 141
Harbord, James G. 68, 71–72, 75, 85, **86**, 88–91, 96, 98, 103–104, 146, 240, 247
Harding, Warren G. 223, 227–229, 233, 235, 245
Harllee, William C. 35, 193–194, 207
Harriman, W. Averill 206
Harrison, Benjamin 13
Harrison, Horace W. 187
Hart, USMC Corporal 214
Harvard University 19, 21, 195
Heddesdorf, Germany **182**
USS *Henderson* 55
Herbst, G. A. **109**
Hertling, Georg von 104
Heywood, Charles 16, 33
Hicks, Fred C. 232–233
Hill 142 73, 75, 79–81, 84, 87, 91, 124, 212–214, 247
Hill 165 212–213
Hill 176 73
Hindenberg Line 122, 151–152
Hines, John L. 149
Hitler, Adolf 121
Hoff, Kleve Corporation 220–221
Hoffman, Charles F. 80–81, 111, 214, 247–248, 255; Ernest A. Janson 247–249, 255
Holcomb, Thomas 64, 87, 106, 204
Hoover, Herbert 240
Hotchkiss 50
Hotel Astor 249
Hotel Commodore 230, 232
Howze, Robert D. 133
Hubbard, Mr. and Mrs. Elbert 34
Hughes, Charles, E. 41
Hughes, John A. 87
Hulbert, Henry L. 111, 134–135
Hungary 33, 111
Hunt, Leroy P. 52, 74, 100, 126, 133, 135–136, **137**, 138, 142, 144, 156, 158–159, 161–162, 183, 204

Independence Day 56, 92, 227; as July 4th 167, 190
Inter-Allied Games 185, 187
International League of Nations 202
Ireland 34, 83

Isleboro, Maine 135
Islington, England 9
Italian military forces 96, 114

Janson, Ernest A. *see* Hoffman, Charles F.
Jauiny-Exammes Ridge 174
Jefferson, Thomas 203
Johnson, Gillis, A. 136
Johnson, Royal C. 215
Jones, George 36
Jones, Theos J. 228
Jordan, Jack 136
Jutland, Denmark 39; Battle of Jutland 40

Kelly, Francis J. Jr. 137
Kelly, John J. 128, 255
Keyser, Ralph S. 102, 204
Kieren, Francis S. 81, 136, 213
Kilgore, Fred D. 204
Kindig, Henry 163
Kingman, Matthew H. 88
Kirby, Maxwell 216
Kittering, Charles F. 232–233
Klein, Charles 34
Knight, Austin M. 217
Knight Board 217
Kocak, Matej 111, 135, 255
Korea 37
Korean War 245
Krulak, Victor H. 257
Kukoski, John 83

Lafayette, Marquis de 56, 90
Lafayette Park 209
La Guardia, Fiorello H. 233
Lamonte, Missouri 136
Landres-et-St. Georges, France 149, 151, 219–220
Landreville, France 150
Langley Field 226
Lansing, Robert 32
Larsen, Henry L. 130–131, 157
"The Last Night of the War" **161**, 251
La Tuilerie Farm 153
Lauchheimer, Charles H. 35
Lawler, Robert A. 178
leatherneck (as term) 46
Leatherneck magazine 4
LeBlanc, Frank 160
Le Droit Park 12–13, 21
Lee, Burton 172
Lee, Harry 126, 131, 150, 204
Lejeune, John A. 5, 44, 93–94, 104, **105**, **109**, 110, 114–115, 117–118, 122–123, 126, 132, 139–142, 146–147, 149, 151–153, 164, 168–169, 174–175, 178, **182**, 185–186, 191, 195–196, **197**, 198, 200, 204, 215, 221,

Index

224–225, 234, 239, 246–249; appointed 13th Commandant 221
Lemly, Wiliam B. 204
Les Islettes, France 144
Les Mares Farm 76
Letanne, France 155, 157
Lewis Gun (description) 50
Lewiston, New York 85
Liggett, Hunter 110, 149, 216
Ligon, Mary T. 39, **40**
Ligon, Thomas W. 39, **40**
Lincoln, Abraham 20, 229; family 235
Lincoln Memorial 235; construction 20
Lincoln Standard Tourabout 235
Lindbergh, Charles A. 235
Lindgren, Everette E. 136
Livermore, George K. 206, 209, 215
Liverpool, England 9, 34, 191
Lloyd, C. A. 228
Locksun 43
Lodge, Henry Cabot 202–203
Loening, Grover Cleveland 234
London, England 187, 224
Long, Charles G. 204
Longstreet, James 85, 236
Lorraine, France 115, 168
Lost Battalion 122
USS *Louisville* 191, 193, 225
Ludwig's Rucken 132
Lufbery, Raoul 64
Lusitania 33, 34
Luxembourg 178, 180–181
Lyng, Arthur E. 52, 137, 214, 247–248

Mackin, Elton E. 7, 85, 108, 110, 115–116, 140, 146–147
Madagascar 60
Maestre, French General 147
Manhattan *see* New York City
Manney, Henry N., Jr. 240
Marbache (Metz Sector) 104, **105**
Marigny, France 211
Marine Brigade *see* 4th Brigade
Marine Corps 2–5, 16, 26–28, 30–31, 33, 35–36, 41, 45–47, 52, 54, 62–63, 68, 72, 79, 83, 86, 88, 91, 94, 104–106, 120, 135–136, 140, 143, 158, 163, 165, 168, 170–172, 184–188, 191, 193–195, 198–199, 203–204, 205–208, 210–211, 215, 217–221, 223–225, 227–228, 233, 235–236, 239–241, 246, 248–251, 253–254, 257; Art Collection 161; aviation 226, 233; established 2; insignia 58; museum 2, 251–252; rifle team 106
Marine Corps Band 12–13, 17, 22, 199, 229, 239; Quantico band 201; Regimental band 65, 201

Marine Corps Commandant 3, 16, 33, 90, 204, 221, 225, 239, 246–247
Marines' Hymn 3, 108, 199, 257
Marion Daily Star 223
Marmion, Paul 194, 196
Marne River 69–70, 174, 188
Marryat, Frederick 9
Marsh, Clinton 160
Marshall, Thomas R. 203
Martin, George R. 236–237
Maryland 227
Maryland Agricultural College 22
Massachusetts 83, 202
Massachusetts Institute of Technology 56, 227
Matthews, Calvin B. 35
Matthews, H.L. **109**
Maxim, Hiram 50
Maximilian, Prinz Von Baden 143
May-en-Multien, France 70
Mayflower 19
Mayo, Henry T. 39
McCarthy, Thomas, A. 160
McClellan, John M. 61
McCormick, Joseph M. 217
McCracken, Arnold W. 160
McDonald, Clyde A. 214
McGabe, John C. 135
McKinley, William 16, 229
McLendon, Preston. A. 127
Meaux, France 70
Médéah Farm 126; ridge 138
Medal of Honor 229, 256; Boone 240; Catlin 68; Chamberlain 190; Cukela 111, 135, 165, 247, 255; Daly 84; Hamilton 3, 4, 90–91, 93, 201, 210, 246–249, 255; Hoffman 81, 111, 214, 247–248, 255; Hulbert 111, 135; Kelly 128, 255; Kocak 111, 135, 255; Neville 68, 90; Pruitt 128, 255; Robinson 255; Stockham 255; Talbot 255; Roovevelt 255–256; Unknown Soldier 230; Whittlesey 122; York 1, 122
Memorial Day 69, 193, 226, 235
Menaucourt, France **59**
Mercer's School 9
Meredith, James E. "Ted" 200
Messersmith, Robert E. 128, 131
Metcalf, Clyde H. 2, 157, 186, 191, 192, 194, 196, 198, 200, 204, 252
Metropolitan Club 226
Meuse-Argonne (Argonne) 118, 120, **121**, 124, 149, 151, 168, 172, 175, 186, 219
Meuse River 3–4, 107, 123, 146–148, 153–156, **161**, 162, 166, 168–169, 175–176, 183, 200, 210, 215–216, 220, 241, 246–247, 254–255
Mexico 42

Index

Military Affairs Committee 209
Miller, Thomas A.O. 135
Minos, Alexix P. 172
Missouri 203
USS *Missouri* 245
Mitchell, Jack 216
Mitchell, W.A. 96–97, 101, 103
Mitchell Field 221
Moffett, William A. 232–233
Mokeley, (Chaplain) *177*
Mon-Le-Vignoble, France 116
Monroe, James 203
Monroe Doctrine 202
Montana 21, 41
Montmedy, France 179
Morocco 96
Morse, Edmond H. 52
Mortensen, Ove E. 87, 111, 115, 134, 141, 160, 165, 181, 185, **205**, 206
Mortenson, Norma J. 3
Moslems 96
Mouzon, France 157
Musolf, Edward, J. 160
"My Rifle" 30, 31
Myers, Fred 212–213

Naegle, Hans M. 160, 162
Naismith, James 185
Naix-aux-Forges, France 58
Nanteuil-le-Haudouin, France 104
Nantucket, Massachusetts 41
National Capital Press Club 12
National Guard 45, 117, 254
National Press Club 243, 249, 251
National Rifle Association 35, 41
National Rifle Matches (National Matches) 35–37, 193–196, 198, 204, 206, 227–228
National Savings and Trust Co. 26–27
Native Americans 22, 117, 221
Naulin, Stanislas 126, 128
Naval Act 208
Naval Heritage Center 161
Naval War College 40
Navy Cross 90
USS *Nebraska* 52
Neiderbreitach, Germany 183
Nelms, James A. 132
USS *Nevada* 38
Neville, Wendell C. 63, 68, 71, 75, 90, 93, 96, 100, **112**, 113, 126, 140, 144, 150, 162, 164–165, 167, 175, **197**, 201, 211, 239, 246–247, 249; as 14th Commandant 3, 90, 239
New England Military Rifle Association 36
USS *New Hampshire* 225; *see also* Hamilton, George W.
New Hampton, Iowa 67
New Mexico 42

New Orleans, Louisiana 83
New York 222, 233; Long Island 95, 221, 232, 236; Yankees 215; *see also* New York City
USS *New York* 38, 42
New York City 11, 17, 38, 54, 141, 191, 193, 196, 198, 200–201, 220, 221, 224, 226–227, 229–230, 232, 244, 249; Polo Grounds 41
New York Navy Yard 37–39, 41–42
New York Shipbuilding Corp. 37
New York Times 41, 86, 175, 188, 203
New York Tribune 56
Newberry, Senator Truman H. 217
Newfoundland 245
Newport, Rhode Island 40
Niagara Falls, New York 13, 85
Nicaragua 37
Nice, France 88
Nice, William 55–56, 63, 82, 85, 102, 130, 135, 144, 214
Niederbreitbach, Germany 196
Nieuport 64, 95
19th Amendment 221
9th Regiment 103, 115, 126, 149, 151–153, 172
90th Division 110, 149
92d Division 206, 209, 215
94th Squadron 64, 191–192, 216, 225
95th Squadron 95, 190, 216
Nobel Peace Prize 256
Nome, Alaska 221
Norfolk 19
Norfolk, Virginia 19, 42; *see also* Hamilton, George W.
Northern Bombing Group 188, 218
Norway 220

Oberndorff, Alfred von 163
O'Connor, Charles A. 83, 213
O'Donoghue, Michael T. 136
Oklahoma 117
USS *Oklahoma* 39
Oldroyd, Harold J. 160
"Old-Timers" 243
O'Leary, Arthur J. "James" 106, 108, 116
Olympics (Olympic) 22–23, 25, 35, 41, 185
142nd Regiment 117
167th Field Artillery Brigade 206, 215
Orly, France 190
Oshkosh, Wisconsin 83
Osterhout, George H. 186, 191–192
Ottoman Empire 147
Oyster Bay, New York 95, 185

Palestine 123
Pall Mall, Tennessee 122
Palmer, Frederick 146–147, 151

Index

Panama 37
Panama Canal 17, 32
Pan-American Exposition 15
Paris, France 23, 54, 56, 61, 68–70, 85, 89, 92, 164, 174, 176, 183, 185, 190, 254; as capital city 86
Paris-Metz 75
Parris Island Training Depot 87, 111, 160, 194, 231
Patrick, Mason M. 232–233
Pearl Harbor, Hawaii 43
Pennsylvania 130
USS *Pennsylvania* 42
Penrose, Boies 25
Pensacola, Florida 227, 230, 235
Pershing, John J. 45–46, 48, 54–56, 58–60, 64, 67–69, 85, 89, 91–92, 94, 103–104, 109–110, 114–117, 142, 144–148, 155, 164–166, *182*, 185–186, 195, 204, 209–210, 215, 226, 229, 233, 240, 255; "Pershing's Own" 172; Pershing Stadium 185; "Pershing's Veteran Engineers" 47
Persons, Ida M. 10; *see also* Hamilton, Ida P.
Pétain, Henri P. 60, 67, 69, 109, 117, 143
Petersburg 132
Peterson, William C. 78, 81, 213
Philadelphia, Pennsylvania 226, 244; hospital 208; Navy Yard 35, 53–54, 208, 210, 214–215, 225
Philippines 37, 111
Pickett, George 237
Picpus Cemetery 56
Pittman, Key 217
Platt, Jonas H. 81, 213
"The Pocket" 122
Poincaré, Raymond 115
Pont-a-Mousson, France 116, 186
Porter, David D. 204
Potomac River 235
Pottstown, Pa. 136
Pouilly, France 153, 176, *177*, 183
Praeger, Otto 233
Prince of Wales 245
Princeton University 21, 136, 187
Progressive Party 23–24
Prohibition 217
Pruitt, John H. 128, 255
Prussians xii, 58, 85, 126; 5th Division 75; 10th Division 74; 87th Division 75; 197th Division 74; 237th Division 74; 460th-462nd Regiments 75
Puryear, Bennett Jr. 240
Pyramid Farm 72

Quantico, Virginia 31, 44, 46, 52–54, 83, 143, 160, 194, 198–199, 201, 204, 206, 215, 231, 234, 240, 252

Recruiters' Bulletin 188
Red Baron *see* Von Richthofen, Manfred
Red Cross 93, 198, 200, 208
Reilly, Sergeant 214
Remagen, Germany 183
Remarque, Erich Maria 7
Republican Party 23, 222, 223
Reuter, Fritz 21–22
Rhea, James C *109*
Rheims Massif 118, 141–142, 174
Rhine River 176, 178, 182–184, 186
Richards, Fredrick G. 39, **40**
Richards, George 204
Richeson, Welby P. 160
Richmond, Virginia 61
Richmond, Clarence L. 113, 147, 163, 167
Rickenbacker, Edward V. 54, 64, 95, 113–114, 124, 190–191, 216, 225–226, 232–233
Rixey, Presley M. 204
Robinson, Robert G. 255
Rochester, New York 195
Rochester Post Express 247
Rockefeller, William A. 233
Roosevelt, Ethel Carow 96
Roosevelt, Franklin D. 38, 170, 198, 204–206, 243, 245, 251; as Acting Secretary of Navy 186
Roosevelt, Kermit 153
Roosevelt, Quentin 17, 95, 153, 184–185, 238
Roosevelt, Theodore D. 13, 16–17, 19, 23, 25, 45, 94–95, 132, 184–185, 238, 241, 243, 255–256
Roosevelt, Theodore D. Jr. 153, 239
Rough Riders 13, 31, 133, 185
Roycrofter Society 34
Rupertus, William H. 30, 32, 36
Rupt de Mad River 114
Russell, Arthur 83
Russell, John H., Jr. 204
Russell Senate Office Building 17
Russia 33, 221; Russian 83
Ruth, George H. Jr. 215
Rutlidge, Lance 160
Ruzie, Madame 194

Sac and Fox Nation 22
Sagamore Hill 185
St. Clair Street 221, 232–233
Saint Croix 14
St. Etienne, France 4, 120, 124, 130–131, 134, 137, 142; Somme Py-St. Etienne Rd. 138
Saint John 14
St Louis World's Fair 15
Saint-Mihiel, France 107–108, *109*, 111, 114, 127, 131, 146, 172, 186, 219, 247, 254
St. Nazaire, France 55–56

St. Quentin, France 122, 142
Saint Thomas 14
Samaritan, Frank 213
San Antonio, Texas 187
San Juan Hill 256
Santo Domingo, D.R. 37, 214, 219, 231, 234
Santolmann, William H. 199
Saturday Evening Post 246
Sauer River 180–181
Scharfen, John C. 253
Scott, Evan W. 136
Scott, Milton R. 239; U.S. Navy Chaplain 242
Scribner's 246
Sea Grit, New Jersey 36
Second Army 164, 166
2nd Battalion 5th Regiment (USMC) 47, 53–55, 57–58, *59*, 72, 87, 102, 113, 126, 128–129, 131–133, 147, 150, 156–159, *161*, 162–163, 165, 168, 175–176, 200
2nd Battalion 6th Regiment (USMC) 64, 87, 106, 126, 128, 157, 186, 196, 200
2nd Division 47, 62–63, 65–66, 69–70, 72, 85–86, 89, 90, 93, 95–101, 103–104, 110, 114–119, 122–123, 128–131, 140, 142, 146, 149–154, 156–157, 164, 167–168, 170–172, 174–175, 178, 181, 184, 186, 193, 195–196, 198, 200, 204, 239, 250; Division Headquarters 113; Indian Head 106, 137, 160, 197; Lejeune's Division 126, 132, 149; Race Horse 148–149, 151, 171, 181; Second to None 171
2nd Engineers 47, 96–97, 101, 103, 138, 148, 154, 157, 168, 214, 255; A Company 157–159; B Company 157–159; engineers 104, 176; "Pershing's Veteran Engineers" 47
2nd Field Artillery Brigade 47, 127; Second Division Artillery 157
2nd Squadron 236
Second World War *see* World War II
Selfridge, Thomas E. 241–242
Semper Fidelis 166
Senegalese 96, 98, 102, 172
Serbia 33, 111
17th Company (USMC) 74, 76, 84, 100, 126, 128, 133, 135, 138, 144, 154, 156, 162, 252
7th Field Artillery 153
71st Infantry Regiment 36
73rd Machine Gun Company 126
77th Division 122, 149, 164, 177
77th Machine Gun Company 126
78th Company (USMC) 128
78th Division 149
Shearer, Maurice E. 88, 102, 204, 240
Sherburne, John H. 215
Shuler, George K. 52, *53*, 55, 61, 84, 108, 135, 150, 157–158, 194, 196, 198, 200, 204, *222*, 223, 245–246, 249
Sibert, William L. 55, 60
Sibley, Berton 84, 87
Signal Corps 49, 54, 241, 244
Sioux City Journal 13
Sitka, Alaska 136
6th Machine Gun Battalion (USMC) 64, 186, 201
6th Regiment (USMC) xii, 46, 62, 64, 68, 71, 87, 100, 103, 115, 126–128, 130–131, 149–151, 157–158, 163, 200–201, 206
64th Brigade 94
66th Company (USMC) 52, 76, 100, 111, 126, 134–135, 137–138, 141, 144, 154, 156, 160, 165, *177*, *205*, 206
66th Field Artillery Brigade 178
67th Company (USMC) 52, 75–76, 78, 81, 85, 100, 107, 110, 126, 136, 138, 140, 144, 154, 156, 211, 213, 252
skipper (definition) 52
Skull and Bones Society 206
Slover, Robert 213
Smith, Holland 240
Snyder, Harold C. 204
Soissons, France 92, 97, 101, 103–104, 110–111, 117, 127, 131, 146, 172, 174, 186, 240, 254; July 18th 219
Solace 42
Somers, Vernon L. 82, 213
Somervell, Brehon B. 154
Somme-Py, France 119, 123, 127
songs 107, 179; *see also* Marines' Hymn
Sopwith Camel 188
Souain, France 127; Souain-Suippes 119
Sousa, John Philip 12
Spanish-American War 13–14, 31, 133
Spad 190
Spanish flu 50–51, 143, 154
Spokane, Washington 61, 107
Springfield, Massachusetts 31, 185
Springfield Rifle (origin) 31
Stahl, John J. 214, 248
Standing Committee of Correspondents 245
Stanford University 253
Stapleton, New York 54
Stars & Stripes 180
Stinson, Eddie 233
Stockham, Fred W. 255
Stowell, George A. 157, 204
Subcommittee on Naval Affairs 217
Suffrage Amendment 221
Suippe River 123
Sumay, Guam 231
Summerall, Charles P. 96, 146–149, 151–152, 156, 159, 162, 164, 168–169, 175, 178, 203
Sumner, Charles P. 33

Swindler, Harold F. 213
Switzerland 94, 143

Taft, William H. 19, 20, 22, 25, 228–229, 235, 241
Talbot, Ralph 255
Teapot Dome scandal 228, 245
Temple of Music 15–16
Tesla, Nikola 13
Texas 42, 117, 141, 246; Fort Worth 136
USS *Texas* 38–39, 41–42
Theall, Elisha S. 204
Thiacourt, France 114, 174
Third Army 164, 178
3rd Army Corps (Third Corps, III Corps) 97–98, 104, 149, 178
3rd Battalion 5th Regiment (USMC) 53–55, 58, 75, 87–88, 102, 126, 128, 130–133, 150–151, 157–158, 200, 211, 213, 240
3rd Battalion 6th Regiment (USMC) 47, 84, 87, 126, 150, 157, 200
3rd Brigade 47, 102–103, 106, 113, 126, 128, 140, 151–152, 172, 179
3rd Division 69, 171, 178, 195
Thirkield, Wilbur P. 22
30th Division 171
30th Regiment 178
32nd Division 94, 178
33rd Division 171
36th Division 117
39th Division 164
Thomason, John W. Jr. 85, 89, 98, 101, 113, 134, 140, *141*, 154, 246, 249, **250**
Thorpe, Jim 22, 25
306th Machine Gun Battalion 122
308th Infantry 122
314th Engineers 154
356th Infantry 157
Thurmont, Maryland 236
Tintera, Louis 160
Titanic 21, 34
Torcy, France 75, 80
Toronto, Canada 196, 257
Torrey, Henry P. 52
Toul (Toulon), France 64, 66, 68
Tourquin, France 188–189
Tousic, Frank 172
Trammell, Park 217
Treaty of Versailles 195
The Troy Times 246
Turkey 147; Turk 123
Turnbull, Archibald D. 187
Turner, Thomas C. 239–240
Turrill, Julius S. 52, 54, 60, 64, 71, 75–76, 78, 83–84, 87, 94, 102, 106, 178, 211, 239–240
20th Company 1st Brigade (USMC) 35

23rd Machine Gun Company (USMC) 126, 161
23rd Regiment 103, 115, 126, 149, 151–153
26th Regiment 153
28th Division 171

Union Station 18, 200, 204, 206
U.S. Army 3, 41, 45–47, 49, 54–55, 66, 68, 72, 81, 86, 91–92, 94, 104, 113, 146, 153, 170, 198, 204–205, 209, 218, 224, 226, 233, 247, 254–255, 257
U.S. Capital (Capital Hill) 16, 18, 21, 23, 32, 53, 194, 200, 203, 235; Rotunda 16, 229
U.S. Congress (House) 11, 20, 41–43, 45, 63, 91, 143, 187, 190, 202, 207, 209, 217, 219, 221, 223, 226, 249; Congressional appropriation 231; Congressional hearings 194, 207, 215; Congressional information 175; Congressional Library 53; Congressional MOH 247, 255; Military Affairs Committee 209; reference to Congressman and Congressional House Representatives 17, 25, 184, 200, 206, 233, 243; Thirty-Sixth Congressional District 222; *see also* Congressional Press; War Investigation Committee No. 3
U.S. Forest Service 21
U.S. Naval Academy 19, 22, 46, 88, 227, 231, 233, 245
U.S. Navy 37, 41–43, 45, 54, 81, 91, 187, 190, 194, 198, 204, 206–207, 217–218 224, 226–227, 233–234, 241–242, 244–245, 254, 257
U.S. Senate 17, 30, 43, 61, 108, 184, 200–201, 203, 217; Committee on the Geological Survey 27; Military Affairs Committee 45, 209; Rules Committee 11; Senate floor 202; Senators 25; Subcommittee on Naval Affairs 217; *see also* "Old-Timers"
U.S. Soldiers Home Band 199
University of Buffalo 10
University of California 144
University of Illinois 78
University of Michigan 21
University of North Carolina 24
University of Pennsylvania 21, 25
University of Tennessee 113
University of Texas 187
University of Virginia 21, 23–24
Unknown Soldier 229; as Unknown Warrior 230
Usher, Nathaniel R. 38

Vancours, O. M. 189
Vanderbilt, Alfred G. 34
Van Duesen, Robert 136
Van Dyke, Thomas J. 160

Van Dyne, George 23–24, 26
Vanselow, Ernst 163
Vaux, France 174
Vera Cruz 37, 198
Verdun, France 64–65, 107, 168, 172, 186, 219
Veterans Administration 241
Veteran's Day *see* Armistice Day
Victory Parade: New York City 196; Washington D.C. **201**, **202**
Vierzy, France 102
Villemontry, France 157
Villers-Cotterets, France 98
Vineland, New Jersey 136
Virginia Military Institute (V.M.I.) 61
Vitry-en-Perthois, France 68
Von Lumm, William 135
Von Richthofen, Manfred 67; "Red Barron" 71
USS *Von Stuben* 191
Von Winterfeldt, Detlof 163
Vought VE-7 234

Wake Forest University 253
Wakefield, Massachusetts 36, 228
Waldorf, Germany 181, 183
Wallis, Margaret 11
War Expenditure Hearings 206
War Investigation Committee No. 3 206; Congressional hearings 215
Ware, Arthur F. 83
Warner, Glenn S. 25
Warren, Frances 45
Washington, Booker T. 17
Washington, George 203
Washington, D.C. 11–12, 15, 18, 26, 28, 30, 34, 42, 46, 53, 63, 67, 193, 200, 207–209, 221, 225–227, 236, 240–241, 244, 248–249, 251–253; home city 230; nation's capital 11, 18, 53, 199, 208, 251; *see also* Capital City; District of Columbia
Washington Athletic Association 22, 24
Washington Mall 235
Washington Monument 12, 16, 235
Washington Post xii, 13–14, 19, 21, 32, 52, 66–67, 203, 237, 243
Washington Press Club 243
Wear, Eugene W. 83
Webber, Michael P. 160
Wemyss, Rosslyn 163
West Point Military Academy 25, 45, 68
Western Front 2, 3, 7, 30, 46–49, 51, 64–65, 70, 76, 85, 94, 107, 118, 140, 149, 153–154, 157, 163, 165–167, 175, 209, 224, 231, 256

Western Union Telegraph 49
Westinghouse 13
White House 12–13, 16–17, 53, 94, **201**, 207, 229, 243, 251
Whitehead, Frank 100, 110, 136, 142, 154, 240–241
Whittlesey, Charles 122
Wilcox, Ansley 16
Willard Hotel 222
Williams, Lloyd W. 72
Williams, John S. 203
Wilson, Henry 67
Wilson, Woodrow 1, 25, 32, 34, 41–43, 45–46, 62–63, 66, 115, 143, 145, 180, 184, 195–196, 199–200, **201**, 202, 207, 217, 220, 223, 229; reference to 218, 224
Winchester, Massachusetts 206
Winchester A5 50
Winthrop, Maryland 31, 35
Wise, Frederick 87
Woods, Elliott 17
World War I (WW I) 1–7, 14, 32, 39, 47, 50–51, 66, 91, 97, 165–167, 170, 175, 195, 200, 223–225, 228, 230, 233, 235, 239–240, 244, 247, 249–252, 254–255, 257; U.S. declared war 43
World War II (WW II) 1, 5–6, 206, 243–245, 251, 257
Wounded Knee 25
Wright, Carlton H. (cousin) 19, 21–22, 43, 67, 244–246
Wright, George Charles (cousin) 67–68, 227, 244–246
Wright, George Cyrus (uncle) 19, 67, 107, 246
Wright, James L. (cousin) 21, 52, 67, 244, 246
Wright, Lee W. 240, 241
Wright, Mary H. (aunt) 67
Wright, Orville 17, 221, 233, 241
Wright, Wilbur 17, 221
Wright Trophy 234
Wyoming 245–246
USS *Wyoming* 37–39, 41–42

Yale University 2, 19, 21, 206
Yeaton, Guy M. 135
Yohn, Fredrick C. **161**
York, Alvin C. 1, 122
Younger, Edward F. 229

Zimmermann, Arthur 42
Zimmermann, John S.M. 199
Zinner, Fred J. 136

www.ingramcontent.com/pod-product-compliance
Ingram Content Group UK Ltd.
Pitfield, Milton Keynes, MK11 3LW, UK
UKHW041925140426
5217IPUK00014B/316